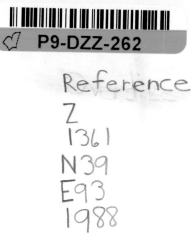

ACKNOWLEDGMENTS

We gratefully acknowledge the contribution of Alain Dessaint in supporting and guiding this project; the contribution of Marybelle Alverson in modifying computer programs to structure the output of the data from the PsycINFO database; the assistance of Maurine Jackson in writing the programming and photocomposition specifications; the assistance of Barbara McLean, Marion Russell, and Jody Kerby in proofreading and correcting the data; the assistance of Carolyn Gosling, Linda McKenney, and Sarah Mulholland in formulating the search strategy; the assistance of Donna Stewart and Stephanie Selice in designing the cover; and the assistance of Mark Brady in desktop publishing parts of this book.

Table of Contents

Section III. Selected Citations to the Dissertation Literature on Black Males in the United States

Section IV. Subject Index

Appendixes

FOREWORD

Statistics can tell us much about Black males in America. In 1988, Black males numbered 15,204,000 or 6.3% of the population of the United States. They represented 13% of the U.S. male population, and they comprised 52.6% of the U.S. Black population. Black males are twice as likely to die in infancy than White males. Black males graduate from high school only 77% as frequently as White males. Black males of all ages are 3 times as likely as White males to live below the poverty line. Black males aged 20-44 are twice as likely to die as White males. Black males are almost 6 times as likely as White males to be victims of homicide. Black male heads of household earn 70% of the income of their White male counterparts. Although they constitute only 6.3% of the total U.S. population, Black males comprise 42% of jail inmates and over 50% of men executed for any reason over the last 50 years!

But these statistics do not present a complete picture. The socio-psychological aspects of the behaviors of a historically discriminated against minority group must be taken into account in order to understand the broad meaning of these statistics. Research on Black males is adding to our knowledge about social and psychological issues — as well as about the changes that must be made both in how such research is conducted and how it is interpreted. For example, Black males are characteristically skilled in effective use of body language in communication, decoding nonverbal and paralinguistic cues, improvisational problem solving, and multilingual/cultural expression. The latter characteristics are considerably less well researched, and, where such findings exist, their interpretations often carry a negative or deficit cast. Black psychologists have produced the bulk of the research that takes a non-normative, idiographic approach and that seeks knowledge on the sources of survival, adaptation, and strength in the Black male psyche. There are many critical problems that this body of research must address. For example, in a society dominated by men, racial conflict has over the centuries been conflict between Black men and White men. When customary avenues of accomplishment have been systematically denied Black men, yet clear cultural demands for strong male identities are projected, what behavioral strategies are or could be pursued—with what psychological and emotional consequences?

Psychology's Growing Involvement

The status of the Black male in the United States was selected by President Raymond Fowler as the theme for a mini-convention within the 1988 annual APA convention. This reflects a continued interest of the discipline of psychology, which has long been concerned with race and societal issues. And the nature of the psychological research and the way in which it has been interpreted have changed with society. Early work on intelligence testing focused attention on racial differences among Army recruits. Social concerns with racial issues were reflected in research on social distance and racial animosity among ethnic and religious groups. Racial differences in temperament, child rearing practices, and moral and social development topped the research agendas of psychologists from the mid-1920s until the 1950s.

The Supreme Court decision of 1954 focused massive attention on the effects of segregation on Black children's psychological development, and the research by Kenneth and Mamie Clark helped document these negative consequences. Much of the psychological literature since that time has focused on cognitive, social, and emotional development of Black children, including IQ testing and achievement motivation. A large body of that literature shows consistent and perplexing race-by-sex interactions that suggests not only differences between Blacks and Whites, but between Black men and Black women.

The American Psychological Association's concern with racial issues goes back to the mid-1960s when special reports on equal opportunity were commissioned. By 1968, the rise of the Association of Black Psychologists triggered demands for APA to be more forthcoming, and, led by the Council of Representatives, a national office of the Black Student Psychological Association was housed at APA central headquarters.

The social concerns reflected in these activities of the 1960s were formalized in a broader context by APA President Kenneth B. Clark, whose presidency led to the formation in 1971 of the Board of Social and Ethical Responsibility (BSERP) — and established organized psychology's comprehensive concern for justice, social equality, and opportunity. Subsequently, APA initiated the Minority Graduate Fellowship Program in 1974. In the late 1970s, the APA-sponsored Dulles Conference of Ethnic Minority Psychologists led to the establishment of an Office of Ethnic Minority Affairs in 1980 and a Board of Ethnic Minority Affairs (BEMA) in 1981.

Although these initiatives have been broadly concerned with a range of ethnic minority group issues, the particular behavioral, social, and psychological factors that have dramatically affected the status of the Black male in American society became a focus of attention for both BSERP and BEMA. As a result, a joint BSERP/BEMA Task Force on the Status of the Black Male was recently created. The Task Force will help to focus issues of particular relevance to psychology and will serve to stimulate knowledge dissemination.

The Value of This Bibliography and Computerized Searching

This annotated bibliography on the *Status of Black Males in America* will guide the reader through a substantial body of the empirical literature focusing on the Black male. We anticipate that it will stimulate research activity focused on the critical and pressing issues that affect Black males and help focus attention on these issues as important research, application, and public policy concerns for psychology. In undertaking research in this area, we call your attention to the need to institute proper controls and implement appropriate operational procedures that are sensitive to the ethnic, racial, gender, and cultural context in which human subjects live and to which they adapt.

The published research literature on Black males is expanding. Keeping up with it is becoming a matter of concern to psychologists, behavioral scientists, and social scientists. A major but sometimes overlooked tool for staying abreast of developments and research is the *Psychological Abstracts* and its electronic counterparts, PsycINFO and PsycALERT online, and PsycLIT on CD-ROM (Compact Disc-Read Only Memory). Searching the *Abstracts* and the other computerized databases can be extremely useful. More complex searches are feasible on the electronic databases.

This bibliography is a demonstration: A carefully thought-out search strategy described in a comment by Evans and Whitfield in the May 1988 *American Psychologist* (and fully explained in Appendix B of this volume) has resulted in the retrieval of the largest abstracted and indexed corpus of materials yet published concerning psychological and behavioral perspectives on Black males in America. The search strategy can be used again by readers who wish to update this bibliography with the very latest references on PsycALERT (which makes available citations and indexing within weeks of an article's publication) or PsycINFO (when complete abstracting and indexing is desired). The strategy can also serve as a model for conducting bibliographic research on other topics.

James M. Jones, Ph.D.
    Executive Director for Public Interest, APA
Christine C. Iijima Hall, Ph.D.
    Director, Office of Ethnic Minority Affairs, APA
Lois W. Granick
    Director, PsycINFO, APA
Gary R. VandenBos, Ph.D.
    Executive Director, Office of Publications
    and Communications, APA

June 1988

This section contains a selective bibliography of annotated references from the journal literature focusing on Black males in the United States. References were retrieved from the PsycINFO database by searching for the concept *Black males* (or synonyms) in the title, descriptor, and identifier fields. Entries are organized alphabetically within the major/ minor classification categories used by *Psychological Abstracts* and the PsycINFO database.

PSYCHOMETRICS

1. Borgen, Fred H. & Harper, Gregory T. (1973). **Predictive validity of measured vocational interests with Black and White college men.** *Measurement & Evaluation in Guidance,* 6(1), 19–27.
Studied the validity of the Strong Vocational Interest Blank for predicting career choices at the end of college using 79 Black and 780 White males who were winners of National Achievement and National Merit Scholarships in 1966. Blacks and Whites moving in different career paths were differentiated before college in similar and meaningful ways by the interest dimensions. Multiple discriminant function weights were determined for 511 of the Whites, with cross-validation hit-rates determined for the remaining Whites and all of the Blacks. Membership in career groups was predicted at least as well for these able Blacks as it was for the Whites.

2. Convey, John J. (1975). **The application of simultaneous confidence intervals for multinomial populations to an inventory of plans and goals.** *Florida Journal of Educational Research,* 17, 1–12.
Reviews several procedures for constructing simultaneous confidence intervals for judging contrasts among multinomial populations. The procedures are illustrated by applying them to the responses of a systematic sample of male and female, Black and White 8th graders who responded to a section of a state-wide 8th grade testing program entitled "Your Plans and Goals."

3. Elion, Victor H. & Megargee, Edwin I. (1975). **Validity of the MMPI Pd scale among Black males.** *Journal of Consulting & Clinical Psychology,* 43(2), 166–172.
Conducted 3 studies to investigate the validity of the MMPI Psychopathic Deviate (Pd) and Pd plus .4K scales in discriminating levels of social deviance among young Black men. Study 1 established that 102 Black inmates at a federal correctional institution had significantly higher scores on both scales than 120 culturally deprived Black male university students. Study 2, using Ss from Study 1, demonstrated that (a) among the inmates recidivists had significantly higher scores than first offenders, and (b) among the students there were significant differences in the expected directions among subgroups differing in self-reported delinquency. Study 3 showed that the Black Ss from Study 1 had higher scores than comparable samples of 60 White male college students and 51 White male prison inmates. It is concluded that Pd and Pd plus .4K both validly differentiate levels of social deviance among young Black men but that the norms for the scales appear to show racial bias. (19 ref).

4. Grace, William C. & Sweeney, Mary E. (1986). **Comparisons of the P > V sign on the WISC-R and WAIS-R in delinquent males.** *Journal of Clinical Psychology,* 42(1), 173–176.
Among 40 White (mean age 16 yrs 2 mo) and 40 Black (mean age 15 yrs 8 mo) delinquents, a larger split between mean Verbal (V) and mean Performance (P) IQ was found on the Wechsler Intelligence Scale for Children—Revised (WISC—R) than on the Wechsler Adult Intelligence Scale—Revised (WAIS—R). Frequency analyses revealed no differences in the number of Ss who showed the P > V sign on each test. Results suggest that the WISC—R and WAIS—R may not be equivalent measures of this sign and that caution should be exercised in applying results of research on the WISC and WAIS to the revisions of those tests. (11 ref).

5. Hennessy, Michael. (1985). **Path analysis using LISREL: Comparing income attainment of White and Black men.** *Journal of Applied Behavioral Science,* 21(1), 51–63.
Contends that the use of standardized regression coefficients makes a comparison of causal models difficult to perform. Using O. Duncan's (1969) path model for White and Black men, the author shows how to use the linear structural relationships (LISREL) software package to analyze such models with unstandardized coefficients and compare them in terms of overall goodness of fit, tests of differential specifications across groups, and assumptions of equality or inequality of corresponding regression coefficients. (37 ref).

6. Humphreys, Lloyd G. (1972). **Implications of group differences for test interpretation.** *Proceedings of the Invitational Conference on Testing Problems,* 56–71.
Discusses the fairness of inferences based on test scores. On the basis of a review of the adequate research involving a comparison of regression equations, it is concluded that there is relatively little difference in the slopes or intercepts of regression lines of different demographic groups. Despite some small differences, a single regression equation can be used for males and females and for Blacks and Whites unless there is intervention in training or unless the criterion measures for the groups differ. Reasons are listed for not drawing inferences about capacity to learn on the basis of aptitude or intelligence test scores.

7. Rosso, Martin; Falasco, Sharon L. & Phelps, LeAdelle. (1984). **Implications of regression analysis and correlational data between subtests of the WISC-R and the PPVT-R for a delinquent population.** *Journal of Clinical Psychology,* 10(3), 811–814.
Computed correlations between the subscales of the WISC—R and the Peabody Picture Vocabulary Test—Revised (PPVT—R), using 72 predominantly Black adjudicated male delinquents aged 13.10–16.11 yrs. Significant relationships at the .0001 level were obtained for 10 subtests with only one, Object Assembly, computed at the .001 level. A forward selection multiple regression analysis resulted in 6 subtests of the WISC—R correlating to the PPVT—R with a R value of .78. (9 ref).

8. Smith, Patricia M. & Barclay, Allan G. (1975). **Q analysis of the Holtzman Inkblot Technique.** *Journal of Clinical Psychology,* 31(1), 131–134.
The Q analysis for refinement of the diagnostic effectiveness of projective tests was used and the Holtzman Inkblot Technique was administered to 3 behaviorally distinct groups of Ss: 20 normal, 20 delinquent, and 20 retarded Black male adolescents who resided in socioeconomically depressed neighborhoods. Median and quartile scores were obtained from 19 of the 22 Holtzman variables, and 4 factors were derived from factor analysis. Definable subfactors appeared within the delinquent and retarded groups, but loadings for normal Ss were primarily on 1 factor.

9. Terrell, David L. (1982). **The TCB in clinical–forensic psychological evaluation: A case study of exceptionality.** *Journal of Non-White Concerns in Personnel & Guidance,* 10(2), 64–72.
Demonstrates how the Themes Concerning Blacks (TCB) test was able to facilitate the establishment of rapport, cooperative behavior, and a high level of verbal productivity and creativity in a 35-yr-old Black male alleged forger referred for a clinical, forensic psychological evaluation. The S was also administered the Rorschach and the WAIS. Results indicate that the S was competent at the time of the alleged offense.

10. Triplett, Sheila & Brunson, Phyllis. (1982). **TCB and TAT response characteristics in Black males and females: A replication.** *Journal of Non-White Concerns in Personnel & Guidance,* 10(2), 73–77.
Hypothesized that (1) no differences would exist between TAT and Themes Concerning Blacks (TCB) test story length; (2) Ss would correctly identify the race of the stimulus figures in the TCB and TAT; and (3) the feeling-tone would be more positive in the TCB than in the TAT stories. Ss were 48 5–8 yr old Blacks grouped according to age and sex. Findings support the hypotheses and confirm those of V. J. Weaver (1978).

11. Valecha, Gopal K. & Ostrom, Thomas M. (1974). **An abbreviated measure of internal-external locus of control.** *Journal of Personality Assessment,* 38(4), 369–376.
Administered an abbreviated version of Rotter's Internal–External Control Scale (developed by eliminating all filler items and excluding items whose content themes were neither work related nor global in their referents) to a national probability sample of 4,330 16–26 yr old males. Psychometric properties (distributional characteristics, scale reliability, and item-test correlations) of the abbreviated scale were similar to the full 29-item scale. Comparable factor structures were obtained for both Black and White Ss. Blacks gave more external responses than Whites.

Test Construction & Validation

12. Bailey, Bruce E. & Green, Jules. (1977). **Black Thematic Apperception Test stimulus material.** *Journal of Personality Assessment,* 41(1), 25–30.
Used a factorial design to test variations of the TAT based on racial characteristics. Ss consisted of 135 Black southern males divided into 3 test groups of 45 Ss each. The H. Murray TAT, the C. E. Thompson TAT, or an experimental version of the TAT for Blacks was group administered to each test group of 45 Ss. Each of the 3 groups was further divided into 3 age groups of 15 Ss each designated as residents, college students, or high school students (25–45, 19–22, and 17–18 yrs of age, respectively). Ss' responses to the racial characteristics and needs content across tests and age groups were examined. Data reveal that (a) Ss could distinguish the racial characteristics of Black and White TAT material, (b) Ss indicated that Black TAT material facilitated the writing of their stories, (c) Ss viewed the Black TAT characters as more like "people in general," (d) both figure and background stimuli were important to Ss, and (e) content differences on need for achievement were found between age groups.

13. Bradley, Robert H. & Caldwell, Bettye M. (1981). **Home environment and infant social behavior.** *Infant Mental Health Journal,* 2(1), 18–22.
18 Black male, 18 White male, 18 Black female, and 18 White female infants and their families participated in a study to examine the validity of the Home Observation for Measurement of the Environment (HOME) in terms of its relation to early indices of social behavior. Early social behavior was assessed using the Infant Behavior Record taken from the Bayley Scales of Infant Development. A factor analysis produced 5 behavior dimensions: (1) Positive Orientation and Involvement, (2) Fear and Reticence, (3) Enthusiasm and Alertness, (4) Activity Level, and (5) Self-Absorption. In general, findings show a similar but somewhat stronger relation between HOME scores and social behavior for females than males. For males, Positive Orientation was significantly related to organization of the environment and provision of appropriate play materials. Self-Absorption was moderately related to avoidance of restriction and punishment. For infant girls, both Positive Orientation and Activity Level were significantly related to 4 of the 6 HOME subscales. (28 ref).

14. Bradley, Robert H.; Caldwell, Bettye M. & Elardo, Richard. (1977). **Home environment, social status, and mental test performance.** *Journal of Educational Psychology,* 69(6), 697–701.
Compared an environmental process measure (Home Observation for Measurement of the Environment Inventory— HOME) and socioeconomic status (SES) measures in terms of their relations with Stanford-Binet Intelligence Scale IQ at 3 yrs of age. Separate analyses were made for 68 Blacks and 37 Whites and for males and females. Results indicate that the HOME measure predicted IQ as well as a combination of HOME and SES measures, whereas there was some loss in predictive power when SES was used by itself (especially in the case of Blacks). It is concluded that HOME appears to be a more accurate index of environmental quality across groups than does SES. (26 ref).

15. Covin, Theron M. (1976). **Alternate form reliability of the Peabody Picture Vocabulary Test.** *Psychological Reports,* 39(3, Pt 2), 1286.
Collected data for 870 Black and White male and female 1st-10th graders to determine alternate form reliability coefficients for the Peabody Picture Vocabulary Test. Mean IQs on Form B were significantly lower than Form A IQs for Blacks, Whites, males, and females, and for the total sample. Pearson correlation coefficients between the 2 forms were as follows: 0.85, Blacks; 0.75 Whites; 0.88, males; 0.72, females; and 0.83, total sample.

16. Cross, Donald T. & Burger, Gary K. (1982). **Ethnicity as a variable in responses to California Psychological Inventory items.** *Journal of Personality Assessment,* 46(2), 153–158.
Compared the responses of 218 Black female, 213 White female, 136 Black male, and 181 White male undergraduates to the California Psychological Inventory items. On the average, 34% in each of the 18 scales showed significant differences. Approximately two-thirds of the significant items for the males were also significant for the females. It is suggested that future development of tests of this nature carefully consider the sociocultural factors that might contribute to differential responses to test items on objective personality tests as assessment devices. (13 ref).

17. DeWolfe, Alan S. & Ryan, Joseph J. (1984). **Wechsler Performance IQ > Verbal IQ index in a forensic sample: A reconsideration.** *Journal of Clinical Psychology,* 40(1), 291–294.
Among 39 White and 31 Black males (aged 16–73 yrs) accused or convicted of felonies, the WAIS Performance IQ > Verbal IQ index was more prevalent among Whites and was significantly related to reading disability, as assessed by the Wide Range Achievement Test. The index was most frequent in Ss charged with sex crimes and least frequent in Ss convicted of murder; with murder excluded, the index occurred more frequently in those accused of violent than nonviolent crimes. The significant relationships between the index and both type of crime and reading disability were most likely independent of ethnicity and each other. (12 ref).

18. Dill, John R. et al. (1975). **Sex-role preference in Black preschool children using a modification of the IT Scale for Children.** *Perceptual & Motor Skills,* 42(3), 823–828.
Used the facial features of the "IT" figure in the IT Scale for Children to measure sex-role preferences of 46 male and 47 female Black 4–6 yr olds. Data show that the majority identified "IT" as their own sex. Significant differences were obtained between the present sample of Black males and those in a comparison sample. No differences existed between the present sample and the original normative White male sample. Black females in the present sample were as feminine as both the Black and White comparison samples. Results indicate that the facial features version is appropriate when using the IT Scale. Black Ss seemed to manifest sex-role preference similar to their White peers, although females' scores were more variable. Previous assumptions regarding the socialization of sex-role behavior of Black children are challengeable and must be reconsidered. (23 ref).

19. Elliott, Stephen N. & Boeve, Kurtis. (1987). **Stability of WISC—R IQs: An investigation of ethnic differences over time.** *Educational & Psychological Measurement,* 47(2), 461–465.
Examined the 3-yr stability of Wechsler Intelligence Scale for Children—Revised (WISC—R) IQs for 168 White, Black, and Mexican-American handicapped males (aged 5–6 yrs). Ss had been categorized as learning disabled, behaviorally impaired, educable mentally retarded, or unclassified. Results show no significant differences in mean IQs across the 3 groups, although over the 3-yr test–retest period, WISC—R Verbal and performance IQs were observed to vary significantly. Verbal IQs decreased by an average of 2 points, while Performance IQs increased by an average of nearly 3 points. It is concluded that the influence of 3 yrs' time on intelligence test performance was clinically insignificant.

20. Evenson, Richard C. & Cho, Dong W. (1987). **Norms for the Missouri Inpatient Behavior Scale: Sex, race and age differences in psychiatric symptoms.** *Journal of Clinical Psychology,* 43(2), 254–261.
Means and standard deviations for 12 subscales of the Missouri Inpatient Behavior Scale were calculated for 12,106 unduplicated patients. Data were subdivided by sex, race, and age. Females consistently were rated as more symptomatic than males, and Blacks were rated as more symptomatic than Whites, except for depression. Ss aged 65+ yrs were more symptomatic than all other age groups.

21. Helsel, William J. & Matson, Johnny L. (1984). **The assessment of depression in children: The internal structure of the Child Depression Inventory (CDI).** *Behaviour Research & Therapy,* 22(3), 289–298.
Conducted 3 experiments to investigate the subcomponents of childhood depression and their relation to social behavior. In Exp I, the internal structure of the CDI, with 108 female and 108 male White, Black, and Hispanic 4–18 yr olds, was evaluated through factor analysis and by various internal-reliability measures. Four factors were established, and internal reliability of the scale was high. The relationship of the factor structure of the CDI to Kendell's (1976) Types A and B categorization of depression is discussed. In Exp II, the relationship of demographic variables to the CDI using the same group of Ss as in Exp I was investigated. The characteristics of depression across factors such as age and sex were examined. Age was a significant factor in depression scores, although race and gender were not. With respect to age, older Ss tended to display more symptomatology. Comparisons of depressed Ss to nondepressed Ss also showed that age was a factor in the obtained scores and range of severity in both groups. Depressed Ss differed from nondepressed Ss on all 27 items, indicating that all the items on the CDI seem to be measuring a unitary concept. Exp III compared CDI scores to a measure of social behavior, the Matson Evaluation of Social Skills with Youngster. 76 4–10 yr olds were evaluated. The factor Appropriate Social Skills was negatively correlated with childhood depression, and Inappropriate Impulsive/Assertiveness was positively correlated with depressive features described under the factor Guilt/Irritability. (38 ref).

22. Hobbs, Steven A.; Walle, Dennis L. & Hammersly, Gail A. (1984). **Assessing children's social skills: Validation of the Behavioral Assertiveness Test for Children (BAT-C).** *Journal of Behavioral Assessment,* 6(1), 29–35.
44 4th graders and 51 5th graders (52 Black, 43 White; 50 male, 45 female) completed peer nominations of their best friends and the children they most admired, peer ratings of likeability, and the BAT-C. SES was determined by classifying each S as either high or low on peer nominations and peer ratings. Examination of the effects of SES as moderated by race and sex revealed several significant differences in BAT-C responses. Ss who were more highly liked or were often named as best friends were significantly less compliant. Differential responding on several additional verbal categories was observed as a function of the interaction between SES and race and/or sex. These findings not only demonstrate the validity of several response categories observed on the BAT-C but also suggest that in social skills training, different component responses may be targeted across child populations. (10 ref).

23. Hogan, H. Wayne. (1975). **Validity of a symbolic measure of authoritarianism.** *Psychological Reports,* 37(2), 539–543.
A symbolic, nonverbal measure of authoritarianism, the SF (Symbolic Fascism) Test, was responded to by 287 male and female, White and Black business school students, undergraduates, and graduate social work students. Scores on the measure showed low (0.35–0.39) predictable "known groups" validity and were generally correlated, as theoretically anticipated, with both objectively measured and self-perceived conservatism, birth order, religious fundamentalism, subjective social-class position, and intrafamilial consistency of psychological attributes and sociopolitical ideologies. Given the methodological limitations of verbal authoritarianism measures, these results suggest some potential advantages of the presently reported nonverbal test of the authoritarianism dimension. (15 ref).

24. Hunter, Ned & Kelley, Crystal K. (1986). **Examination of the validity of the Adolescent Problems Inventory among incarcerated juvenile delinquents.** *Journal of Consulting & Clinical Psychology,* 54(3), 301–302.
Investigated the validity of the B. J. Freedman et al (see PA, Vol 62:6248) Adolescent Problems Inventory (API), a measure of social competence in situations related to antisocial behavior in adolescence, in 60 incarcerated male 14–18 yr olds. Criterion variables included historical and current behavioral indices of antisocial and disruptive behavior. Statistical analyses revealed no significant relationships in the expected direction between the API and the criteria in either the full sample or in the Black or White subsamples. Results challenge the validity of the API, and recommendations for a more refined assessment of social skills in juvenile delinquents are made. (5 ref).

25. Lira, Frank T. & Fagan, Thomas J. (1978). **The Profile of Mood States: Normative data on a delinquent population.** *Psychological Reports,* 42(2), 640–642.
Profile of Mood States normative data for 246 young adult delinquents representing Black, White and Puerto Rican ethnic groups are presented and compared with normative data previously reported for 340 male college students. Delinquents scored significantly lower on 3 of the 6 factors—Confusion, Tension, and Fatigue. Results are discussed in

terms of differences in the diagnostic and demographic characteristics of the populations compared.

26. McCallum, R. Steve & Bracken, Bruce A. (1981). **Alternate form reliability of the PPVT-R for White and Black preschool children.** *Psychology in the Schools,* 18(4), 422–425.
Pearson product moment correlation coefficients from the Revised Peabody Picture Vocabulary Test (PPVT—R) for 18 White males, 18 Black males, 18 White females, and 18 Black females (35–81 mo old), and for the total sample, were significant; values ranged from .74 to .86. Using standard scores for analyses, differences between Form L and Form M mean scores were nonsignificant for Whites, males, females, and the total group. However, for Black Ss, Form L was more difficult to complete successfully than Form M. (12 ref).

27. McGiboney, Garry W. & Huey, Wayne C. (1982). **Hand Test norms for disruptive Black adolescent males.** *Perceptual & Motor Skills,* 54(2), 441–442.
Administered the Hand Test to 51 Black adolescent males of low socioeconomic status. Ss had been referred for chronic disruptiveness in the classroom. Results show that (1) interscorer reliability was .88, (2) the Acting-Out Ratio exceeded high school norms, and (3) the Interpersonal-Environment Response Ratio was significantly imbalanced toward the Interpersonal. It is concluded that possible use of this ratio as a predictor of overt behavior should be studied. (9 ref).

28. Mims, Howard A. & Camden, Carl T. (1986). **Congruity and predictability between two measures of nonstandard dialect usage on four grammatical forms.** *Journal of Speech & Hearing Disorders,* 51(1), 42–52.
Investigated whether Nonstandard English (NSE) dialect responses to an examiner-constructed sentence completion test were congruent with and predictive of use of NSE during spontaneous conversation. The sentence completion test was designed to evoke either NSE or Standard English dialect variants of 4 grammatical forms (verb–subject agreement in the 3rd-person singular, negative concord, possessive suffix, and continuative *be*) for which the NSE dialect variants are highly stigmatized. The 76 Black male Ss were aged 15 yrs 8 mo to 23 yrs 5 mo. Responses to the sentence completion test were predictive of NSE during conversation for more than 90% of the Ss only for the negative concord grammatical form. (16 ref).

29. Newmark, Charles S.; Gentry, Lee; Warren, Nancy & Finch, Alfred J. (1981). **Racial bias in an MMPI index of schizophrenia.** *British Journal of Clinical Psychology,* 20(3), 215–216.
Assessed racial bias in the MMPI using 50 White male, 50 Black male, 50 White female, and 50 Black female 20–33 yr old psychiatric patients matched for IQ, education, and degree of pathology (WAIS and the Mental Status Schedule). MMPI criteria for diagnosing schizophrenia correctly identified 29 Black males, 38 White males, 35 Black females, and 36 White females. Although statistical analysis revealed no significant racial difference, the need to cross-validate is emphasized. (8 ref).

30. Panda, Kailas C. & Lynch, William W. (1973). **Relationships among scores on intellectual achievement responsibility and cognitive style measures in educable mentally retarded children.** *Indian Journal of Mental Retardation,* 6(2), 55–66.
Tested 33 Black and 25 White 9–13 yr old intermediate educable mentally retarded children (EMRs), IQ 50–83, on a modified version of the Intellectual Achievement Responsibility Questionnaire (IARQ) and on the Matching Familiar Figures Test (MFFT). This version of the IARQ, modified for use with EMRs, yielded a Spearman-Bowman reliability coefficient of 0.66. The relationship of the IARQ to the 1st response latency or to the total number of errors on the MFFT was low and insignificant for both Black and White

retardates. Whites and Blacks performed equally well on both instruments. Study 2 tested junior high school EMRs (157 boys and 92 girls 13–16 yrs old, IQ 50–83) on the modified IARQ, and tested 92 of the boys on the Children's Embedded Figures Test (CEFT). Results on the IARQ indicate that boys were slightly more internal than girls. The reliability coefficient was 0.67 for boys and 0.76 for girls. No significant relationship was found between IARQ and CEFT scores. (20 ref).

31. Penk, W. E. et al. (1982). **MMPI differences of Black and White male polydrug abusers seeking treatment.** *Journal of Consulting & Clinical Psychology,* 50(3), 463–465.
The hypothesis that among clinical samples of substance abusers Blacks score lower than Whites on the MMPI was supported when comparing 494 White and 159 Black male veterans (mean age 28 yrs) seeking treatment for polydrug abuse. Blacks scored lower on the Depression, Hysteria, Psychopathic Deviate, and Psychasthenia scales when age, education, socioeconomic status, and intelligence were controlled. The findings do not support the notion of ethnic bias in the MMPI. Rather, the results underscore the need for identifying moderator variables that differentially interact to produce lower Black profiles among substance abusers in comparison to Whites, but higher Black profiles among psychiatric patients. (8 ref).

32. Reinehr, Robert C.; Swartz, Jon D. & Dudley, Harold K. (1984). **Ethnic differences in the measurement of hostility in forensic patients.** *Revista Interamericana de Psicología,* 18(1–2), 53–64.
130 White, 109 Black, and 34 Hispanic male forensic patients (median age 27 yrs) admitted to the maximum security unit of a large Texas mental hospital during a 12-mo period were administered the Buss-Durkee Hostility and Guilt Inventory (HGI) and Form A of the Holtzman Inkblot Technique (HIT), a projective technique. Results reveal no significant differences between the White and Hispanic Ss, but differences appeared between the Hispanic and Black Ss on the HGI Resentment and HIT Form Definiteness subscales. White and Black Ss differed significantly on 3 HGI subscales—Guilt, Suspicion, and Resentment—and on 7 HIT variables—Form Definiteness, Form Appropriateness, Movement, Integration, Hostility, Barrier, and Popular. Black Ss scored higher on all HGI subscales and lower on all HIT variables. Results suggest that ethnic group differences may exist on both objective and projective measures of hostility. Hypotheses concerning ethnic differences in this patient population and the relationship of scores on the HGI and HIT are discussed. (Spanish abstract) (19 ref).

33. Reynolds, Cecil R. (1980). **Differential construct validity of intelligence as popularly measured: Correlations of age with raw scores on the WISC-R for Blacks, Whites, males, and females.** *Intelligence,* 4(4), 371–379.
Correlated raw scores on the 12 WISC—R subtests and the Verbal, Performance, and Full Scale IQ scales with age in years for 938 White males, 137 Black males, 927 White females, and 153 Black females. Ss were 6–16.5 yrs old. Highest and lowest correlations from the 4 groups were then contrasted for each of the 15 WISC—R variables to determine whether the magnitude of the relationship between age and performance on current tests of intelligence is constant across race and sex. None of the 15 comparisons of corrections yielded differences that were significant. Regression coefficients between age and raw scores across groups differed only with respect to the Full Scale IQ, showing smaller incremental changes with age for Black males than for other groups. Results indicate that the relationship between age and intelligence test performance is relatively constant across race and sex. Findings also support the construct validity of the WISC—R as a measure of children's intelligence for Blacks, Whites, males, and females, although some evidence was

found to indicate slower development of "g" in Black males as compared to the other groups. (28 ref).

34. Reynolds, Cecil R. & Paget, Kathleen D. (1981). **Factor analysis of the Revised Children's Manifest Anxiety Scale for Blacks, Whites, males, and females with a national normative sample.** *Journal of Consulting & Clinical Psychology,* 49(3), 352–359.
Factor analyzed responses to "What I Think and Feel," the Revised Children's Manifest Anxiety Scale (RCMAS), using 4,972 6–19 yr olds (2,208 White males, 2,176 White females, 289 Black males, and 299 Black females) who participated in a nationwide standardization of the instrument. Three anxiety factors emerged that were consistent with earlier studies employing more limited samples. The Lie scale of the instrument separated into 2 distinct factors. The resulting 5-factor (3 anxiety and 2 lie) solution was then separately applied to males, females, Whites, and Blacks. The 5-factor solution was equally appropriate for all groups. Comparative analysis of the factors across groups indicated that the factor structure of the RCMAS was invariant with regard to race and sex. (25 ref).

35. Shaffer, John W.; Kinlock, Timothy W. & Nurco, David N. (1982). **Factor structure of the MMPI-168 in male narcotic addicts.** *Journal of Clinical Psychology,* 38(3), 656–661.
Factor analyses of abbreviated clinical and validated scales derived from the MMPI-168 yielded essentially the same solutions reported for full-length versions of the inventory. However, previously derived item-level factor scales did not emerge as distinct factors. Although the factor structures associated with 460 Black and White narcotic addicts (mean age 28.7 yrs) were highly similar, significant mean differences between the racial groups on many of the scales suggested the presence of greater psychopathology among White addicts. (17 ref).

36. Sheffey, Marie A.; Bingham, Rosie P. & Walsh, W. Bruce. (1986). **Concurrent validity of Holland's theory for college-educated Black men.** *Journal of Multicultural Counseling & Development,* 14(4), 149–156.
Expanded on J. L. Holland's (1985) theory of vocational choice—that individuals enter occupational environments consistent with their personality types—by examining the influence of race on vocational choice. 151 college-educated Black males (aged 23–74 yrs) were chosen from 6 occupations (engineers, physicians, attorneys, coaches, music teachers, and accountants) corresponding to Holland's environmental classifications (realistic, artistic, investigative, social, enterprising, and conventional). Ss responded to 2 scales developed by Holland: the Vocational Preference Inventory (VPI)—Seventh Revision and the Self Directed Search (SDS): A Guide to Educational and Vocational Planning. Results indicate that the VPI and SDS discriminated among environmental choice groups more effectively than among the occupational groups. It is suggested that the VPI and the SDS are somewhat appropriate for Black American adults.

37. Terrell, Francis & Terrell, Sandra L. (1981). **An inventory to measure cultural mistrust among Blacks.** *Western Journal of Black Studies,* 5(3), 180–184.
Developed an inventory designed to measure cultural mistrust among Blacks in the domains of Education and Training, Interpersonal Relations, Business and Work, and Politics and Law. The initial 72-item Cultural Mistrust Inventory (CMI) was administered to 172 Black male undergraduates by a Black male examiner. Psychometric strategies were used to examine the internal construction of the CMI and to eliminate items of low discriminatory value or those that significantly correlated with the Social Desirability Scale. In an examination of external validity, it was found that Ss with a high exposure to racial discrimination had higher mistrust

scores than those with lower exposure to racial discrimination. A 2-wk test–retest revealed adequate temporal stability. A copy of the final 48-item CMI is appended. (21 ref).

38. Terrell, Francis & Taylor, Jerome. (1978). **The development of an inventory to measure certain aspects of Black nationalist ideology.** *Psychology,* 15(4), 31–33.
Defines the 4 domains of the Black nationalist position and offers a Black Ideology Scale (BIS) sensitive to a person's identification with Black nationalism. 134 11th- and 12th-grade Black males were given the Jackson Social Desirability Scale; the Taylor, Wilson, and Dobbins Racialism Scale; and the Penick Inventory. The BIS was developed using an item discrimination analysis, an index of homogeneity, and a measure of social desirability. Items were tested for convergent and divergent validity. The hypotheses were offered: (a) Ss obtaining high scores on the BIS would be more familiar with Black customs, as measured by the Penick Inventory, than would low-scoring BIS respondents. (b) Ss responding high on the BIS would be less likely to accept White stereotypic values of Blacks, as measured by the Racialism Scale, than low-scoring BIS respondents. Significant F tests were obtained for both hypotheses. It is concluded that the BIS can describe specifics about attitudinal differences in the Black population and can be used to provide information on the behavioral correlates of individual differences in ideological orientation. (6 ref).

39. Terrell, Francis; Terrell, Sandra L. & Taylor, Jerome. (1981). **Effects of race of examiner and cultural mistrust on the WAIS performance of Black students.** *Journal of Consulting & Clinical Psychology,* 49(5), 750–751.
100 Black males (17–19 yrs old) were given the Terrell Cultural Mistrust Inventory, and groups with high and low levels of mistrust of Whites were identified. Half of the Ss in each group were then administered the WAIS by a White examiner. The remaining were tested by a Black examiner. The Black examiner/high mistrust group scored significantly higher than the White examiner/high mistrust group. In addition, the White examiner/low mistrust group scored significantly higher than the White examiner/high mistrust group. (4 ref).

40. Terrell, Francis; Taylor, Jerome & Terrell, Sandra L. (1978). **Effects of type of social reinforcement on the intelligence performance of lower-class Black children.** *Journal of Consulting & Clinical Psychology,* 46(6), 1538–1539.
Examined the effects of different types of reinforcement on the performance of 80 Black 2nd grade males on the WISC—R. Ss given candy or culturally relevant social reinforcement obtained significantly higher scores than Ss given either no reinforcement or traditional social reinforcement. (2 ref).

41. Terrell, Francis; Terrell, Sandra L. & Taylor, Jerome. (1980). **Effects of race of examiner and type of reinforcement on the intelligence test performance of lower-class Black children.** *Psychology in the Schools,* 17(2), 270–272.
Selected a total of 120 Black 9–11 yr old males and assigned them to either a White or Black examiner. Ss were given no reinforcement, tangible reinforcement, traditional social reinforcement, or culturally relevant social reinforcement after each correct response on the WISC—R. Ss given tangible rewards, regardless of race of examiner, obtained significantly higher scores than did Ss given no reinforcement or Ss given traditional social reinforcement. Also, Ss given culturally relevant social reinforcement by a Black examiner obtained significantly higher scores than did Ss given culturally relevant reinforcement by the White examiner. (3 ref).

42. Walters, Glenn D. et al. (1983). **Racial variations on the MacAndrew Alcoholism Scale of the MMPI.** *Journal of Consulting & Clinical Psychology,* 51(6), 935–936.

27 Black and 46 White male alcoholic and 27 Black and 46 White male nonalcoholic psychiatric inpatients (aged 18–45 yrs) were administered the MacAndrew Alcoholism Scale (MAC). Black and White alcoholics performed similarly in terms of mean score and accuracy of identification by cutting scores. Black nonalcoholics scored significantly higher than White nonalcoholics. The MAC discriminated successfully between White alcoholics and nonalcoholics, but not between Black alcoholics and nonalcoholics. (5 ref).

43. Walters, Glenn D.; Greene, Roger L. & Jeffrey, Timothy B. (1984). **Discriminating between alcoholic and nonalcoholic Blacks and Whites on the MMPI.** *Journal of Personality Assessment,* 48(5), 486–488.
Investigated the influence of race (Black, White) on the MMPI performance of 27 Black (mean age 33.41 yrs) and 46 White (mean age 34.89 yrs) male alcoholic inpatients and 27 Black (mean age 24.41 yrs) and 46 White (mean age 26.26 yrs) male nonalcoholic psychiatric inpatients. Findings show that while Black and White alcoholics failed to differ on the MMPI, White alcoholics presented as less disturbed and Black alcoholics as less defensive and distressed, compared to their respective nonalcoholic counterparts. Only White alcoholics were accurately identifed by the MMPI 2–4/4–2 high-point pair combination and only White alcoholics achieved more high-point pairs containing Scale 4 relative to nonalcoholic controls. It is suggested that the MMPI may be more efficient in identifying alcoholism in Whites than in Blacks. (5 ref).

44. Wen, Shih-Sung. (1976). **Item validity of the Lie Scale of the Eysenck Personality Inventory.** *Psychological Reports,* 39(3, Pt 1), 880–882.
Assessed the item validity of the 9-item Lie scale of the Eysenck Personality Inventory, Form A, using the responses of 320 White and 320 Black males and females. The corrected point-biserial correlations indicated that only 2 items were significantly valid across race and sex. The remaining 7 items were valid for either race only or specific race–sex combinations. Results support the hypothesis that social desirability in personality assessment may vary from one ethnic group to another and from one race–sex combination to another as well.

45. Whitworth, Randolph H. & Gibbons, Ruth T. (1986). **Cross-racial comparison of the WAIS and WAIS—R.** *Educational & Psychological Measurement,* 46(4), 1041–1049.
Presents a cross-racial comparison of the Wechsler Adult Intelligence Scale (WAIS) with the Revised WAIS (WAIS—R), using 25 Anglo, 25 Black, and 25 Mexican-American male undergraduates. Ss were administered both versions of the WAIS on the same day, using a procedure that precluded the repetition of identical test items. Significant differences were found among the racial groups, with the Anglos scoring higher than the Blacks or Mexican-Americans. The WAIS and WAIS—R scores were all highly correlated, but the WAIS—R produced significantly lower scores than the WAIS for all 3 groups. Despite significant differences for ethnicity and test form, no significant interaction (form by race) was found, confirming that the WAIS/WAIS—R differences were consistent across racial groups. Results are discussed in terms of sociocultural and bilingual factors affecting test bias. (9 ref).

46. Widerstrom, Anne H.; Miller, Lucy J. & Marzano, Robert J. (1986). **Sex and race differences in the identification of communicative disorders in preschool children as measured by the Miller Assessment for Preschoolers.** *Journal of Communication Disorders,* 19(3), 219–226.
1,204 preschoolers, approximately 100 boys and 100 girls at each of 6 age groups (3 yrs, 3.5 yrs, 4 yrs, 4.5 yrs, 5 yrs, and 5.5 yrs) were administered the Miller Assessment for Preschoolers (MAP). Scores on the Verbal Index of the MAP were analyzed for each of the age groups by sex and race

using 6 2-way analyses of variance (ANOVAs). Results indicate that boys and girls in all 6 age groups were equally identified as being at risk for communication disorders. At 3, 3.5, and 5 yrs, Black Ss had a greater likelihood of being identified at risk than White Ss. It is concluded that the MAP Verbal Index is not biased for sex and that it is less culturally biased against older preschool children than the Peabody Picture Vocabulary Test (PPVT), the Test for Auditory Comprehension of Language, the Carrow Elicited Language Inventory, and the Boehm Test of Basic Concepts. (24 ref).

47. Woodbury, Roger & Shurling, James. (1975). **Factorial dimensions of the Jesness Inventory with Black delinquents.** *Educational & Psychological Measurement,* 35(4), 979–981.
Identified the personality dimensions in the Jesness Inventory among 250 adjudicated Black delinquent males (mean age 14.6 yrs). A principal components factor analysis with a varimax rotation identified 3 factors: self-estrangement, social isolation, and immaturity. The proportions of total common-factor variance accounted for by the 3 factors were .511, .286, and .203, respectively. Results suggest that the factors might be a part of a larger alienation construct in Black delinquents.

48. Yater, Allan C.; Boyd, Miller & Barclay, Allan. (1975). **A comparative study of WPPSI and WISC performances of disadvantaged children.** *Journal of Clinical Psychology,* 31(1), 78–80.
Administered the WISC and the Wechsler Preschool and Primary Scale of Intelligence (WPPSI) to 60 Black disadvantaged children from Head Start preschool and Follow-Through kindergarten and 1st grade. Results show (a) there were no sex differences for either the WPPSI or the WISC, (b) the WPPSI consistently overestimated the Verbal and Full Scale IQs obtained from the WISC, and (c) there were no significant WPPSI–WISC differences for Performance and Full Scale IQs.

EXPERIMENTAL PSYCHOLOGY (HUMAN)

49. Ball, Portia M. & Cantor, Gordon N. (1974). **White boys' ratings of pictures of Whites and Blacks as related to amount of familiarization.** *Perceptual & Motor Skills,* 39(2), 883–890.
120 4th- and 5th-grade White boys were shown photographs of 4 White and 4 Black boys, which were presented 1, 5, 10, or 20 times. Ss then rated these photographs, plus 2 (1 White, 1 Black) not previously exposed, on a scale indicating the extent to which they "would like to bring the boy home to spend some time with them and their families." The Black pictures were rated more favorably than were the White pictures, and increasing familiarization was associated with an increase in favorability for Black pictures but a decrease for White pictures. The attitudinal effects of stimulus familiarization are discussed.

50. Busse, Thomas V. (1968). **Establishment of the flexible thinking factor in fifth-grade boys.** *Journal of Psychology,* 69(1), 93–100.
A battery of 14 tests was administered to 61 lower-class Negro boys in order to locate a flexible thinking factor. The tests included 6 predicted to tap flexible thinking (Match Problems A and B, Water Jug Test, insight problems, closure speed, Embedded Figures Test), as well as 8 reference tests (measures of impulsivity in problem solving, unusual uses, and marking speed, plus 5 primary mental abilities). A factor analysis of the 14 tests yielded 3 factors, the largest of which was clearly identified as flexible thinking. (20 ref).

51. Doty, Richard L.; Applebaum, Steven; Zusho, Hiroyuki & Settle, R. Gregg. (1985). **Sex differences in odor identification ability: A cross-cultural analysis.** *Neuropsychologia,* 23(5), 667–672.

To ascertain the generality of a sex difference noted in odor identification ability, the University of Pennsylvania Smell Identification Test developed by the 1st author and colleagues (see PA, Vol 72:5611) was administered to 4 groups of Ss: 660 male and 899 female White Americans (mean ages 39.1 and 41.1 yrs, respectively); 210 male and 228 female Black Americans (mean ages 29.7 and 36 yrs, respectively); 53 male and 53 female Korean-Americans (mean ages 14.1 and 14.3 yrs, respectively); and 117 male and 191 female native Japanese (mean ages 25.5 and 21.8 yrs, respectively). The women of all 4 groups outperformed the men to the same relative degree. The Korean-American group performed better than the Black and White American groups, who, in turn, outperformed the native Japanese. Analyses of the proportions of Ss correctly answering each of the test items revealed considerable similarity of relative item difficulty among the S groups. Data suggest that sex differences in odor identification ability are probably not due to ethnic or cultural factors per se. (33 ref).

52. Lietz, Enno S. (1972). **Perceptual-motor abilities of disadvantaged and advantaged kindergarten children.** *Perceptual & Motor Skills,* 35(3), 887–890.
Individually administered a revised form of the Purdue Perceptual-Motor Survey to 50 disadvantaged and 50 middle-class kindergartners. Advantaged Ss performed significantly better than disadvantaged Ss. Boys performed as well as girls, and the White and Black disadvantaged Ss performed equally well except on perceptual-motor match.

53. Norton, Darryl E. & Hodgson, William R. (1973). **Intelligibility of Black and White speakers for Black and White listeners.** *Language & Speech,* 16(3), 207–210.
Investigated the auditory discrimination ability of 10 Black and 10 White male undergraduates. Ss listened to phonetically balanced word lists spoken by 10 Black and 10 White speakers. No significant differences were found between the discrimination ability of the 2 groups. However, both groups obtained better discrimination scores when listening to White rather than Black speakers.

54. Payne, R. B. & Turkat, Ira D. (1982). **Sex, race, and psychomotor reminiscence.** *Bulletin of the Psychonomic Society,* 19(6), 336–338.
Extended the search for boundary conditions of the well-known female dominance in psychomotor reminiscence by comparing Ss of Caucasoid and Negroid ancestries. Apportioned equally among the 4 combinations of sex and race, 72 Ss (mean age 19.6 yrs) engaged in alternating periods of massed practice and rest on a mirror tracking task. Females of both races reminisced more than their male counterparts, but race contributed virtually nothing to the variance of reminiscence. However, Whites maintained an essentially constant margin to task proficiency over Blacks across the practice sequence. Various hypotheses concerning this effect are discussed. (17 ref).

55. Prestrude, A. M. & Larson, Carl. (1980). **Visual thresholds during dark adaptation: Comparison in Black and White observers.** *Journal of Cross-Cultural Psychology,* 11(2), 203–211.
The alleged lack of color vocabulary for short wavelength discriminations among linguistic groups with darker skin pigmentation has been thought to be due to a correlated increase in melanin pigment in the ocular media. The presence of this tritanopiclike condition in Black observers was tested by comparing the dark adapted thresholds of 13 White and 10 Black male undergraduates with white, red, green, and blue test lights. There were no significant differences between White and Black Ss for any of the test lights. The range of cone and rod thresholds for each group was the same. Results do not support the hypothesis that linguistic deficiencies in color

discrimination terms reflect a tritanopiclike condition due to increased ocular pigmentation. (12 ref).

PHYSIOLOGICAL PSYCHOLOGY

56. Brunswick, Ann F. & Collette, Patricia. (1977). **Psychophysical correlates of elevated blood pressure: A study of urban Black adolescents.** *Journal of Human Stress,* 3(4), 19–31.
Reports the results of a broad-ranged health study conducted in the late 1960s of a community probability sample of 496 urban Black adolescents. Certain conditions that have been found to be correlated with elevated blood pressure (BP) later in life were analyzed. On the basis of 3 BP readings taken during the course of a ½-hr medical examination, the sample of Black 12–17 yr olds was classified into 3 groups: consistently high readings (diastolic 90 mm Hg or greater on all 3 or on 2 out of 3 readings, 37 Ss); labile or only 1 high reading (49 Ss); no high BP reading (410 Ss). Percentage cross-tabulation and multiple discriminant analyses were performed. Findings point to the significance of obesity as an indicator of elevated BP in adolescence. Differences were observed between boys and girls in conditions associated with elevated BP and in the strength of the association. Smoking was a significant correlate for boys, but not for girls. It was the strongest discriminator of elevated BP for young male adolescents and was more distinctive of fluctuating or labile high pressures than consistently high pressures. In general, the social and psychophysical correlates were stronger definers of elevated BP for adolescent boys than for girls. Fluctuating or labile BP in itself comprised a distinct condition among teenaged boys but not girls, with determinants significantly different from those observed in relation to consistently elevated BP. (30 ref).

57. Friedman, Sarah L. & Jacobs, Blanche S. (1981). **Sex differences in neonates' behavioral responsiveness to repeated auditory stimulation.** *Infant Behavior & Development,* 4(2), 175–183.
Used 6 response measures to evaluate the responsiveness of 9 not-yet circumcised Black male neonates and 9 Black female neonates to pure tone stimuli. The females were quicker to respond than the males. On the initial trials, females responded with more or bigger responses; they also tended to be more responsive to the auditory stimulation as indicated by the duration of their responsiveness to repeated stimulation and by their activity level. Results are presented in the context of no previous report of sex differences in neonates' auditory responsiveness and an existing data base indicating that female children and adults are more responsive than males to auditory stimulation. (36 ref).

COMMUNICATION SYSTEMS

58. Brown, Jane D. & Campbell, Kenneth. (1986). **Race and gender in music videos: The same beat but a different drummer.** *Journal of Communication,* 36(1), 94–106.
Compared how men and women and Blacks and Whites are portrayed in 75 videos from Music Television (MTV) and 37 videos from the Black Entertainment Television (BET) channel. Data indicate that 83% of all videos shown on MTV featured White male singers or bands led by White males; White female singers or band leaders were featured in only 11% of the videos, and non-Whites accounted for only 5% of the leaders of the groups shown. Among videos aired on BET, 54% featured Black male leads and 19% featured Black female leads. White men were the center of attention and power and were more often aggressive and hostile; women and Blacks were rarely part of the foreground.

59. Bryant, Ernest & O'Connell, Daniel. (1971). **A phonemic analysis of nine samples of glossolalic speech.** *Psychonomic Speech,* 22(2), 81–83.
Analyzed 9 tape-recorded samples of glossolalia from a middle-aged Caucasian business man, a young Roman Catholic woman, and an elderly Negro woman. A remarkably low correlation was found with English samples from the same Ss, ascribable primarily to variation in vowel frequency. Nonetheless, all glossolalic phonemes were within the normal phonemic repertoire of native speakers of English. There was a divergence of syllables/pause rates between glossolalia and English. It is concluded that optional articulatory choices characteristic of glossolalic samples can evidently be studied by means of accepted scientific procedures independently of theological or religious explication.

60. Drabman, Ronald S. & Thomas, Margaret H. (1977). **Children's imitation of aggressive and prosocial behavior when viewing alone and in pairs.** *Journal of Communication,* 27(3), 199–205.
Compared the behavior of 40 5-yr-old Black males who viewed a 3.5-min prosocial or aggressive film individually or in pairs. The aggressive film showed an adult male physically and verbally assaulting an adult costumed as a clown. The prosocial film showed the model and clown engaging in friendly and cooperative play. The Ss, individually or in pairs, then participated in a 5-min free play session in an experimental room containing both the adult clown and the toys seen in the film. Ss who participated in pairs showed more aggression than those who participated alone. Aggression toward the clown was higher for those who watched the aggressive film. Ss who viewed the prosocial film engaged in more constructive play, particularly for those participating in pairs. There was no difference between individuals and pairs in prosocial behavior for those Ss in the aggressive film condition.

61. Gerken, Kathryn C. & Deichmann, John W. (1979). **The ability of listeners to report oral responses of Black and White children.** *Language, Speech & Hearing Services in the Schools,* 10(1), 35–46.
A group of 20 Black and 20 White college students viewed videotapes of 8 1st-grade boys and recorded in writing the boys' responses to 10 vocabulary items from the WISC. The 8 boys represented 4 dialect groups: Black standard, Black nonstandard, White standard, and White nonstandard. Analysis of the data showed significant interactions between race and dialect of child relative to (a) a listener's ability to report in writing a child's verbatim responses without producing a change in the WISC scoring of the responses, and (b) a listener's ability to restate in writing a child's responses without producing a change in the scoring of the responses. Further, both dialect and race of child were significantly related to the total number of errors the listener made in writing the child's responses. Significant interaction occurred between race of listener and race of child and among race of listener, race of child, and dialect of child relative to the total number of errors the listener made in writing the child's responses. (55 ref).

62. Hudson, Amelia I. & Holbrook, Anthony. (1982). **Fundamental frequency characteristics of young Black adults: Spontaneous speaking and oral reading.** *Journal of Speech & Hearing Research,* 25(1), 25–28.
Investigated the speaking fundamental vocal frequency (FVF) of 200 18–29 yr old Blacks during prompted spontaneous speech and reading and compared the results with previous findings for White Ss of comparable age. Central tendency and dispersion values were calculated from data obtained with a fundamental frequency analyzer. The mean modal FVF for spontaneous speaking was 108.05 Hz for men and 188.85 Hz for women. The mean range was 80.70–166.65 Hz (6.27 tones) for men and 132.55–270.80 Hz (6.18 tones) for women. Men showed smaller excursions from the mean mode to the lower limit of the mean range than from the mean mode to the upper limit of the mean range. Women had a range of 81.95 Hz above and 56.30 Hz below the mean mode but approximately equal tonal intervals above and below. A comparison of prompted spontaneous speech to reading for the same Ss indicated that the mean modal FVF was significantly lower and the mean range was significantly greater for speaking than for reading. Both men and women had a mean speaking range of 1 octave. In comparison to values for Whites, Black Ss had a lower mean FVF. (15 ref).

63. Shuter, Robert. (1979). **The dap in the military: Hand-to-hand communication.** *Journal of Communication,* 29(1), 136–142.
Interviewed 95 servicemen about "the dap"—a series of ritualized hand movements performed by Black enlisted men stationed outside the US during the 1960's and early 1970's. The military often went to extremes to eliminate the use of this symbol of Black solidarity. With improved racial conditions in the services overseas, use of the dap declined and the regulations prohibiting it have been abolished. It is still employed, however, by Black veterans working in Black veteran agencies, and it has been found effective in therapy with Black veterans. (12 ref).

64. Szalay, Lorand B. & Bryson, Jean A. (1973). **Measurement of psychocultural distance: A comparison of American Blacks and Whites.** *Journal of Personality & Social Psychology,* 26(2), 166–177.
Used the distribution of verbal associations produced in continued association tasks to compare a blue-collar sample of 50 White and 50 Black male US Army recruits on 3 dimensions: dominance, affinity structure, and intergroup similarity of concepts. The study focused on 60 concept themes selected in the representation of 15 broader problem domains. The distance between the White and the Black groups showed considerable variations across domains. The "social" domain showed an especially sizable distance with respect to both relative priorities and meaning similarity. When results were compared with domestic and foreign samples studied previously by L. Szalay, the Black–White distance in the 3 dimensions was consistently greater than the distance between White urban workers and farmers, but smaller than between White students and workers. The distance between US and Korean culture groups was of a much larger magnitude. Implications for the measurement of trends of social development and culture changes are discussed. (34 ref).

65. Terrell, Francis; Terrell, Sandra L. & Golin, Sanford. (1977). **Language productivity of Black and White children in Black versus White situations.** *Language & Speech,* 20(4), 377–383.
Tested the hypothesis that Ss would have increased language productivity when talking to members of their own ethnic group than when talking to members of a different ethnic group. 148 7–9 yr old males participated in this study. Ss consisted of 22 Blacks who were required to give a speech to all Black Ss; 22 Blacks who were required to give a speech to all White Ss; 22 Whites who were required to give a speech to all Black Ss; and 22 Whites required to give a speech to all Black Ss. The speeches were recorded and analyzed. Results support the hypothesis. Since language productivity depended on the interaction of race and context, the results are not in accord with the deficiency theory of Black–White differences in language productivity. (15 ref).

66. Weigel, M. Margaret & Weigel, Ronald M. (1985). **Directive use in a migrant agricultural community: A test of Ervin-Tripp's hypotheses.** *Language in Society,* 14(1), 63–79.
Tested Ervin-Tripp's hypotheses concerning the relationship between the variables (the relative social ranks of the speaker and recipient, their ages, their familiarity, the presence/ab-

8

sence of outsiders, territorial location, task expectations) and the choice of the identified syntactically based directive variants (imperatives, imbedded imperatives, need statements), using a sample of predominantly Black male migratory agricultural labor population. Data indicate that the imperative form was used almost exclusively in those contexts where the syntactically based directive variants were expected to occur, thus contradicting most predictions derived from Ervin-Tripp's model for these directive variants. The preference for imperatives is suggested to be largely a consequence of the antagonistic relationships within the migrant farmworker community. Results also suggest that the set of decision rules used in choosing among directive variants according to social criteria is a function of crosscultural (i.e., social class and ethnic) variation and social and physical characteristics of the interaction setting. (45 ref).

DEVELOPMENTAL PSYCHOLOGY

67. Biller, Henry B. (1968). **A note on father absence and masculine development in lower-class Negro and White boys.** *Child Development,* 39(3), 1003–1006.
Explored the relation of father absence and sociocultural background to masculine development. Ss were 29 6-yr-old lower-class Negro and White boys. In terms of projective sex-role orientation (the It Scale for Children), White father-present boys were the most masculine; there was no significant difference between White father-absent and Negro father-present boys; and the Negro father-absent boys were the least masculine. No significant differences relating to either direct sex-role preference or teacher's ratings of masculinity on a multidimensional scale were found. The results suggested that underlying sex-role orientation is more influenced by father availability and family background than are more manifest aspects of masculinity.

68. Bloom, Richard D. (1968). **Dimensions of adjustment in adolescent boys: Negro-White comparisons.** *Journal of School Psychology,* 7(3), 63–69.
Performed separate factor analyses on the responses of a random sample of 30 White and 30 Negro adolescent boys to 40 closed-end questions dealing with adjustmental states. There was apparent overlap between the 2 factor structures. For both samples, the following factors were tentatively identified: global distress, aggressive impulses, physical distress, social isolation, optimism vs. pessimism, test anxiety, general anxiety, and guilt reactions. While there was comparability between the 2 factor structures, the factors extracted for the Negro sample exhibited less coherency and organization.

69. Brown, Duane; Fulkerson, Katherine F.; Vedder, Marilyn & Ware, William B. (1983). **Self-estimate ability in Black and White 8th-, 10th, and 12th-grade males and females.** *Vocational Guidance Quarterly,* 32(1), 21–28.
Extended the work of R. P. O'Hara and D. V. Tiedeman (1959) and R. J. Tierney and A. Herman (see PA, Vol 51: 3977) by conducting a cross-sectional study of self-awareness among 8th, 10th, and 12th graders; examined racial differences in making self-estimates; and investigated sex-related differences in ability of make self-estimates. Ss were 92 8th, 89 10th, and 88 12th graders; there were 146 females and 123 males, and 58 were Black and 211 White. Ss completed a personal data sheet, the Self-Estimate Questionnaire, Work Values Inventory, Career Decision Making Inventory, and Differential Aptitude Test. Results show a significant difference between Black and White Ss' ability to self-estimate, and there were no differences between abilities of males and females to self-estimate, with the latter finding supporting the finding by Tierney and Herman. The lack of differences among Ss at the 3 grade levels does not support the findings of O'Hara and Tiedeman. Overall results suggest that career

counselors need to consider means of increasing self-awareness. (27 ref).

70. Burnes, Kay. (1970). **Patterns of WISC scores for children of two socioeconomic classes and races.** *Child Development,* 41(2), 493–499.
Negro and White 8-yr-old boys from lower- and upper-middle-class homes were given the WISC in order to determine group patterns of intellectual abilities. Results show lower-class Ss of both races obtaining the lower scores, but configurations of scores for each group are similar. A few differences are found between socioeconomic groups, not between races.

71. Burnes, Kay. (1971). **Clinical assumptions about WISC subtest score and test behavior relationships.** *Journal of Consulting & Clinical Psychology,* 36(2), 299.
Administered the WISC to 40 White and 38 Negro 8-yr-old boys. The experimenter and an observer independently scored the S's behavior for attention, energy level, social skill, task persistence, and concern about performance. 13 clinical psychologists completed a questionnaire ranking behaviors considered important to performance on each of the WISC subtests. 15 hypotheses resulted, 8 involving attention and none involving concern about performance. Analysis of scores and ratings produced 8 significant relationships, 3 involving concern about performance. Emphasis on attention was found to be greatly overestimated. 16 correlations were significant for race and socioeconomic status. Results indicate that (a) most of the clinically assumed relationships do not exist, and (b) the importance of test behavior to performance may vary among groups of children and tasks.

72. Busse, Thomas V. (1969). **Child-rearing antecedents of flexible thinking.** *Developmental Psychology,* 1(5), 585–591.
Related the behavior, attitudes, and social class of 48 Negro mothers and 48 Negro fathers to the development of their 5th-grade boys' flexible thinking, defined as the ability to consider alternative means to a given end. Linear relationships were found linking flexible thinking with mother commands, father love, father total words, social class, and 2 father factors, powerlessness vs powerfulness and rigid, absolute vs warm, sympathetic standards. Quadratic relationships were found linking flexible thinking with mother manipulation, mother commands, mother pointing, father manipulation, and 3 father factors active vs ignoring role with children, discouraging vs tolerating physical aggression in children, and powerlessness vs powerfulness.

73. Cheong, Keywon; Toney, Michael B. & Stinner, William F. (1986). **Racial differences among young men in the selection of metropolitan and nonmetropolitan destinations.** *Rural Sociology,* 51(2), 222–228.
Results from the cohort of 5,222 males (aged 14–24 yrs) of the Center for Human Resource Research's (1983) National Longitudinal Surveys indicate that young Black males are much less likely than White males to select nonmetropolitan destinations. Migration increases racial segregation. Findings are discussed in both demographic and socioeconomic contexts.

74. Doll, Paddy A.; Fagot, Hacker J. & Himbert, Joanna D. (1971). **Experimenter effect on sex-role preference among Black and White lower-class male children.** *Psychological Reports,* 29(3, Pt. 2), 1295-1301.
Administered the It Scale for Children to 120 White and 120 Black lower-class male children at 6-, 9-, and 12-yr-old age levels. Neither sex of the experimenter (E) nor the age and race of S had any main effects on sex-role preference scores, but there were significant interactions between sex of E, race of S, and administration method. (19 ref.).

75. Epstein, Ralph & Komorita, S. S. (1970). **Self-esteem, success-failure, and locus of control in Negro children.** *Developmental Psychology,* 4(1, Pt. 1), 2–8.
Evaluated personality and situational parameters related to internal–external control by investigating self-esteem and success–failure treatments. A 3 by 2 factorial design was employed with 20 4th-6th grade Negro boys in each of 6 experimental conditions. Results confirm the predictions that (a) failure rather than success experiences were attributed to external causes, and (b) high-self-esteem Ss were more internal than low- or moderate-esteem Ss. Results imply that the belief in one's powerlessness, arising from membership in a stigmatized minority group, may be cushioned by a positive self-concept. (25 ref).

76. Ewing, Dorlesa B. (1971). **The relations among anomie, dogmatism, and selected personal-social factors in asocial adolescent boys.** *Journal of Social Issues,* 27(4), 159–169.
Studied Black, Mexican, and White American high school boys to examine relations between observed asocial behavior and anomie, dogmatism, and selected personal-social variables. Hypotheses were predicted on the assumptions that belief systems of anomic adolescent boys would center about a dim world view, indicating closed-mindedness (dogmatism); and that such boys would be more likely than their counterparts to pursue illegitimate goals in order to reduce their anomic condition. The study investigates whether boys who exhibit observed asocial school behavior also manifest high anomie, dogmatism, and self-reported asociality (tested predelinquency).

77. Fulkerson, Katherine F.; Furr, Susan R. & Brown, Duane. (1983). **Expectations and achievement among third-, sixth-, and ninth-grade Black and White males and females.** *Developmental Psychology,* 19(2), 231–236.
Hypothesized that (a) boys in 3rd, 6th, and 9th grade would have higher expectations than girls, but only 9th-grade boys would have higher achievement; (b) achievement would increase with grade; (c) Whites would have higher expectations and achievement than Blacks; and (d) realism would increase with grade level. 112 Black and White 3rd, 6th, and 9th graders recorded their expectations and then attempted to perform tasks of math, mazes, or geometric drawings. Contrary to predictions and most previous studies, no significant sex differences were found. Whites achieved higher scores on mazes and drawings than did Blacks. The expectations of Blacks rose with grade level, regardless of concomitant achievements; but expectations of Whites did not. (26 ref).

78. Goffeney, Barbara; Henderson, Norman B. & Butler, Bruce V. (1971). **Negro–White, male–female eight-month developmental scores compared with seven-year WISC and Bender Test scores.** *Child Development,* 42(2), 595–604.
A total of 626 Bayley scale of infant tests scores at about 8 mo significantly correlated with WISC Full, Verbal, and Performance, and Bender-Gestalt scores at 7 yrs. For Black boys, no 8-mo measure correlated significantly with any 7-yr measure. Mental and fine motor scores of girls correlated significantly with Full, Verbal, Performance, and Bender scores, but gross motor did not. Except for gross motor, female scores contributed most to total group relationships. Generally, mental and fine motor measurements had significant but low predictive value for girls of both races and White boys but nonsignificant value for Black boys.

79. Gottesman, Ruth L. (1972). **Auditory discrimination ability in Negro dialect-speaking children.** *Journal of Learning Disabilities,* 5(2), 94–101.
Selected 3 groups of 40 1st grade boys: Negro dialect-speaking, Negro standard English-speaking, and Caucasian standard English-speaking. Ss were given an auditory discrimination test composed of word pairs pronounced as (a) homonyms in Negro dialect but as contrasting words in standard English, and (b) contrasting words by all Ss. The word pairs were presented on tape by both Negro dialect and standard English speakers. Results indicate that there were no significant group differences in auditory discrimination performance on those word pairs which could be commonly differentiated in the speech of all Ss. However, both groups of standard English-speaking Ss scored significantly higher than the group of Negro dialect-speaking Ss on those word pairs pronounced as homonyms in Negro dialect when they were presented contrastingly by standard English speakers. (19 ref.).

80. Harris, Helena. (1970). **Development of moral attitudes in White and Negro boys.** *Developmental Psychology,* 2(3), 376–383.
White and Negro boys of 4 social class levels were compared in maturity of moral attitudes. A Piaget-type interview was individually administered to 200 9.5–11.5 yr old Ss, equally distributed in an 8-cell 2-by-2 ANOVA. The interview yielded 5 moral attitude scores for each S. The WISC Vocabulary test was also administered. The hypotheses tested were that maturity of moral attitudes was positively related to: (a) social class, (b) white race, and (c) vocabulary skills. Results of (a) were supported on all 5 subtests while (b) was supported on only 2 subtests. The hypothesis relating to (c) was supported. Complex interrelationships on the 3 variables are suggested. (16 ref).

81. Hartnagel, Timothy F. (1970). **Father absence and self-conception among lower class White and Negro boys.** *Social Problems,* 18(2), 152–163.
Explored the effects of fatherlessness and race on the self-conceptions of lower-class adolescent males using the orientation of symbolic interactionism and the semantic differential for measurement. A distinction was made between actual and normative self, and the categories of White and Black, father-absent and father-present boys were examined. All categories exhibited significant differences between actual and normative self, but the magnitude of differences varied among categories: Black father-absent boys had smaller differences than White father-absent boys; there was no difference between White and Black father-present boys. The smaller differences of the Black father-absent boys was the result of their more potent actual self-conceptions. Several interpretations of these results are discussed.

82. Hauser, Stuart T. (1972). **Black and White identity development: Aspects and perspectives.** *Journal of Youth & Adolescence,* 1(2), 113–130.
Constructed empirical definitions and 5 variants of identity formation, using a technique for studying multiple self-images and applied the method to 22 Black and White lower socio-economic class male adolescents. Ss were tested and given in-depth interviews twice a yr for the last 3 yrs of high school. Results disclose that the Ss had emphatically different patterns of identity formation. Blacks were characterized by unchanging configurations of self-images. Both the content of their self-definitions and the interrelations for these self-definitions remained strikingly stable over time. Whites displayed a progressive integration of different self-images and stabilization of the content of these images. The patterns displayed by the Blacks were consistent with the definition of identity foreclosure, a disruption in ego identity development. The Whites' patterns, however, were consistent with progressive identity formation. Sociocultural as well as cognitive aspects of racial differences in identity development are discussed in conclusion. (30 ref).

83. Hendricks, Leo E.; Montgomery, Teresa A. & Fullilove, Robert E. (1984). **Educational achievement and locus of control among Black adolescent fathers.** *Journal of Negro Education,* 53(2), 182–188.
Interviewed 48 unmarried adolescent (under 21 yrs of age) Black fathers and 50 unmarried adolescent Black males who

had not fathered out-of-wedlock children. Questions pertained to the social and demographic characteristics of the Ss; their sexual knowledge, attitudes, and practices; and the problems they encountered as adolescent males and ways in which they coped. Chi-squared and discriminant function analyses were used to assess the key variables identified for the study: educational achievement, contraception use, and external locus of control. Data show that the fathers were more similar than they were different on the SES variables, but there were 3 significant differences between them. Fathers were more likely to be employed, were less inclined to use contraceptives during sexual intercourse, and were more likely to be out of school than were the nonfathers. It is suggested that educators and counselors must strive to help adolescent fathers learn to make decisions that will have positive results in their lives. Unmarried Black adolescent fathers should be encouraged to seek birth control counseling. If other forms of counseling are needed, attention should be paid to the issue of locus of control, for if they can see themselves as being in control of their lives, young Black males may be more likely to remain in school and less likey to become unmarried adolescent fathers.

84. Johnson, Daniel & Brody, Nathan. (1977). **Visual habituation, sensorimotor development, and tempo of play in one-year-old infants.** *Child Development,* 48(1), 315-319.
The pattern of relationships between rate of visual habituation, sensorimotor development, play tempo, and motor activity was examined in 168 1-yr-old Black infants. Ss were exposed to 3 consecutive series of a repeated visual stimulus and the rate of habituation determined for each series. The measures of sensorimotor development included both standard psychometric and Piagetian scales. Measures of play tempo and motor activity were obtained from observations of free play. Longer fixation time to the initial stimulus presentation and faster habituation on the original series were associated with advanced sensorimotor development for girls. Longer initial fixation time in boys was associated with a slower tempo of play. The magnitude of these relationships, however, was dependent on whether the S completed the entire experimental session or was terminated early due to irritability or drowsiness. Results suggest that both the sex and state of the infant are important moderators of the relationship between measures of visual attention and other individual difference variables.

85. King, William L. & Seegmiller, Bonni. (1973). **Performance of 14- to 22-month-old Black, firstborn male infants on two tests of cognitive development: The Bayley scales and the Infant Psychological Development Scale.** *Developmental Psychology,* 8(3), 317-326.
Tested 51 14-22 mo old Black infants living in Harlem (unselected for socioeconomic status) at 3 ages. The mean Bayley mental score was elevated at 14 mo but fell to a level similar to the standardization sample at 18 mo and remained stable to 22 mo. The mean Bayley psychomotor score was significantly greater than that of the standardization sample at all 3 age levels. Variability on both the Bayley Mental and Psychomotor Scales was small at 14 mo and increased significantly with age to equal the standardization sample at 22 mo. The mental scale showed good predictive validity, while the psychomotor scale showed almost none. The Infant Psychological Developmental Scale appears to measure specific abilities and to be most applicable below 18 mo of age. Individually, the scales showed almost no predictive validity. The Bayley Mental Scale showed the greatest number of intercorrelations with all other scales at all age levels. With increasing age, vocalization and verbal ability became more important determinants of test performance. (19 ref).

86. Kohn, Martin & Rosman, Bernice L. (1973). **Cognitive functioning in five-year-old boys as related to social-emotional and background-demographic variables.** *Developmental Psychology,* 8(2), 277-294.
Applied hierarchical multiple regression analysis to determine the extent to which cognitive functioning at the preschool level is a function of 2 major classes of variables: background-demographic variables and measures of social-emotional functioning. A sample of 287 male kindergartners (half Black and half White) served as Ss. Background variables as a group accounted for 6-22% of the variance in 7 measures of cognitive functioning; social-emotional variables as a group accounted for 4.8-20.6% of the variance in these measures; jointly they accounted for 12.7-34.5% of variance. The most potent background variables were social class and race. The most potent social-emotional variables were interest-participation and task orientation; a 3rd social-emotional variable, cooperation-compliance, was not related to cognitive functioning. (1½p ref).

87. Kuvlesky, William P. & Dameron, Jane. (1971). **Adolescents' perceptions of military service as a vehicle for social mobility: A racial comparison of rural youth.** *Journal of Vocational Behavior,* 1(1), 57-67.
Examined attitudes toward military service held by Black and White teen-age males from rural east Texas. It was hypothesized, but not supported, that Black males are more positively inclined toward military service than Whites; and that regardless of race, youths from lower socioeconomic levels with high-status aspirations are more positively oriented toward military service than other youths.

88. Lee, Courtland C. (1985). **An ethnic group–gender comparison of occupational choice among rural adolescents.** *Journal of Non-White Concerns in Personnel & Guidance,* 13(1), 28-37.
Examined the occupational choice processes among 520 10th graders in 4 rural county school systems in the southeastern US: 92 Black males, 87 White males, 70 Native American males, 114 Black females, 82 White females, and 75 Native American females. All 4 counties were experiencing significant industrial and technological growth. Analyses of Ss' responses to a questionnaire about occupational aspirations indicated that females, regardless of ethnicity, aspired to and expected to attain higher-level occupations than males. Most males, regardless of ethnicity, aspired to and expected to attain intermediate-level occupations. Implications for guidance and vocational counseling are discussed. (30 ref).

89. Liebert, Robert M., Sobol, Michael P. & Copemann, Chester D. (1972). **Effects of vicarious consequences and race of model upon imitative performance by Black children.** *Developmental Psychology,* 6(3), 452-456.
Exposed a total of 96 Black male 1st and 2nd graders to Black or White adult male models who received positive or negative reinforcement to study acceptance and recall measures of imitation. Results are comparable to previous findings with White children. Ss exposed to vicarious reward showed more imitative acceptance than controls who had seen a model perform without consequences. Ss exposed to vicarious punishment showed the least imitation. Vicarious reward also facilitated recall of model's behavior, although vicarious punishment did not. A simple main effect for race of model was accounted for by the fact that Ss were more likely to match the responses of White models.

90. Longabaugh, Richard. (1973). **Mother behavior as a variable moderating the effects of father absence.** *Ethos,* 1(4), 456-465.
Tested the hypotheses that father-absent boys have a more feminine semantic style than father-present boys, and that father-absent homes have a higher rate of mother-son interaction than father-present homes. 51 mother-child dyads were

selected for study from a group of Black, lower-class households. Children ranged in age from 5 to 12 yrs, and 18 were from households in which the father had been absent for at least 2 yrs prior to the study. Mother–child interactions were observed and coded with a resource process coding system, and each child was administered a modified semantic differential test. No significant relationship was found between father absence and masculinity of semantic style of either sons or daughters. Father absence was related to alterations in the behavior of mothers toward sons. It is concluded that increased mother–son interaction moderates the impact of father absence on the femininity of the son's semantic style.

91. Massari, David J. & Schack, Mary L. (1972). **Discrimination learning by reflective and impulsive children as a function of reinforcement schedule.** *Developmental Psychology,* 6(1), 183.
Classified 28 lower-class Black male 1st graders as impulsive or reflective using J. Kagan's Matching Familiar Figures Test. Ss were then administered a 2-choice discrimination learning task under conditions of 70% positive and 30% negative or 70% negative and 30% positive social reinforcement. Based on the hypothesis that impulsive children are more concerned with speed of response and reflective children are more concerned with accuracy, it was predicted that (a) the negative condition would lead to better performance of both groups, (b) reflective Ss would perform better than impulsive Ss in both conditions, and (c) impulsive Ss in the negative condition would perform better than impulsives in the positive condition. Results support the predictions; however, impulsive Ss in the negative condition performed similarly to reflective Ss in the positive condition. The influence of feedback on response style and the interaction between reinforcer effectiveness and socioeconomic status are discussed.

92. McNair, David & Brown, Duane. (1983). **Predicting the occupational aspirations, occupational expectations, and career maturity of Black and White male and female 10th graders.** *Vocational Guidance Quarterly,* 32(1), 29–36.
Investigated the relationship of self-concept to career maturity and occupational aspirations and expectations and attempted to clarify the relationship of SES and parental influence to career maturity and occupational aspirations and expectations, using 54 Black females, 80 White females, 38 Black males, and 87 White males in the 10th grade. Ss completed the Attitude scale of the Career Maturity Inventory, a student data form, the Tennessee Self-Concept Scale, and questions regarding parental influence. Findings show that Whites scored higher on career maturity measures than did Blacks and that females scored higher than males on career maturity. Self-concept added significantly to the prediction of career maturity for White males only. Parental influence was the variable that added the greatest degree of predictability in 9 of 12 stepwise regression analyses. Data suggest that counselors must be aware of the potential influence of race, sex, and SES on career development. (22 ref).

93. McNevin, Tony E. & Rosencranz, Howard A. (1967). **Racial differences in life satisfaction and adjustment between welfare and non-welfare noninstitutionalized, aged males.** *Proceedings of the 20th Annual Meeting of the Gerontological Society,* 35.
Data consisted of 4 subsets of aged, male respondents living in natural neighborhoods in a city of 29,000 inhabitants. One group of 50 persons included an equal number of Negroes and Whites. The comparison group of 50, also racially divided, was selected by area probability sampling from among nonwelfare, aged males. Differences in life satisfaction and adjustment were examined by the Life Satisfaction Index–A, health ratings, and family and social participation ratings. Statistical analyses were made between welfare and nonwelfare groups, and between each of the 4 subgroups, yielding a total of 7 categorical comparisons. It was found that significant differences on the above variables existed between welfare and nonwelfare groups and between race subcategories within each of the 2 main groups. Further, health and economic differences appeared to significantly function as correlative factors contributing toward racial distinctions for both objective and subjective evaluations of life satisfaction and general adjustment patterns.

94. Mezei, Louis. (1974). **The development of time perspectives by race and socio-economic class in males between the ages of 11 and 19.** *Personality & Social Psychology Bulletin,* 1(1), 330–332.
Data from 13 groups of students from public schools of varying socioeconomic class neighborhoods and a private university indicate that the American Dream of a better future transcends racial and socioeconomic class differences. From TAT data, the most consistent finding is that, in all groups, the rank order of evaluations tends to rate the future the best, followed by the present, and the evaluation of the past as the worst.

95. Palmer, Francis H. (1970). **Socioeconomic status and intellective performance among Negro preschool boys.** *Developmental Psychology,* 3(1), 1–9.
Tested the assumption from studies of Negro elementary school children that differences in intellective performance are a function of the operation of socioeconomic status at earlier stages of development of the Negro child. With sampling procedures and adaption to the testing situation highly controlled, no differences were found by socioeconomic status among 240 Negro children up to age 3.8 yr. and 70 matched controls when measures assessing a variety of intellective behaviors were used.

96. Ratusnik, David L. & Koenigsknecht, Roy A. (1975). **Normative study of the Goodenough drawing test and the Columbia Mental Maturity Scale in a metropolitan setting.** *Perceptual & Motor Skills,* 40(3), 835–838.
Found that the performance of a total of 144 4–5 yr old Black and White preschoolers on Goodenough's Draw-A-Man Test and the Columbia Mental Maturity Scale was influenced by socioeconomic background and sex rather than race. While no overall difference in IQ was noted between the 2 tests, analysis displayed uniformly somewhat lower scores by Blacks on the Draw-A-Man Test.

97. Rubin, Roger H. (1974). **Adult male absence and the self-attitudes of Black children.** *Child Study Journal,* 4(1), 33–46.
Administered a self-concept and background questionnaire to 280 Black 5th and 6th graders to investigate the finding that the frequent absence of adult males from the households of lower-class Blacks results in boys perceiving themselves as less worthwhile persons compared to boys who live with adult males and to girls who live with and without an adult male. This is attributed to a lack of male role models for boys and to negative female attitudes about males. No support for this hypothesis was found for the Ss. The availability of male role models outside the home and the significance of adult males within the home are suggested as explanations for the nonsignificant results. (29 ref).

98. Ryckman, David B. (1967). **A comparison of information processing abilities of middle and lower class Negro kindergarten boys.** *Exceptional Children,* 33(8), 545–552.
50 middle-class and 50 lower-class Negro kindergarten boys were administered a battery of 8 instruments designed to assess specific information processing abilities. An analysis of 19 variables produced 5 reasonably meaningful components, with a general language ability component the most significant. When class groups were compared, this component discriminated most significantly between the groups. Implica-

tions for educational definition, diagnosis, and program planning are discussed. (37 ref).

99. Schab, Fred. (1974). **Adolescence in the South: A comparison of Black and White home, school, religion and personal wishes.** *Adolescence,* 9(36), 565–568.
Used an open-ended questionnaire to ascertain the wishes of 1,092 White and 714 Black US adolescents from the states of Georgia, Tennessee, and Florida. Results indicate that the Ss were not committed to school, home, or church. They wished for more consideration and understanding and were not completely satisfied with themselves. They had a desire to be smarter. Sex and race made little difference, except that when affluence was involved, Black males more than the others wished for more than their environment was giving them.

100. Tuck, Samuel. (1971). **Working with Black fathers.** *American Journal of Orthopsychiatry,* 41(3), 465–472.
Describes a strategy used to mobilize Black fathers (4 initially) to provide new experiences for their preschool children within the ghetto. A much larger-scale neighborhood involvement evolved that included the fathers engaging their wives in a neighborhood social event and sponsoring a local business venture. A concerted drive for community control resulted. It is suggested that if an indirect rather than a direct approach is used to engage Black fathers, many of them can be mobilized to provide the emotional and positive experience necessary for the development of their children. 7 operating principles are suggested.

101. Vroegh, Karen & Handrich, Millicent. (1969). **The validity of the Howard Maze Test as a measure of stimulus-seeking in preschool children.** *Educational & Psychological Measurement,* 29(2), 495–502.
The Howard Maze Test for children and the Goodenough-Harris Draw-a-Man Test were administered to 31 disadvantaged Negro and 42 Caucasian advantaged 4 and 5 yr. olds. Teachers rated each child for stimulus seeking. IQ was unrelated to maze and to Draw-a-Man scores. Advantaged children had higher stimulus-seeking scores than did the disadvantaged. Correlations of maze scores with stimulus-seeking ratings were low.

102. Westney, Ouida E.; Jenkins, Renee R.; Butts, June D. & Williams, Irving. (1984). **Sexual development and behavior in Black preadolescents.** *Adolescence,* 19(75), 557–568.
Assessed sexual maturation and sociosexual behaviors in 101 9–11 yr old middle- and low-income Black males and females using criteria developed by J. M. Tanner (1955). Involvement in heterosexual behaviors was elicited through self-reports and was classified on a 5-point heterosexual physical activity scale. Data show that female Ss were more advanced than males in the process of sexual maturation. Considerable variation in stages of maturation for CA existed in both males and females, but it was more pronounced in females. For females, there was no association between heterosexual physical activity and degree of biologic maturation. However, genital development in males was significantly related to sexual behavior. (21 ref).

Cognitive & Perceptual Development

103. Bondy, Andrew S. & Erickson, Marilyn T. (1977). **Effects of manipulating objects in modeling films on selection of imitative response class.** *Perceptual & Motor Skills,* 45(3, Pt 1), 871–881.
40 Black male kindergartners individually observed 1 of 4 films in which a model was (a) swinging a baseball bat, (b) pantomiming swinging, (c) swinging a nonbat-like stick, or (d) exercising (an activity-control film). Each S then entered a standard playroom and was observed for 10 min. The room contained 3 bat-like objects, 2 nonbat-like but swingable ob-

jects, and a pail and shovel. Contact time with each object and number of swings were recorded. Results indicate that those Ss who saw a bat being swung displayed frequent swings with the bat objects. Ss who observed pantomime swinging did swing sooner but not more often than controls. Ss who observed the nonbat-object being swung imitated the modeled response class but not with the object used by the model. Rather, these Ss imitated using culturally familiar objects. The advantages of using several available objects within imitative testing environments and using multiple dependent measures (e.g., frequency and latency) are discussed.

104. Feagans, Lynne & Haskins, Ron. (1986). **Neighborhood dialogues of Black and White 5-year-olds.** *Journal of Applied Developmental Psychology,* 7(3), 181–200.
Employed linguistic and dialog measures to examine the language used by 37 Black low-income (BLI) and White middle-income (WMI) 5-yr-olds (18 males and 19 females) in their respective neighborhoods. Results show no differences between White and Black Ss on any linguistic or dialog measure, although it was noted that Black boys talked more than Black girls. Correlational analysis revealed a positive relationship between language use in the neighborhood and school language measures for the WMI group, but not for the BLI group. Findings are discussed in relation to previous studies that found substantial language differences between Black and White children and to the possible cultural and societal influences that might have affected the relationship between linguistic skill and school success in the BLI group. (49 ref).

105. Heisel, Marsel A. (1985). **Assessment of learning activity level in a group of Black aged.** *Adult Education Quarterly,* 36(1), 1–14.
Developed a learning activity level (LAL) scale to assess the learning efforts of 132 urban Black Ss (aged 60–94 yrs) with a mean educational attainment of 6 grades. Learning was broadly defined to include all purposeful attempts to acquire knowledge and information. The scale consisted of 3 components—reading, educational use of TV and radio, and formal and informal learning endeavors in the recent past—and had a reliability coefficient of .81. A multiple regression analysis showed that sex, age, educational attainment, participation in organized adult education, self-perceived reading ability, health, and life satisfaction accounted for over 40% of the variance associated with LAL scores, with sex and self-perceived reading ability emerging as the most significant predictors. Older women were more likely than older men to engage in information getting activities, and Ss who assessed their reading ability as being good, regardless of their sex, tended to be much more active learners than those who considered their reading ability to be poor. The LAL scale and scoring criteria are appended. (26 ref).

106. Hogan, H. Wayne & Mookherjee, Harsha N. (1980). **Some developmental and racial dimensions of cognitive complexity.** *Social Behavior & Personality,* 8(1), 85–89.
Explored 2 facets of cognitive complexity: (1) the examination of selected developmental, socialization correlates of cognitive complexity; and (2) the examination of cognitive complexity as a potentially differentiating factor vis-a-vis the racial categories of Blacks and Whites. Based on the responses of 280 White and 154 Black undergraduates, the principle findings are: (a) nearly twice the amount of variance in complexity scores accounted for by 17 presumably antecedent variables was associated with Black rather than White Ss, (b) the findings noted in (1) were truer of Black males than for any other category of S, and (c) it was for Black females that the independent variables were most strongly correlated with complexity scores. It is suggested that cognitive complexity research advance beyond correlation and into the area of causation. (12 ref).

107. Horn, Alan J. & Medway, Frederic J. (1984). **The effect of peer and adult feedback on young children's task performance and imitative behavior.** *Child Study Journal,* 14(2), 123–136.
80 Black 1st and 2nd graders (40 in each grade) were assigned to 8 experimental cells containing an equal number of males, 1st graders, and students from the same classroom. The basic experiment was an extension of that of S. E. Henry et al (see PA, Vol 63:794). Ss were administered a shape-mark substitution task; 2 wks later they were administered a digit-substitution task during which they received either positive or neutral videotaped feedback from 1 of 2 sets of agents—either 2 Black children or 2 adults. After Ss had completed the problems, the videotaped agents selected 1 of 5 toys and proceeded to play with it. Immediately and 1 wk later, Ss were shown the same 5 toys and told they could play with any of them. Results show that the differential responsiveness of boys and girls to peer and adult feedback found in the study by Henry et al was not replicated. Praise had divergent effects on the task performance of boys and girls. Praising agents were imitated more often than nonpraising agents immediately following the praise induction, but this effect was not found at the 1-wk follow-up. (22 ref).

108. Samuel, William. (1983). **Sex differences in spatial ability reflected in performance on IQ subtests by Black or White examinees.** *Personality & Individual Differences,* 4(2), 219–221.
Investigated sex differences in spatial ability using scores on the Performance subtests of the WISC. The sample consisted of 832 adolescents (aged 12–16 yrs), divided by race (Black or White) and sex. Within both racial groups, males outscored females on all of the spatially oriented subtests, but females outscored males on a subtest emphasizing rote memory. It is suggested that the similarity of patterning of sex differences within each racial group may be interpreted as indicating that something more than social experience alone is involved in this phenomenon. (19 ref).

109. Sung, Yong H. & Dawis, René V. (1981). **Level and factor structure differences in selected abilities across race and sex groups.** *Journal of Applied Psychology,* 66(5), 613–624.
Administered 16 aptitude tests and a rhythm test adapted from the Seashore Measures of Musical Talent to 545 female and 464 male high school seniors of Black, Hispanic, and White ethnic backgrounds. Race and sex accounted for .7% (for Finger Dexterity/Left) to 65% (for Grip/Right) of the test score variance, with a median of 13%. Race accounted for most of the explained variance for Idea Fluency, Tonal Memory, Pitch Discrimination, Inductive Reasoning, Paper Folding, Vocabulary, Ideaphoria, Shape Assembly, and Analytic Reasoning. Sex was more influential than race for Clerical, Word Association, Writing Speed, Finger Dexterity (Left and Right), and Grip (Left and Right). Factor analyses for the separate race and sex groups showed highly similar factor structures, with 10 well-defined factors replicated across all groups, despite pronounced socioeconomic status differences among the race groups. Simplicity of factor patterns for the tests and the well-defined factor structure indicated that redundancy was minimal for the aptitude tests. (21 ref).

110. Wasik, Barbara H.; Day, Barbara D. & Wasik, John L. (1980). **Basic concepts and conservation skill training in kindergarten children.** *Perceptual & Motor Skills,* 50(1), 71–80.
17 White males, 15 White females, 6 Black females, and 5 Black males were randomly assigned within level of race and sex to 4 groups: Group 1, basic skills training and conservation training; Group 2, basic skills training; Group 3, conservation training; and Group 4, contact control. The experimental design called for Groups 1 and 2 to receive training on basic concepts, specifically "more than," "less than," "same," and "different." Following a 2nd test session,

Groups 1 and 3 then received training on conservation while Group 4 served as a contact control group for both training sessions. Only the conservation training programs resulted in significant effects, and that was only for the White Ss. A retention testing administered several months after the conservation training showed a significant drop for those Ss who had received the conservation training and a significant increase for the contact control group. (16 ref).

Psychosocial & Personality Development

111. Alston, Doris N. & Williams, Nannette. (1982). **Relationship between father absence and self-concept of Black adolescent boys.** *Journal of Negro Education,* 51(2), 134–138.
Investigated the relationship between father absence and self-concept in 35 9th-grade boys of lower socioeconomic status, 21 of whom were from father-present homes, and 14 of whom were from father-absent homes. Ss were administered the Self-Appraisal Inventory and the Personal Background Data Sheet. Socioeconomic status and GPA were also assessed. A significant positive relationship was found between father presence and self-esteem. Ss whose fathers were present also exhibited more stability in peer relations and stronger scholastic endeavors than those whose fathers were absent. It is concluded that a father–son relationship facilitated the adoption of an adequate self-concept by Ss who were able to model after their fathers and were, in addition, given training by them.

112. Badaines, Joel. (1976). **Identification, imitation, and sex-role preference in father-present and father-absent Black and Chicano boys.** *Journal of Psychology,* 92(1), 15–24.
Investigated (a) the effect of race of model and S on imitation of behavior, and (b) the effect of paternal status on choice of a male or female model and masculine sex-role preference. 26 Black and 26 Chicano 7-yr-old boys, half of whom were from father-absent homes, were exposed to filmed models. Black Ss expressed a significant preference for the Black model, but for Chicano Ss no significant preferences among the Black, White, and Chicano models were obtained. Father-present Ss had a significantly higher male sex-role preference score as compared to father-absent Ss. Both father-absent and father-present Ss imitated the male model significantly more than the female model, but these scores did not correlate significantly with the sex-role preference. It is concluded that by age 7, masculine preference appears well-established but is more marked for father-present Ss. (23 ref).

113. Bauman, Karl E. & Udry, J. Richard. (1981). **Subjective expected utility and adolescent sexual behavior.** *Adolescence,* 16(63), 527–535.
Administered questionnaires that examined the relationship between subjective expected utility (SEU) and sexual behavior. Ss were 67 White males, 73 White females, 38 Black males, and 65 Black females in the 7th–9th grades. One measure of sexual behavior determined whether S had had sexual intercourse, while a 2nd measure derived responses to 12 items that represented progressively intimate interaction with a person of the opposite sex. For both measures and for each race and sex group, the correlation was significant and in the hypothesized direction of more intimate behavior as SEU became more positive. Findings show that males had more positive SEU than females. Blacks were also found to have more positive SEU than Whites. (16 ref).

114. Billy, John O. & Udry, J. Richard. (1985). **The influence of male and female best friends on adolescent sexual behavior.** *Adolescence,* 20(77), 21–32.
Panel data on 579 White and 114 Black students, initially in Grades 7–9, were used to examine whether Ss' best same-sex and best opposite-sex friends' sexual intercourse behavior would increase the likelihood that Ss who were virgins at

Round 1 would make the transition to intercourse between rounds of the study. No significant influence effects of friends of either sex were found for Black males or females or White males. In contrast, White females were influenced by the sexual behavior of both their best female friend and best male friend. A virgin White female whose best friends of both sexes were sexually experienced at Round 1 was almost certain to have sexual intercourse within the 2 yrs of the study. (41 ref).

115. Brown, Duane et al. (1984). **Locus of control, sex role orientation, and self-concept in Black and White third- and sixth-grade male and female leaders in a rural community.** *Developmental Psychology,* 20(4), 717–721.
Examined locus of control among 43 Black boys, 36 White boys, 35 Black girls, and 47 White girls from the 3rd and 6th grades. Ss had been selected as class leaders by their peers. Ss completed the Piers-Harris Children's Self-Concept Scale, the Who Should Test, and the Intellectual Achievement Responsibility Questionnaire. White female leaders were more internally controlled than were Black leaders and attributed good outcomes to personal attributes more often than did Black leaders. White female leaders were also more willing to accept responsibility for bad outcomes than were Black female leaders. Self-concept data and sex-role orientation data were not helpful in interpreting the findings but did serve to suggest several avenues for future research in the area of locus of control. Results do not support the findings of other researchers who found that girls attributed their success to luck or to luck and effort while boys attributed their success to effort. (15 ref).

116. Dawkins, Marvin P. (1981). **Mobility aspirations of Black adolescents: A comparison of males and females.** *Adolescence,* 16(63), 701–710.
Examined data from the National Longitudinal Study of the High School Graduating Class of 1972 to compare 1,369 Black males with 1,369 Black females in terms of educational and occupational aspirations. Results show that both groups held high educational aspirations. However, with the exception of professional occupations, fewer females aspired to careers outside the fields in which women tend to be concentrated. A multiple-regression analysis revealed that the most important predictors of educational aspirations for both males and females were high school curriculum, academic aptitude, and self-concept of ability. Predictors of occupational aspirations tended to differ by sex—with community size and social class being important for males and community size, high school curriculum, aptitude, and self-concept being important for females. Findings suggest that greater attention should be given to sex differences within race in the development of mobility aspirations among minority adolescents. (9 ref).

117. Ensminger, Margaret E.; Brown, C. Hendricks & Kellam, Sheppard G. (1984). **Social control as an explanation of sex differences in substance use among adolescents.** 45th Annual Scientific Meeting of the Committee on Problems of Drug Dependence, Inc: Drug abuse treatment (1983, Lexington, KY). *National Institute on Drug Abuse: Research Monograph Series,* 49, 296–304.
Examined whether social bonds relate to substance use for males and females and if so, whether they operate in similar ways for both sexes. Data were gathered prospectively on a total population of 939 1st-grade children in a poor Black urban community and 705 Ss were reassessed 10 yrs later. At 10-yr follow-up, interviews were conducted with 939 mothers or mother surrogates. Results show that for females, stronger family bonds were associated with less use for all substances except cigarettes. For males, family bonds had no relation to substance abuse. Both males and females with weak bonds to school were at 4 times greater risk for marihuana, cigarette, and alcohol use. Males who reported strong attachments to

peers reported heavier use of beer or wine, hard liquor, marihuana, and cigarettes; the relationship of peer attachment to subtance use was weaker for females. It is suggested that in prevention efforts the school context is an important arena for both sexes and that sex differences, school, and the home environment should be considered in future research designs. (10 ref).

118. Evans, Dwight L.; Dalton, Richard & Greenwood, Jeffrey D. (1984). **Psychic trauma in early adolescence.** *Psychiatric Forum,* 12(1), 45–54.
Presents the case of a 13-yr-old Black male who experienced psychic trauma resulting from a truck accident in which he received burns over approximately 80% of his body. The authors discuss the S's case from the standpoint of M. J. Horowitz's (1976) theory of stress response syndromes and extend this model to include aspects of the adolescent period of development. S's sudden, violent stress evoked several of the universal responses to trauma and reactivated both the themes of earlier trauma and earlier conflicts. (13 ref).

119. Fields, A. Barrett. (1981). **Perceived parent behavior and the self-evaluations of lower-class Black male and female children.** *Adolescence,* 16(64), 919–934.
Examined relationships between Black children's perceptions of mothers' behavior and their self-evaluations. Ss were 180 males and 173 females, mostly 10–13 yrs old, from several Southern states. Perceptions, similar to those previously linked to the self-evaluations of other populations of children, were measured and characterized as expressions of mother affection toward children, as emphasizing companionship, as encouraging the child's independence, and as monitoring the child's actions. Results reveal that lower-class Black male and female children make fine distinctions in their perceptions of their mothers' behavior. Although females perceive more of their mothers' behavior as expressing affection, companionship, encouragement of independence, and monitoring than males do, these perceptions are more important to the self-evaluations of males. (40 ref).

120. Fine, Michelle & Bowers, Cheryl. (1984). **Racial self-identification: The effects of social history and gender.** *Journal of Applied Social Psychology,* 14(2), 136–146.
In a replication of K. Clark and M. Clark's (1947) research in the early 1940's, 35 males and 23 females (aged 4–6 yrs) enrolled in a private alternative school for Black children were tested to study their self-identification. Ss were tested individually after rapport was established. Each S was given 2 infant dolls, identical except for skin color (Black vs White) and asked to show which doll he/she would like to play with, which doll looked nice, which looked bad, which looked like a Negro child, and which looked like the S. Results show that males were significantly more likely than females to identify with the White doll. It is suggested that the current political climate that places Blacks at a significant social and economic disadvantage may reduce children's willingness to identify with a Black stimulus. It is further suggested that Black females, who often score higher on self-esteem measures and lower on fear of success measures than Black males, and who enjoy more academic success, may take greater comfort in or suffer less from being Black in today's society. (36 ref).

121. Greenberg, Martin S. & Holmes, Robert. (1978). **Effect of experimenter's race, sex, and presence of rewards on delay preference of Black males.** *Social Behavior & Personality,* 6(2), 155–162.
Examined the effect of experimenter's (E's) race and sex and the visual presence or absence of rewards on Black children's preference for larger delayed rewards vs smaller immediate rewards. 48 Black males (mean age of 5 yrs 7 mo) were randomly assigned to 1 of 8 cells of a 2 factorial design. Using a paradigm developed by W. Mischel and E. B. Ebbesen (see PA, Vol 45:2138), the experiment placed Ss in a

situation in which they could receive a preferred reward if they waited 15 min or a less preferred reward if they chose not to wait. The dependent variable was amount of time waited. Where previous research has shown that reward absence facilitates preference for delayed rewards, the significant 3-way interaction found in the present study indicates that when the E was White and female, the absence of rewards inhibited rather than facilitated preference for delayed rewards. Results are viewed as supporting the situational specificity of delay preference. (9 ref).

122. Griffin, Quincy D. & Korchin, Sheldon J. (1980). **Personality competence in Black male adolescents.** *Journal of Youth & Adolescence,* 9(3), 211–227.
Explored the nature and antecedents of personality competence in 13 competent and 10 average (as determined by their teachers) Black male college students. Ss completed the California Q-Sort, Offer Self-Image Questionnaire, and the WAIS Vocabulary subtest. In general, the personality qualities of the 2 groups were more alike than different, though the competent Ss were more inner- than outer-directed and more sensitive to personal qualities than to outward appearances and their own acceptability to others. They were more ambitious, more motivated for success, and seemed to strive more vigorously, perhaps even to sidestep some moral precepts. The competent Ss differed importantly, although not always significantly, from average Ss in being earlier and more thoroughly committed to a work ethic. They came from more stable homes, had more social contact with the White culture, and were more likely to be 1st or only children. It is suggested that both the nature and antecedents of competence are probably transracial. Additional analyses show that competence can be empirically distinguished from social desirability, though the 2 concepts are related. (19 ref).

123. Handal, Paul J. & Hopper, Saul. (1985). **Relationship of sex, social class and rural/urban locale to preschoolers' AML scores.** *Psychological Reports,* 57(3, Pt 1), 707–713.
Determined the effects of race, social status, and geographic location (urban–rural) on an aggression-moodiness-learning problems (AML) scale scores of 345 male and 334 female 4- and 5-yr-olds. Results indicate that boys evidenced more aggression, learning problems, and adjustment problems than girls. An interaction of race by social status suggested that middle-status Blacks showed more aggression, moodiness, and adjustment problems than middle-status Whites, low-status Blacks, and low-status Whites. The finding that boys are rated higher than girls on aggression, learning, and adjustment has been reported earlier in the works of E. L. Cowen et al (1973) and A. Carberry and P. Handal (see PA, Vol 66:155). This replication of sex differences supports the recommendation of Carberry and Handal that norms and cutoff scores should be established separately by sex. Data from the present study and from Carberry and Handal's study (1980) are presented in a table that provides preliminary norms against which investigators may compare scores. (10 ref).

124. Hansell, Stephen. (1984). **Cooperative groups, weak ties, and the integration of peer friendships.** *Social Psychology Quarterly,* 47(4), 316–328.
Investigated the strength of ties between students of different races and sexes and tested a cooperative-group intervention designed to increase weak ties between naturally occurring peer groups. Ss were 5th- and 6th-grade students from an inner-city school; 117 Ss were in control classrooms, and 200 were in experimental classrooms. The sample was 53% White, 47% Black, 56% male, and 44% female. All classes studied a 10-wk language mechanics curriculum on grammar, punctuation, and English usage. The treatment was composed of an interdependent cooperative-task structure and a cooperative-reward structure that enabled the Ss to learn about each other as individuals. Results support several hypotheses derived from the theory of the strength of weak ties. Friendships

between races and sexes tended to be weak rather than strong, and ties between peer groups also tended to be weak. The cooperative-group intervention stimulated new weak ties between students of different race and sex. However, these did not form a bridge between groups but instead were concentrated within existing peer groups. Findings confirm that cooperative groups stimulate new weak ties between individuals of different race and sex but raise doubts about whether this intervention directly improves intergroup relations among preexisting peer groups. (29 ref).

125. Hendricks, Leo E. (1982). **Unmarried Black adolescent fathers' attitudes toward abortion, contraception, and sexuality: A preliminary report.** *Journal of Adolescent Health Care,* 2(3), 199–203.
Assessed the attitudes of 95 unmarried Black adolescent fathers using standardized data collected in Tulsa, Oklahoma; Chicago, Illinois; and Columbus, Ohio. A majority of the Ss in each city were opposed to abortion. Two-thirds indicated a willingness to share contraceptive responsibility with the female. These data suggest that if family planning agencies offered sex education programs for adolescent fathers, particularly in relation to contraceptive responsibility, the incidence of repeat unwed adolescent fatherhood might be reduced. (7 ref).

126. Hendricks, Leo E. & Fullilove, Robert E. (1983). **Locus of control and the use of contraception among unmarried Black adolescent fathers and their controls: A preliminary report.** *Journal of Youth & Adolescence,* 12(3), 225–233.
Presents preliminary data from a study of 48 unmarried Black adolescent fathers and 50 matched controls who had never been fathers. The fathers were more likely to have an external locus of control, to be non-churchgoers, and not to believe in using birth control. Policy implications of this research indicate that unmarried Black adolescent fathers should be given birth control counseling and that if other forms of counseling are warranted, attention should be paid to issues of locus of control. (9 ref).

127. Hendricks, Leo E.; Robinson-Brown, Diane P. & Gary, Lawrence E. (1984). **Religiosity and unmarried Black adolescent fatherhood.** *Adolescence,* 19(74), 417–424.
48 unmarried Black adolescent fathers and 50 unmarried Black adolescent nonfathers under age 21 yrs were interviewed with regard to their religious behavior and attitudes; social and demographic characteristics; sexual knowledge, attitudes, and practices; and problems and coping methods to examine the relationship between religiosity and unmarried adolescent fatherhood. Results indicate that fathers did not differ from nonfathers in the degree that they were religiously oriented but in the manner that they gave expression to their religious involvement. Fathers were more likely to be responsive to nongroup modes of institutionalized religion (i.e., media forms), whereas nonfathers' religious involvement was likely to be within institutionalized groups. Findings also suggest that unmarried Black adolescent fathers are more likely to be employed, drop out of school, and not to use contraceptives. Media forms are recommended to practitioners as useful ways of reaching out to young Black fathers. (7 ref).

128. Hunt, Larry L. & Hunt, Janet G. (1975). **Race and the father-son connection: The conditional relevance of father absence for the orientations and identities of adolescent boys.** *Social Problems,* 23(1), 35-52.
Examined interview data from 445 paid male Black and White juniors and seniors in high school to determine the effects of father presence/father absence on personal identity and attitudes toward conventional success goals in early adulthood. Results indicate that father absence has quite different consequences by race, with father absence being associated with damaging effects only among White males. By

contrast, father absence seems to have some slightly positive effects on Black males. This pattern of costs for Whites and gains for Blacks is general across social class levels. The lack of evidence of detrimental effects of father absence among Black males raises questions about the role of the Black family in sustaining intergenerational patterns of racial inequality. (36 ref).

129. Johnson, Glenn M.; Shontz, Franklin C. & Locke, Thomas P. (1984). **Relationships between adolescent drug use and parental drug behaviors.** *Adolescence,* 19(74), 295–299.
Administered an anonymous questionnaire to 145 difficult students who were primarily Black 15–18 yr old males in an inner-city secondary school in an investigation of the previously reported relationships between drug use by adolescents and perceived attitudes and behaviors of their parents. Results indicate that relationships between parental use of drugs and Ss' use of the same drugs were moderate and roughly equivalent across drugs. However, parental use of marijuana was strongly related to Ss' use of opiates, cocaine, amphetamines, and barbiturates. This finding is explained within the framework of D. Kandel and R. Faust's (see PA, Vol 54:9490) postulated stages of drug initiation. (9 ref).

130. Jorgenson, David E. (1985). **Transmitting methods of conflict resolution from parents to children: A replication and comparison of Blacks and Whites, males and females.** *Social Behavior & Personality,* 13(2), 109–117.
Tested the findings of S. Steinmetz (see PA, Vol 58:7368), which indicated that husband and wife set the pattern for conflict resolution (CR) and that this pattern is used in their CR with their children and modeled by their children in their CR with each other. A structured questionnaire and a conflict tactics scale were administered to 164 White and 82 Black (100 males) students on 2 college campuses. With one exception the results were similar to those of Steinmetz: the transmission of the method of verbal aggression from husband and wife to sibling and sibling was not born out. Siblings were found to use a method of CR similar to the one used with them by mother and father and similar to the method mother and father used with each other. Further analyses suggested that transmission was complete primarily for females and Blacks and that the adoption of physical aggression as a method for CR by siblings was influenced by their adoption of verbal aggression as a method for CR and by their being male. (16 ref).

131. McCartin, Rosemarie; Freehill, Maurice F. & Greig, Laurie M. (1984). **Profile of preadolescent values: Revisited.** *Journal of Early Adolescence,* 4(3), 223–230.
Compared the findings obtained from a survey of values among 6th-grade pupils with those of a survey by R. A. Cole (1972) from an earlier generation of pupils using the same questionnaire in the same schools and at the same grade level. The 1982 Ss included 22 White males, 20 Black males, 16 White females, and 24 Black females. The SES of the 1982 Ss appeared to be lower than that of the 1972 Ss. The revised value survey from the Cole study was used with the Ss. Results indicate complete agreement on 3 of the highest values, all indicating a preference for love and affection. Differences in ranking across the decade were for mid-level items, with the 1982 group elevating a few relatively individualistic values and reducing the rankings of more social values such as Politeness and A Secure Country. Comparisons were also made for subgroups of the 1982 population by sex and ethnicity. The proportion of each subgroup that ranked an item above the mean for the generational group is reported. Only 8 of 116 values were significantly different across groups, a finding consistent with evidence that agreement within a generational group tends to be strong. (26 ref).

132. McGhee, Paul E. & Duffey, Nelda S. (1983). **The role of identity of the victim in the development of disparagement humor.** *Journal of General Psychology,* 108(2), 257–270.
In Study 1, 238 low-income White, Black, and Mexican-American 3–6 yr old boys and girls were presented with pairs of drawings differing only in the identification of the victim of the mishap and were asked to choose the funnier of the 2. Study 2 followed the same procedure with 79 middle income 4–6 yr old White boys and girls. The pairs of humorous drawings included the following comparisons of victims: boy vs girl, son vs father, son vs mother, daughter vs father, and daughter vs mother. Findings for middle-income children and low-income boys from all 3 racial-ethnic backgrounds were consistently in the direction predicted by the disposition theory of humor: Humor victimizing a parent was funnier than humor victimizing one's own sex. For low-income girls, however, humor victimizing one's own sex was funnier than humor victimizing the opposite sex. Sex-difference data are interpreted in terms of the importance of extent of traditional sex-role development. (19 ref).

133. McGhee, Paul E.; Ethridge, LaNelle & Benz, Nancy A. (1984). **Effect of level of toy structure on preschool children's pretend play.** *Journal of Genetic Psychology,* 144(2), 209–217.
Two studies, with 30 low-SES Black and 30 middle-SES White male 2.5–5 yr olds, examined the amount of pretend play as a function of the realistic structure level of toys. Ss were presented one structure level at a time and were allowed to play with the toys for as long as they wished. Comparable findings were obtained for the 2 samples. More frequent pretend behavior was shown with unstructured toys, but Ss played longer with high-structure toys. Unstructured toys were associated with high playing time only when they were presented before high- or moderate-structure toys. Data are consistent with the notion that children show a greater variety rather than amount of pretend behavior with unstructured objects. (11 ref).

134. Miller, Mark J. & Stanford, Thomas J. (1986). **Sex differences in occupational choices of second-grade Black children.** *Psychological Reports,* 59(1), 273–274.
40 female and 44 male 2nd-grade Black children were asked about their most preferred occupations. Both sexes chose traditionally sex-stereotyped occupations.

135. Montare, Alberto & Boone, Sherle L. (1980). **Aggression and paternal absence: Racial-ethnic differences among inner-city boys** *Journal of Genetic Psychology,* 137(2), 223–232.
Obtained aggression scores from 3-dimensional puzzle games for 132 preadolescent (9–13 yrs old) inner-city males to test the hypothesis that paternal absence may differentially influence aggressive behavior. A significant 2-way Race by Paternal Absence interaction indicated that, when compared to their racial-ethnic counterparts living with both parents, father-absent Puerto Ricans were equally aggressive, father-absent Blacks were less aggressive, and father-absent Whites were more aggressive. Tentative interpretations of these findings are developed with a view to the demographic realities of an American innercity. (22 ref).

136. Murray, David M.; Matthews, Karen A.; Blake, Susan M.; Prineas, Ronald et al. (1986). **Type A behavior in children: Demographic, behavioral, and physiological correlates.** *Health Psychology,* 5(2), 159–169.
Provides descriptive data on the Type A (coronary prone) behavior pattern from an urban, biracial sample of 8–10 yr old children. Type A behavior was assessed using K. A. Matthews and J. M. Siegel's (1982) youth test for health (MYTH). High MYTH scores were more prevalent in males relative to females and in Black males relative to White males. Parent self-reports suggested that Type A Ss were more

outgoing, talkative, and physically active than Type B Ss; they were more aggressive in their interactions with others and were more likely to experience a greater number of aversive significant life events than Type B Ss. No differences in resting heart rate or diastolic or systolic blood pressure were found between Type A and Type B Ss; there were no differences on measures of the family environment.

137. Pitcher, Brian L.; Stinner, William F. & Toney, Michael B. (1985). **Patterns of migration propensity for Black and White American men: Evidence from a cohort analysis.** Special Issue: Methodology and aging research. *Research on Aging,* 7(1), 94–120.
Investigated age, period, and cohort patterns of migration for Blacks and Whites by applying cohort analysis models to panel data from 5,225 14–24 yr old males and to 5,218 45–59 yr old males surveyed by the National Longitudinal Surveys. The simultaneous inclusion of these 4 variables represented an important refinement of previous studies that considered only 1 or 2 of them at a time. Principal findings are that age, period, and cohort had independent effects on migration and that the effects differed markedly by race. Blacks not only had lower migration rates, but these rates were fairly homogeneous and varied less across age, period, and cohort than for Whites. These findings have significant implications for the development of causal models of migration. (63 ref).

138. Rao, V. Prakasa & Rao, V. Nandini. (1982). **Determinants of life satisfaction among Black elderly.** *Activities, Adaptation & Aging,* 3(2), 35–48.
Examined the relative influence of social, economic, health, and familial variables in explaining the sex differences in the life satisfaction of the Black elderly. The dependent variable was measured using the Life Satisfaction Index (Form A) on a sample of 240 retired elderly Blacks living in a southern metropolitan area. Multiple regression analysis revealed that nearly 52% of variance in life satisfaction for males was explained by all (24) independent variables while only 19% of variance in the dependent variable for females was explained by the same independent variables. Stepwise regression analysis yielded a 6-variable optimal model for life satisfaction for males while a 2-variable model was found for females. The most important of the 6 variables for males were income level and number of children. Females who saw siblings once a week or more and who visited people less often tended to be most satisfied with their lives. (25 ref).

139. Sagar, H. Andrew & Schofield, Janet W. (1980). **Racial and behavioral cues in Black and White children's perceptions of ambiguously aggressive acts.** *Journal of Personality & Social Psychology,* 39(4), 590–598.
Examined the way in which the interpretation of ambiguous social behavior is influenced by racial stereotypes and cultural differences. 40 Black and 40 White 6th-grade males were shown a variety of ambiguously aggressive behaviors performed by Black and White stimulus figures. As predicted, both Black and White Ss rated these behaviors as more mean and threatening when the perpetrator was Black than when he was White. In contrast, ratings of personal characteristics were in general determined by individual behavior rather than by group stereotypes, although Blacks, whether they were the perpetrator or the recipient of the behaviors, were rated as stronger than their White counterparts. Cultural differences between S groups were apparent in the greater tendency of the White Ss to read threat into ambiguously aggressive behaviors involving no physical contact and to assume that the perpetrators of such behaviors were stronger than the recipients. (24 ref).

140. Schab, Fred. (1982). **Early adolescence in the South: Attitudes regarding the home and religion.** *Adolescence,* 17(67), 605–612.
Summarizes the perceptions, attitudes, and beliefs regarding religion and the home situation of 751 8th graders (180 White males, 181 Black males, 92 White females, and 198 Black females) from 22 middle schools in Georgia. Differences attributable to sex and race were evident. Living with both parents or with just one (this was usually the mother for Blacks) was an obvious cause for perceptual dissimilarities. Black mothers were seen as more restrictive than White parents. White males claimed to have more social freedom than the other 3 groups. Black females conformed to their mothers' dictates yet more had run away from home than their White counterparts, and more Black than White males had considered doing so. Black males were more adamant about having fewer children of their own and indicated that they would treat them differently from the way they themselves were treated. The Black experience in the South was an important factor in Black Ss' views on the home. Ss felt that many adults were hypocritical in their religiosity, but they did not alter their childhood ideals despite lapses in religious education. Religious traditions are still very strong in the South, perhaps more so among Blacks than Whites. (8 ref).

141. Severy, Lawrence J.; Forsyth, Donelson R. & Wagner, Peggy J. (1979). **A multimethod assessment of personal space development in female and male, Black and White children.** *Journal of Nonverbal Behavior,* 4(2), 68–86.
To obtain evidence of the effects of demographic parameters and measurement techniques on personal space, several different assessments were used to determine the impact of S age, race, and sex on interpersonal distancing. 144 7-, 11-, and 15-yr-old children served as Ss. 13 variables representing stimulation, paper-and-pencil, and behavioral techniques indicated that as age increased, personal space requirements decreased, particularly for Whites. Blacks as compared to Whites required less space at age 7, and mixed-sex dyads tended to require more space than same-sex dyads. Results indicate that while some previous findings appear to be measurement-method specific, others show intermethod consistency. (30 ref).

142. Shade, Barbara J. (1979). **Regional differences in personality of Afro-American children.** *Journal of Social Psychology,* 107(1), 71–76.
Investigated whether regional differences could be found in an Afro-American population as they had been in previous studies of the general population. With the use of the Early School Questionnaire, 120 6- and 8-yr-olds from 2 cities (Atlanta and Los Angeles) were compared by region, sex, and age. An ANOVA revealed no differences within groups but found differences according to regions, along with some expected age differences. It is concluded that if geographical differences are considered along with those usually found for socioeconomic status, age, and sex, perhaps ethnicity is not nearly as important a variable as is currently maintained. (13 ref).

143. Shikiar, Richard & Coates, Carolie. (1978). **A multidimensional scaling study of person perception in children.** *Multivariate Behavioral Research,* 13(3), 363–370.
Asked 48 Anglo and Black children at 2 age levels and of both sexes to judge the similarity of 12 stimulus persons, using a proximity setting technique. The stimuli consisted of cardboard caricatures of individuals representing policemen, male and female teachers, parents, male and female peers, and self. Where appropriate, stimuli of both Black and Anglo races were present. The judgments were used as inputs for an individual difference multidimensional scaling program. The resultant dimensions of social perception are interpreted as racial identification, sex, and age. Some differences in perception between Ss were obtained. Implications of the present investigation for future research are discussed. (15 ref).

144. Smith, Thomas E. (1981). **Adolescent agreement with perceived maternal and paternal educational goals.** *Journal of Marriage & the Family,* 43(2), 85–93.
Multiple regression analysis of questionnaire data from 2,466 6th, 8th, 10th, and 12th graders showed that educational expectations were substantially related to perceived maternal and paternal educational goals for offspring. The statistical effect of perceived maternal goals was 50% greater than that of perceived paternal goals, indicating the importance of differentiating between parents. Tests of hypotheses in multiple-classification analyses showed that rates of agreement with perceived maternal and paternal goals were positively associated with self-reported school grades, formal education of the parent, and perceived agreement between the mother's and father's goals for the adolescent. Also, agreement with perceived paternal goals was somewhat more frequent among 6th- and 8th- than among 10th- and 12th-grade Ss. Whites agreed with perceived maternal goals at a slightly higher rate than Blacks. (36 ref).

145. Sun, Se-wen & Lull, James. (1986). **The adolescent audience for music videos and why they watch.** *Journal of Communication,* 36(1), 115–125.
Explored the patterns of exposure to and motivations for viewing music television (MTV) in 587 high school students. The influence of race, gender, membership in one's peer group, and attitudes toward school were also examined. Data from questionnaires indicate that Latino Ss were more likely than all other groups to watch MTV during the week. Reported motivations for watching MTV included music and visual appreciation, entertainment, information/social learning, passing time, and social interaction. Weekday MTV viewing was negatively related to how happy Ss were at school, positively related to the amount of time spent with friends, and negatively related to Ss' socioeconomic status (SES).

146. Thomas, Veronica G. & Shields, Leslie C. (1987). **Gender influencers on work values of Black adolescents.** *Adolescence,* 22(85), 37–43.
Examined work values and key influencers of a sample of 145 Black adolescents (median age 16.3 yrs), 66.2% of whom were female. Ss responded to 10 work outcomes on a Likert-type scale. Results indicate that boys and girls valued both the intrinsic and extrinsic rewards of work; however, girls reported slightly stronger extrinsic values than did boys. In addition, the sexes reported differences in the importance of specific work values such as "making lots of money." When naming a key influencer, Ss tended to cite a same-sex and race individual. Because males cited males more often as their key influencer, it is suggested that Black males are, contrary to belief, a viable part of the Black community.

147. Verna, Gary B. (1981). **Use of a free-response task to measure children's race preferences.** *Journal of Genetic Psychology,* 138(1), 87–93.
Examined the racial preferences of 225 3rd grade White children (107 males and 118 females) in a task that required Ss to decide how close or far away a figure representing themselves (self-figures, SFs) should be placed in relation to various target-figures (TFs; Black or White male or female). Results show that both males and females placed the SFs significantly farther from Black than from White TFs. Regardless of race of TFs, each sex placed the SFs closer to same-sex than to opposite-sex TFs. However, distances were shortest to TFs of the same sex and race as the S, whereas distances were farthest from TFs of the opposite sex and race from the S. (6 ref).

148. Ward, Wanda E. (1986). **Comment on Brown et al.'s "Locus of control, sex role orientation, and self-concept in Black and White third- and sixth-grade male and female leaders in a rural community."** *Developmental Psychology,* 22(1), 95–96.
D. Brown et al (see PA, Vol 71:25593) reported that White leaders were more internally controlled and more willing to attribute good outcomes to personal attributes than were Black leaders. They also found that White female leaders were more willing to accept responsibility for bad outcomes than were Black female leaders. The present author discusses the absolute and the relative statuses of the relevant groups on locus of control and suggests that because of the widespread appeal of this theoretical construct, extreme care should be taken when attempting to generalize the existence of internality–externality across varied populations. (8 ref).

149. Welte, John W. & Barnes, Grace M. (1985). **Alcohol: The gateway to other drug use among secondary-school students.** *Journal of Youth & Adolescence,* 14(6), 487–498.
Examined the "stepping-stone" theory of progression into drug use, based on the alcohol and other drug use of 27,335 7th–12th grade students. An anonymous, self-administered questionnaire was completed, and the data show that Ss did not use illicit drugs unless they also used alcohol. White, Black, and Hispanic Ss tended to initiate the use of drugs in the following order—alcohol, marihuana, pills, and hard drugs. Among Blacks and Hispanics, pills were not considered to be as important a transition between marihuana and hard drugs as they were among Whites. Cigarettes formed a step between alcohol and marihuana use for younger Ss, particularly for females. It is concluded that since alcohol serves as the gateway to all other drug use, prevention approaches that control and limit alcohol use among adolescents may be warranted. (12 ref).

150. Whitley, Bernard E.; Schofield, Janet W. & Snyder, Howard N. (1984). **Peer preferences in a desegregated school: A round robin analysis.** *Journal of Personality & Social Psychology,* 46(4), 799–810.
Analyzed children's sociometric ratings of their classmates in a desegregated school by both conventional and round robin ANOVAs. 49 Black male, 51 Black female, 36 White male, and 27 White female 6th graders indicated how much they would like to play and work with each of their classmates. Unlike conventional ANOVA, which aggregates each S's ratings of the members of a group, the round robin procedure permits the assessment of the effects of individual dyadic relationships on expressed preferences, and can therefore provide additional information on the processes involved in preference formation. The impact of both race and sex on sociometric choices was explored using these 2 techniques. Although conventional ANOVA showed strong same-race preferences, round robin ANOVA revealed that individual relationships were more important than race in forming peer preferences. A high degree of reciprocity of Ss' ratings of each other was found both within and between racial groups. Both conventional and round robin analyses found strong same-sex preferences, and much less reciprocity of ratings between the sexes than within the sexes. The complementary uses of conventional and round robin analyses of sociometric data are discussed. (36 ref).

151. Williams-McCoy, Janice E. & Tyler, Forrest B. (1985). **Selected psychosocial characteristics of Black unwed adolescent fathers.** *Journal of Adolescent Health Care,* 6(1), 12–16.
24 unwed adolescent fathers and 27 unwed adolescent non-fathers completed a questionnaire containing Rotter's Internal–External Locus of Control Scale, Rotter's Interpersonal Trust Scale, a measure of individual coping style, and a scale measuring family pattern of unwed parenthood. All Ss were Black and aged 15–19 yrs. A discriminant function

analysis showed that adolescent fathers were usually older, more likely to have been born out of wedlock, and less trusting than nonfathers. The 2nd author's (see PA, Vol 62: 11071) model of psychosocial competence did not effectively differentiate between the 2 groups. Implications for casework with adolescent fathers are discussed. (18 ref).

152. Young, Timothy W. & Shorr, David N. (1986). **Factors affecting locus of control in school children.** *Genetic, Social & General Psychology Monographs,* 112(4), 405–417.
1,899 Black, Mexican-American, and White 4th, 5th, and 7th graders completed a locus of control questionnaire and the Stanford Achievement Test or California Achievement Tests. Greater internality was found in girls and in Ss in the higher grades. Internality was related to socioeconomic status (SES), middle and upper SES Ss being more internal, and ethnicity, Whites being more internal. A comparison of White and Mexican-American Ss indicated that SES was a stronger correlate of locus of control than was ethnicity. Correlations between internality and academic achievement remained significant when controlling for the effects of SES, ethnicity, and sex. (38 ref).

153. Zabin, Laurie S.; Hardy, Janet B.; Smith, Edward A. & Hirsch, Marilyn B. (1986). **Substance use and its relation to sexual activity among inner-city adolescents.** *Journal of Adolescent Health Care,* 7(5), 320–331.
A study of inner-city Blacks and Whites in 2 junior and 2 senior high schools provided data on sexual knowledge, attitudes and behaviors, and substance use based on over 2,500 anonymous, voluntary self-administered questionnaires. Substance use was high among Whites, particularly females. Females smoked more cigarettes than males, and males drank more alcohol. Marihuana smoking showed only small racial, age, and gender differences. Compared with Blacks, Whites used more hard drugs. Sexually active Ss scored higher on an index of type and frequency of substance abuse than nonactive Ss in all subgroups, with those who initiated intercourse early scoring highest. A regression model explaining 21% of the variance in substance use showed independent effects of age, race, gender, and sexual activity.

SOCIAL PROCESSES AND SOCIAL ISSUES

154. Adams, Paul L. & Horovitz, Jeffrey H. (1980). **Coping patterns of mothers of poor boys.** *Child Psychiatry & Human Development,* 10(3), 144–155.
Examined the coping styles of mothers of 201 impoverished, urban dwelling Black and Cuban boys. Mothers were classified according to their firstborn sons' ages, their ethnicity, and the presence or absence of a father in their household. Scored according to scales *L, F, K,* 1–4 and 6–9 of the MMPI, the women were profiled and a descriptive comparison employed. In most instances the null hypothesis was confirmed: Mothers of fathered boys did not differ in their coping strategies from mothers of fatherless boys regardless of the family's ethnicity and the boy's psychopathology or age. There were high scores on the Paranoia scale of MMPI, indicating that it may be functional and adaptive to use projection in an urban slum. (4 ref).

155. Block, Gerald H. (1969). **Alienation: Black and White, or the uncommitted revisited.** *Journal of Social Issues,* 25(4), 129-141.
The research of K. Keniston's (see PA, Vol 40:6523) *The Uncommitted* and E. Liebow's *Tally's Corner* is utilized to compare similarities in alienated White Harvard students and Black streetcorner men. The sufferings of each group are then related to their societal origins where a common causality is described. With reference to a solution, recent literature and a movement are viewed. Working with the values indicated by these sources and the concept of Blacks as the "weathervanes of the future," the present crisis in Black leadership is described. From this discussion, an attempt is made to indicate in which way the term radical is being misused, and in which direction our nation must turn for new and viable values.

156. Blum, Zahava D. (1971). **Income changes during the first ten years of occupational experience: A comparison of Blacks and Whites.** *Center for Social Organization of Schools Report, Johns Hopkins U.,* (Serial No. 122).
Analyzed income changes for 30–39 yr old White and Black males in 1968. Educational level was the most important determinant of initial income for both groups, but the relationship was weaker for Whites than for Blacks. 10 yrs later, education showed a stronger relation to income growth for Whites than for Blacks. The differential impact of levels of education and other background resources of initial income and income 10 yrs later was examined. For initial income, Black resources were more efficacious than those of Whites, but the greater average resource levels of Whites created an initial income difference in favor of the Whites. 10 yrs later, the efficacy of White background resources for income growth was greater than that for Blacks. Intervening events and experiences, whose efficacy favored Blacks, kept the income gap from becoming even wider. A comparison of this income analysis with a previous analysis of occupational status suggests that Whites may be using their resources to obtain jobs with a high status, with the expectation that the job status will in the long run bring high income, while Blacks do the opposite. It is suggested that such a strategy is effective for Whites, but would not be for Blacks.

157. Blum, Zahava D. & Coleman, James S. (1970). **Longitudinal effects of education on the incomes and occupational prestige of Blacks and Whites.** *Center for Social Organization of Schools Report, Johns Hopkins U.,* (Serial No. 70).
Analyzed the life history data of a national sample of Black and non-Black males who reached the ages of 30–39 in 1968 to examine differences in occupational growth. The lower levels of occupational growth attained by Blacks in income and prestige were found to be due to lower growth rates rather than lower starting points. The relatively small continuous effect of education on income was slightly smaller for Blacks than for non-Blacks. For Blacks, the positive effects of education were eroded by unmeasured factors which made high incomes less stable than for non-Blacks. The continuing effects of educational levels on occupational prestige were somewhat larger than on income. While these effects were greater for non-Blacks, the occupational prestige of Blacks was more stable. The effect of education and the greater regression effect seemed to balance each other, with the result that the Black and non-Black distributions of prestige remained in the same relative positions. For Blacks, mother's education was of greater importance to son's educational attainment than father's education and occupation. For non-Blacks, these 3 factors were of approximately equal weight. When the son's own education was controlled, these factors had minimal effect on income and prestige, except for the direct effect of mother's education on the income of Blacks. (24 ref.).

158. Clark, Russell D. (1974). **Effects of sex and race on helping behavior in a nonreactive setting.** *Representative Research in Social Psychology,* 5(1), 1-6.
Used S. Gaertner and L. Bickman's 1972 wrong telephone number technique to assess Southern Whites' willingness to help Black and White callers. 10 White male, 14 White female, 3 Black male, and 4 Black female callers called a random sample of 665 White residents of a southern city supposedly trying to reach a garage that would come out and repair their car. Callers indicated that they were using their last dime and asked if the S could call the garage for them.

Race of the caller was manipulated by varying speech characteristics. If Ss did not offer to help immediately, 2 prods were given; if S still refused, he was relieved of concern by the caller indicating that he had secured help from a police car. Ss helped both Black and White females more frequently than Black and White males, with White males receiving more assistance than Black males. Males were more likely to be hung up on than were females. Results are partially attributed to differences in the perceived seriousness of the situation.

159. Donini, Gerald P. (1967). **An evaluation of sex-role identification among father-absent and father-present boys.** *Psychology,* 4(3), 13–16.
Attempted to evaluate whether or not father absence affects sex-role identification as measured by the degree of sexual differentiation on the Draw-A-Person test. 60 Negro adolescent males enrolled at a regional Job Corps center were selected and equally divided into father-present and father-absent groups. Contrary to what the defensive, developmental, and role-playing theories of identification would expect, no significant differences were found between the groups on the measure of the sex-role identification. However, a nonsignificant but consistent trend was found relating father absence with poor and excellent sexual differentiation. These findings were interpreted as suggesting possible disturbance in sex-role identification, with poor sexual differentiation being associated with less masculinity and excellent sexual differentiation being associated with compensatory masculinity.

160. Dunn, Joe R. & Lupfer, Michael. (1974). **A comparison of Black and White boys' performance in self-paced and reactive sports activities.** *Journal of Applied Social Psychology,* 4(1), 24–35.
Tested M. Worthy and A. Markle's thesis (see PA, Vol 45: 4035) that Whites excel at self-paced and Blacks at reactive sports activities, by assessing the performance of 55 White and 122 Black 4th-grade boys playing a modified soccer game. The research also explored the relationships between several dimensions of socialization (e.g., father presence–absence) and relative performance on the self-paced–reactive dimension. Two significant correlations emerged: regardless of their own racial identity, boys who excelled at the self-paced activity tended to have several younger siblings and to attend schools with a sizeable representation of White students. Subsequent interviews revealed that Black and White boys did not differ in their preference for self-paced and reactive sports activities.

161. Edwards, Daniel W. (1974). **Blacks versus Whites: When is race a relevant variable?** *Journal of Personality & Social Psychology,* 29(1), 39–49.
Derived from literature reviews 5 generalizations about Black–White differences considered most representative of current thinking on racial differences. Samples of 8th-, 9th-, and 11th-grade boys from 4 schools responded to questionnaire measures that would allow tests of these generalizations. Black adolescents had lower socioeconomic status and lower matrices scores in between-schools comparisons, although a within-schools comparison showed no differences between Blacks and Whites with reversed trends in mean scores. No significant and meaningful differences were found between Black and White Ss on replicated studies of self-esteem, internal-external control, social desirability, or social exploration. Findings suggest that while race may be relevant for studies of discrimination, for rectifying social injustice, and for providing a rallying point for minority groups, race is not a relevant variable for personality research or theory. (29 ref).

162. Flanagan, J. & Lewis, G. (1969). **Comparison of Negro and White lower class men on the General Aptitude Test Battery and the Minnesota Multiphasic Personality Inventory.** *Journal of Social Psychology,* 78(2), 289–291.

When some (imperfect) attempt was made to control for socioeconomic status, lower class Negro men obtained lower (.05 level) scores on all the General Aptitude Test Battery (GATB) scales except the Motor Coordination scale than did lower class Whites. However, with socioeconomic status at least partially controlled, none of the Negro–White differences on the MMPI were statistically significant (.05 level) except the *Ma* scale. Results are interpreted as being congruent with J. McV. Hunt's theory that early experiences are more important for cognitive functions than for emotional functions.

163. Garza, Joseph M. (1969). **Race, the achievement syndrome, and perception of opportunity.** *Phylon,* 30(4), 338–354.
Interviews with Negro and White mothers and TAT data from their 5th-grade sons indicate that training for achievement is related to the child's level of need for achievement and level of educational aspiration is related to level of occupational aspiration. The degree to which mothers perceive that suitable opportunities and rewards exist for their sons permit more specific understanding of factors underlying these relationships.

164. Gitter, A. George; Mostofsky, David I. & Satow, Yoichi. (1972). **The effect of skin color and physiognomy on racial misidentification.** *Journal of Social Psychology,* 88(1), 139–143.
Examined the effects of race, sex, and age of 80 Black and White 4–6 yr olds on racial misidentification. Ss were shown 6 slides of dolls differing in skin color (light, medium, and dark) and anthropologically based physiognomy (White, mulatto, and Black). Race and sex effects were significant for both color and physiognomic misidentification.

165. Hall, William S. (1971). **Two variables associated with differential productive cultural involvement among lower class Negro and Caucasian young men.** *Journal of Social Psychology,* 83(2), 219–228.
Investigated the relationship between productive cultural involvement, racial group membership, and personality among lower-class young men in the United States. Level of culturally productive behavior and environmental press were employed as independent variables. The dependent variables were 2 aspects of personality achievement orientation and locus of control. The sample consisted of 30 Negro and 30 Caucasian young men, all of whom had dropped out of school at some point in their lives. While found, racial differences seem secondary to those reflecting different degrees of productive involvement.

166. Hamm, Norman H.; Williams, David O. & Dalhouse, A. Derick. (1973). **Preference for black skin among Negro adults.** *Psychological Reports,* 32(3, Pt. 2), 1171–1175.
Required 24 Black males (age 15–25, 35–45, and 55–65 yrs) to choose a real and ideal face from 11 faces which differed in skin color and attribute desirable and undesirable behavioral characteristics to 20 figures, 10 of which were Black. Analyses of the former task showed neither a significant preference on the part of all Ss for dark skin colors nor an increasing tendency for older Ss to prefer light skin; analyses of the latter task also indicated that across all age groups there was no preference for dark skin. However, Ss in the youngest age group attributed significantly more positive behavioral attributes to black skin than Ss in the older age categories.

167. Harburg, Ernest, et al. (1973). **Socio-ecological stress, suppressed hostility, skin color, and Black–White male blood pressure: Detroit.** *Psychosomatic Medicine,* 35(4), 276–296.
Selected 4 areas in Detroit by factor analysis of all census tracts as varying widely in socioecological stressor conditions. High-stress areas were marked by rates of low socioeconomic status, high crime, high density, high residential mobility, and

high rates of marital breakup; low-stress areas showed the converse conditions. All areas were racially segregated. The sample in each area provided about 125 25–60 yr old married males, living with spouse, with relatives in the city. Blood pressure levels were highest among Black high -stress males and showed no difference among Black low-stress and White areas. Suppressed hostility (keeping anger in when attacked and feeling guilt if one's anger is displayed when attacked) was related to high blood pressure levels and percent hypertensive for Black high-stress and White low-stress males; Black low-stress men with high pressures were associated with anger in but denying guilt. White high-stress high readings were most associated with guilt after anger. For Blacks, skin color was related positively to blood pressure, and high-stress males had darker skin color than Black middle-class males. Black high-stress men with dark skin color and suppressed hostility had the highest average blood pressure of all 4 race–area groups. (47 ref).

168. Henretta, John C. (1979). **Race differences in middle class lifestyle: The role of home ownership.** *Social Science Research,* 8(1), 63–78.
Analyses of data from the National Longitudinal Studies of Middle-aged Men (H. S. Parnes, 1970) showed that (a) while Whites at any earnings level are very likely to own homes by ages 50–64, only at relatively high earning levels do Blacks begin to approach the home ownership rates of Whites; (b) the net worth of Blacks is substantially lower than that of Whites after adjusting for variables in a standard status attainment model; and (c) among home owners the race difference and the effects of other variables are much smaller than they are among renters. (26 ref).

169. Hicks, Jack M. (1972). **The validation of attractiveness judgments as an indirect index of social attitude.** *Journal of Social Psychology,* 88(2), 307–308.
92 White psychology students at a midwestern state university participated in an attempt to validate an attractiveness judgment task as an indirect index of attitudes toward Blacks. Ss judged photographs depicting White and Black males and females, and completed a questionnaire measuring attitudes towards Blacks in independent experimental sessions. Attractiveness judgments of Black males correlated significantly with attitudes toward Blacks. Judgments of Black females, White males, and White females correlated nonsignificantly with attitudes toward Blacks. Convergent correlations pertaining to Black males were significantly higher than corresponding discriminant correlations, indicating validity for judgments of Black males only.

170. Howell, Frank M. & Frese, Wolfgang. (1983). **Size of place, residential preferences and the life cycle: How people come to like where they live.** *American Sociological Review,* 48(4), 569–580.
Uses a life-cycle interpretation of the size-of-place mobility process to specify a longitudinal LISREL model, estimated with data from a 4-wave panel covering the adolescent to adulthood period. The model examines the process through which residential origin influences adulthood residence as well as the temporal relationship between residential preferences and location. It is argued that the "first move" subsequent to the completion of high school is important in redirecting size-of-place preferences during early adulthood. Moreover, adulthood residence tends to bring contemporaneous residential preferences in line with actual location. Results present a plausible life-course explanation of the observation, based on cross-sectional surveys of adults, that the modal residential preference is current size of place. Race/sex variations in this model are assessed and suggest models that are not invariant. Theoretical directives and problems for continued research using a life-course perspective are discussed. (36 ref).

171. Kuvlesky, William P. & Ohlendorf, George W. (1968). **A rural-urban comparison of the occupational status orientations of Negro boys.** *Rural Sociology,* 33(2), 141–152.
Discusses the occupational status orientations of Negro youth through analysis of data obtained from a recent study of high school sophomores in Texas. Rural and urban differences among Negro boys were explored on the following aspects of occupational orientations: aspirations, expectations, and anticipatory deflection from goals. Findings indicated that both groups maintain generally high level goals and expectations. Given this broad similarity, the urban boys had higher goal and expectation levels than the rural. Rural-urban differences were greater for goals than expectations. Rural and urban respondents were found to experience very similar rates of anticipatory deflection from occupational goals, but differences were observed in reference to the nature of anticipatory deflection experienced.

172. Lefebvre, Andre. (1973). **Self-concept of American Negro and White children.** *Acta Psychologica Taiwanica,* 15, 25–30.
Hypothesized that urban Black children have a lower self-concept than their White counterparts. 40 Black male 7th and 8th graders from an all-Black parochial school and 40 White male 7th and 8th graders from an all-White parochial school were matched in terms of age, IQ, and socioeconomic status. Both groups were administered the Tennessee Self-Concept Scale. Blacks scored significantly lower than Whites on total scores and the following scales: Behavior, Physical Self, Personal Self, Moral-Ethical Self, Identity, and Self-Satisfaction. Scores on the other subscales were all in the expected direction.

173. LeVine, Elaine S. & Bartz, Karen W. (1979). **Comparative child-rearing attitudes among Chicano, Anglo, and Black parents.** *Hispanic Journal of Behavioral Sciences,* 1(2), 165–178.
The childrearing attitudes of 152 Chicano mothers and fathers were compared to those of 143 Anglo and 160 Black parents within a low socioeconomic urban community. Ss responded to a 25-item oral interview administered in English or Spanish by interviewers of matched ethnicity. Factor analysis revealed 7 main attitude clusters with Chicanos differing from Anglos and/or Blacks on 6 categories. Chicanos were characterized as emphasizing early assumption of responsibility. In contrast to Blacks, fewer support and control attitudes were expressed. Chicanos ascribed to more permissiveness than Anglos and were less equalitarian in childrearing attitudes than were either Anglos or Blacks. Although attitudes of Chicano mothers and fathers were not significantly different from one another, cross-ethnic differences were more attributable to Chicano fathers than mothers. Comparisons and contrasts are drawn to the widely held assumptions about the Hispanic family. (Spanish summary) (23 ref).

174. Money, John; Clarke, Florence & Mazur, Tom. (1975). **Families of seven male-to-female transexuals after 5-7 yrs: Sociological sexology.** *Archives of Sexual Behavior,* 4(2), 187–197.
Examined 7 male-to-female sex reassignments as events in family sociology, with special reference to social stigmatization, publicity, and concealment. Data were obtained from interviews with 4 Black and 3 White families who had a male-to-female transexual member surgically reassigned more than 5 yrs ago. The Black families were more open than the White in declaring the reassignment within the family and community. Thereby they relieved themselves and the transexual member of a need for deception, defiance, or defensiveness, and they were less scheming and manipulative. Without the anxiety of concealment, they could feel more positive about sex reassignment as a form of rehabilitation. A formal public declaration of sex reassignment, analogous to a

declared change of citizenship, would be advantageous in transexual rehabilitation.

175. Moulton, Robert W. & Stewart, Lawrence H. (1971). **Parents as models for mobile and low-mobile Black males.** *Vocational Guidance Quarterly,* 19(4), 247–253.
Attempted to provide data on the relative roles of mothers and fathers in the lives of 27 27–57 yr old high-mobile Black males and 71 17–52 yr old low-mobile Black males. Each S completed a questionnaire and all but 5 high-mobile Ss were interviewed. Results indicate that high-mobile Ss reported somewhat stronger attempts to be like their fathers than low-mobile Ss, somewhat more pressure from mothers to identify with the father, and a greater sense of similarity to him. It is felt that these Ss did develop the clear masculine identity that may facilitate upward mobility which has been reported in the literature. High-mobile Ss reported that as children they made strong attempts to identify with their mothers, and it is suggested that the families with a relatively matriarchal structure are capable of producing highly achieving males. Although the data suggest that under certain circumstances the relevant behavior can be acquired by males even in the absence of a strong male model in the home there is further information which tends to corroborate the idea that contacts outside the home may be important. In the absence of massive changes in the social system which will overcome the general effects of unequal opportunities, diagnostic or predictive efforts will remain important to determine who can respond to relatively traditional educational-economic pathways to upward mobility. (15 ref).

176. Myers, Vincent. (1978). **Drug-related sentiments among minority youth.** *Journal of Drug Education,* 8(4), 327–335.
Interviews with a nationwide sample of young and low-income Black, Chicano, and Caribbean men and women, as well as their nonminority counterparts (1,357 Ss, 70% male) reveal that the large majority disapprove of illicit drug phenomena. Caribbean youth were most likely and White youth least likely to disapprove. And, although women and older youth were more likely to disapprove than men and younger youth, sentiments did not vary by formal educational attainment or urban/rural backgrounds. Within groups' White men and women were in greatest attitudinal discord, and Black men and women were in greatest accord. Although half of the youth reported having had illicit drug experiences, two-thirds of these currently disapproved of illicit drugs and illicit drug users. Even so, youth who had used illicit substances were less likely to disapprove of drug phenomena than those who had abstained or confined their use to licit substances. Despite these findings, interviews with adults who staffed the programs in which the youth were involved perceived the sentiments to be different from those reported. Accordingly, it is concluded that young people with the attributes of these Ss may bring a set of drug-related sentiments, cognitions, and behavior to programs that are different from those that many professionals in the social interventions might expect. (11 ref).

177. Paige, Jeffery M. (1971). **Political orientation and riot participation.** *American Sociological Review,* 36(5), 810–820.
Analyzed the relationship between political trust, political efficacy, and riot participation in a survey of 237 15–35 yr old Black males in Newark, New Jersey. Self-reported riot participants are more likely to be found among the dissident those high on political efficacy but low on political trust, rather than among the alienated, those who are both distrustful and ignorant of government. When compared to civil rights activists and voters, rioters are similar in their generally higher levels of political information but lower in trust of the government. Rioting appears to be a disorganized form of political protest rather than an act of personal frustration,

or social isolation, as has been suggested in some past research. (15 ref).

178. Porter, James N. (1974). **Race, socialization and mobility in educational and early occupational attainment.** *American Sociological Review,* 39(3), 303–316.
Investigated the applicability of a recently developed path model of the process of educational and early occupational attainment to a longitudinal study of a national sample of 14,891 White and 435 Black males using data obtained 5 yrs after Grade 12. The model that explains the White data does not explain the Black data. 10 major departures of the Black data from the results expected on the basis of studies of Whites are noted (origin socioeconomic status, creativity, IQ, significant others' influence, conformity, occupational aspiration, occupational expectation, school grades, educational attainment, and occupational attainment). It is concluded that these racial differences reflect the existence of 2 different ideal-typical systems of mobility in America. Implications of this distinction are observed in the operation of social-structural and social-psychological values.

179. Ransford, H. Edward. (1970). **Skin color, life chances, and anti-White attitudes.** *Social Problems,* 18(2), 164–179.
Among 312 Negro males interviewed shortly after the Watts riot, dark Negroes were found to be in lower occupational and income positions than light Negroes, even with education (as a measure of skill) held constant. Thus, skin color per se appears to structure opportunity, irrespective of educational investment (college graduates are an exception to this statement). Further, dark Negroes expressed more "anti-White system" feelings than light Negroes with higher proportions willing to use violence, expressing hostility toward Caucasians, and opposed to integration as a goal. However, color was a strong predictor of "anti-White system" feelings only among working- and lower-class persons, among those with no social contact with Caucasians, and among those who felt powerless to exert control through institutional channels.

180. Robins, Lee N.; Murphy, George E. & Breckenridge, Mary B. (1968). **Drinking behavior of young urban Negro men.** *Quarterly Journal of Studies on Alcohol,* 29(3-A), 657–684.
A longitudinal study was conducted on the drinking behavior of 235 Negro males. Results differed considerably from those of a similar study conducted with White Ss. Detailed results are given. (18 ref.).

181. Ross, Harvey L. & Glaser, Edward M. (1973). **Making it out of the ghetto.** *Professional Psychology,* 4(3), 347–356.
Conducted a pilot study to identify factors differentiating upward-mobile and nonupward-mobile men. 60 men in a 2 by 2 matrix of successful or unsuccessful Blacks and Mexican-Americans (a) were interviewed using a questionnaire structured around 14 life factors distilled from the literature, (b) took the Science Research Associates Non-Verbal Form mental ability test, and (c) participated in group sessions. Using a chi-square significance of p > .10, 34 items differentiated successful and nonsuccessful Ss in both ethnic groups, while mental ability was not significantly different. The resultant clusters of differences were compared to the characteristics of mainstream life and street or gang life and differences in parental influence between ethnic groups. Recommendations for modifying training and employment programs include (a) explaining the steps to program completion; (b) breaking programs into subgoals; (c) minimizing failure and maximizing success; (d) fostering group cohesiveness; (e) utilizing counselors to provide personal relationships, interpret expectations, and discuss values and goals; (f) using the "unsuccessful's" expertise for planning; and (g) using former unsuccessfuls for recruiting. (15 ref).

182. Sank, Zachary B. & Strickland, Bonnie R. (1973). **Some attitudinal and behavioral correlates of a belief in militant or moderate social action.** *Journal of Social Psychology,* 90(2), 337–338.
Differentiated 74 Negro college males active in civil rights movements on belief in militant vs moderate social action. Groups were then compared on Rotter's Internal-External Control Scale, the Rokeach Dogmatism Scale, and a behavioral task measuring level of aspiration. Locus of control and dogmatism were not related to the other variables except that when nonactivists were included, moderate Ss were significantly more likely to believe in internal control. Moderate activists were significantly more likely than militants to give aspiration responses following performance that reflected realistic and adaptive expectancies of future success.

183. Sciara, Frank J. (1971). **Perceptions of Negro boys regarding color and occupational status.** *Child Study Journal,* 1(4), 203–211.
Examined whether the changed social milieu has resulted in a greater acceptance of blackness. 70 4th grade Negro males were administered the Projective Picture Inventory (PPI), consisting of 36 photographs of adult Negro males judged to be light, medium, or dark in skin color. Ss were asked to select 1 photograph which he thought represented a person of a certain occupational group for each of 6 high and 6 low status occupations. The null hypothesis was adopted that there would not be a difference in the responses of Ss to the selection of pictures representing blackness (dark Negroes) in the high and low occupational groups. The null hypothesis was rejected at a high level of statistical significance: high status jobs were ascribed to light Negro males. Methods by which a more positive acceptance of blackness can be attained are discussed.

184. Sciara, Frank. (1972). **A study of the acceptance of blackness among Negro boys.** *Journal of Negro Education,* 41(2), 151–155.
Administered the Projective Picture Inventory (PPI), constructed by the author, to a sample of 70 4th grade Black males from two schools in a large midwestern city. The schools had student populations more than 90% Black, and 1 school had a Black male principal and the other a Black female principal. Ss selected photographs from the PPI which represented high or low status occupations. Results show that high status occupations were assigned to Black men with light coloring and low status occupations to Black men with dark coloring. It is concluded that "Black is beautiful" is more a concept in rhetoric than actuality, at least for these Ss.

185. Shulman, Arthur D. (1974). **Exploratory literary analysis of interracial behaviors.** *Journal of Social Psychology,* 92(1), 127–132.
Literary analysis of 20 Black biographies written by White and Black authors during the 1960's revealed 6 major dimensions which describe interactions between adult Black and White, male and female Americans. An attempt to order Race by Sex dyadic interactions on these dimensions is reported. Analyses suggest that much more is going on in interracial relationships than can be captured by the 2 dimensions of dominance and affiliation employed in most interracial behavior studies. (15 ref).

186. Staples, Robert E. (1970). **Educating the Black male at various class levels for marital roles.** *Family Coordinator,* 19(2), 164–167.
Explored the necessity and feasibility of preparing the Black male, at various class levels, to take on the marital roles of husband and father. A pragmatic approach is presented as it involves revitalization of the cultural heritage pertaining to the family. Criterion for Black educators in a premarital education program is presented.

187. Stoloff, Peter H. & Lockman, Robert F. (1973). **Development of the Navy Human Relations Questionnaire.** *Proceedings of the 81st Annual Convention of the American Psychological Association, Montreal, Canada,* 8, 731–732.
Designed a questionnaire to measure racial attitudes of Naval personnel. About 1,000 White and 200 Black enlisted men, and 300 White officers, rated item alternatives on a 5-point Likert-type scale. 3 factors emerged from analyses of the correlations among items about race, discrimination, and conditions in the Navy; these were designated "racial generalizations," "Navy climate," and "perceived discrimination." Scores for each S population are discussed. Subsequent administration of the questionnaire to a large worldwide sample of White and Black Army enlisted men produced the same 3 attitude factors and percentage distributions found in the Navy sample. Also, the 3 factors correlated with other explanatory items in the questionnaire.

188. Theiner, Eric C. (1969). **Current approaches to symbolization: The Kahn Test of Symbol Arrangement.** *International Journal of Symbology,* 1(1), 52–58.
The Kahn Test of Symbol Arrangement represents a basically projective test employing objective scoring criteria. It provides a template for evaluating symbolic productions according to 9 different levels of abstraction. Study I sought to assay potential difference in thought processes among 3 variant cultures, American, German, and Vietnamese. Findings suggest that the Vietnamese demonstrated less reliance on formal objective characteristics, whereas the German and American samples employed more. The Vietnamese, conversely, showed greater reliance on abstract associations. Study II was an assessment of thought processes among ghetto resident, Negro males. Findings suggest that this population was more conceptually concrete, rigid, and structure-seeking than either a normative population or the 3 experimental populations. Conversely, variation was not great, both studies therefore supporting the hypothesis that emotionally healthy men, regardless of culture, possess relatively comparable capacities to employ abstraction in thought.

189. Thomas, Charles W. (1969). **Boys no more: Some social psychological aspects of the new Black ethic.** *American Behavioral Scientist,* 12(4), 38–42.
Explores some of the underlying social psychological factors of the new Black ethic. The movement is seen "as a corrosive operation against those harsh, oppressive elements of the social structure that have either misinterpreted the humanness of Black people or compelled them to believe that psychosocially they had infantile or animal-like motivational systems."

190. Turner, Barbara F. & Turner, Castellano B. (1974). **Evaluations of women and men among Black and White college students.** *Sociological Quarterly,* 15(3), 442–456.
L. Rainwater's 1966 assertion that Blacks have low self-evaluations because they receive more negative evaluations from other Blacks than Whites receive from other Whites is challenged here by reference to P. Heiss and S. Owens's 1972 evidence that negative self-evaluation among Blacks is limited to work-related traits. Substantial support was found for the major hypotheses that, compared to Whites, Blacks would report more negative evaluation of "most men" but not of "most women" (since the provider role is traditionally ascribed primarily to men), and that the more negative evaluation of "most men" by Blacks would be limited to work-related traits. Data were obtained from 59 Black and 82 White freshmen at a large university. (23 ref).

191. Turner, Jonathan H. (1972). **Structural conditions of achievement among Whites and Blacks in the rural South.** *Social Problems,* 19(4), 496–508.
Studied achievement motives and value orientations among Black and White adolescent males in 8 small communities in

the rural South. Significant differences between White and Black achievement scores were observed, leading to a search for the structural conditions best accounting for these differences. The generally low achievement among Blacks was attributed to general patterns of community oppression. Low achievement motives were linked to the caste-like occupational structure as it apparently influenced Black family socialization, whereas low achievement value orientations were associated with perceptions of opportunities for mobility among Blacks. These conclusions are felt to have implications for the general literature on achievement as well as for the current "culture of poverty" controversy.

192. Unger, Rhoda & Raymond, Beth. (1974). **External criteria as predictors of values: The importance of race and attire.** *Journal of Social Psychology,* 93(2), 295–296.
To determine whether the appearance of youth reflects their value system, the Rokeach Value Survey was given to a total of 30 Black and White young men classified as conventional or deviant on the basis of attire and hairstyle. Results show that appearance was related to value systems, although value differences occurred more as a function of race than attire.

193. Ward, William D. (1972). **Sex-role preference and parental imitation within groups of middle-class Whites and lower-class Blacks.** *Psychological Reports,* 30(2), 651–654.
Examined the responses of 16 White middle-class and 16 Black lower-class 2nd graders (8 males and 8 females in each group) on the It Scale for Children and W. Hartrup's Imitation Schedule. The middle-class White boys were more masculine in preference than the middle-class White girls were feminine, and lower-class Black girls tended to be more mother imitative than the lower-class Black boys were father imitative. No such differences were found in sex-role preference for Blacks or in imitation for Whites. Results indicate a dominant masculine influence in the development of sex-role preference among middle-class White children and a dominant feminine influence in parental imitation among lower-class Black children.

194. Willie, Charles V. (1981). **Dominance in the family: The Black and White experience.** *Journal of Black Psychology,* 7(2), 91–97.
Compared male and female roles in decision making in Black and White households. Ten college professors represented the middle class, and 10 tradesmen represented the working class for each of the racial groups. Respondents were aged 20–49, had been married at least 2 yrs, and had at least 1 child. A 15-item questionnaire involving family decisions was filled out separately by each spouse, and then the couples arrived at a joint decision on items to which they had given differing responses. If the joint decisions matched the initial responses of 1 partner 75% of the time, that partner was considered to dominate the relationship. Equal roles in decision making were found in 17 of the Black families, but in only 13 of the White families. White middle-class couples shared equally in decision making only in 6 cases. This study refutes the idea of a Black matriarchy and indicates that the tendency, if any, toward a matriarchy is most visible among Whites, especially in the middle-class nuclear White family. (9 ref)

195. Wind, Yoram; Green, Paul E. & Jain, Arun K. (1973). **Higher order factor analysis in the classification of psychographic variables.** *Journal of the Market Research Society,* 15(4), 224–232.
Discusses the use of higher order factor analysis in the classification of life styles into a taxonomic structure. In a pilot study, 26 leisure-time activities were rated on a 9-point Likert-type scale by 346 17–50 yr old Black males in 4 major US cities. Data indicated that the Ss were fairly representative of urban nonghetto Black residents. 1st-order factor analysis revealed 8 factors accounting for 62% of variance. 2nd-order factor analysis resulted in 3 factors accounting for 50%

of the variance. The 2nd-order factors were (a) homebody with emphasis on home, family, and church activities; (b) loner with emphasis on drinking and movies; and (c) social-sport enthusiast with emphasis on musical, social, athletic, and game activities. Limitations of the study and possible applications of the procedures to marketing research are discussed. (20 ref).

Social Structure & Social Roles

196. Dressel, Paula. (1986). **An overview of the issues.** *Gerontologist,* 26(2), 128–131.
Argues that policy concerns in aging are ultimately inseparable from social policies directed toward the nonaged adult population. Landmark civil rights initiatives in education, employment, and other arenas for today's nonaged will have had a life-long impact on cohorts who reach retirement age in the 21st century. A historical and conceptual framework for assessing the relative impact of these civil rights initiatives is presented. The framework is helpful in determining whether the disproportionate hardships characterizing the lives of current aged Black and Hispanic men and aged women of all racial and ethnic groups will diminish in future cohorts.

197. Hout, Michael. (1984). **Occupational mobility of Black men: 1962 to 1973.** *American Sociological Review,* 49(3), 308–322.
W. J. Wilson (1978) argues that the gains in employment and occupational status that Blacks made during the 1960's bred Black class cleavages that did not exist prior to that time. In the present paper, the data on the inter- and intragenerational mobility of Black men from the 1962 and 1973 Occupational Changes in a Generation surveys (P. M. Blau and O. D. Duncan [1967] and D. L. Featherman and R. M. Hauser [1978], respectively) were analyzed. Results support Wilson's argument; 3 types of class effects were found. (22 ref).

198. Sorensen, Aage B. (1975). **The structure of intragenerational mobility.** *American Sociological Review,* 40(4), 456–471.
Analyzes mobility rates for Black and White male adults, using life-history data on intragenerational mobility. Mobility is linked to the process of occupational achievement, and it is argued that job mobility is generated by persons' attempts to maximize their status and income. Since opportunities for better jobs will be fewer the higher the occupational achievement already attained, the rate of mobility will depend on time in the labor force. The mathematical formulation of this time dependency is derived from a simple change model for the occupational achievement process, making a redefinition of time possible and job shifts in the redefined time scale described a Poisson process. This enables a component in the formulation of a realistic and theoretically meaningful stochastic model of mobility to be obtained. The empirical analysis indicates that the proposed model describes the observed change in mobility rates over time reasonably well. (22 ref).

199. Watson, Betty C.; Smith, Willy D. & Williams, Louis N. (1984). **Differential economic status of Black men and women: Perception versus reality.** *Papers in the Social Sciences,* 4, 47–60.
Administered a questionnaire containing 10 presuppositions about Black female economic superiority to 55 male and 86 female undergraduates and compared Ss' beliefs with corroborative data from the US Department of Labor and Census Bureau. The sample included 84 Black and 57 White Ss. Results show that all Ss, and especially Black Ss, were carriers of myths about the differential economic status of Black females and males. Although Ss believed that Black females earn more than Black males, the labor and census data showed that earnings of Black males have been historically

and continue to be higher than that of Black females. It is suggested that the disparity between Ss' beliefs and statistical facts can be explained through the sociology-of-knowledge theory by R. Merton (1957). The principles of consistency and discounting in attribution theory could also explain why some Ss accepted, while others rejected, certain presuppositions. (37 ref).

Culture & Ethnology & Religion

200. Carroo, Agatha W. (1986). **Other race recognition: A comparison of Black American and African subjects.** *Perceptual & Motor Skills,* 62(1), 135–138.
Assessed the ability of 10 Black American (mean age 21.5 yrs) and 10 Black African (mean age 24.8 yrs) men to recognize previously seen White male faces. Relationships between recognition, performance scores, and quality of interracial experience were also examined. Black Americans performed significantly better and made fewer false responses than the Nigerian Ss. Significant positive relationships were found between performance scores and interracial experience. Differential use of cues for discriminating White male faces by both groups was also found.

201. Cazenave, Noel A. (1983). **Black male–Black female relationships: The perceptions of 155 middle-class Black men.** *Family Relations: Journal of Applied Family & Child Studies,* 32(3), 341–350.
155 22–83 yr old middle-class Black males were surveyed through questionnaires to obtain data on their perceptions of problems affecting Black male–Black female relationships. A majority of Ss reported that Black women had more opportunity than Black men; and a large minority felt that Black women were, in part at least, responsible for the relative low status of Black men. Those Ss who had a pessimistic view of Black male–Black female relationships also tended to feel that they had been affected little by racial discrimination and preferred traditional gender roles for men and women. Results suggest that salient issues affecting Black male–Black female relationships may vary by SES, political and ideological orientations, and the overall social circumstances experienced by Black men and women during any given historical period. It is concluded that the feeling of strained relationships and antagonism between Black men and women is not limited to lower-class Black men. (25 ref).

202. Clark, M. L. (1985). **Social stereotypes and self-concept in Black and White college students.** *Journal of Social Psychology,* 125(6), 753–760.
Examined favorability of racial and gender stereotypes and their relationship to self-concept for 51 Black and 66 White middle-class college students. Ss were administered an adjective checklist and were told to describe themselves, Black and White Americans, and women and men. Ratings were then converted into favorability scores. Blacks and Whites both held more favorable stereotypes of their own racial group. Own-race ratings were related to the self-concepts of Blacks. Own-gender stereotypes were unrelated to self-concept, suggesting that group identity may not be an integral part of the evaluation. Disassociation from low-status groups might also insulate self-concepts from negative stereotypes. However, females' self-concept was related to their ratings of men. (36 ref).

203. Glenn, Norval D. & Weaver, Charles N. (1981). **Education's effects on psychological well-being.** *Public Opinion Quarterly,* 45(1), 22–39.
Used data from the 1973–1978 General Social Surveys to estimate, by means of multiple regression analysis, the effects of years of school completed on 8 dimensions of psychological well-being for White men, White women, Black men, and Black women. Estimates are provided of total effects; of effects net of socioeconomic variables; and of effects net of socioeconomic variables, family situation, and frequency of attendance of religious services. There is little evidence for negative effects, the only significant negative coefficient being that for satisfaction with community among White men. There is some evidence that education has positive effects on psychological well-being in all subpopulations except Black men, the strongest evidence being for White women. Dummy variable regression estimates of the effects of different increments of education indicate greater effects from 4 yrs of high school than from 4 yrs of college. There is tentative evidence that mothers' education may have an important positive effect on their offspring's psychological well-being. (29 ref).

204. Hogan-Garcia, Mikel M.; Martinez, Joe L. & Martinez, Sergio. (1979). **The semantic differential: A tri-ethnic comparison of sex and familial concepts.** *Hispanic Journal of Behavioral Sciences,* 1(2), 135–149.
Investigated the responses of a tri-ethnic sample of 201 Chicano, Black, and Anglo undergraduates on a semantic differential to concepts related to sex and familial roles as well as to a series of questions related to sociocultural status. Results demonstrate the utility of using the semantic differential in conjunction with questions relating to sociocultural status, since not all ethnic differences on the semantic differential are related to sociocultural differentiation. Furthermore, the semantic differential reveals subcultural differences among groups that speak the same language. The responses of the Chicanos and Blacks were always polar to the responses of the Anglos. In no case were Chicanos and Blacks polar. The overall pattern of results suggests that minority experience was more important than cultural experience in producing the observed differences. In addition, there were sex differences that cross-cut ethnic lines, and males were more stereotypic in their responses than females. (Spanish summary) (27 ref).

205. Jacobson, Cardell K. (1977). **Anxiety and personal control effects in biracial dyads.** *Psychological Reports,* 41(1), 239–245.
36 Black and 36 White junior high school boys participated in a biracial group task. Based on initial testing on the task Ss were paired with a partner of the opposite race. One-third were paired with a slower partner, one-third with a faster partner, and one-third with a partner of approximately equal ability. Debilitating anxiety among some of the Blacks affected their performance on the initial task so that the performance biracially was confounded. Implications of this anxiety and its changes over time are discussed briefly. (18 ref).

206. Kerckoff, Alan C. & Campbell, Richard T. (1977). **Race and social status differences in the explanation of educational ambition.** *Social Forces,* 55(3), 701–714.
Investigated the antecedents of educational ambitions of 12th-grade boys, comparing Blacks with high- and low-status Whites. The Black–White comparison revealed major differences in the total explanatory power of the antecedents as well as their relative importance. Level of education of head of household had far less importance and one's view of the opportunity structure (fatalism) had more importance for Blacks than for Whites. High- and low-status Whites resembled each other much more than Blacks, although education of head of household was a stronger source of explanation of ambition for high-status Whites. When mother's education was substituted for education of head of household, it sharply reduced the effect of socioeconomic status (SES) of origin among high SES Whites, sharply increased it for Blacks, and had little effect for low SES Whites. These findings suggest that models of educational ambition need to be quite different for Blacks than Whites, and they suggest nonlinear relationships among Whites. (18 ref).

207. Kunz, Phillip R. (1979). **Blacks and Mormonism: A social distance change.** *Psychological Reports,* 45(1), 81–82.
Examined the effects of a basic doctrinal change (i.e., admission of Black males to the priesthood) on attitudes of Mormons toward Blacks. 84 Mormon undergraduates in 1975 (before the change) and 132 similar Ss in 1979 (the year after the change) completed the Social Distance Scale for 30 ethnic groups. Scores for 27 ethnic groups decreased over the 3 yrs, with scores for Blacks showing the greatest decrease. Results suggest that doctrinal change can bring about attitudinal change.

208. Milliones, Jake. (1980). **Construction of a Black consciousness measure: Psychotherapeutic implications.** *Psychotherapy: Theory, Research & Practice,* 17(2), 175–182.
Describes the Developmental Inventory of Black Consciousness (DIB-C). Empirical, theoretical, autobiographical, and biographical studies suggest there are 4 distinct stages of Black consciousness: the preconscious stage, confrontation, internalization, and integration. Items were written for each of these domains and administered to 160 Black male undergraduates. The DIB-C was analyzed by using a sequentially organized psychometric strategy of item discrimination and tests of homogeneity, social desirability, and differential validity. A construct validational study was also performed using the unpublished "Nadanolitization Scale," which measures the degree of internalization by Blacks of stereotypic attitudes held by Whites about Blacks. Results show 65 items remaining for the DIB-C following the sequential analysis. Construct validation showed an inverse linear relationship between the degree of "Nadanolitization" and progressive DIB-C scores. Psychotherapeutic implications are discussed. (12 ref).

209. Panzarella, Robert & LaMar, Ansley. (1979). **Attitudes of Blacks and Whites toward Native American revolutionary tactics for social change.** *Human Relations,* 32(1), 69–75.
75 male Blacks and Whites in New York City responded to a questionnaire concerning the Native American seizure of Wounded Knee, South Dakota, while the events were occurring. Younger Whites expected more favorable outcomes for the militants themselves, and there was a tendency to predict more favorable outcomes for the militants when the investigator was Black. (4 ref).

210. Price-Williams, Douglass R. & Ramirez, Manuel. (1977). **Divergent thinking, cultural differences, and bilingualism.** *Journal of Social Psychology,* 103(1), 3–11.
63 Mexican-American, 61 Black, and 59 Anglo 4th graders of low socioeconomic status (approximately evenly divided on the basis of sex) were tested with the Unusual Uses (UU) subtest of the Torrance Tests of Creative Thinking and the Peabody Picture Vocabulary Test. Anglo Ss scored higher than the Blacks and Mexican-Americans on the Peabody test. Mexican-American and Black males scored higher than Anglo males on both fluency and flexibility as measured by the UU. Black males scored higher on fluency than any of the other subgroups. On the other hand, Anglo females scored higher on fluency and flexibility than the other females. Furthermore, Anglo females scored higher on flexibility than any of the other subgroups. Black females obtained the highest flexibility/fluency ratio. ANOVA showed a significant ethnic effect for the Peabody data and the UU flexibility data, but not for fluency. The Ethnic by Sex interactions were significant for both fluency and flexibility. Results of the male Ss supported the hypothesis that children of minority groups and children who are "balanced" bilinguals tend to do better on the UU. Female results, however, did not support this hypothesis and could not be explained by the study.

211. Snyder, David & Hudis, Paula M. (1976). **Occupational income and the effects of minority competition and segregation: A reanalysis and some new evidence.** *American Sociological Review,* 41(2), 209–234.
Investigated the causal dynamics underlying the negative relationship between occupational income and concentrations of minority (female and Black male) workers, specifically, the value of competition (entrance of minorities depresses occupational income) vs segregation (minority workers are excluded from higher paying occupations) arguments. Regression analyses of 1950–1970 US Census data on detailed occupations indicated that competition and segregation are race- or sex-specific processes. Females competed with White males, but there was no support for wage segregation of women. Conversely, findings show segregation but not competition in the case of Black men. However, neither competition nor segregation was empirically very important during the period covered by the census data. Instead, "historical" factors that have largely determined the occupational distributions of income and minorities (in the lower paying jobs) were the most important sources of the lesser economic rewards of heavily Black or female occupations. (2 p ref).

212. Thomas, Charles B. (1986). **Values as predictors of social activist behavior.** *Human Relations,* 39(3), 179–193.
Investigated values as correlates of social activist behavior by interviewing a stratified random sample of 33 White Catholic, 24 White Protestant, and 18 Black Protestant male clergy in mainline denominations in Boston and in the 1st ring of suburbs surrounding Boston during the midst of the major Boston school desegregation controversy in 1975. Ss completed the terminal values section of the Rokeach Value Survey and answered questions about the extent of their participation in activities to support the peaceful implementation of the school desegregation process. Zero-order correlations between social activism and specific values were computed for the present sample and were compared to previous research with student populations (e.g., N. T. Feather, 1975). Partial correlations between social activism and specific values (controlling for the effects of intercorrelations among the values) revealed that equality and freedom were significantly and positively correlated with social activism. Results are discussed in terms of M. Rokeach's (1973) 2-value law of political activism, which asserts that those individuals who have high levels of political involvement will also have an extreme regard (either positive or negative) for freedom or equality or both. (28 ref).

213. Wilkinson, Doris Y. (1980). **Play objects as tools of propaganda: Characterizations of the African American male.** *Journal of Black Psychology,* 7(1), 1–16.
Presents a psychocultural analysis of toys as material objects that are instrumental in attitude formation and value transmission, with emphasis on toys distributed from the years following the Civil War up to and including the Depression years. Content analysis was used to assess the meaning and labeling function of racial play objects as socialization tools. Data were obtained from department store catalogs and selected historical volumes on toys. Five categories of communication bias were used to determine stereotypes and propaganda content: attribution, adjective, adverbial, contextual, and photographic. Data show that racial games and toys have functioned for decades as disseminators of racially biased images. Results provide a framework for evaluating the content of contemporary media portrayals of Afro-American males. (2½p ref).

214. Young, Robert L. (1985). **Perceptions of crime, racial attitudes, and firearms ownership.** *Social Forces,* 64(2), 473–486.
Tested the hypothesis that because of prevailing public image of criminals as young Black males, racial prejudice leads to aggressive attitudes toward criminals, which increases the

likelihood of gun ownership. Concern about crime, in turn, produces a greater increment in gun ownership among highly prejudiced than among less prejudiced White males. These expectations are supported by data from 229 White males from the 1979 Detroit Area Study. The model is also supported by patterns of ownership of passive forms of household protection, which was unrelated to racial prejudice. The impact of prejudice was sufficiently strong that the proximity of a relatively large Black population was sufficient to increase gun ownership among highly prejudiced Ss, even in the absence of concerns about crime.

Marriage & Family

215. Ball, Richard E. & Robbins, Lynn. (1986). **Marital status and life satisfaction among Black Americans.** *Journal of Marriage & the Family,* 48(2), 389–394.
Examined the relationship between marital status and overall life satisfaction among Black Americans in a probability sample of 373 Black women and 253 Black men (aged 18 yrs). For women, the married, widowed, and divorced were more satisfied with their lives than were the separated or single. When controls for age, social participation, health, adjusted income, and education were introduced, differences were no longer statistically significant. For men, the married were the least satisfied Ss of any category. When the controls were added, married men were significantly less satisfied than the divorced, separated, and widowed.

216. Carlson, James M. & Iovini, Joseph. (1985). **The transmission of racial attitudes from fathers to sons: A study of Blacks and Whites.** *Adolescence,* 20(77), 233–237.
Examined relationships between racial attitudes of 100 White fathers and sons and 100 Black fathers and sons. Fathers indicated their own racial attitudes, while sons indicated their perceptions of their fathers' racial attitudes as well as their own. Sons of both races perceived their fathers to be more prejudiced than they actually were. There was a relationship between fathers' perceived racial attitudes and sons' attitudes in the White sample, but Black fathers appeared to have no influence on the racial attitudes of their sons. It appeared that adolescents' perception of parental attitudes is more relevant to socialization than actual attitudes. With regard to racial attitudes, Black families appeared to be less influential in the socialization process. (5 ref).

217. Carter, Jo A. (1985). **Maternal acceptance of Black and White school-aged boys and girls.** *Journal of Genetic Psychology,* 146(3), 427–428.
Administered a parental acceptance scale to 43 Black and 27 White low socioeconomic status (SES) mothers of children 84–126 mo. Findings indicate that White Ss tended to have slightly higher acceptance scores than Black Ss. Results suggest that when SES was not a factor, Ss were alike in their attitudes toward childhood autonomy. All Ss showed more respect for boys' than they did for girls' feelings. (6 ref).

218. Earl, Lovelene & Lohmann, Nancy. (1978). **Absent fathers and Black male children.** *Social Work,* 23(5), 413–415.
Studied 53 Black 7–12 yr old boys from low- and middle-income homes to determine whether they had access to their fathers or other Black males as role models and male images. Contrary to much of the literature, many boys saw their fathers with surprising frequency, and all the boys in the study had access to some Black male who could, at least potentially, serve as a role model. Implications for social workers are noted.

219. Gilman, Richard & Knox, David. (1976). **Coping with fatherhood: The first year.** *Child Psychiatry & Human Development,* 6(3), 134–148.
Examined fantasy (thinking back to pre-baby times) and holidays (going out alone with the wife) as methods used by 95 White first-time fathers to cope with parenthood. Results suggest that only the holiday mechanism is associated with maintaining or improving marital satisfaction. The use of fantasy actually decreases marital satisfaction. These data suggest that the discrepancies in the conclusions of previous "parenthood as crisis" studies may be accounted for by analyzing the coping mechanisms that various fathers utilize. A separate analysis of 7 Black first-time fathers suggests that they were significantly more successful than Whites in adapting to fatherhood.

220. Glenn, Norval D. & McLanahan, Sara S. (1981). **The effects of offspring on the psychological well-being of older adults.** *Journal of Marriage & the Family,* 43(2), 409–421.
Used data from 6 national surveys, conducted from 1973 through 1978, to estimate the effects of having had offspring on the global happiness and 5 dimensions of satisfaction of persons age 50 and older who had no children under age 18 living at home. 1,055 White males, 1,310 White females, 101 Black males, and 117 Black females were interviewed. All estimated effects on global happiness were either negligible or negative, the strongest evidence for negative effects being for high-education White males. The estimated effects on the dimensions of satisfaction were mixed and generally moderate in magnitude, being most distinctly negative for Black males and high-education White males and most distinctly positive for unmarried White females. Overall, there was little evidence that important psychological rewards are derived from the later stages of parenthood. (44 ref).

221. Glenn, Norval D. & Weaver, Charles N. (1981). **The contribution of marital happiness to global happiness.** *Journal of Marriage & the Family,* 43(2), 161–168.
Used data from 6 US national surveys to compare the estimated contributions to global happiness of marital happiness and satisfaction with each of 7 aspects of life, ranging from work to friendships. Separate estimates are provided for White males, White females, Black males, and Black females. Except for Black males, the estimated contribution of marital happiness was far greater than the estimated contribution of any of the kinds of satisfaction, including satisfaction with work. These findings, considered in conjunction with other evidence, indicate that Americans depend heavily on their marriages for their psychological well-being. (11 ref).

222. Hobbs, Daniel F. & Wimbish, Jane M. (1977). **Transition to parenthood by Black couples.** *Journal of Marriage & the Family,* 39(4), 677–689.
Replicates, using Black parents, 2 earlier studies of the amount of difficulty reported by White parents in adjusting to their 1st infant. Ss were 38 couples who were parents for the 1st time and whose child was under 1 yr of age. Mothers reported significantly more difficulty than fathers in adjusting to their infants, as had been found earlier with White parents, and mean difficulty scores were slightly higher for Black parents than for White parents. Of 15 potential predictor variables, postbirth marital satisfaction, age of self, whether pregnancy was planned and/or desired, number of additional children desired, and preference for sex of baby were associated with fathers' adjustment to their 1st child, while age for self and age of baby were associated with adjustment by mothers. It is concluded that Black parents' difficulties in adjusting to their 1st child were slightly greater than and somewhat different from difficulties reported in the prior studies of White parents, but their difficulties were not of crisis proportions. (22 ref).

223. King, Karl; Abernathy, Thomas J. & Chapman, Ann H. (1976). **Black adolescents' views of maternal employment as a threat to the marital relationship: 1963-1973.** *Journal of Marriage & the Family,* 38(4), 733–737.

Conducted 2 surveys of 9th grade Black adolescents, one in 1963 (N = 842) and one in 1973 (N = 533), in 2 metropolitan areas in the southeast using the same procedures to determine adolescent attitudes toward working wives as a threat to the marital relationship. In general, hypotheses were supported that adolescents whose mothers were employed viewed employment as less threatening; adolescents from higher status families perceived mother employment as less threatening, as did females when compared to males in 1963 and 1973. (22 ref).

224. Landerholm, Elizabeth. (1984). **Teenage parenting skills.** *Early Child Development & Care,* 13(3–4), 351–364.
Investigated the relationship between teenage mothers' interactions with their male and female infants. 17 Black 16–19 yr old mothers were videotaped interacting with their 5–8 mo olds (9 male, 8 female) on 10 tasks. Later, trained observers watched the videotapes and coded the parents' interactions with their infants on 5 variables: physical contact, social/verbal stimulation, object/material play, effectiveness, and responsiveness. These variables were observed and recorded on 3 coding sheets adapted from T. J. Koller (1979) and K. A. Clarke-Stewart (see PA, Vol 53:7086). Data were analyzed by means of a t-test on all variables. Mothers of female infants called their child's name significantly more often than the mothers of male infants. Mothers of female infants used significantly more object/material play to get their child's attention than mothers of male infants. Mothers of female infants more often demonstrated toy use than mothers of male infants. The mothers of male infants were significantly more affectionate and physical than the mothers of female infants. (29 ref).

225. McAdoo, John L. (1979). **Father–child interaction patterns and self-esteem in Black preschool children.** *Young Children,* 34(2), 46–53.
Trained 4 Black male recorders to interview and observe 36 suburban, middle-class, Black working families with 19 boys and 17 girls. Questionnaires included the Cognitive Home Environment Scale and the Thomas Self-Concept Values Test. Results show much interaction between father and child, and the majority (77%) of observed interactions were warm, loving, and supportive. Fathers perceived themselves to be strict in controlling their children's behavior, were vitally concerned about their children, and actively involved in decisions regarding the child's welfare. The Black children in this sample felt good about themselves and felt valued by both parents, by their teachers, and by peers. The fathers did not fit the stereotype of the invisible man, although some of them had outside stress related to their employment that limited the amount of nurturance they could give their children. (25 ref).

226. McAdoo, John L. (1986). **A Black perspective on the father's role in child development.** *Marriage & Family Review,* 9(3–4), 117–133.
Examines the origins of some common stereotypes of the Black father's role. The present author maintains that the absent father as a by-product of slavery is a myth, as is the existence of a Black matriarchy. Empirical research is reviewed as it relates to the provider role, decision making, parenting style, parent–child relationships, and father–child interaction in Black families. It is noted that when economic sufficiency rises within the Black family, an increase in the active participation of the Black father in his children's socialization is observed. Black fathers, like fathers of other ethnic groups, take an equal part in childrearing decisions. Unlike other fathers who are authoritarian, the Black father appears to be socializing their daughters to be more competent and independent at an early age.

227. Price-Bonham, Sharon & Skeen, Patsy. (1979). **A comparison of Black and White fathers with implications for parent education.** *Family Coordinator,* 28(1), 53–59.
Interviewed 160 Black and White fathers to investigate differences and similarities in their family characteristics and participation in and attitudes toward the father role. Analysis of data indicated that Black and White fathers were more similar than dissimilar. (26 ref).

228. Semaj, Leahcim T. (1982). **Polygamy reconsidered: Causes and consequences of declining sex ratio in African-American society.** *Journal of Black Psychology,* 9(1), 29–43.
The declining ratio of Black males to females, particularly at higher educational and income levels, makes it necessary to evaluate various family life-styles since it is impossible for every Black woman to enter into a monogamous relationship with a Black man. To assess the relative evaluation of some options, a male–female relationship survey was administered to 90 Blacks (mean age 25.3 yrs). Both sexes ranked monogamy the most desirable option, but overt sharing was second. Both men and women ranked as least desirable women being lesbians, giving up, or finding a White mate. Rankings of options were affected by age, marital status, and education. Findings suggest that overt sharing relationships may be a viable option augmenting monogamy among Black families. (34 ref).

229. Wilkinson, Charles B. & O'Connor, William A. (1977). **Growing up male in a Black single-parent family.** *Psychiatric Annals,* 7(7), 50–59.
Describes a study of 101 16- and 17-yr-old Black males for whom the mother had functioned as sole parent from infancy through high school entrance. Demographics and ratings of the amount and type of social practices employed in each of 13 ecosystem areas were analyzed. Ratings for the 13 areas were made for both mother and son for the periods kindergarten through 3rd grade and Grades 4–6, and a single current area was rated to determine the son's social competence. Results indicate significant associations between maternal emphasis on the development of social, educational, and community-oriented skills and the son's social and academic competence. Overall, the findings suggest that when sources of employment or community participation exist, particularly the former, mothers engage in childrearing practices that encourage social competence and educational attainment. (29 ref).

Political & Legal Processes

230. Davis, John A. (1974). **Justification for no obligation: Views of Black males toward crime and the criminal law.** *Issues in Criminology,* 9(2), 69–87.
Interviewed 150 Black males, over a 15-mo period in Los Angeles, in the age groups approximately 15-19, 20-25, and 26-30 yrs, to determine their attitudes toward the legal system. A central core of explanation emerged, unique to Blacks, indicating motives for criminal law violations. The most significant justifications were the incompatability of White-Black interests, unequal access to institutional participation, the injustice of the unequal access, the weight of history of unjust treatment (400 yrs), the initial involuntary servitude of Blacks, the lack of rights and privileges under the law and citizenship, and the feeling that Blacks are a conquered people. With a few exceptions by income class and age, these attitudes were found throughout the Black community. Hence the law is perceived by many as an instrument of racial suppression. These attitudes do not necessarily lead to criminal behavior, but a Black who finds himself entering a life of crime will be aware of a network of justifications to explain legal misbehavior.

231. Erez, Edna. (1984). **Self-defined "desert" and citizens' assessment of the police.** Annual Meeting of the American Society of Criminology (1983, Denver, Colorado). *Journal of Criminal Law & Criminology,* 75(4), 1276–1299.

Studied the link between experience and assessment of police, using data (1) collected in the follow-up study *Delinquency in a Birth Cohort* by M. Wolfgang et al (1972) on 971 males born in Philadelphia in 1945 and (2) from interviews with 567 of the Ss at age 26 yrs. Frequencies of contact with the police were compared by race and by official offender status. Data indicate that the frequency of police contacts with Ss in terms of questioning, chasing, or warning did not vary by race but varied by offender status. Findings also suggest that something other than actual experience may account for Blacks' negative assessment of the police.

232. Sigelman, Lee & Sigelman, Carol K. (1982). **Sexism, racism, and ageism in voting behavior: An experimental analysis.** *Social Psychology Quarterly,* 45(4), 263–269.
To assess the impact of candidate characteristics and candidate–voter similarity on voting preferences, descriptions of candidates were presented to 1,158 voters in a simulated mayoral election. Five experimental candidates (a 47- or 53-yr-old White female, 47- or 53-yr-old Black female, 47- or 53-yr-old Black male, 31-yr-old White male, and 72-yr-old White male) were pitted in 2-candidate races against a middle-aged, White male opponent. Ageism in voting patterns was stronger overall than either sexism or racism. The hypothesis that similarity breeds attraction received strong support in the form of pro-female bias among women, pro-Black bias among Blacks, and pro-White male bias among White males. (30 ref).

233. Unnever, James D. (1982). **Direct and organizational discrimination in the sentencing of drug offenders.** *Social Problems,* 30(2), 212–225.
Analyzed archival data on 171 White, 108 Black, and 34 Mexican-American males convicted and sentenced for drug offenses. After correcting for the methodological and statistical deficiencies of prior research, it was found that direct economic/organizational and racial/ethnic discrimination occurred in the sentencing of Ss. (42 ref).

Psychosexual Behavior & Sex Roles

234. Brenner, O. C. & Tomkiewicz, Joseph. (1986). **Race difference in attitudes of American business school graduates toward the role of women.** *Journal of Social Psychology,* 126(2), 251–253.
Hypothesized that Blacks would be more liberal in their attitudes toward women than Whites and that the difference between Black men and Black women would be less than that between White men and White women. 157 White men, 113 White women, 51 Black men, and 53 Black women who were graduating seniors majoring in business completed a questionnaire. Both hypotheses were supported. White men were the most conservative in their attitudes toward women, and Black women were the most liberal.

235. Carr, Peggy G.; Thomas, Veronica G. & Mednick, Martha T. (1985). **Evaluation of sex-typed tasks by Black men and women.** *Sex Roles,* 13(5–6), 311–316.
Examined the relationship of sex of S, sex-typing of tasks, and prior task experience on self-confidence ratings of 105 Black men and 115 Black women in 2 studies. In both studies, women's self-confidence tended to vary as a function of task type, with women scoring lower on the masculine task than on the feminine or neutral tasks, while men's self-confidence remained relatively stable across all tasks. Prior experience with the task was highly correlated with self-confidence ratings for men and women and moderated the effects. Findings support the view of women's self-confidence as responsive to situational variations. (18 ref).

236. Cazenave, Noel A. (1984). **Race, socioeconomic status, and age: The social context of American masculinity.** *Sex Roles,* 11(7–8), 639–656.
In a paper presented at the National Institute of Child Health and Human Development conference on gender role research in Bethesda, Maryland, in September–October 1981, the author examined the effects of race, SES, and age on the masculine role perceptions of 155 Black middle-class men (aged 22–83 yrs). Comparative data from previous research by the author (1979) on 54 Black working-class men are discussed. Comparisons were also made to findings reported by C. Tavris (1977) from a survey sample consisting primarily of middle-class White men. It was found that age was an important factor in determining male role identity, while SES was a major determinant of the degree and nature of male involvement in familial roles. Data exemplify the importance of studying masculine roles within a framework that takes into account the relative social location of American men. (24 ref).

237. Davis, Gary L. & Cross, Herbert J. (1979). **Sexual stereotyping of Black males in interracial sex.** *Archives of Sexual Behavior,* 8(3), 269–279.
Beliefs about Black males' sexuality are pervasive in this society, but little studied. This investigation used a semantic differential to measure 360 White undergraduates' perceptions of Black and White characters in sexually explicit stories, some of which depicted interracial pairings. The perceptions were then examined in relationship to authoritarianism and sexual repression as measured by an F scale (R. Lee and P. Warr, 1969) and the Sex Guilt Scale. Results suggest that Black males are stereotyped as more potent than White males. (20 ref).

238. Finn, Jerry. (1986). **The relationship between sex role attitudes and attitudes supporting marital violence.** *Sex Roles,* 14(5–6), 235–244.
Explored the relationship between attitudes toward sex roles and attitudes endorsing the legitimacy of physical force by men in the marital relationship among 80 White male, 80 Black male, 70 White female, and 70 Black female undergraduates who completed a personal opinion scale. Findings show a strong positive relationship between traditional sex role preferences and attitudes supporting the use of physical force. In addition, men were found to hold more traditional sex role attitudes than women and were more likely to endorse the use of physical force in the marital relationship. Whites were more traditional in their sex role attitudes than Blacks, but no racial differences were found with regard to attitudes endorsing physical force. Further analysis revealed that traditional sex role attitudes were the most powerful predictor of attitudes supporting marital violence, while race and sex played a relatively unimportant role. (21 ref).

239. Franklin, Clyde W. (1985). **The Black male urban barbershop as a sex-role socialization setting.** *Sex Roles,* 12(9–10), 965–979.
Investigated an urban barbershop's role as a sex-role socialization setting for Black males during a 2-mo period. Two middle-aged Black males served as field workers and 2 Black male barbers served as informants over 280 hrs. Eight hours of informal interviews with informants were conducted. Analyses revealed that the barbershop perpetuated sex-role stereotypes, encouraged sexist attitudes toward women, and, in general, was a sex-role socialization setting that promoted sex-role inequality. (23 ref).

240. Gary, Lawrence E. (1986). **Predicting interpersonal conflict between men and women: The case of Black men.** *American Behavioral Scientist,* 29(5), 635–646.

Interviewed and administered the Center for Epidemiological Studies Depression Scale to 142 Black males (aged 18–65 yrs) to explore how demographic and sociocultural factors predict interpersonal conflict between Black men and women. The dependent variable, Conflict Between the Sexes, was defined as the number of disagreements with mates during the past few weeks. Most Ss did not perceive themselves as having a high level of conflict with Black women. Among Ss who did experience considerable conflict with their mates, irritating personal habits, how to spend leisure time, being away from home too much, time spent with friends, and the job were the major areas of conflict. Ss who experienced higher levels of conflict also evidenced higher levels of depression.

241. Hansen, Sally L. (1977). **Dating choices of high school students.** *Family Coordinator,* 26(2), 133–138.
Dating is experienced by most adolescents in our society as a prelude to mate selection. 354 15–19 Black and White high school students were studied to measure their dating-mating choices. Ss completed a dating-rating checklist on which they selected internal and external traits they perceived to be important to (a) their peers in date selection (perceived level of popularity), (b) themselves in date selection (dating level), and (c) themselves in mate selection (mate selection level). Results show that (a) gender differences exist at mate selection and popularity levels, (b) Black Ss chose external traits at both popularity and dating levels, and White Ss chose internal traits at the dating level, and (c) Ss chose more external traits at the popularity level than at dating and mate selection levels.

242. Icard, Larry. (1986). **Black gay men and conflicting social identities: Sexual orientation versus racial identity.** Special Issue: Social work practice in sexual problems. *Journal of Social Work & Human Sexuality,* 4(1–2), 83–93.
Explores the negative influences of the Black and the gay communities in terms of social identity elements of the self-concept of Black gays. It is suggested that the Black community holds negative attitudes about homosexuality and that Blacks may be viewed as inferior members of the gay community and may be unable to find the positive consequences necessary for closure of sexual identity, especially during the coming-out period. Suggestions for social workers are included to aid in the understanding of the uniqueness of the life experiences and needs of Black, gay men and to enhance therapeutic intervention.

243. Intons-Peterson, M. J. & Samuels, Arlene K. (1978). **The cultural halo effect: Black and White women rate Black and White men.** *Bulletin of the Psychonomic Society,* 11(5), 309–312.
In an exploratory study, 21 Black and 21 White college women rated Black and White men on traits associated with masculinity, femininity, and social desirability using the Bem Androgyny Scale. Black women rated Black men as more masculine than White men, whereas White women characterized both Black and White men as less masculine than the ratings assigned by Black women to Black men but as more masculine than the ratings assigned by Black women to White men. Both Black and White women attributed feminine socially desirable traits to Black and White men in approximately equal proportions. Data are consistent with a "cultural halo" hypothesis. (15 ref).

244. Korolewicz, Mitchell & Korolewicz, Ann. (1985). **Effects of sex and race on interracial dating preferences.** *Psychological Reports,* 57(3, Pt 2), 1291–1296.
32 undergraduates from New Jersey and 32 undergraduates from Mississippi, evenly divided between Black and White and male and female, completed an interracial dating-preference questionnaire consisting of dating scenarios involving White and Black participants, White participants only, and Black participants only. A 2-way analysis of variance

(ANOVA) showed that sex and race affected interracial dating preferences. Blacks, particularly Black females, were more apt to prefer interracial dating than Whites. Among the Whites, males tended to prefer interracial dating more than females. Findings do not confirm the findings of F. Petroni (1973), who reported that Black females were the least likely to date interracially. It is suggested that the present results may differ from those of Petroni because Petroni investigated behavior and the present study examined attitudes. The scenarios used on the questionnaire are appended. (16 ref).

245. Millham, Jim & Smith, Lynette E. (1981). **Sex-role differentiation among Black and White Americans: A comparative study.** *Journal of Black Psychology,* 7(2), 77–90.
160 evening community college students (mean age 24 yrs) judged the desirability of the 218 personality characteristics selected by S. L. Bem (1974) for either of the sexes. 300 other students completed the Sex-Role Survey (A. P. McDonald, 1974). Both samples were divided evenly between males and females, and between Blacks and Whites. Males made more distinctions on the basis of sex than did females, and Whites of both sexes made more than Blacks. Among Whites, competitive and vocationally-oriented traits were valued more highly for males than for females, and emotional expression was valued more for females. The Black sample placed minimal value on sex roles differentiated on the basis of trait-descriptive characteristics. White Ss' endorsement of statements of sexual equality could be described by 3 general attitudinal sets, while Blacks responded to such statements as largely independent beliefs. (10 ref).

246. Price-Bonham, Sharon & Skeen, Patsy. (1982). **Black and White fathers' attitudes toward children's sex roles.** *Psychological Reports,* 50(3, Pt 2), 1187–1190.
Using the Bem Sex-Role Inventory, the authors collected sex-role attitudes from 100 White and 60 Black middle-class fathers. A stepwise-regression analysis indicated that both Black and White Ss held significantly more masculine sex-role attitudes toward their sons and more feminine sex-role attitudes toward their daughters. White Ss expressed significantly more androgynous attitudes toward daughters and sons than did Black Ss. (11 ref).

247. Rao, V. Prakasa & Rao, V. Nandini. (1985). **Sex-role attitudes: A comparison of sex-race groups.** *Sex Roles,* 12(9–10), 939–953.
Investigated the differences in the 3 dimensions of sex-role attitudes among 4 sex-race groups (White male, White female, Black male, Black female) and the ability of sex and race jointly to condition the effects of background characteristics on these attitudes. 409 undergraduates (40% male, 60% female, 48% Black, 52% White) were asked to state preferences for numbers of children desired and to complete scales on traditional wife, mother, and father roles. Significant differences were found on all 3 dimensions of sex-role attitudes between the 2 sex groups but not between the 2 racial groups, implying that gender is the most significant variable in eliciting differences in sex-role attitudes. Findings fail to support the contention that sex-role attitudes will be jointly influenced by the respondent's sex and race. (59 ref).

248. Rubin, Roger H. (1981). **Attitudes about male–female relations among Black adolescents.** *Adolescence,* 16(61), 159–174.
The literature on Black persons in the US suggests that family structure, peer groups, social class, and sex membership are important factors in the development of attitudes concerning male–female relations. 46 male and 39 female Blacks aged 13–20 yrs, constituting almost the entire Black population of never married, not engaged adolescents in a rural, Pennsylvania community, were studied. Research was conducted in the school, poolroom, streets, and homes, using a questionnaire and a structured interview. It is concluded that the aforemen-

tioned variables are not good predictors of attitudinal differences, but rather that general community norms and values may be more influential. (62 ref).

249. Smith, Patricia A. & Midlarsky, Elizabeth. (1985). **Empirically derived conceptions of femaleness and maleness: A current view.** *Sex Roles,* 12(3–4), 313–328.
Investigated the nature and type of conceptions of femaleness and maleness generated by Blacks and Whites in an open-ended questionnaire. 251 male and 249 female respondents (aged 17–74 yrs) from 13 vocational schools, community colleges, 4-yr colleges, and universities generated 718 conceptions, which were then rated on degree of maleness and femaleness and social desirability by a sample of 297 respondents fairly evenly distributed across gender and race from that same population. Ss completed a maleness–femaleness conceptions form and a conceptions rating scale. Results indicate that females and males (races combined) and Blacks and Whites (genders combined) differed significantly in their male–female conceptions scores. White Ss had higher maleness and femaleness scores than did Black Ss. Females generated positive conceptions of personality traits and emphasized socially desirable recreational and social activities in descriptions of their own gender, contrary to the relatively negative portrait of women provided by men. Women tended to use fewer personality trait items in their descriptions than men. Males' descriptions of maleness focused on strong, adaptive personalities and interesting lifestyles, while females' descriptions of maleness concentrated on activities and occupations. (34 ref).

250. Stack, Carol B. (1986). **The culture of gender: Women and men of color.** *Signs,* 11(2), 321–324.
Discusses C. Gilligan's assertion that there is a female model for moral development (1982) as it relates to minority men and women. An African-American model of moral development appears different from that of Gilligan. Gender construction may not be the same in all societies.

251. Staples, Robert. (1978). **Masculinity and race: The dual dilemma of Black men.** *Journal of Social Issues,* 34(1), 169–183.
Examines the special status of Black men in contemporary society. Considering some of the common stereotypes of Black men from a historical perspective, alternative explanations are posited to counter prevailing views of the Afro-American male as emasculated, dominated by women, and lacking in positive self-esteem. The socialization process and problems of Black youth are examined, and the special roles of lover, husband, and father are analyzed as Black men interpret and carry them out. Black male sexism and the response of Black feminism are discussed, as are the problems and prospects for Black men in American society. (46 ref).

252. Vadies, Eugene & Hale, Darryl. (1977). **Attitudes of adolescent males toward abortion, contraception, and sexuality.** *Social Work in Health Care,* 3(2), 169–174.
Young males appear to be reassessing their roles in preventing unwanted conception. This article reports the findings of a study of the attitudes of 1,017 young men toward pregnancy, family planning, and sexuality. A questionnaire was used over a 2-yr period, administered before educational sessions conducted by the Planned Parenthood Association of the Chicago Area. Findings indicate that young males are tending to see the responsibility for contraception more as a dual responsibility than as that of the female alone. Findings also reveal a strong sentiment against abortion on the part of Black teenagers, with the opposite being reported by White teens.

Drug & Alcohol Usage

253. Connors, Gerard J.; Watson, Donnie W. & Maisto, Stephen A. (1985). **Influence of subject and interviewer characteristics on the reliability of young adults' self-reports of drinking.** *Journal of Psychopathology & Behavioral Assessment,* 7(4), 365–374.
Interviewed 48 male and 48 female undergraduates, equally divided between Blacks and Whites, concerning their drinking practices. Effects of S race and sex and interviewer race and sex on self-reports were analyzed. Half of the Ss were used to assess the test–retest reliability of the self-reports. Each S was interviewed individually in a counterbalanced manner and coded into 1 of 3 mutually exclusive categories. Results show that Ss provided highly reliable self-reports regarding their use of alcohol. Test–retest correlations for a criterion interval of 90 days were .96, .93, and .97 for the numbers of abstinent, moderate-drinking, and heavy-drinking days, respectively. Analyses also showed that White female Ss generally provided more reliable reports of abstinent and heavy-drinking days and that White female interviewers gathered more reliable reports across the 3 drinking disposition categories. Findings show several race/gender differences in Ss' drinking practices and suggest that nonalcoholic young adults' retrospective reports of their drinking behavior can be reliably assessed using the time-line methodology. (14 ref).

254. Galchus, Donna S. & Galchus, Kenneth E. (1978). **Drug use: Some comparisons of Black and White college students.** *Drug Forum,* 6(1), 65–76.
Administered a questionnaire concerning drug use to 342 Black undergraduates from a predominately Black private college and to 374 White undergraduates from a predominately White state-supported college. Results are as follows: (a) Approximately 50% of both Black and White Ss were occasional or frequent users of marihuana. (b) No racial difference was found in marihuana use. (c) A significant racial difference was found in the use of heroin and cocaine, and amphetamines and barbiturates. (d) No significant difference was found between male and female use of marihuana. (e) Tobacco was associated with marihuana use for both Black and White Ss. (f) The correlation between marihuana use and that of heroin and cocaine was low for both samples. (g) Religious beliefs were negatively correlated with an S's decision to use marihuana.

255. Marini, James L.; Bridges, C. I. & Sheard, M. H. (1978). **Multiple drug abuse: Examination of drug-abuse patterns in male prisoners.** *International Journal of the Addictions,* 13(3), 493–502.
Pre-incarceration drug-use patterns were investigated retrospectively in 58 male prisoners, average age 18.6 yrs. 50% of the Ss were White, 43% Black, and 7% Hispanic. 55% were classified as drug-dependent, 36% as regular, and 9% as casual users of at least 1 drug. Classification according to numbers of "hard" drugs used regularly gave equal percentages of Ss using none, 1–2, or more than 2 (polydrug) users. The polydrug users were predominantly White and often used amphetamines or hallucinogens, while those using 1–2 "hard" drugs regularly were predominantly Black, eschewed hallucinogens, and preferred narcotics. (22 ref).

256. Milavsky, J. Ronald; Pekowsky, Berton & Stipp, Horst. (1976). **TV drug advertising and proprietary and illicit drug use among teenage boys.** *Public Opinion Quarterly,* 39(4), 457–481.
Reports results of a 5-wave panel study, conducted by the National Broadcasting Company over a 3½-yr period, which investigated the relationships between exposure to drug advertisements on TV and (a) use of proprietary drugs, (b) use of illicit drugs, and (c) an attitude of readiness to take proprietary drugs. Data were collected from teen-age boys and their

families, in 2 midwestern cities, representing low- and middle-income Black and White groups. Procedures are described in detail. The major finding was a negative relationship between exposure to drug advertising on TV and use of illicit drugs, which remained negative under a large number of controls. No negative relationship between the 2 variables was found via the use of proprietary drugs or via an attitude of readiness to take proprietary drugs. (16 ref).

257. Watson, Donnie W. & Sobell, Mark B. (1982). **Social influences on alcohol consumption by Black and White males.** *Addictive Behaviors,* 7(1), 87–91.
32 Black and 32 White male undergraduate normal drinkers participated in a beer taste test either simultaneously (co-action condition) with a heavy drinking Black or White experimental accomplice or while the accomplice completed an art-rating task (control observer condition). Ss in the co-action condition drank significantly more beer than Ss in the control observer condition, regardless of their race or the race of the accomplice. Ss' postexperimental questionnaire answers indicated they did not perceive themselves to be in competition with the accomplice. The mechanism underlying the robust co-action facilitation effect on drinking, now demonstrated in several studies (e.g., B. D. Caudill and G. A. Marlatt, see PA, Vol 54:5173 and W. K. Garlington and D. A. DeRicco, PA, Vol 59:12289) and extended to Black males in the present study, remains unexplained. (18 ref).

EXPERIMENTAL SOCIAL PSYCHOLOGY

258. Bankart, C. Peter. (1972). **Attribution of motivation in same-race and different-race stimulus persons.** *Human Relations,* 25(1), 35–45.
40 male Caucasian and 40 male Negro undergraduates were shown a set of videotapes of a stimulus person involved in a problem-solving task. 1 stimulus person was Caucasian and the other Negro, and each was shown at high and low motivation levels. Analysis of questionnaire responses revealed that Caucasian Ss perceived less motivated Caucasian and Negro stimulus person as less anxious than highly motivated stimulus persons. Negro Ss perceived this same relationship for Caucasian stimulus persons only. Negro Ss perceived less motivated Negro stimulus persons as more anxious than Negro stimulus persons with high motivation. The stereotyped view of the Negro as casual, likeable, friendly, and lazy, was held by Negro Ss as well as Caucasians in describing the Negro stimulus person. Attribution of high motivation was found to be associated with a wide range of positive personality attributes. This effect was spread over both races of Ss and both races of stimulus persons.

259. Bauer, Ernest A. (1973). **Personal space: A study of Blacks and Whites.** *Sociometry,* 36(3), 402–408.
15 male and 15 female Blacks and equal numbers of Whites all college age were asked to approach, "as close as comfortable," a confederate of their own sex and race whom they did not know. Data were analyzed to investigate differences in the distances chosen attributable to race, sex, or their interaction. It was found that White males chose the most distant positions (17.8 in.), White females were next (13.4 in.), Black males followed (11.4 in.), and Black females were most proximal (8.1 in.). No significant differences were found for sex and the interaction of sex and race, but White Ss chose significantly greater distances than did Black Ss. Results are interpreted as possibly being due to different cues eliciting distancing in the 2 groups. It is also suggested that the verbal instructions may have been construed differently by members of the 2 groups.

260. Blumenthal, Monica D. (1972). **Predicting attitudes toward violence.** *Science,* 176(4041), 1296–1303.

Developed and tested a model for predicting attitudes toward violence. It was assumed that attitudes are likely to be reflected in behaviors and that basic cultural values, identifications, and definitions will affect attitudes. 1,071 White and 303 Black 16–64 yr old males were interviewed in the summer of 1969. Ss' attitudes toward violence for social change and for social control were assessed. It was found that attitudes toward violence were related to values and attitudes toward the contending parties. Attitudes on retributive justice and self-defense were positively oriented toward violence. A strong relationship was found between what acts an S defined as violence and his attitudes toward violence for social control. Many of the Ss considered acts of dissent to be violence (e.g., 22% of the Ss defined sit-ins as violent and 58% so defined draft-card burning). It is concluded that there is a strong relationship between attitudes toward violence and basic values, attitudes toward others, and the language that is used to describe events. Implications for law enforcement officials are noted. (23 ref).

261. Blumenthal, Monica D. (1973). **Resentment and suspicion among American men.** *American Journal of Psychiatry,* 130(8), 876–880.
Interviewed a representative national sample of 1,046 White and 303 Black 16–64 yr old males with respect to their levels of resentment and suspicion and their attitudes toward violence. Results show that resentment and suspicion appeared to be related both to race and to social class. However, these variables were not related to attitudes toward the use of violence for gaining social control, suggesting that such attitudes are normative rather than expressive in nature.

262. Christian, Walter E. & Greene, Joel E. (1976). **Ethnicity as an input variable to equity theory.** *Journal of Psychology,* 94(2), 237–243.
Used the equity model to study ethnic relations, hypothesizing that within a homogeneous dyad (composed of members of the same ethnic group), greater equity would occur than in a heterogeneous dyad (composed of members of different ethnic groups). A secondary hypothesis was that greater equity would occur in a dyad composed of members of 2 different minority groups than in a dyad composed of a minority group member and a White individual. Ss were 18 Anglo, 18 Black, and 18 Chicano male college students. The task involved an S and a stooge working in partnership to identify correctly 18 American slang words for a reward. An analysis of variance indicated partial support for the primary hypothesis, in that homogeneous Chicano dyads were the most equitable, and full support for the secondary hypothesis. The findings show the validity of using equity theory to study intergroup relations. (17 ref).

263. Coates, Brian. (1972). **White adult behavior toward Black and White children.** *Child Development,* 43(1), 143–154.
24 male and 24 female White undergraduates used verbal statements to train 9-yr-old Black or White male Ss on a discrimination problem. Bogus information on Ss' performance was given to the adults and the dependent variable was the adults' statements to the Ss. A Sex of Adult by Race of Child interaction was found. Males were more negative with Black Ss than with White, whereas there was a nonsignificant difference between the 2 races for females. On trait ratings of Ss following the training session, both males and females rated Black Ss more negatively than White.

264. Cohen, Elizabeth G. (1972). **Interracial interaction disability.** *Human Relations,* 25(1), 9–24.
19 4-member groups were formed from boys in the 7th and 8th grade and observed as they played a game of strategy. Each group contained 2 Black and 2 White boys matched for height and combined index of socioeconomic and school attitude. The groups were systematically observed by both Black and White observers (Os) using an observation scheme

derived from status characteristic theory. No systematic differences were found between Black and White Os. Three hypotheses were confirmed: (a) Race was strongly associated with differences in rank order on the number of acts initiated, with Whites more likely to have a higher rank than Blacks. (b) On an independent measure of influence, a White S's suggestion became the group's decision more frequently than a Black's, especially where decisions were contested. (c) The indices of influence and rate of initiation were strongly positively related. It is concluded that Blacks are more inhibited and less willing to argue for their point of view in an integrated work situation, and therefore less influential than Whites.

265. Foley, Linda A. (1976). **Personality and situational influences on changes in prejudice: A replication of Cook's railroad game in a prison setting.** *Journal of Personality & Social Psychology,* 34(5), 846–856.
Attempted to replicate S. W. Cook's (1972) laboratory study of racial prejudice in a natural setting. The objective was to determine the influences of personality and situational factors on changes in prejudice. The environment studied was a maximum security state prison for males. Ss were 83 Black and White inmates admitted to the institution during a 1-mo period. The different environments within the institutions were defined in terms of the norms as perceived by the residents of the different living areas. Ss were pretested for cognitive complexity, self-esteem, and attitudes toward people in general. Interracial attitudes of these Ss were measured at 2 time periods: as the Ss entered the institution and 3 wks later. Results indicate that an individual tends to change racial attitudes toward the norms of his living area, and the amount of change is dependent on the individual's cognitive complexity, self-esteem, and attitudes toward people in general. (24 ref).

266. Hepler, Ruth & Stabler, John R. (1976). **Children's perception of the origin of personal evaluations: Broadcast simultaneously from a white box and a black box.** *Psychology,* 13(2), 26–28.
Conducted an experiment with black and white colored "talking boxes" from which positive and negative statements reflecting appraisals of individual Ss were broadcast (e.g., "You are a good-looking boy (girl)," "You are a winner," "You're stupid," "You are a loser"). 10 positive and 10 negative statements were recorded by a Euro-American adult male who was not identifiable as to race or sex by 2 samples of children. Ss were 15 female and 15 male Black and 15 female and 15 male White 2nd graders. More positive than negative statements were perceived as originating from the white box. The race variable approached significance, and inspection of the group means indicated a greater tendency for Blacks than Whites to associate negative statements with the white box.

267. Keller, Peter A. & Murray, Edward J. (1973). **Imitative aggression with adult male and female models in father absent and father present Negro boys.** *Journal of Genetic Psychology,* 122(2), 217–221.
After mildly frustrating Black male 6-yr-olds from homes where the father was absent ($n = 28$) or present ($n = 31$), Ss were shown films of either an adult Black male or an adult Black female behaving aggressively with a number of toys. Later, Ss were allowed to play with similar toys and their aggressiveness was rated. There were no differences between the father-absent and father-present Ss in imitative aggression. The female model significantly inhibited aggression in both groups. Both groups showed a strong preference for identifying with pictures of males in a supplementary test of masculine preference.

268. Larsen, Knud S.; Colen, Leonard; von Flue, Doug & Zimmerman, Paul. (1974). **Situational pressure, attitudes towards Blacks, and laboratory aggression.** *Social Behavior & Personality,* 2(2), 219–221.
Investigated the effects of racial attitudes on 40 male undergraduates' willingness to shock a Black or White "victim." 2 wks after the laboratory experiment, Ss were approached by a different experimenter and asked to complete the Steckler Anti-Negro Survey. Results show that attitudes toward Blacks were not related to the level of shock administered to Black victims. A Black victim was shocked less than a White victim. Results are interpreted in terms of the social pressures of a university community as influenced, for example, by affirmative action and equal opportunity programs.

269. Lerner, Richard M. & Frank, Phyllis. (1974). **Relation of race and sex to supermarket helping behavior.** *Journal of Social Psychology,* 94(2), 201–203.
Conducted a study of 66 White women and 36 White men as potential helpers to determine the relationship of the race and sex of a person in need of help to the frequency of helping behavior. Ss could help, or not help, a White or a Black male or female, respectively, whose bag of groceries had just broken in front of a supermarket. Overall, the White females tended to help more than the White males, but the overall percentages of help given to males or females, or to Blacks or Whites, were not significantly different. The distribution of the White males' and females' helping did differ in relation to the sex and race of the person in need of help. Despite these differences, no support was found for a racial- or sexual-congruence-increased-helping-frequency relation.

270. Lynch, Denis J. (1974). **A-B type and the relationship between police officers and ghetto citizens.** *Community Mental Health Journal,* 10(4), 434–440.
Investigated the A-B therapist-type distinction in a study in which police officers interviewed Black male ghetto citizens with the goal of eliciting personal information. Analysis was based on 13 dyads, 7 with a B-type interviewer and 6 with an A-type interviewer. Police Ss were White and had a mean age of 34.4 yrs. Citizen Ss were Black and had a mean age of 23.5 yrs. Contrary to predictions, As were not more successful than Bs; further, Bs were better liked by the citizens and tended to be rated as more trustworthy. In turn, Bs rated the citizens as more likable than did As. Citizens interviewed by As tended to rate themselves as less active and potent following the interview than did citizens interviewed by Bs. The value of the complementary hypothesis in interpreting the results is noted, as well as the contribution of the citizens' social class to the superior performance of the Bs.

271. Paige, Jeffery M. (1970). **Changing patterns of anti-White attitudes among Blacks.** *Journal of Social Issues,* 26(4), 69–86.
Anti-White attitudes among Blacks are related to the changing social context of group conflict. Attitudes are part of a broader political ideology suggesting practical strategy for dealing with the White majority. As usefulness of a strategy increases, associated attitudes become more widespread. Three strategies—moving away, moving toward, and moving against—are discussed in terms of associated anti-White attitudes. A survey of 236 15–35 yr old Black males is reported. Attitudinal changes are described, and comparisons with earlier studies are made. (20 ref).

272. Patterson, David L. & Smits, Stanley J. (1974). **Communication bias in Black-White groups.** *Journal of Psychology,* 88(1), 9–25.
Defined prejudice as a statistically significant bias in the direction of verbal statements in T groups whose membership was balanced by race and sex. 3 major hypotheses were tested with a total of 16 White and Black male and female graduate students. Results are discussed in relation to the

nature of prejudice and communication dynamics. 2 *T*-group methodologies were contrasted as an exploration of potential intervention strategies. Results indicate that both race and sex contributed to significant biases, although race seemed to be the more substantive contributor. (22 ref).

273. Turner, Barbara F. & Turner, Castelleno B. (1974). **The political implications of social stereotyping of women and men among Black and White college students.** *Sociology & Social Research,* 58(2), 155–162.
Administered semantic differential scales on the concepts "most women are..." and "most men are..." to 28 Black female, 31 Black male, 45 White female, and 37 White male undergraduates. White females were the only group to rate the opposite sex significantly more positively than their own sex. Black females rated men as more unreliable than did the other groups and were the only group to rate men as significantly more unreliable than they rated women. Otherwise, Black females' evaluations of men did not differ from male evaluations. (16 ref).

274. Veltman, Calvin J. (1972). **The resistance of respondents in inter-ethnic interviewing.** *Sociology & Social Research,* 56(4), 513–521.
Interviewed 135 graduating male White seniors to determine whether the traditional research methods model, which indicates that respondents tailor their answers to the social characteristics of interviews, would be supported. Utilizing 1 Black and 2 White interviewers, (1 "racial" and 1 "conservative"), results suggest that when respondents knew answers were being evaluated, they followed the traditional assumption. However, the use of an unobtrusive major revealed a resistance on the part of the White respondents to accept a definition of the situation from a Black interviewer.

275. Webber, Ross A. (1974). **Majority and minority perceptions and behavior in cross-cultural teams.** *Human Relations,* 27(9), 873–889.
Studied majority and minority perceptions and behavior in cross-cultural teams of White American male, White American female, Black American male, and foreign male business students. 456 Ss in 114 4-person cross-cultural teams with White American male (WAM) majorities performed case analysis tasks for 13 wks. Data on roles claimed for self and attributed to others were collected by questionnaire and essays with supplementary interviews. Results show that the WAM majority claimed task leadership for themselves or attributed it to other WAMs and perceived all minorities as generally following and contributing relatively little. Most minority members did not claim leadership, and those few that did were usually rejected. American White females tended to respond with complementary stereotypic behaviors (e.g., relative passivity and claims of nonleadership). American Black, European, and Latin American males tended to violate group norms and frequently withdrew from the team. (23 ref).

276. Weitz, Shirley. (1972). **Attitude, voice, and behavior: A repressed affect model of interracial interaction.** *Journal of Personality & Social Psychology,* 24(1), 14–21.
Investigated the relationship between verbal attitudes, voice tone, and behavior toward Blacks among a sample of 80 White college males in the North identified as "liberal" on the basis of Schuman and Harding's Irrational Pro and Anti Scales. A simulated interracial encounter in which Ss expected to interact with a Black (or White) stimulus person was used. A general pattern of overt friendliness and covert rejection was found. Voice tone and behavior were positively related to each other, but negatively related to friendliness of attitude toward Blacks. Results suggest a repressed affect model leading to conflicting cues in interracial interaction.

277. Winter, Sara K. (1971). **Black man's bluff.** *Psychology Today,* 5(4), 39–43.
3 racially mixed groups of undergraduates met for 3 hr/wk for 10 wk to study the groups' functioning. In each group a Black male became the accepted leader. They were rated as upward-negative-backward types by the other group members using Bales' Interpersonal Rating System. The Blacks were able to maintain leadership roles, in spite of being in the minority, at least partially because group members shared (but did not discuss) cultural myths concerning Blacks and Whites.

278. Woodbury, Roger. (1973). **Delinquents' attitudes toward the juvenile justice system.** *Psychological Reports,* 32(3, Pt. 2), 1119–1124.
Administered Attitudes Toward the Police, Attitudes Toward the Juvenile Court, Attitudes Toward Probation, and the T. Elmore Scale of Anomie to 73 White and 73 Black 14-yr-old male delinquents. White Ss had more unfavorable attitudes toward the juvenile court and more feelings of valuelessness and hopelessness, while Blacks had more hostile attitudes toward the police and more feelings of powerlessness. Correlations suggest that attitudes toward legal agencies and anomie may be acquired independently.

279. Word, Carl O.; Zanna, Mark P. & Cooper, Joel. (1974). **The nonverbal mediation of self-fulfilling prophecies in interracial interaction.** *Journal of Experimental Social Psychology,* 10(2), 109–120.
Conducted 2 experiments designed to demonstrate the existence of a self-fulfilling prophecy mediated by nonverbal behavior in an interracial interaction. Exp I, which employed 14 White job interviewers (male university students) and 5 trained White and Black job applicants, demonstrated that Black applicants received (a) less immediacy, (b) higher rates of speech errors, and (c) shorter amounts of interview time. Exp II employed 30 naive, White applicants (male university students) and 2 trained White interviewers. In this experiment Ss received behaviors that approximated those given either the Black or White applicants in Exp I. Results indicate that Ss treated like the Blacks of Exp I were judged to perform less adequately and to be more nervous in the interview situation than Ss treated like the Whites. The former Ss also reciprocated with less proximate positions and rated the interviewers as being less adequate and friendly. Implications for Black unemployment are discussed. (16 ref).

Group & Interpersonal Processes

280. Barlow, David H. et al. (1977). **A heterosocial skills behavior checklist for males.** *Behavior Therapy,* 8(2), 229–239.
Social skills necessary to function heterosexually (heterosocial skills) include at least 3 overlapping categories of social behavior: initiating a heterosocial relationship, initiating sexual behavior, and maintaining the heterosocial relationship over a period of time. The purpose of this experiment was to pinpoint social behaviors important in initiating a heterosocial relationship in males. 10 White and 10 Black high school and college males, judged socially attractive by a panel of popular females in their schools, were videotaped interacting with female research assistants. 10 patients with sexually variant behaviors who reported and were judged to be heterosocially inadequate were also videotaped interacting with a female. Behaviors in 3 categories—form of conversation, affect, and voice—significantly discriminated the adequate from inadequate males. The relationship of these data to general social skills training and the importance of investigating other aspects of heterosocial behavior are discussed. (25 ref).

281. Dean, Larry M.; Willis, Frank N. & la Rocco, James M. (1976). **Invasion of personal space as a function of age, sex, and race.** *Psychological Reports,* 38(3, Pt 1), 959–965.

Reactions to the invasion of personal space in terms of age, sex, and race of the invaders were investigated. Children, grouped by sex (male and female), race (Black and White), and age (5, 8, and 10 yrs old), invaded the personal space of 192 adults grouped by sex (male and female) and race (Black and White). The 6 types of behavioral responses were avoidance, aggression, exploratory behavior, facilitative behavior, excess motor activity, and failure to respond. Responses to personal space invasion were not affected by sex. Blacks responded more often than Whites but did not differ with regard to any particular type of behavioral response. Age of the invader had a significant effect on type of response given by adults whose personal space was invaded. It is concluded that the age of the invader was much more important than race or sex in determining the response to invasion of personal space. (22 ref).

282. Garratt, Gail A.; Baxter, James C. & Rozelle, Richard M. (1981). **Training university police in Black-American nonverbal behaviors.** *Journal of Social Psychology,* 113(2), 217–229.
Empirically derived differences in nonverbal behavior and personal space arrangements between Black and Anglo Americans were incorporated into 2 interview procedures during a standing police interview. Ss were 30 Black male undergraduates. One interview involved the use of several specified nonverbal behaviors and personal space arrangements typical of Blacks; the other included behaviors and spatial arrangements typical of Anglos. The interviews were conducted by 2 uniformed Anglo university police officers (approximately 30 yrs of age) who had been trained and rehearsed in both the Black and Anglo styles of interview. Following the interviews, each S reported his preferences for the police officer performing in either the Black or Anglo interview within a personal, social, and professional context. As predicted, Black Ss showed a significant preference in all contexts for those interviews in which the policeman employed Black nonverbal behaviors and spatial arrangements. A recency effect and a preference for a particular officer were also found. (16 ref).

283. Peretti, Peter O. (1976). **Closest friendships of Black college students: Social intimacy.** *Adolescence,* 11(43), 395–403.
Used ego perception to study social intimacy of closest friendships and social intimacy based on structural characteristics of groups formed by members of the same and the opposite sex. 77 male and 120 female Black college students completed a "closest friendship diagram" and questionnaires about group stability and social intimacy. Results found different degrees in the range of social intimacy between closest friendships of same and opposite sex members. Among the structural networks of both heterosocial and homosocial friendships, dyadic forms of relations tended to be the most socially intimate.

284. Peretti, Peter O. (1976). **Closest friendships of Black college students: Structural characteristics.** *Psychology,* 13(1), 11–18.
Studied friendship structures among Black college students. 197 male and female students in 8 social science classes were asked to draw diagrams depicting their closest friendships with members of the same sex, members of the opposite sex, and members of both sexes together. Results are presented in detail for males and females and for all Ss combined. In general, the dyad, the double dyad, and the triple dyad were the structures most frequently represented, indicating that students tend to develop close one-to-one relationships with people who do not know each other. The great majority of friendships with the opposite sex are dyadic.

285. Ruhe, John & Eatman, John. (1977). **Effects of racial composition on small work groups.** *Small Group Behavior,* 8(4), 479–486.

Compared the work attitudes and behaviors of Blacks and Whites in small segregated and integrated groups. 96 male undergraduates were randomly selected to participate as subordinates and supervisors in problem-solving groups of various racial compositions. The variables assessed were (a) productivity in each of 3 tasks (e.g., knot-tying, ship routing, and letter writing), (b) duration of individual speech during each of the 3 tasks, (c) total duration of speech for all tasks, (d) group cohesiveness, (e) self-esteem, (f) satisfaction with work, (g) satisfaction with supervisor, and (h) satisfaction with coworkers. Whites in segregated groups or in integrated groups did not differ significantly on any of the measures. Blacks in integrated groups performed significantly better in the letter-writing task and had significantly higher self-esteem than Blacks in segregated groups. The only significant difference between Whites and Blacks in segregated groups was that the Whites performed better in the letter-writing task. Blacks in integrated groups had significantly better attitudes toward self and others than Whites in integrated groups. Results show that work in an integrated setting improves the performance and attitudes of Blacks without adversely affecting the performance and attitudes of Whites. (17 ref).

286. Smith, Althea. (1983). **Nonverbal communication among Black female dyads: An assessment of intimacy, gender, and race.** *Journal of Social Issues,* 39(3), 55–67.
Research in the area of the effects of gender and race on social and psychological behavior has been limited in its approach, only reporting differences between Blacks and Whites or males and females. The present study expands race and gender effects to include both within- and between-race comparisons, as well as gender comparisons across race. Using the results of a naturalistic observation of nonverbal cues between same-sex dyads, the behavior of 19 Black female/Black female dyads was compared to 22 White female/White female and 18 Black male/Black male dyads. Similarities and differences among the groups provide further evidence for previously reported race and gender effects. Specifically, Black females did not smile more often than Black males when interacting in same-sex dyads; Black females looked less often than White female dyads; and Black females leaned synchronously more often than White female and Black male dyads. There were no significant differences in smiling behavior between Black males and Black females. Other examples from the nonverbal literature are discussed using this "simple effects" comparative strategy. (36 ref).

287. Thomas, Veronica G. & Littig, Lawrence W. (1985). **A typology of leadership style: Examining gender and race effects.** *Bulletin of the Psychonomic Society,* 23(2), 132–134.
Assessed 4 leadership style typologies, each representing a different mix of consideration and structure orientation, using the Leadership Opinion Questionnaire with 121 White and 129 Black male and 101 White and 179 Black female business administration and management undergraduates. Results reveal a significant relationship between race and leadership typology, with Blacks making use of significantly more consideration- and structure-oriented leadership behaviors than Whites. Gender was not significantly related to leadership typology. (28 ref).

288. Weigel, Russell H. & Quinn, Thomas E. (1977). **Ethnic differences in cooperative behavior: A non-confirmation.** *Psychological Reports,* 40(2), 666.
74 pairs of 13-yr-old males participated in a task requiring cooperative interaction for successful resolution. Ss were randomly assigned to 1 of 6 conditions: White-White, Black-Black, Puerto Rican-Puerto Rican, White-Black, White-Puerto Rican, and Black-Puerto Rican. No significant differences obtained among these 6 conditions with respect to degree of cooperative behavior exhibited. The relation of these findings to previous research of ethnic differences in cooperative behavior is discussed briefly.

Social Perception & Motivation

289. Brown, Clifford E. (1981). **Shared space invasion and race.** *Personality & Social Psychology Bulletin,* 7(1), 103–108.
Observed the tendency of shoppers at a suburban shopping mall to walk between conversing Black, White, or mixed-race male dyads. Both male and female shoppers (*N* = 508, 93.7% White) were more likely to walk through the Black dyad than through the White or the mixed-race dyads. Results are interpreted as indicating a relative lack of consideration for the Black dyad's interaction territory. When walking around a mixed-race dyad, shoppers more often chose to pass behind the White member. Findings suggest that the often subtle effects of racial attitudes can be studied unobtrusively using the invasion of shared space paradigm. (9 ref).

290. Buckalew, L. W. & Coffield, K. E. (1978). **Relationship of reference group to perception of humor.** *Perceptual & Motor Skills,* 47(1), 143–146.
Psychosocial importance of humor in reduction of anxiety and communication was developed, with specific consideration of group influence on perception of humor. Ss were 15 Black females, 20 White females, 13 Black males, and 16 White males; all were psychology graduate students. Cartoons depicting 7 humorous themes were rank ordered in terms of "funniness." Group mean ranks were transformed into ordinal integers. Groups applied similar concepts of humor to rankings, although rank correlations showed significant relationships only between White females, Black females, and White males. (16 ref).

291. Coleman, Lerita M. (1976). **Racial decoding and status differentiation: Who hears what?** *Journal of Black Psychology,* 3(1), 34–46.
Tested the ability of 20 White and 20 Black students to distinguish sex, race, and status of 24 tape-recorded voices. The stimulus voices represented 3 categories: professors, students, and workers. The simple standard statement spoken by the voices controlled for syntax, grammatical construction, vocabulary, and reading ability. Analysis of variance (ANOVA) was used to examine abilities to decode and encode race. Although Blacks scored significantly higher on the task as a whole, correct identification appeared to be dependent upon the race of the listener: Blacks did better on Black voices; Whites did better on White voices. Better performance by Blacks may reflect greater exposure to both races. Scores were highest for Black females, followed by Black males, White males, and White females. Status was a more difficult task; no major differences were found in scores. Analysis for vocal stereotyping showed that Black listeners heard more Black voices, and that placement of the voices in a particular status category was dependent upon the race and sex of the listener and race of the speaker. ANOVA for sex and status showed assignation of status category to be contingent upon sex of speaker. Black female voices were hardest to detect, followed by Black males, White females, and White males. Student status was easiest to detect; professor was the most difficult. (12 ref).

292. Crane, Valerie & Ballif, Bonnie L. (1976). **Effects of Black or White adult modeling with rule structure on adopting a standard for self-control in Black boys.** *Journal of Educational Research,* 70(2), 96–101.
Assessed the effects of modeling, modeling with rule structure, and race of model on adopting standards for self-control. 108 6-11 yr old Black males were exposed to a Black or a White adult male model who consistently chose a self-control response as a reaction to an intentional act of transgression combined with either a rule statement (rule-structure group) or a summary of the story (no-rule-structure group). 54 Ss in a control group were not exposed to a model. Treatment consisted of exposure to modeling procedures and testing over a 3-wk period. Results indicate that modeling is an effective means of modifying verbal responses in Black boys. A significant interaction of Race of Model with Repeated Sessions indicated that from baseline to treatment sessions, Black Ss exposed to a Black model increased in the number of self-control responses to a greater degree than did Black Ss exposed to a White model. There were no significant differences between the self-control scores and rule-statement scores of the rule-structure and no-rule-structure groups. However, Ss in the no-rule-structure group as well as the rule-structure group gave more rule statements than the control group. This finding is explained in terms of J. Aronfreed's (1969) concept of social facilitation.

293. Donnerstein, Edward & Donnerstein, Marcia. (1975). **The effect of attitudinal similarity on interracial aggression.** *Journal of Personality,* 43(3), 485–502.
Examined the influence of expected retaliation and attitudinal similarity on aggression and reward delivered by 122 male undergraduates to Black and White targets. Results show that both retaliation and attitudinal similarity increased the level of reward and reduced the level of aggression delivered to Black targets. However, modifications in these direct behaviors induced through retaliation were generally accompanied by increases in less direct forms of aggressive behavior. No such increase accompanied modifications induced through attitudinal similarity. Results are discussed in terms of the usefulness of instigation-based vs inhibition-based strategies in the control of interracial aggression. (25 ref).

294. Forgas, Joseph P. & Brown, L. B. (1978). **The effects of race on observer judgments of nonverbal communications.** *Journal of Social Psychology,* 104(2), 243–251.
Studied the effects of race on observer judgments of nonverbal communications (NVC) with the use of 2 sets of stimulus slides, showing (a) White or Black males individually and (b) same race (White) or mixed race (Black male, White female) interacting couples. For both sets of stimuli, 2 levels of nonverbal behavior were programmed, a neutral stance and a positive, or in the case of couples, an intimate stance. The stimuli were presented to a 60-student sample, and judgments were recorded on a set of 6 bipolar scales. Multivariate ANOVAs indicated that while NVC effects were highly significant for both sets of stimuli, race effects were only significant on evaluative scales, and this effect could be wholly attributed to an interaction of race and NVC cues. Thus, for individual stimulus persons, the effects of positive NVC are relatively attenuated for Black models, and for couples the effects of nonverbal intimacy are more accentuated for mixed-race couples.

295. Frable, Deborrah E. & Bem, Sandra L. (1985). **If you are gender schematic, all members of the opposite sex look alike.** *Journal of Personality & Social Psychology,* 49(2), 459–468.
96 male and 96 female undergraduates classified on the basis of the Bem Sex-Role Inventory were asked to recall "who said what" after listening to a taped conversation either among 3 men and 3 women (the gender study) or among 3 Blacks and 3 Whites (the race study). Analysis of Ss' errors revealed that both sex-typed and cross-sex-typed Ss confused the members of the opposite sex with one another significantly more than androgynous or undifferentiated Ss did. In contrast, no individual differences related to sex typing emerged in the race study, which suggests that the greater gender schematicity of sex-typed individuals is specific to gender, as S. L. Bem's (see PA, Vol 66:5685) gender schema theory implies. The finding that cross-sex-typed Ss were significantly more gender schematic than anyone else and the apparent inconsistency of the data with the self-schema theory of H. Markus et al (see PA, Vol 68:3588) are discussed. (18 ref).

296. Hurwitz, Don; Wiggins, Nancy H. & Jones, Lawrence E. (1975). **A semantic differential for facial attribution: The face differential.** *Bulletin of the Psychonomic Society,* 6(4A), 370–372.
Four groups of 10 college students each (Black males, Black females, White males, and White females) associated a total of 2,400 personality descriptive adjectives to slides of 20 Black and White male faces. Adjectives were grouped into synonym classes, and important adjective groups and their antonyms were selected on the basis of (a) frequency of association, (b) judged relevance of adjective to faces, (c) judged commonness of opposite, and (d) judged commonness of adjective. This procedure was conducted for the whole group of 40 Ss by 1 investigator and for each of the 4 subgroups by another investigator. The 2 adjective lists were compared, and a final set of 27 bipolar adjective scales was selected as appropriate for the study of personality attributions to faces. Race and sex differences in the use of these adjectives were explored.

297. Katz, Irwin; Cohen, Sheldon & Glass, David. (1975). **Some determinants of cross-racial helping behavior.** *Journal of Personality & Social Psychology,* 32(6), 964–970.
Tested the hypothesis that White Americans will favor Black over White help-seekers when both display socially valued characteristics. Male confederates posing as college students telephoned 2,340 White adult males and asked them to answer several questions about a consumer product. Confederates identified themselves as Negro or Black or used no racial label. In addition, callers used either high, medium, or low levels of assertiveness. Ss' racial attitudes were assessed 1 mo later in another telephone survey. Amount of compliance was greater for Negro callers than for Black or nonminority (i.e., no label) callers. Compliance rates declined with increasing assertiveness, especially for minority callers. In the Negro condition helpers had less favorable racial attitudes than nonhelpers. In a 2nd experiment confederates asked males of both races on subway platforms to participate in a brief consumer survey interview. All Ss favored Black confederates, and the effect was enhanced when confederates described themselves as college students. In another subway study male confederates asked for change for a quarter. Compliance was greater for White confederates. Results are consistent with the perceived social desirability hypothesis. An ambivalence interpretation of cross-racial altruism is suggested by the obtained attitude–behavior relationship.

298. Kempler, Bernhard & Shatzer, Craig. (1976). **Attributions of helpful and blameworthy behavior by Black and White boys and girls.** *Perceptual & Motor Skills,* 42(3, Pt 1), 795–800.
30 Black and 30 White boys and girls, aged 5, 8, and 11 yrs, were shown 4 pictures depicting conflict and 4 pictures depicting cooperation between a Black and a White figure. Ss were instructed to tell stories that included the attribution of helpfulness and blameworthy behavior to 1 of the 2 figures. No age trends were found, and helpfulness was attributed on a racial basis; however, females, particularly White females, blamed their own race, while males did not make racially based blame attributions. The traditional female sex-role of accepting blame in resolving conflict situations may be involved. Methodologically, studies of racial attitudes should concentrate on specific attributions in emotionally arousing situations.

299. Maruyama, Geoffrey & Miller, Norman. (1980). **Physical attractiveness, race, and essay evaluation.** *Personality & Social Psychology Bulletin,* 6(3), 384–390.

Three experiments with 530 males examined the impact of race and facial attractiveness on evaluations received by essay writers. Results suggest that attractiveness favorably influenced White raters' perceptions of Blacks as well as of Whites. Other hypotheses predicting a main effect for race and an interaction between race and attractiveness were not supported. (9 ref)

300. Moore, Clifford L. (1976). **The racial preference and attitude of preschool Black children.** *Journal of Genetic Psychology,* 129(1), 37–44.
Conducted a study to investigate the racial preference and attitude of low socioeconomic preschoolers toward female models and to determine whether the race of the examiner influenced these factors. 42 Black male and female preschoolers were randomly assigned to 3 Black female and 3 White female examiners who administered a preference measure that was a variant of the Clark doll test. Although Black males preferred the Black model, they viewed the Black model negatively and the White model positively. Black females preferred the Black model and viewed her positively. The evidence indicates that more than half of all Ss preferred the Black model. The choices made by Ss were not influenced by the race of the examiner. (22 ref).

PERSONALITY

301. Baron, Reuben M.; Cowan, Gloria; Ganz, Richard L. & McDonald, Malcolm. (1974). **Interaction of locus of control and type of performance feedback: Considerations of external validity.** *Journal of Personality & Social Psychology,* 30(2), 285–292.
Conducted 2 studies with 85 White male 10–11 yr olds, 85 Black male 10–11 yr olds, and 72 White male undergraduates to establish the generality of R. M. Baron and R. L. Ganz's (see PA, Vol 47:10627) finding of a significant Locus of Control by Type of Performance Feedback interaction. Locus of control was assessed by administering the Crandall Intellectual Achievement Responsibility Questionnaire to the children and Rotter's Internal–External Control Scale to the adults. Study 2 (with adults) also used a different problem-solving task and new procedures for operationalizing the type of feedback variable. The superior performance of internals to externals under a condition of self-discovery of success (intrinsic feedback), as opposed to the superior performance of externals to internals when unverifiable verbal praise was used (extrinsic feedback), was found for lower-class White as well as lower-class Black 10–11 yr olds and for adults. Taken together, these studies provide strong evidence of the generality and usefulness of the Personality by Treatment interaction design in the area of locus of control. (19 ref).

302. Diener, Robert G. & Maroney, Robert J. (1974). **Relationship between Quick Test and WAIS for Black male adolescent underachievers.** *Psychological Reports,* 34(3, Pt 2), 1232–1234.
Although the Quick Test underestimated Wechsler Adult Intelligence Scale (WAIS) IQs at the lower ranges of intelligence, it approximated WAIS IQs adequately as the average range was approached. It is recommended that a regression equation based on local norms be computed to minimize the risk of misclassifying Black male adolescent underachievers.

303. Dressler, William W. (1985). **The social and cultural context of coping: Action, gender and symptoms in a southern Black community.** *Social Science & Medicine,* 21(5), 499–506.
Examined the relationships of coping styles, chronic economic stressors, and symptoms of distress among 285 residents of a Black community in the rural South. It was found that the effect of an active coping style in moderating the effects of stressors was different for males and females. For females,

active coping buffered the effects of stressors; for males, active coping exacerbated the effects of stressors. These results are consistent with the social and cultural context of the community and with cultural norms governing gender roles within the community. Findings demonstrate the need to incorporate cultural and social structural factors in models of the stress process. It is concluded that cultural norms and structural constraints interact to systematically alter the meaning of different factors in the stress process and in turn alter the effects of those factors on health.

304. DuCette, Joseph; Wolk, Stephen & Friedman, Sarah. (1972). **Locus of control and creativity in Black and White children.** *Journal of Social Psychology,* 88(2), 297–298.
Administered the Intellectual Achievement Responsibility Questionnaire and the Wallach and Kogan Pattern Meanings Test to 20 Black and 20 White lower-class male 9–11 yr olds. Internal Ss gave more creative responses and were more efficient than externals, regardless of race. Implications for locus of control theory are discussed.

305. DuCette, Joseph; Wolk, Stephen & Soucar, Emil. (1972). **Atypical patterns in locus of control and nonadaptive behavior.** *Journal of Personality,* 40(2), 287–297.
Investigated the relationship between locus of control and disruptive, maladjusted behavior in young children. Moderator variables of this relationship were examined through racial membership in Study 1 and intellectual ability in Study 2. 40 8–10 yr old males participated in Study 1, while in Study 2 the Ss were 76 8–14 yr olds. Locus of control was assessed by the Crandall Intellectual Achievement Responsibility Questionnaire. Results in both studies suggest that a discrepancy between the assumption of responsibility for positive and negative events might be conducive to maladaptive behavior. (18 ref).

306. Durand, Douglas & Shea, Dennis. (1974). **Entrepreneurial activity as a function of achievement motivation and reinforcement control.** *Journal of Psychology,* 88(1), 57–63.
Gave reinforcement control and achievement motivation measures (Rotter's Internal–External Control Scale and the Thematic Apperception Test, respectively) to 22 male and 7 female Black adults engaged in operating small businesses. Level of business activity was assessed 18 mo later. Ss with a high need to achieve were found to be significantly more active than those whose achievement motivation was low. Activity scores of internal locus of control Ss were significantly higher than those of externals. Internals with a high need to achieve were significantly more active than all others. Data suggest that thoughts are most successfully translated into action when the individual feels in control of his/her fate and recognizes the steps that are instrumental in reaching goals.

307. Fields, B. Celestine. (1976). **The psychology of death.** *Journal of Black Psychology,* 3(1), 100–111.
A Black Death Questionnaire (BDQ), which concerned feelings, attitudes, and emotions toward death and dying was given to 50 Black men and women (most aged between 20 and 24 yrs) in the Saint Louis and Washington, DC, areas. The intent was to determine whether Blacks have their own unique thoughts on these issues or whether their thinking is similar to that of the American public in general. Questions involved feelings about mourning and grief rituals, life expectancy, life after death, the meaning of death, the terminally ill, open/closed casket, cost of funerals, disposal of body after death, and death acceptance. Respondents appeared to view death as a significant happening, as important as life. Though they have become somewhat Americanized, in most areas they seemed to have their own unique coping mechanisms. Further research, especially cross-cultural, is strongly urged, as are death education, seminars and symposiums, and more literature on the subject. (30 ref).

308. Fleming, Jacqueline. (1982). **Fear of success in Black female and male graduate students: A pilot study.** *Psychology of Women Quarterly,* 6(3), 327–341.
To test M. S. Horner's (1969) assumption that the intensity of fear of success arousal increases with the S's success potential, 14 Black female and 21 Black male graduate students at a prestigious university were administered a verbal TAT and a 54-item sex-role questionnaire developed by the author. Fear of success was scored according to a new, experimentally derived scoring system for this motive (M. S. Horner and the author, 1977). Contrary to expectation, results do not provide any evidence of success avoidance in either sex. However, fear of success in females was clearly associated with striving to develop career interests compatible with their strong commitment to home and husband, while among similarly motivated males it was suggested that the pragmatic career orientation observed was the product of compensatory motivational dynamics. It is concluded that these Ss were motivated to avoid what they perceived to be role-inappropriate behaviors while conforming to socially accepted values internalized in earlier years. (36 ref).

309. Gardner, William E. (1985). **Hope: A factor in actualizing the young adult Black male.** Special Issue: The Black male: Critical counseling, developmental, and therapeutic issues: II. *Journal of Multicultural Counseling & Development,* 13(3), 130–136.
Investigated the extent to which 60 productive (employed or in school) and 61 nonproductive (unemployed and not in school) 18–23 yr old Black males tended to perceive and transform into constructive actions the elements of hope. Indicators of motivation that constitute major operational elements of hope taken from E. Stotland's (1969) schema were used. Ss rated goal expectation, environmental relevance, and goal importance alike in terms of strength and importance. They differed, however, in their ratings of the likelihood that action would take place in the pursuit of a goal. Productive Ss were more prone to take action; the nonproductive Ss were not able to sustain hope and, thereby, experienced productivity dysfunction. (11 ref).

310. Glautz, Oscar. (1976). **Family structure, fate control, and counter-normative political beliefs among lower-class Black students.** *College Student Journal,* 10(2), 121–126.
Survey data from 140 aspiring Black students in an open-admissions college program pointed to father-present vs father-absent differences on a 4-item index of internal–external control (for males and females equally) and on 4 measures of political disaffection (3 of the 4 for males alone). Political differences attributable to family structure, however, were minimized among males when variations in fate control were taken into account, thereby lending support to the hypothesis that internality is negatively associated with counter-normative political beliefs. By contrast, the hypothesis was not supported by the data for females. (28 ref).

311. Guagnano, Greg; Acredolo, Curt; Hawkes, Glenn R.; Ellyson, Steve et al. (1986). **Locus of control: Demographic factors and their interactions.** *Journal of Social Behavior & Personality,* 1(3), 365–380.
Explored the relation of gender, socioeconomic status (SES), and ethnicity to locus of control, using 625 White, Hispanic, Black, Asian-, and Native American Ss who were administered an abridged version of a locus-of-control questionnaire. The influence of age, sex, income, education, and ethnicity was examined through regression analyses and multivariate and univariate analyses of variance. Results show few significant interactions. It is concluded that individual differences in locus of control are more a function of individual personality dynamics than of simple demographics.

312. Humphreys, Lloyd G.; Pang-Chieh Lin & Fleishman, Allen. (1976). **The sex by race interaction in cognitive measures.** *Journal of Research in Personality,* 10(1), 42–58.
Analyzed data consisting of 79 cognitive measures from Project TALENT (M. F. Shaycoft, 1967) for 100,000 White and Black high school students for possible Race by Sex interactions. Control variables included geographical area, grade in high school, and socioeconomic class. Race by Sex interactions are largest when socioeconomic class is controlled and are highly related to the size of the main effect of Sex as well. White boys and girls differ more than Black boys and girls whether the overall sex difference favors males or females. Sex by Grade, and to a lesser extent, Sex by Area interactions are also moderately large and consistent with the size of the main effect of Sex. Since there are no consistent relationships with other main effects, and since the measures producing sex differences also tend to produce the interactions, it is concluded that sex differences and the interactions with sex share the same causes. Differences between these results and those of A. R. Jensen (1971) are also discussed.

313. Hunt, Janet G. & Hunt, Larry L. (1975). **The sexual mystique: A common dimension of racial and sexual stratification.** *Sociology & Social Research,* 59(3), 231–242.
Compares low-status Black males with high-status White females and presents some propositions concerning similar personal consequences of racial and sexual stratification. The view formulated draws extensively on the ideas of Elliot Liebow and Betty Friedan and suggests that, while many dimensions of their circumstances and the content of their personal identities may differ radically, low-status Black males and high-status White females may evidence similar responses to structural barriers to achievement on the level of identity integration and in the compensatory nature of sex-role identification. (36 ref).

314. James, Sherman A.; Hartnett, Sue A. & Kalsbeek, William D. (1983). **John Henryism and blood pressure differences among Black men.** *Journal of Behavioral Medicine,* 6(3), 259–278.
132 17–60 yr old Southern, working-class Black men were administered a scale designed to measure the degree to which they felt they could control their environment through hard work and determination. Since the legend of John Henry—a Black steeldriver of American folklore—can be understood as a cultural statement about how Black Americans must often attempt to control behavioral stressors through hard work and determination, items for the scale were developed to reflect the theme of "John Henryism." In accordance with the experimental hypothesis, Ss who scored low on education and high on John Henryism had significantly higher diastolic blood pressures than did those who scored above the median on both measures. Findings are discussed in terms of the meaning that education and John Henryism may have for raising or lowering autonomic arousal when individuals encounter behavioral stressors in everyday life. Preliminary evidence for the construct validity of the John Henryism Scale is presented. (60 ref).

315. King, Harriet F.; Carroll, James L. & Fuller, Gerald B. (1977). **Comparison of nonpsychiatric Blacks and Whites on the MMPI.** *Journal of Clinical Psychology,* 33(3), 725–728.
The literature indicates inconsistent results when MMPI differences between Black and White Ss were investigated. In general, most studies found that Blacks responded in a more pathological direction. However, previous studies can be criticized because they have used students, prisoners, and hospital patients as Ss with variables that were controlled inconsistently and varied widely. In the present study, comparison was made of MMPI scales for 56 Black and 56 White males who were full-time employees of a large chemical company. Ss were matched for age, education, occupation, seniority, mental ability level, and socioeconomic level. The 10 stan-

dard clinical and 3 validity MMPI scales were recorded for each S as well as 6 experimental scales: Control (*C*), Dependency, Dominance (*Do*), Ego Strength (*Es*), Anxiety Index, and Internalization Ratio. Using *K* corrected T-scores for the MMPI scales, a repeated measures analysis of variance indicated that subtests and group by subtests were significant. More specifically, Blacks scored significantly higher than White Ss on the *Ma* scale, and White Ss scored significantly higher than Blacks on the *Pa, C, D,* and *Es* scales. While the present study did find significant differences between Black and White Ss on the MMPI, the scores were all well within the normal range.

316. Krug, Samuel E. (1986). **Preliminary evidence regarding Black–White differences in scores on the Adult Personality Inventory.** *Psychological Reports,* 58(1), 203–206.
Investigated the relationship between test respondents' race and test scores, using 214 White and 37 Black men (aged 21–60 yrs) who completed the Adult Personality Inventory. Results show that within a relatively homogeneous sample of employed adults, statistically significant relationships were found for only 2 of the scales: Creative, on which Whites scored higher, and Uncertainty, on which Blacks scored higher. The magnitude of the observed relationships suggests that race was not a significant source of bias in the remaining scales of the inventory studied.

317. Lairson, David; Lorimor, Ronald & Slater, Carl. (1984). **Estimates of the demand for health: Males in the preretirement years.** *Social Science & Medicine,* 19(7), 741–747.
Estimated the demand for health for 569 Black and 1,471 White males in the preretirement years using data from the 1st wave of the 1966 National Longitudinal Survey of men aged 45–59 yrs. Findings for Whites generally corroborate M. Grossman's (1972) estimates of the demand for health. In contrast to Whites, Blacks showed a much stronger wage effect and a significant positive effect of wife's education, with no other factors being significant. The issue of reverse causality between wage and health was addressed via a simultaneous equations, health–wage model, which yielded an even larger wage effect. (21 ref).

318. Levy, Marguerite F. (1976). **Deferred gratification and social class.** *Journal of Social Psychology,* 100(1), 123–135.
Hypothesized that choice of immediate reward may be explained by variables other than impulse control. Ss were 429 13–16 yr old boys stratified by social class and racial category. Questionnaire measures were taken of generalized attitudes on subjective power, optimism, delay, and risk-taking. After manipulation of task comprehension, Ss made choices between specific prizes under different conditions of delay and/or task performance. Ss trained on task principles chose the larger reward significantly more often than those not trained. Middle-class Ss reported more favorable attitudes toward risk-taking and were more likely than lower-class Ss to choose the immediate reward. Blacks reported less favorable attitudes toward risk-taking and were more likely than Whites to attribute control to external sources. High scores on optimism and risk-taking were associated with choice of larger reward. It is concluded that differences in preference for immediate reward are not a simple function of impulse control. (17 ref).

319. Littig, Lawrence W.; Allen, Juanita & Briggs, Yvette M. (1980). **Locus of control, historical context, and Black physical self-perception.** *Journal of Research in Personality,* 14(1), 40–48.
Examined effects of locus of control on the physical self-perception of 63 Black male undergraduates in 1968 and 1975. Ss completed Rotter's Internal–External Locus of Control Scale. External Ss were hypothesized to perceive themselves to be more Negro in appearance than they were judged to be by observers. The hypothesis was tested by comparing

Ss' own appearance judgments with the mean judgment of 3 observers on a scale of 15 faces that changed incrementally from Negro to Caucasian. The hypothesis was contradicted in the 1968 study and supported in the 1975 study. These discrepant results are interpreted in terms of historical events at the time of data collection. (17 ref).

320. Moore, Thom L. & Baltes, Paul B. (1975). **Training of White adolescents to accurately simulate Black adolescent personality.** *Adolescence,* 10(38), 231–239.
30 White male high school students responded to the Personality Research Form as they believed a Black student would; 10 Black students responded under self-endorsement. A 2-session training program was aimed at increasing the accuracy of cross-racial simulation. Posttest resulted in near perfect simulation on Achievement and Understanding, the 2 scales with the highest original discrepancy. No generalization to other personality dimensions was obtained.

321. Moses, E. Gnanaraj; Zirkel, Perry A. & Greene, John F. (1973). **Measuring the self-concept of minority group pupils.** *Journal of Negro Education,* 42(1), 93–98.
Administered the Self-Esteem Inventory (SEI) and the McDaniel Inferred Self-Concept Scale to 61 male and 59 female 5th- and 6th-grade disadvantaged Negro, Puerto Rican, and White students from 3 schools in Connecticut. Results of analysis of variance indicate that Puerto Ricans scored significantly lower on the SEI. Analysis of variance on the McDaniel showed no differences. Scores on the SEI and McDaniel were significantly correlated for all Ss.

322. Oberle, Wayne H.; Stowers, Kevin R. & Falk, William W. (1978). **Place of residence and the role model preferences of Black boys and girls.** *Adolescence,* 13(49), 13–20.
Explored differences between urban and rural Black adolescents in role model preferences. Samples of 101 urban males, 93 rural males, 154 urban females, and 96 rural females were obtained from the sophomore classes of 1 all-Black urban high school and 13 all-Black rural high schools. The role model preferences of the Ss were determined by their replies to the forced-choice question, "Think of the person whom you would most want to fashion your life after." Analysis of the results showed that urban males were significantly more likely than rural males to prefer a relative not in their immediate family or a close friend and less likely to prefer their father or mother or "glamor figures." Urban females were significantly more likely than rural females to prefer a close friend and less likely to prefer glamor figures.

323. Pandey, R. E. (1975). **Factor analytic study of attitudes toward death among college students.** *International Journal of Social Psychiatry,* 21(1), 7–11.
Compared the factorial structures of the cognitive and feelings components of attitudes toward death among college students, using 132 Whites and 101 Blacks (81 males and 152 females). A test of 40 items having 5 Likert-type responses was constructed. The hypothesis that people of different races and sexes, having divergent temperaments and beliefs, will also show different factors involved in their attitudes toward death was not supported, because the factors of escape, depressive-fear, mortality, and sarcasm were common to them all.

324. Rochester, D. E. & Bodwell, A. (1970). **Beta-WAIS comparisons for illiterate and indigent male and female Negroes.** *Measurement & Evaluation in Guidance,* 3(3), 164–168.
A representative sample of 50 male and 50 female adults from an evaluation and training center in a large metropolitan area was used to study the feasibility of using the Revised Beta Examination to assess the intellectual functioning level of indigent Negro adults. Beta IQs were compared with scores on the WAIS Verbal and Performance and the Full Scale IQs. The WAIS–Beta comparisons revealed significant positive

correlations; r's ranged from .29 to .79. Findings suggest that the Beta holds promise for assessing intellectual functioning of illiterate and indigent Negroes.

325. Scott, James D. & Phelan, Joseph G. (1969). **Expectancies of unemployable males regarding source of control of reinforcement.** *Psychological Reports,* 25(3), 911–913.
Used Rotter's Internal–External Locus of Control Scale to test 3 groups of 60 22–28 yr old males, matched for age, socioeconomic status, and scholastic aptitude and classified as hard core unemployables. No significant differences in alienation scores were noted between Group A Whites and White undergraduates. Group B Black Ss were significantly more externally controlled with greater variability of scores. Group C Mexican-Americans showed an even greater tendency in the external direction and greater variability than the others. Blacks and Mexican-Americans did not differ significantly in expression of external control. Lack of feeling for any relation between individual effort and reward may account for the difficulty in equipping these groups with knowledge and skill to improve their lot.

326. Vernon, Philip A. & Jensen, Arthur R. (1984). **Individual and group differences in intelligence and speed of information processing.** *Personality & Individual Differences,* 5(4), 411–423.
A battery of 8 RT tests, measuring the speed with which individuals perform various elementary cognitive processes, and the Armed Services Vocational Aptitude Battery (ASVAB) were given to 50 Black and 56 White male vocational college students. The regression of the general factor scores of the ASVAB on the RT measures yielded a shrunken multiple correlation of .465. Although discriminant analyses, when applied separately to the ASVAB subtests and to the RT variables, showed highly comparable overall discrimination between the Black and White groups, factor scores derived from the general factor (labeled speed of information processing) of the RT battery showed only about one-third as large a mean Black–White difference as the mean group difference on the general factor scores derived from the AS-VAB. Comparisons were also made between the 106 Ss and 100 university students of higher average academic aptitude who had previously been tested on the same RT battery by the 1st author (see PA, Vol 71:16923). These groups showed marked differences on the RT variables, especially on tests that required more complex cognitive processing. The more complex RT tests also correlated most highly with the psychometric measures of ability within each group. (16 ref).

327. Vining, Daniel R. (1982). **On the possibility of the reemergence of a dysgenic trend with respect to intelligence in American fertility differentials.** *Intelligence,* 6(3), 241–264.
National Longitudinal Surveys data on 5,172 men and 5,097 women aged 25–34 yrs support the hypothesis that persons with higher intelligence tend to have fertility rates equal to or exceeding that of the population as a whole in periods of rising birth rates, whereas the reverse is true in periods of falling birth rates. The relationship between fertility and IQ was less negative for White males than for White females, and for White females than for Black females. If realized, the stated intentions of this cohort with respect to future fertility will moderate the degree of this relationship but not change its sign. (81 ref).

PHYSICAL AND PSYCHOLOGICAL DISORDERS

328. Berger, Stephen E. & Tedeschi, James T. (1969). **Aggressive behavior of delinquent, dependent, and "normal" White and Black boys in social conflicts.** *Journal of Experimental Social Psychology,* 5(3), 352–370.

Modified the Prisoner's Dilemma game by giving an option to S after every 7th iteration of the game of taking $10 from a dummy other than at a cost to himself of 2, 5, 8, or $11. A 4 by 3 by 2 orthogonal design was used, with 1 dimension representing the 4 opportunity cost levels. The 2nd dimension consisted of adjudicated delinquent, adjudicated dependent, and normal preadolescent boys of 10–13 yrs of age. The 3rd dimension was race. Each S played 50 trials against a dummy, who played a preplanned 50% cooperative strategy. It was found that Black Ss cooperated more and won less than White Ss. There were no differences related to frequency of exercising the option of punishing the other. Only analyses based on the cue of the dummy's cooperation yielded differences in aggression. When the dummy had cooperated on the trial preceding the option, Black Ss were more aggressive than White Ss, dependents were more aggressive than delinquents, and delinquents were more aggressive than normals. White Ss were more sensitive to the costs of using their power than were Black Ss, and normals were more sensitive to costs than delinquents. Dependent Ss were not affected by opportunity costs. A cue/personality/aggression hypothesis is used to interpret the data. (61 ref).

329. Bixenstine, V. Edwin & Buterbaugh, Ralph L. (1967). **Integrative behavior in adolescent boys as a function of delinquency and race.** *Journal of Consulting Psychology,* 31(5), 471–476.
Explored integrative behavior (i.e., behavior maximizing reward over time) in 88 adolescent boys all evincing, via intelligence test performances, comparable symbolizing capacity. The findings show that delinquency is related to integrative failure as measured by choice of a small but immediate reward over a large but remote reward (candy). However, contrary to expectancy, Negro boys behaved more integratively than White boys. The findings are discussed in connection with results found on auxiliary measures made on all Ss.

330. Burgess, P. K.; Tedeschi, James T. & Berger, Stephen E. (1971). **Aggressive behavior of delinquent, dependent, and "normal" White and Black boys in social conflicts.** *Journal of Experimental Social Psychology,* 7(5), 545–559.
Presents criticisms of the methodology and conclusions of S. Berger and J. Tedeschi's (see PA, Vol. 44:5345) study on aggression. A reply by Tedeschi and Berger is presented along with further comments by Burgess.

331. Cashdan, Sheldon. (1967). **The use of drawings in child psychotherapy: A process analysis of a case study.** *Psychotherapy: Theory, Research & Practice,* 4(2), 81–86.
The drawings of an 8-yr-old Negro boy were used to index 5 progressive stages in his psychotherapy. Indices were required to chart the presence or absence of movement in therapy. With adults, these indices characteristically take the form of certain verbal statements; with children, artistic productions can be used.

332. Cloninger, C. Robert; Reich, Theodore & Guze, Samuel B. (1975). **The multifactorial model of disease transmission: II. Sex differences in the familial transmission of sociopathy (antisocial personality).** *British Journal of Psychiatry,* 127, 11–22.
A study of 58 male and 28 female felons and their families shows that sociopathy was highly familial in both White and Black families. Sociopathy in males and females clustered in the same families, but was much more frequent in males than in females. It was more prevalent among relatives of sociopathic females than among relatives of sociopathic males. The sex difference in its prevalence appeared to be due to sex-related cultural or biological factors causing the threshold to be more deviant in females. There was no evidence of a genetic difference in its prevalence and transmission according to race. The 2-threshold multifactorial model of disease transmission provided an explanation for the striking sex

difference in the transmission of sociopathy. Assortative mating accounted for a large proportion of the observed similarity between relatives. However, the familial clustering of male and female sociopaths was not dependent on assortative mating. The high correlation among siblings that is expected under conditions of random mating indicates that environmental factors common to siblings contribute to the etiology of sociopathy. The greater deviance of the parental home experiences of sociopathic females compared to sociopathic males is further evidence of the importance of familial environment. (42 ref).

333. Cross, Herbert J. & Tracy, James J. (1971). **Personality factors in delinquent boys: Differences between Blacks and Whites.** *Journal of Research in Crime & Delinquency,* 8(1), 10–22.
Interviewed 119 boys who were either institutionalized or in active contact with the juvenile court and classified them into interpersonal maturity categories. Internal–external locus of control, future time perspective, legal status, socioeconomic status, intelligence, age, and 5 aspects of guilt were assessed. Interpersonal maturity was directly related to internal locus of control for the whole sample, while future time perspective and guilt were not. When these variables were analyzed with respect to race of the delinquents, a different pattern of relationships emerged. Interpersonally mature Blacks were more external and had a shorter time perspective, whereas interpersonally mature Whites were more internal but their time perspective was no different from immature Ss. Results suggest that the acquisition of interpersonal maturity is related to the expectation of rewards (opportunities) and suppression by society and that these have differentially damaging effects on Black and White male delinquents.

334. Davids, Anthony & Falkof, Bradley B. (1975). **Juvenile delinquents then and now: Comparison of findings from 1959 and 1974.** *Journal of Abnormal Psychology,* 84(2), 161–164.
Measures of time orientation and delay of gratification were obtained from 40 male and 10 female juvenile delinquents (mean age 15-16 yrs) who were institutionalized in 1974. Similar measures were available from studies of delinquents by A. Davids et al conducted in the same institutions in 1959. Within the 1974 sample, comparisons were made between males and females, Blacks and Whites, and younger and older delinquents. Many similarities and some interesting differences among these subgroups were found on indices of future orientation, accuracy of time estimation, and seeking of delayed rewards. In general, the 1974 delinquents appeared to be more impulsive, present oriented, and in need of immediate gratification than were the delinquents in 1959.

335. Deitz, George E. (1972). **The influence of social class, sex, and delinquency–nondelinquency on adolescent values.** *Journal of Genetic Psychology,* 121(1), 119–126.
Solicited value preferences from 280 male and 281 female 12-18 yr olds in 3 groups: middle-class Whites, lower-class Blacks, and juvenile delinquents of both races. Ss were given the following open-ended instructions: "Write down as many personal qualities as you can think of that you regard as important for people to have." Where delinquents valued traits underlying the making of a favorable social impression, nondelinquents valued traits concerned with social responsibility. Males focused slightly more upon physical attractiveness and females upon traits functioning in interpersonal relationships. The middle class was distinguished from the lower class in their preference for the possession of intelligence and ambition.

336. Frankel, Steven A. & Frankel, Ellen B. (1970). **Nonverbal behavior in a selected group of Negro and White males.** *Psychosomatics,* 11(2), 127–132.

Studied the nonverbal behavior of 11 Negro and 11 White surgical patients. Each S was interviewed, and specific gestures and actions and subdivisions (behavioral dimensions) of autistic and communicative nonverbal behavior categories were rated. Analysis by the chi-square test showed significance for 1 gesture, the frequent turning of palms up and out, and 1 body posture, the clasping of hands together, for greater than 50% of the interview. Both were shown primarily by the Negro group. The former gesture is customarily thought to denote helplessness and the latter to reflect inhibition in an individual's manner. The behavioral-dimension findings were analyzed by analysis of variance and t tests. Findings convey the impression of inhibition by the Negro Ss. Data yielded no impressive age-related findings. It is uncertain whether these observations reflect differences in behavior in the 2 races or whether they are a result of interacting with White professionals in an institution of White society.

337. Guze, Samuel B.; Goodwin, Donald W. & Crane, J. Bruce. (1970). **Criminal recidivism and psychiatric illness.** *American Journal of Psychiatry,* 127(6), 832–835.
Describes a study of criminal recidivism during an 8–9 yr period; Ss were 125 White and 51 Black convicted male felons. Recidivism was measured by percentage rearrested, reimprisoned, and reconvicted of a felony at least once and more than once for each criterion. Increased recidivism rates were found to be associated with the following factors: "flat-timer" status (reflecting a more extensive criminal career), relative youth, and diagnoses of sociopathy, alcoholism, and drug dependency. Remission of the latter 2 conditions was correlated with a decline of recidivism.

338. Hammer, Max. (1969). **Suicide, and White reformatory girls' preference for Negro men.** *Corrective Psychiatry & Journal of Social Therapy,* 15(3), 99–102.
Reformatory girls' deep-seated feelings of worthlessness tend to cause them to seek love from Negro men who are also rejected by society and have feelings of worthlessness. The girl thus becomes very possessive, may end up destroying the relationship, and then turn to suicide to act out her self-destructive feelings.

339. Harcum, Phoebe M. & Harcum, E. Rae. (1973). **Tempo modification in visual perception of EMR children.** *Perceptual & Motor Skills,* 37(1), 179–188.
Gave nonintellectual tasks which involved visual perception and spatial relationships to 45 White and 42 Black 7–12 yr old educable mental retarded Ss in urban schools. Ss copied visible patterns and also reproduced patterns from memory after tachistoscopic exposure. The major variable was perceptual tempo, manipulated by instructions to adopt a reflective rather than impulsive style of responding. Other variables were sex and race. Perceptual accuracy was increased by instructions to adopt a reflective attitude, presumably because the latency of responding was increased. Blacks improved more than Whites with reflective instructions, showing superior performance afterward.

340. Hoiberg, Anne. (1983). **Health effects associated with minority status among U.S. Navy officers.** *US Naval Health Research Center Report,* (Serial No. 83-30).
Investigated the health risks unique to various minority groups in the Navy Officer Corps and whether or not being a member of a minority group had an impact on an individual's health, especially for stress-related disorders. Five subpopulations of Navy officers were identified: 133,818 White males; 1,486 Black males; 46,189 male and 3,149 female unrestricted line officers; 1,156 male and 7,410 female members of the Nurse Corps; and 45,409 male and 1,132 female other officers of the Staff Corps. Ss' officer career history files and medical inpatient files were examined for hospital admissions and diagnoses. Results indicate that each minority group studied had significantly higher rates than dominants

for one or more of the stress-related disorders, with women unrestricted line officers having more significant differences than other groups. White male officers had significantly higher rates of circulatory disease than women, and Blacks and women had higher rates than- White males for mental disorders. (17 ref).

341. Holmes, George R. & Heckel, Robert V. (1970). **Psychotherapy with the first Negro male on one southern university campus: A case study.** *Journal of Consulting & Clinical Psychology,* 34(3), 297–301.
Describes the incidents, attitudes, and problems confronting the 1st Negro male since Reconstruction to attend a southern university. Of particular importance in producing stress were pressures from both White and Negro groups. White students produced stress through their hostility, while militant Negro groups created difficulty by their attempts at capitalizing his role.

342. Jaffe, E. D. (1969). **Family anomie and delinquency: Development of the concept and some empirical findings.** *British Journal of Criminology,* 9(4), 376–388.
Describes a concept which is called family value confusion (or family anomie), reviews some of the literature related to the concept, discusses an instrument which was developed to measure family anomie empirically, and presents findings concerning the relationship between family anomie and delinquency proneness. Respondents consisted of a group of 25 institutionalized delinquent Negro boys and a 2nd group of 25 Negro boys nominated by leaders as least likely to become involved with the police. The research findings seemed to establish a relationship between delinquency proneness and value confusion. In addition, we noted specific types of family disorganization from which value confusion may originate.

343. King, Lucy J.; Murphy, George E.; Robins, Lee N. & Darvish, Harriet. (1969). **Alcohol abuse: A crucial factor in the social problems of Negro men.** *American Journal of Psychiatry,* 125(12), 1682–1690.
Associated increasing degrees of alcohol use with increasing evidence of social deviance in an interview study of 223 young urban Negro men. Absence of the father from the childhood home and failure to complete high school strongly predict heavy drinking in adult life. Heavy drinking, with or without these negative factors, is equally predictive of social deviance. It is concluded that alcohol abuse is not simply another symptom of social deviance but an important intervening variable in the ghetto cycle of broken home, delinquency, underemployment, and broken home.

344. Kinsbourne, Marcel & Fisher, Milton. (1971). **Latency of uncrossed and of crossed reaction in callosal agenesis.** *Neuropsychologia,* 3(4), 471–473.
Studied the performance of a 16-yr-old Black male with callosal agenesis on RT tasks. S manifested no pathological delay in crossed RT to unilateral stimulation. This result is most readily explicable if cerebral hemisphere control of movement was, in this case, bilateral. (French & German summaries).

345. Kunce, Joseph T. & Thelen, Mark H. (1972). **Modeled standards of self-reward and observer performance.** *Developmental Psychology,* 7(2), 153–156.
Randomly assigned 48 Black and 48 White institutionalized, delinquent, teen-age males to 1 of 4 experimental conditions whereby they previewed different stimulus videotapes. The tapes showed either a Black or a White model depicting either liberal or stringent standards of self-reward behavior following his reported scores on a pursuit rotor task. Ss who viewed a stringent model subsequently had significantly higher performance on the last of 6 trials and a significantly greater increase in performance over trials. Race of model and race of S were not significantly related to performance. Observed liberal-stringent model behavior significantly affect-

ed both Ss subsequent self-reward behavior and performance, but S's self-reward behavior and performance were not interrelated.

346. Maksud, Michael G. & Hamilton, Lyle H. (1974). **Physiological responses of EMR children to strenuous exercise.** *American Journal of Mental Deficiency,* 79(1), 32–38.
A battery of physiological tests administered to 62 10–13 yr old Black and White educable mentally retarded boys resulted in no statistically significant physiological differences between the 2 racial groups. The maximal oxygen uptake for Ss appeared to be lower than data reported for nonretarded children; some rationale for this lower aerobic power is discussed. (24 ref).

347. Matranga, James T.; Jensen, Diana E. & Prandoni, Jogues R. (1972). **Bender-Gestalt protocols of adult Negro male offenders: Normative data.** *Perceptual & Motor Skills,* 35(1), 101–102.
Attempted to develop norms for adult, Negro male offenders on the Bender Visual Motor Gestalt Test. The Bender-Gestalt reproductions of 224 15–65 yr old Ss were scored according to E. Koppitz's developmental scoring system and then divided into 7 IQ ranges. Normative data are listed for each range.

348. Mescavage, Alexander A. (1975). **Tyrone the dope fiend: A case of heroin addiction.** *Transactional Analysis Journal,* 5(2), 193–196.
Presents a case study illustrating E. Berne's notion of the importance of the mother's influence on the life choices of some drug addicts. The patient is a Black male with separated parents, a succession of step-fathers, and a 4-yr history of heroin addiction. The patient's difficulties in getting a fair share of strokes from his mother until he adopted the behavior of trying, but always failing, to be the man his mother wanted him to be is described. His therapy concentrated on relieving his feelings of being split off from his body by parental injunctions.

349. Monroe, Jack J. (1971). **The attribution by opiate addicts of characteristics to addict subgroups and to self.** *Journal of Social Psychology,* 85(2), 239–249.
Administered a modification of Monroe and Astin's Addict Identification Scale to 60 Negro male prisoner addicts from the northern US. It was hypothesized that Ss with favorable self-presentations would attribute (a) favorable characteristics to a similar reference group and (b) neutral or unfavorable characteristics to a dissimilar group (i.e., Caucasian voluntarily committed southern addicts). Results support predictions. (15 ref).

350. Mosher, Loren R. (1969). **Father absence and antisocial behavior in Negro and White males.** *Acta Paedopsychiatrica,* 36(6-7), 186–202.
Data from the 1960 US census reveal a rate of delinquency among Negro youth twice that of Whites with socioeconomic status controlled. The higher proportion is linked to early father absence. Lack of high status adult males differentially predisposes the Negro child to exhibit antisocial behavior. Wrath and scorn are experienced for anyone symbolizing effeminate culture, most particularly effeminate men. The psychic economy of the gang demands aggressive independence, a touchy and exaggerated virility, and a deep protective secrecy. The enemy of the gang is the world of people (especially men) too unmanly for survival in what has been described as a social jungle. (37 ref).

351. Murray, Michael E.; Waites, Lucius; Veldman, Donald J. & Heatly, Maurice D. (1973). **Ethnic group differences between WISC and WAIS scores in delinquent boys.** *Journal of Experimental Education,* 42(2), 68–72.
Investigated the patterns of IQ scores of 2,498 delinquent boys of different ethnic groups on the WISC and WAIS.

Variables examined included age, ethnic classification, Verbal IQ, performance IQ, and Full Scale IQ. A 3-factor analysis of variance was computed on the scores. Factors included ethnic group (Anglo, Black, Chicano), test-age level (WISC, WAIS), and subscale (verbal, performance). Results show that the mean IQ scores of the various ethnic groups were spread over a 15-point range with Anglos highest and Blacks lowest. WISC scores were lower than WAIS scores for all groups, although the difference was significantly exaggerated in the Blacks. Performance subscales elicited higher mean scores than did verbal subscales and the performance-verbal difference was twice as large on the WISC as on the WAIS. Blacks performed at about the same low level on both performance and verbal subscales, while the Chicanos did poorly on Verbal IQ, but scored much higher (in the normal range) on the performance subscales. Results are discussed with reference to the present IQ controversy. (22 ref).

352. Palinkas, Lawrence A. & Colcord, Christine L. (1983). **Health risks among enlisted males in the U.S. Navy: Race and ethnicity as correlates of hospital admissions.** *US Naval Health Research Center Report,* (Serial No. 83-31).
Examined whether a significant difference in health risks by race exists for US Navy personnel. Hospital admissions among Black and White enlisted males in the Navy between 1974 and 1979 were examined in a cross-sectional study. During this time, 279,265 enlisted males were hospitalized. Age-adjusted rates for racial subgroups by year hospitalized, occupation, and education were calculated. Results indicate that the health status of Blacks consistently improved such that, by 1979, there were no significant racial differences in total hospitalization rates. Significant racial group differences were discovered, however, in 7 major diagnostic categories. Blacks were at greater risk of hospitalization for mental disorders, diseases of the musculoskeletal system, diseases of the genitourinary system, symptoms and ill-defined conditions, and supplementary classifications. Whites, on the other hand, were found to be at risk for diseases of the skin and subcutaneous tissue, and accidents, poisonings, and violence. These patterns of disease risk were attributed to differences in age, occupation, education, access to health care prior to entrance into the service, and cultural patterns relating to expectations, job satisfaction, and perception of stress. (37 ref).

353. Palinkas, Lawrence A. & Colcord, Christine L. (1985). **Health risks among enlisted males in the U.S. Navy: Race and ethnicity as correlates of disease incidence.** *Social Science & Medicine,* 20(11), 1129–1141.
A cross-sectional study of all Black and White enlisted males in the US Navy between 1974 and 1979 examined 1st hospitalization rates for 16 diagnostic categories, and selected diagnoses were compared on the basis of race, age, year hospitalized, education, and occupation. Findings show that the total disease incidence among Blacks declined from 1,652/10,000 in 1974 to 1,088/10,000 in 1979. Total incidence rates for Whites in the same period declined from 1,347/10,000 to 1,100/10,000. However, Blacks were at significant risk for mental disorders; diseases of the genitourinary, circulatory, musculoskeletal and digestive systems; diseases of the blood and blood-forming organs; symptoms and ill-defined conditions; and supplementary classification. Whites had significantly higher incidence rates for diseases of the skin and subcutaneous tissue and for accidents, poisonings, and violence. There existed numerous subgroups within each racial group, defined on the basis of certain demographic and social characteristics, that were at risk for particular diseases. The relationship between race and disease was mediated by several factors, including genetic predisposition, socioeconomic status (SES), and cultural patterns of belief and behavior. (41 ref).

354. Picou, J. Steven; Cosby, Arthur G.; Lemke, James W. & Azuma, Henry T. (1974). **Occupational choice and perception of attainment blockage: A study of lower-class delinquent and non-delinquent Black males.** *Adolescence,* 9(34), 289–298.
Administered a questionnaire to 73 incarcerated and 68 non-incarcerated Black male 9th-grade students. Results indicate that lower-class Black delinquents and nondelinquents desired prestigious occupational placement and were optimistic enough to plan for it. However, they were aware of possible blocks to their occupational success.

355. Polednak, Anthony P. (1972). **Dermatoglyphics of Negro schizophrenic males.** *British Journal of Psychiatry,* 120(557), 397–398.
Several significant differences were found when specific features of fingerprints and palmprints of 40 Negro male schizophrenics were compared to those of 105 controls. While this is the 2nd study to report such differences, the adequacy of the control groups is questionable. Positive relationships of the skin patterns and psychiatric status remain to be proved.

356. Polednak, Anthony P. (1971). **Body build of paranoid and non-paranoid schizophrenic males.** *British Journal of Psychiatry,* 119(549), 191–192.
Results of a study of 36 Irish-American and 42 Negro male schizophrenic patients showed little difference in body measures between paranoid and nonparanoid subgroups. (17 ref).

357. Rainer, John D.; Abdullah, Syed & Jarvik, Lissy F. (1972). **XYY karyotype in a pair of monozygotic twins: A 17-year life history study.** *British Journal of Psychiatry,* 120(558), 543–548.
Describes a study of a pair of identical dull-normal Black twin boys followed from infancy through adolescence. Ss first showed excess aggressiveness in kindergarten and subsequently grew to be tall, quiet, and aloof. One S now shows less control than the other, has had to leave school, and has escaped disorderly conduct charges by pleading emotional problems. It is suggested that this case material can be useful in the further exploration of the psychiatric, medical, and legal implications of the XYY chromosome abnormality. (22 ref).

358. Richter, Ralph W. & Rosenberg, Roger N. (1968). **Transverse myelitis associated with heroin addiction.** *JAMA,* 206(6), 1255–1257.
Acute transverse myelitis involving thoracic segments was observed as a new complication of heroin addiction in 4 Negro men. Three of the 4 patients had not taken heroin for periods of 1–6 mo either while in prison or the hospital. The acute myelitis developed shortly after heroin was taken again intravenously. At onset, 3 patients suddenly became paraplegic, and moderate paraparesis developed in one. All 4 demonstrated thoracic sensory levels. Myelograms were normal for the 3 patients on whom they were performed. One patient died 5 wks after taking heroin again. Extensive necrosis of the spinal cord in the lower thoracic region was found at necropsy. Another patient died, but no autopsy was performed. Mild paraparesis with sensory loss remains in 1 man, and severe paraparesis with sensory loss persists in the other survivor.

359. Robins, Lee N.; Murphy, George E.; Woodruff, Robert A. & King, Lucy J. (1971). **Adult psychiatric status of Black schoolboys.** *Archives of General Psychiatry,* 24(4), 338–345.
Studied the adult psychiatric status of 235 Black men of average or better intelligence who were urban born and urban educated between 1930 and 1934. The frequency of psychiatric disorders and the childhood variables foreshadowing those disorders are compared with findings from an earlier study of White child-guidance-clinic patients and normal White controls reared in the same city. Despite discrimination, young urban Black men apparently differ little from Whites in rates of psychiatric disorders. Among the 3 childhood variables investigated, the child's own antisocial behavior was a more powerful predictor of adult psychiatric status than was either his family's social status or his father's history of antisocial behavior. This same result had been noted for Whites. All 3 childhood predictors were positively associated with the diagnosis of antisocial personality in adult life. (16 ref).

360. Robins, Lee N.; West, Patricia A. & Herjanic, Barbara L. (1975). **Arrests and delinquency in two generations: A study of Black urban families and their children.** *Journal of Child Psychology & Psychiatry & Allied Disciplines,* 16(2), 125–140.
Obtained the police and juvenile records of 76 Black urban-born males and 145 of their children, 17 yrs old and older, to (a) determine whether there had been changes in delinquency patterns over a generation, (b) establish the extent and nature of the continuity between parents' arrest histories and their children's, and (c) examine other family characteristics that might protect children of arrested parents from repeating the parental pattern. A comparison of juvenile records of parents and children showed similar rates and types of offenses. Parental arrest histories were powerful predictors of their children's delinquency. Children with fewer siblings, even when they had 2 arrested parents, were less likely to be delinquent. This was true of both males and females. Children of 2 arrested parents who had 3 or more siblings were delinquent in 100% of males and 50% of females; with 1 or 2 siblings, rates were 50% for males and 22% for females.

361. Rosen, Lawrence. (1969). **Matriarchy and lower class Negro male delinquency.** *Social Problems,* 17(2), 175–189.
Despite fairly wide speculation, the issue of matriarchy and delinquency among lower-class Negro males has failed to generate significant empirical research. In an attempt to fill this gap, the factors of absent father, sex of main wage earner, main decision maker, and most influential adult were investigated for the households of 921 Negro 13–15 yr old males, who resided in a lower-class Negro high-delinquent area. Even though some significant differences were found for the total sample, not a single variable proved to be a major factor (as measured by Goodman and Kruskal's tau). The suggestion is made that the factor of matriarchy may be only one of numerous "original causes" that "push" a lower-class Negro male into delinquency, thus accounting for the small association for matriarchy and delinquency.

362. Rosner, Fred & Steinberg, Florence S. (1968). **Dermatoglyphic patterns of Negro men with schizophrenia.** *Diseases of the Nervous System,* 29(11), 739–743.
Employed standard statistical procedures to assess the value of dermatoglyphic features as a diagnostic tool for schizophrenia. Finger and palm prints in 207 Negro male schizophrenic inpatients were compared with 105 normal Negro males. Statistically significant differences were found on 4 digits and in 3 palmar areas. These were determined to have no clinical application. A histogram showing the distribution of indices of the digital patterns of Ss and controls also failed to be of clinical value. Differences between controls and the diagnostic subcategories of schizophrenia suggest that inconsistencies in previous investigations may be due to varied proportions of the subgroups studied and that schizophrenics are not a homogeneous group. Future research should be concerned with a population in each diagnostic subcategory large enough for a valid statistical evaluation.

363. Schleifer, Carl B.; Derbyshire, Robert L. & Martin, Jean. (1968). **Clinical change in jail-referred mental patients.** *Archives of General Psychiatry,* 18(1), 42–46.
It is hypothesized and supported that Negroes display more areas of clinical disturbance than Whites when examined at the police station. 50 White and 50 Negro males were evalu-

ated after state hospital certification by 2 police physicians and re-evaluated after 72 hrs in the state hospital ward. Degree of disturbance and clinical change were determined by 14 ratings on an adjustment index. Improvement in both groups and a reduction of the difference between the groups in the re-evaluation were found. In comparing identically matched groups, it was shown that both groups recovered from mental illness at the same rate. The fact that Negroes do not have a higher admission rate than Whites although they are more clinically disturbed is discussed. The importance of getting patients out of jail and into a psychiatric treatment center is stressed.

364. Stephenson, P. Susan & Lo, Nerissa. (1974). **When shall we tell Kevin? A battered child revisited.** *Child Welfare,* 53(9), 576–581.
Presents the case history of a Black male, battered in infancy, in which attempts were made to determine the long- and short-term effects of disclosing his mother's near fatal assault on him.

365. Sutker, Patricia B. & Moan, Charles E. (1973). **A psychosocial description of penitentiary inmates.** *Archives of General Psychiatry,* 29(5), 663–667.
Indepth analyses of family, social, and demographic characteristics, antisocial behaviors, and psychological dimensions of a bi-racial sample of 190 male and 51 female inmates housed predominantly on prison farms in Louisiana showed inmates to be minimally educated, young adults originating from the lower socioeconomic strata of large metropolitan areas, and serving sentences for generally under 10 yrs. Women, characteristically a more homogeneous group than their male counterparts, were most frequently incarcerated for narcotic offenses or homicide and seemed to be serving shorter sentences for the same felony convictions as men. A number of important racial differences, particularly within the male sample, suggest the need for closer scrutiny of the handling of the Black inmate, who represents a probably neglected and specifically overlooked group in the prison environment.

366. Thelen, Mark H.; Fryrear, Jerry L. & Rennie, David L. (1971). **Delayed imitation of self-reward standards.** *Journal of Experimental Research in Personality,* 5(4), 317–322.
Attempted to determine whether Ss would imitate a model, observed 3 mo before, when they had not been previously tested for imitation. 72 15–17 yr old Black and White delinquent adolescent males were assigned to 1 of 3 groups. Within each race, 1 group saw a videotape of a White adult male reward himself liberally for his predetermined performance at a pursuit rotor task. Another group saw the same model reward himself stringently. The 3rd group did not see a model. Three months later, each S was given an opportunity to reward himself for a pursuit rotor performance that was ostensibily equal to that of the model. Results show that the liberal and stringent self-reward behaviors of the model were imitated after the 3-mo delay. There were no differences in imitation between Black and White Ss nor correlation between imitation and assessed racial attitudes.

367. Thelen, Mark H. & Fryrear, Jerry L. (1971). **Effect of observer and model race on the imitation of standards of self-reward.** *Developmental Psychology,* 5(1), 133–135.
Assigned 96 Black and White 15-17 yr. old delinquent males to observe a Black or a White model who employed liberal or stringent standards of self-reward behavior. 24 other Ss did not observe a model. Even with explicit normative information, Ss clearly imitated the self-reward standards of the model. Black and White Ss imitated the liberal White significantly more than the liberal Black model, but imitated the stringent Black and White models about equally. Evaluative semantic differential ratings of racial attitudes showed little relationship to the imitation of self-reward.

368. Tobin, David D.; Goldberg, Harold H. & Shapiro, David N. (1967). **The interpersonal world of a disturbed boy.** *American Journal of Orthopsychiatry,* 37(2), 377.
Explored reality testing in a severely disturbed Negro boy over a 5-yr period between the ages of 10 and 15 yrs.

369. Viamontes, Jorge A. & Powell, Barbara J. (1974). **Demographic characteristics of Black and White male alcoholics.** *International Journal of the Addictions,* 9(3), 489–494.
Studied demographic differences and variations in the reported incidence of alcohol-related symptomatology in 100 Black and 100 White male hospitalized alcoholics. Results support previous findings that Blacks began drinking at an earlier age, were younger at admission, and reported more hallucinatory behavior and convulsions than Whites.

370. Waldo, Gordon P. & Hall, Nason E. (1970). **Delinquency potential and attitudes toward the criminal justice system.** *Social Forces,* 49(2), 291–298.
A questionnaire dealing with attitudes toward the criminal justice system was administered to 626 7th grade boys. Guttman scales were developed for 9 attitude dimensions associated with the criminal justice system. The relationship of these attitudes to measures of delinquency potential was examined. All of the associations were negative, of low magnitude, and differed in strength among the 9 attitude areas as well as between Negroes and Caucasians. The relationship between delinquency potential and attitudes toward the criminal justice system is very complex and many issues must be resolved before a complete acceptance can be made of the generalization that potential delinquents hold more unfavorable attitudes toward the criminal justice system than potential nondelinquents.

371. Walters, Glenn D. (1986). **Screening for psychopathology in groups of Black and White prison inmates by means of the MMPI.** *Journal of Personality Assessment,* 50(2), 257–264.
Administered both the Minnesota Multiphasic Personality Inventory (MMPI) and a structured diagnostic interview based on the Feighner criteria to 225 male offenders (mean age range 23.73–27.95 yrs; 51 Black, 46 White). Results indicate that 51 Ss (25 Blacks, 26 Whites) earned highly elevated MMPI profiles (at least 1 clinical scale greater than or equal to a T score of 90), and 46 (26 Blacks, 20 Whites) achieved profiles that were essentially within normal limits (all clinical scales less than a T score of 70). The concordance between the MMPI and the total number of syndromes reported by the Ss was significantly greater in the White group (classification accuracy, 96%) relative to the Black group (classification accuracy, 71%). However, both Black and White hit rates significantly improved upon chance. It is concluded that the hypothesis that the MMPI would successfully identify general psychopathology in White but not in Black inmates received only partial support. (16 ref).

372. Wax, Douglas E. (1972). **Self concept in Negro and White preadolescent delinquent boys.** *Child Study Journal,* 2(4), 175–184.
Tested the hypothesis that differences in self-concept would be found in a comparison of Negro and Caucasian delinquents. 20 Negro and 35 Caucasian 7–12 yr old adjudicated male delinquents served as Ss. A semantic differential was used to rate 8 relevant concepts on a 5-point scale for 10 bipolar adjectives. A significant difference on means was found only for 1 concept: "Boys who get into trouble." It is concluded that Caucasian boys have a lower concept of boys who get into trouble than Negro boys. The latter perceived boys who get into trouble as stronger, smarter, tougher, and more positively endowed than boys who do not get into trouble. This finding is discussed in terms of opportunities within society, identity problems, and perception of the adult sex role. (21 ref).

Mental Disorders

373. Adams, Paul L. & Horovitz, Jeffrey H. (1980). **Psychopathology and fatherlessness in poor boys.** *Child Psychiatry & Human Development,* 10(3), 135–143.
In this study, the sample of 201 US Blacks and Cuban refugees of White derivation was controlled for the family's economic class position, ethnicity, place of residence, and children's age, gender, and ordinal position; Ss were also matched with a control group of "fathered" children. Instruments used were a mini-MMPI (76 items) and the Louisville Aggression Survey Schedule-1. All of the data obtained were supplied by the mothers—about both themselves and their firstborn male child. No positive association between the boys' psychopathology and their fatherlessness was found. Moreover, the data indicate that poverty exerted a leveling influence that overrode the differentiating characteristics of ethnic and age grouping, family structure, father presence or absence, and linguistic and cultural heritages. (11 ref).

374. Chu, Chung-chou; Sallach, Harriet S.; Zakeria, Saleha A. & Klein, Helen E. (1985). **Differences in psychopathology between Black and White schizophrenics.** *International Journal of Social Psychiatry,* 31(4), 252–257.
Compared the psychopathology of 69 male and 59 female Black schizophrenics (aged 18–58 yrs) and 53 male and 94 female White schizophrenics (aged 19–51 yrs). Data were collected on Ss through structured interviews and ratings on the Brief Psychiatric Rating Scale and a psychopathological rating scale. Findings indicate that Black Ss exhibited more frequent symptoms of angry outbursts, poor communication, disorientation, asocial behavior, and auditory and visual hallucinations than did Whites, whereas Whites showed more frequent symptoms of unsystematized delusions than did Blacks. Black female schizophrenics were found to be more often excited, ambivalent, rigid, and dysphoric than were White female schizophrenics; Black females also exhibited the symptom of split personality more often. Results also show that Black males exhibited asocial behavior more frequently than did White males. It is suggested that differences in psychopathology exist among schizophrenic patients of different cultural backgrounds. (14 ref).

375. Cobrinik, Leonard. (1974). **Unusual reading ability in severely disturbed children: Clinical observation and a retrospective inquiry.** *Journal of Autism & Childhood Schizophrenia,* 4(2), 163–175.
Studied 3 Black and 3 White severely disturbed males (ages 12 yrs 2 mo to 14 yrs 9 mo) who demonstrated unexpected rote reading abilities despite profound developmental arrest. Current functioning (WISC; Illinois Test of Psycholinguistic Abilities) and interviews with parents assessing origins and development of reading and reading-related abilities showed a specific, shared pattern consisting of severe language deficit, tendencies toward perseverative action, and, as the necessary condition, the early manifestation of acute visual imagery and recall. The latter occurred despite generalized instability involving poorly controlled attention and deviant visual regard. Results support, with some modification, the deficit hypothesis of M. Sheerer et al (1945) which accounts for unusual abilities in developmentally arrested individuals.

376. Emsley, Robin A. (1985). **Koro in non-Chinese subjects.** *British Journal of Psychiatry,* 146, 102.
Summarizes the case of a previously healthy 25-yr-old Black male presenting with koro symptoms (the belief that the penis is retracted into the abdomen) who became mute and catatonic under his delusion. Haloperidol resulted in rapid improvement, but the delusion remained. It is suggested that the patient's condition best fits P. C. Ang and M. P. Weller's (see PA, Vol 72:22664) description of an anxiety state and delusional belief due to an underlying psychotic condition.

377. Gary, Lawrence E. (1985). **Depressive symptoms and Black men.** *Social Work Research & Abstracts,* 21(4), 21–29.
Conducted a cross-sectional survey of 142 noninstitutionalized Black men (aged 18–65 yrs) from an urban metropolitan area to determine the association among demographic factors, stressful life events, sociocultural patterns, and depressive symptoms (as measured by the Center for Epidemiological Studies Depression Scale). Two-hour personal interviews were conducted with Ss to ascertain personal data as well as information on life events, identification of problems, psychological symptoms, help-seeking behavior, social participation, and psychosocial adjustment. Findings indicate that demographic and stressful life event variables were better predictors of the presence of depressive symptoms among Ss than were sociocultural variables. Age, family income, household size, employment status, and conflict between the sexes also were significantly related to the presence of depressive symptoms. Ss most likely to be depressed tended to be those who lived in extended family units, had few friends, were inactive in community activities, had a low involvement in religious activities, and were very conscious of racial issues. It is suggested that caution should be used in interpreting this profile, however, since none of the sociocultural variables were significantly related to depression.

378. Gary, Lawrence E. & Berry, Greta L. (1985). **Depressive symptomatology among Black men.** Special Issue: The Black male: Critical counseling, developmental, and therapeutic issues: II. *Journal of Multicultural Counseling & Development,* 13(3), 121–129.
Investigated how demographic factors, stressful life events, and sociocultural patterns predicted depressive symptomatology among 142 Black males (median age 33 yrs). Ss were interviewed about age, marital status, living arrangements, health, employment history, family background, and life events; the interviews also solicited information on Ss' experiences in the previous week according to the 20 symptoms of depression that constitute the Center for Epidemiologic Studies-Depression Scale (CES-D). The Ss had a mean depression score of 12.15, with a standard deviation of 8.44. Of the Ss, 31% had CES-D scores of 16 or more, indicating serious depressive symptoms. Findings indicate that those Ss who were young, poor, unemployed, lived in large households, and had considerable conflict with women had the highest depression scores. Demographic variables and variables involving stressful life events were better predictors of the presence of depressive symptoms among the Ss than were sociocultural variables. (17 ref).

379. Goldstein, Harris S. & Gershansky, Ira. (1976). **Psychological differentiation in clinic children.** *Perceptual & Motor Skills,* 42(3, Pt 2), 1159–1162.
In a clinic population the relationship between children's perceptual differentiation as measured by the rod-and-frame test (RFT) and their self-concept differentiation as evidenced in their human figure drawings (Draw-A-Person test, scored using a Body Sophistication Scale) was studied. In addition, the WISC Vocabulary subtest was employed. Ss were 140 Black and 38 White 8–15 yr olds making an initial visit to a child guidance clinic. The relationship between perceptual differentiation and self-concept differentiation was significantly positive only for White females with a father present. Vocabulary and RFT were positively correlated for the Black and White Ss, while vocabulary and the body-sophistication scores were significantly related for Black males and White females with a father present. Differentiation may then appear in a variety of patterns in different populations.

380. Griffin, Phillip T.; Garey, Richard E.; Daul, George C. & Goethe, John W. (1983). **Sex and race differences in psychiatric symptomatology in phencyclidine psychosis.** *Psychological Reports,* 52(1), 263–266.

The medical records of 153 psychiatric admissions who were determined to be phencyclidine (PCP) toxic were analyzed for the presence of various categories of psychiatric symptoms. Aggression was observed during the hospital stay in 58% of the Ss, followed closely by bizarre behavior (55%) and anxiety (53%). 116 males did not differ from 37 females in observed symptoms, but 112 Blacks showed more bizarre behavior than 41 Whites. Further analysis indicated that the Black–White difference was due to the significantly higher incidence of bizarre behavior, aggression, and looseness of association observed among 26 Black females than 11 White females. These results suggest that White females who are PCP toxic may not resemble the often reported and frequently observed PCP-toxic patient who is violently psychotic and paranoid. (11 ref).

381. Helzer, John E. (1975). **Bipolar affective disorder in Black and White men: A comparison of symptoms and familial illness.** *Archives of General Psychiatry,* 32(9), 1140–1143.
Administered a systematic psychiatric interview to 11 Black and 19 White men in their early to mid thirties with conditions diagnosed as manic-depressive disease, manic type. In addition, as many of their 1st-degree relatives as could be contacted were also interviewed. Demographic, clinical, and family history variables were compared for the 2 races. With the exception of a greater preponderance of alcoholism in the paternal relatives of the Black Ss, few differences were found between the 2 groups in terms of the variables studied. It is concluded that the clinical and familial expression of bipolar affective disorder is similar in the 2 races.

382. Johnson, William G.; Ross, James M. & Mastria, Marie A. (1977). **Delusional behavior: An attributional analysis of development and modification.** *Journal of Abnormal Psychology,* 86(4), 421–426.
Presents the case of a 37-yr-old Black male who complained that he was having sexual intercourse with a "warm form." The otherwise normally functioning S was treated using a reattribution procedure. The case illustrates the utility of attribution theory as a model for understanding the development and maintenance of delusions in addition to providing a basis for their modification. It is argued that the proper focus of attribution theory lies in changing cognitions and not overt behavior by veridical rather than deceptive manipulations. (31 ref).

383. Lazarus, Arthur. (1986). **Folie à deux in identical twins: Interaction of nature and nurture.** *British Journal of Psychiatry,* 148, 324–326.
Presents the case of a pair of Black monozygotic identical male twins born in 1964 to provide evidence for the syndrome folie à deux, which is characterized by the transference of delusional ideas from one person to others in close association with the primary affected person. Psychological assessment revealed schizophreniclike thought processes and evidence of borderline mental retardation in the Ss. Other cases of folie à deux and its treatment are discussed.

384. Malinick, Charles; Flaherty, Joseph A. & Jobe, Thomas. (1985). **Koro: How culturally specific?** *International Journal of Social Psychiatry,* 31(1), 67–73.
Presents the case of a 51-yr-old Black American male with Koro-like symptoms who presented to an emergency room extremely anxious with both tachycardia and tachypnea. The S's history indicated no psychiatric illness, but he maintained a schizoid lifestyle with little contact with family or friends. The Western concept of penis loss is compared to the Chinese or Malaysian concept, and a combined hypothesis for the development of Koro is proposed. (15 ref).

385. Ness, Myrna K.; Donnan, Hugh H. & Jenkins, Jack. (1983). **Race as an interpersonal variable in negative assertion.** *Journal of Clinical Psychology,* 39(3), 361–369.
Investigated assertive behavior among Black male psychiatric patients (aged 19–45 yrs) under White and Black interpersonal partner conditions. 24 high and 24 low scorers in level of measured general assertiveness served as Ss. Responses to familiar and unfamiliar interpersonal stimuli in 2 conditions—role-play and in vivo—were videotaped and rated. Dependent variables in the role-play condition were request for new behavior, compliance, affect, and overall assertiveness. Dependent variables for the in vivo condition were expression of negative opinion, compliance, and overall assertiveness. Although MANOVA revealed no main effect for race, Ss in the unfamiliar condition were more assertive than those in the familiar role-play condition. Ss' responses in role play were more assertive in the unfamiliar-White prompter condition as compared to Ss' responses in the unfamiliar-Black prompter condition. In the in vivo situation for overall assertiveness, responses were rated as more assertive in the White prompter condition. Although Ss were more likely to express negative opinions in the Black prompter condition, they were more likely to comply with an unreasonable request in the White prompter condition. (10 ref).

386. Pellegrini, Adrian J. & Putman, Paul. (1984). **The Amytal interview in the diagnosis of late onset psychosis with cultural features presenting as catatonic stupor.** *Journal of Nervous & Mental Disease,* 172(8), 502–504.
Presents the case of a 48-yr-old Black male with atypical psychosis who exhibited catatonic stupor. Interview procedures using amobarbital sodium and the differential diagnosis for catatonia are discussed. Response to loxapine (60 mg/day) was excellent, though this was clouded by the S's belief in root medicine, a source of cultural incongruity between him and his therapist. Distinguishing between psychosis and cultural belief systems is shown to be essential in therapy. (7 ref).

387. Pfeffer, Cynthia R. et al. (1985). **Variables that predict assaultiveness in child psychiatric inpatients.** Thirtieth Annual Meeting of the American Academy of Child Psychiatry (1983, San Francisco, California). *Journal of the American Academy of Child Psychiatry,* 24(6), 775–780.
Extended a previous study by the 1st author and colleagues (see PA, Vol 69:10561) of assaultive behavior in child psychiatric patients by adding new neuropsychological and neurophysiological variables and using Ss with different racial/ethnic and social status. Clinical assessments of 106 6–12 yr old psychiatric inpatients (primarily White) showed that 28.4% were nonassaultive, 12.7% contemplated assault, and 58.8% made assaultive threats and attempts. The 81 boys were significantly more assaultive than the 25 girls. Highest positive correlations with assaultive behavior were for recent and past aggression and past general psychopathology; highest negative correlations were for sublimation and repression. Parents' assaultive behavior was not significantly correlated with the child assaultiveness ratings. Multiple regression analysis determined that the best predictors of assaultiveness were presence of recent aggression and absence of sublimation. (22 ref).

388. Schaefer, Charles & Brown, Swan. (1976). **Investigating ethnic prejudice among boys in residential treatment.** *Journal of Social Psychology,* 100(2), 317–318.
32 Black, 11 White, and 10 Hispanic 8–13 yr old boys in a residential treatment center for emotionally disturbed children rated all the other boys in their cottages using the Comfortable Interpersonal Distance Scale (CIDS). There were no significant differences between CIDS scores that members of each ethnic group gave to their own vs those given to the other groups. Results support the value of the CIDS as a quick, economical means of assessing ethnic prejudice among youth.

389. Scheftel, Susan; Nathan, Amy S.; Razin, Andrew M. & Mezan, Peter. (1986). **A case of radical facial self-mutilation: An unprecedented event and its impact.** *Bulletin of the Menninger Clinic,* 50(6), 525–540.
Reports the case of a 20-yr-old schizophrenic Black male who removed virtually his entire face in a psychotically analgesic state. The authors compare S with other patients who have performed radical self-mutilations and discuss an unusual aspect of the case—his persistent refusal to admit that he mutilated himself. The reactions elicited in staff members working with this S are also examined. (31 ref).

390. Serafetinides, E. A.; Coger, R. W. & Martin, J. (1986). **Different methods of observation affect EEG measures associated with auditory hallucinations.** *Psychiatry Research,* 17(1), 73–74.
Measured EEG changes related to hallucinatory behavior with verbal and nonverbal reporting methods for the presence of hallucinations. A 36-yr-old Black male with chronic paranoid schizophrenia and a history of auditory hallucinations from 19 yrs of age was studied. Results show that the "ramp" spectra were present between reports of hallucinations, suggesting that the hallucinations are present subsequent to some abnormal subcortical discharge rather than concurrent with it, as has been suggested by J. R. Stevens et al (see PA, Vol 64: 12672). (3 ref).

391. Strahilevitz, Meir et al. (1976). **Immunoglobulin levels in psychiatric patients.** *American Journal of Psychiatry,* 133(7), 772–777.
In a study of 19 schizophrenic patients, 7 schizo-affective and nonschizophrenic patients, and 31 controls (mean ages 34.0, 44.5, and 30.8 yrs, respectively), data show significantly higher mean serum levels of (a) immunoglobulin A in schizophrenic females than in control females and in schizophrenic Blacks than in either schizophrenic Whites or Black controls, (b) immunoglobulin D in schizophrenic Blacks than in schizophrenic Whites, (c) immunoglobulin M in controls than in nonschizophrenic patients, and (d) immunoglobulin G (IgG) in schizophrenics whose urine was positive for phenothiazines than in schizophrenics whose urine was negative for phenothiazines. High serum levels of IgG were associated with no or mild hallucinations and low levels with moderate or severe hallucinations. Black female patients had significantly more severe hallucinations than White female patients. (26 ref).

392. Tousley, Martha M. (1984). **The paranoid fortress of David J.** *Journal of Psychosocial Nursing & Mental Health Services,* 22(2), 8–16.
Describes the case of a 46-yr-old Black male admitted to a state hospital with a diagnosis of schizophrenia, paranoid type. Anecdotes about S's paranoid behavior on the hospital ward are related in an attempt to illustrate the problems of working with chronic paranoiacs. Paranoiacs usually experience late onset, come from authoritarian families in which they were devalued or abused by their parents, have trouble establishing intimate relationships, and retain paranoid ideas that cannot be corrected by experiences. Therapy must begin with the establishment of trust between therapist and patient. (11 ref).

Behavior Disorders & Antisocial Behavior

393. Bonecutter, Bruce E. (1985). **Psychological Evaluation Report.** *Journal of Psychology & Christianity,* 4(2), 57–61.
Presents a fictional psychological evaluation report that was developed on the basis of the author's experiences as a Christian psychologist in a neighborhood church clinic and a public health facility. The report concerns a 23-yr-old suicidal Black male and includes data on referral information, tests administered, background and life history, behavioral observations, interpersonal functioning, and cognitive and intellectual functioning. Implications for the success of pastoral counseling are noted.

394. Borduin, Charles M.; Pruitt, Julie A. & Henggeler, Scott W. (1986). **Family interactions in Black, lower-class families with delinquent and nondelinquent adolescent boys.** *Journal of Genetic Psychology,* 147(3), 333–342.
The interaction patterns of 32 Black, lower-class family triads (mother–father–son), divided into 2 equal groups by the son's delinquency status, were assessed across self-report and observational measures of family affect, conflict, and dominance. In support of previous research (e.g., E. M. Hetherington et al; see PA, Vol 47:9273) with White, middle-, and lower-middle class families, results indicate that families with delinquent boys were less warm and more conflictual than families with nondelinquent boys. Relative to parents of nondelinquents, parents of delinquents were more conflictual in expressive family issues than on instrumental issues. Results show that the content of the family interaction task (expressive vs instrumental) influences observed patterns of intrafamily dominance. (31 ref).

395. Coleman, Philip P. (1986). **Separation and autonomy: Issues of adolescent identity development among the families of Black male status offenders.** Second Annual Conference of the Black Task Force: The Black family: Mental health perspectives (1984, San Francisco, California). *American Journal of Social Psychiatry,* 6(1), 43–49.
Examined the conceptual variables influencing the patterns of relationship and socialization practices (e.g., autonomy, separation) in 11 Black male status offenders (aged 12–18 yrs) and their families. Interviews were conducted with both Ss and their parents, which allowed exploration of the relationship between changing cultural values and factors in the social environment that influenced families' overall subjective experience of the developmental events of separation and autonomy. Findings highlight the recent migration from the rural South to the urban North as an important change in social networks for these families; there were sharp differences in the view of the American Dream that existed between parents and their children. (8 ref).

396. Crawford, Gail A.; Washington, Melvin C. & Senay, Edward C. (1983). **Careers with heroin.** *International Journal of the Addictions,* 18(5), 701–715.
Conducted personal history interviews with 147 Black male heroin addicts and their nonaddicted friends. Based on the extent of their heroin use, Ss were classified into the following sub-groups: light experimenters (mean age 24.3 yrs), moderate experimenters (mean age 24.1 yrs), heavy experimenters (mean age 25.6 yrs), and addicts (mean age 26 yrs). Findings indicate that no single career line or pattern characterized all heroin users and the heroin use does not necessarily lead to heroin addiction. While some users quickly progressed from initiation to heroin to regular, intermittent use or "chipping" to daily heroin use and physical dependence, others were deflected at various points along the way. Some of the sociobehavioral processes or career contingencies associated with movement from one level of heroin use to the next are discussed. Implications for treatment/intervention programs are also discussed. (9 ref).

397. Datesman, Susan K. & Aickin, Mikel. (1984). **Offense specialization and escalation among status offenders.** *Journal of Criminal Law & Criminology,* 75(4), 1246–1275.
Interviewed and collected data on the offense behavior of 689 (107 Black female, 52 Black male, 244 White female, and 286 White male) juveniles following their first referral to juvenile court for status offenses and followed up 6 mo later with a 2nd interview of 502 of the Ss. Official and self-reported data were collapsed into a delinquency category and 3 status of-

fense categories: running away, being ungovernable, and a residual category of other status offenses. Analyses of offense patterns by race and sex indicated that the majority of Ss appeared in official records as pure status offenders, although this was more typical of White females and less so of Black males. According to self-report data, however, almost all admitted to some degree of delinquent activity. Data do not demonstrate that official processing has no effect on producing delinquency, but only that most youths labeled as status offenders do not reappear in court as delinquent offenders. There was no evidence that offense careers follow an escalating pattern.

398. Dean, Anne L.; Malik, Mary M.; Richards, William & Stringer, Sharon A. (1986). **Effects of parental maltreatment on children's conceptions of interpersonal relationships.** *Developmental Psychology,* 22(5), 617–626.
39 maltreated and 60 nonmaltreated Black 6–14 yr olds from lower income families told stories about kind or unkind initiatives from child to child, adult to child, or child to adult and then told what the recipient would do next. In contrast to their nonmaltreated counterparts, maltreated 6–8 yr olds told more stories in which children reciprocated the kind acts of adults and fewer stories in which adults or peers reciprocated the kind acts of children. Maltreated Ss of all ages justified their parents' unkind acts on the basis of their own bad behavior. Developmental trends in story content and story context measures differed for maltreated boys and girls; boys showed less development toward mature interpersonal peer relations. Findings suggest that the modes of adaptation used by abused and neglected children may be cognitively and emotionally similar. (26 ref).

399. Edwards, Dan W. (1985). **An investigation of the use and abuse of alcohol and other drugs among 50 aged male alcoholics and 50 aged female alcoholics.** *Journal of Alcohol & Drug Education,* 30(2), 24–30.
Examined alcohol use and abuse among 50 male and 50 female alcoholics (aged 55 yrs and over) and the extent to which Ss abused other drugs. Ss were randomly selected from case records of a large alcohol counseling center. Findings were derived from Ss' responses to a questionnaire that was administered during interviews. Most Ss reported that they began drinking heavily when they were 55–64 yrs old. Data suggest that most of the older females began drinking heavily between ages 55 and 64 yrs, as compared to most of the males who reported beginning heavy drinking from age 35 to 44 yrs. A large number of the men indicated that they first began drinking heavily between ages 55 and 64 yrs. Conversely, most Black males reported beginning heavy drinking between ages 45 and 64 yrs, whereas more of the Black females reported that they began drinking heavily between ages 55 and 64 yrs. A comparison of the male alcoholics and Ss who reported using other drugs in conjunction with alcohol showed that 29% of the total sample of aged alcoholics reported using other drugs. However, approximately 76% of the total sample of Black alcoholics reported using other drugs, compared with slightly over 19% of the total sample of White alcoholics. Findings suggest that wives of male alcoholics tended to leave or divorce less quickly than did husbands of female alcoholics, suggesting that the marital relationship and family support system is more at risk among aged female alcoholics than that of males. (5 ref).

400. Friedman, C. Jack; Mann, Fredrica & Friedman, Alfred S. (1975). **A profile of juvenile street gang members.** *Adolescence,* 10(40), 563–607.
Studied 499 15–18 yr old Black and White disadvantaged males from correctional facilities, a job training program, the Youth Corps, and an inner-city high school in an attempt to elucidate the factors differentiating street gang members from youths in comparable neighborhoods who remain independent of the gang. A battery of tests and questionnaires were used to obtain psychological, sociological, demographic, and family background information. In addition, traces were conducted of police and court records to provide data on the Ss' past criminal history. A stepwise multiple regression analysis of 73 independent variables yielded a hierarchical structure of the variables most highly associated with street gang affiliation; the most powerful single predictor of gang membership was found to be a high self-reported proclivity for violence. No substantial differences between gang members and nonmembers were noted on traditional psychological, sociological, and family background measures, suggesting that gang affiliation may be highly dependent on the presence of an available peer group as an alternative to an unrewarding family situation. (34 ref).

401. Gaudin, James M. & Polansky, Norman A. (1986). **Social distancing of the neglectful family: Sex, race, and social class influences.** *Children & Youth Services Review,* 8(1), 1–12.
Notes that parents who neglect their children tend to be socially isolated. One explanation for this is that they are shunned by the community because of their deviant lifestyles. A social distance questionnaire (including social intimacy and sharing-childcare indices) was constructed and administered to 52 White males, 63 White females, 54 Black males, and 63 Black females from an urban area. There were 110 middle-class and 122 working-class Ss. Scalogram analysis yielded 2 scales of social-distancing behavior applicable at the neighborhood level. Males and working-class respondents averaged greater distancing than females and members of the middle class among both Blacks and Whites. Implications for social network interventions to prevent neglect are offered. (20 ref).

402. Goldstein, Gerald et al. (1983). **Withdrawal seizures in Black and White alcoholic patients: Intellectual and neuropsychological sequelae.** *Drug & Alcohol Dependence,* 12(4), 349–354.
The 2nd author and colleagues (see PA, Vol 71:1660) found that White alcoholics with histories of withdrawal seizures did not demonstrate neuropsychological differences from White alcoholics without such histories. However, the apparently higher incidence of withdrawal seizures among Blacks noted during the screening of Ss raised the question of whether the consequences of the seizure history might be different among Blacks. This issue was addressed in the present study in which the Halstead-Reitan Neuropsychological Test Battery, including the full WAIS, was administered to 22 White and 20 Black male alcoholic inpatients. Half of each group had a history of withdrawal seizures, while the other half did not. The mean ages of Blacks with and without seizures were 44.10 and 39.80 yrs, respectively; the mean ages of Whites with and without seizure were 47.55 and 43.46 yrs, respectively. Results show that Blacks with seizure histories performed substantially worse than Blacks without such histories; these differences were not observed among Whites, confirming previous findings. Regardless of race, performance on the Picture Arrangement subtest of the WAIS was worse for the Ss with than those without seizures. (11 ref).

403. Halikas, James A.; Darvish, Harriet S. & Rimmer, John D. (1976). **The Black addict: I. Methodology, chronology of addiction, and overview of the population.** *American Journal of Drug & Alcohol Abuse,* 3(4), 529–543.
192 Black male heroin addicts in various phases of treatment and nontreatment, including never-treated active addicts and actively addicted treatment dropouts, were interviewed for early life events, psychosocial variables, and natural history of addiction. The chronology of the addiction problem from childhood is described, and evidence of significant early antisocial activities predating drug use in this population is presented. Data on family characteristics, arrests, problems in formal schooling, and adult activities are summarized. The current work is compared to earlier data on comparable populations.

404. Hickman, Lillian C. (1984). **Descriptive differences between Black and White suicide attempters.** *Issues in Mental Health Nursing,* 6(3-4), 293-310.
Identified and described differences between 958 Black and White suicide attempters from a large general hospital's emergency department in the period 1974-1976. Data indicate that Black females (aged 16-20 yrs), Black males (aged 21-25 yrs), and both White males and females (aged 16-20 yrs) were the high-risk groups according to age. Females, single persons, and persons experiencing disrupted social relationships were at higher risk for attempting suicide.

405. Holcomb, William R. & Adams, Nicholas. (1983). **The inter-domain among personality and cognition variables in people who commit murder.** *Journal of Personality Assessment,* 47(5), 524-530.
Examined the interdomain among personality variables (the MMPI) and cognitive variables (the Peabody Picture Vocabulary Test and Revised Beta Examination), using 91 White and 46 Black males (mean age 26.6 yrs) charged with 1st-degree murder. Two significant canonical correlations were found, one of which was related to ability to focus on problem solving and the other to introspective self-focus. These variates explained the relation between personality and cognitive variables to a greater degree for Black than for White Ss. Both of these variates may affect several mechanisms that contribute to aggression, including environmental cues toward aggression, motivation toward aggression, repertoire of alternative behaviors, and lack of inhibitions. (19 ref).

406. Howze, Beverly. (1977). **Suicide: Special references to Black women.** *Journal of Non-White Concerns in Personnel & Guidance,* 5(2), 65-72.
Discusses the history of suicide in general and suicide as it pertains to Black males and females. Although suicide has taken place for many years, only recently have attempts been made to understand it. Statistics indicate that White males commit suicide 3 times more frequently than Black males. The pattern of Black male suicide is examined. The largest result increase in suicide rates is among Black women. This seems to be due in part to Black women's feelings of loneliness because of fewer Black men to associate with. Analysis of the case histories of 3 Black women who attempted suicide indicates that suicide is the result of a process which occurs over years. This process is created by intrapsychic and external stresses. There is no simple explanation for the higher rate of suicide among Black females, but radical changes are needed to stem this suicide rate.

407. Ingram, Jesse C. et al. (1985). **Recidivism, perceived problem-solving abilities, MMPI characteristics, and violence: A study of Black and White incarcerated male adult offenders.** *Journal of Clinical Psychology,* 41(3), 425-432.
Examined recidivism, perceived problem-solving abilities, type of offense, and personality characteristics in 20 Black males and 32 White males selected systematically from inmate populations and matched for age, IQ, and SES. Ss were administered the MMPI, Shipley-Institute of Living Scale for Measuring Intellectual Impairment, and a problem-solving inventory. Results show that the MMPI *F, L, Re,* and *Do* scales had significant effects. Black nonrecidivists scored significantly higher on the *L* scale than Black and White recidivists and White nonrecidivists. Black nonrecidivists scored higher than Black recidivists and White recidivists scored higher than White nonrecidivists on the *Re* scale. Black recidivists generated significantly higher scores on the *F* scale than did Black or White nonrecidivists. The MMPI *Pd* scale yielded a significant main effect for type of offense. Ss incarcerated for violent crimes scored higher on the *Pd* scale than nonviolent Ss. Findings demonstrate the utility of the MMPI in discriminating between nonviolent and violent criminals. (33 ref).

408. Johnson, Charles F. & Showers, Jacy. (1985). **Injury variables in child abuse.** Special Issue: C. Henry Kempe memorial research issue. *Child Abuse & Neglect,* 9(2), 207-215.
Analyzed the child abuse reporting records of 616 children (aged 4 wks to 17 yrs) seen by the child abuse team in a metropolitan children's hospital. Boys were referred for abuse more often than girls, and Black children were reported disproportionately more often than were White children. Mothers were the most frequent perpetrators of abuse, although males constituted more than half of the abusers. Bruises were the most frequent manifestation of abuse. The types of injury, injury site, and types of instruments used varied with the age and race, but not the sex of the child. The wide variety of instruments used to perpetrate child abuse resulted in a broad spectrum of injury types. It is concluded that if professionals are to recognize common and early manifestations of child abuse, they must be aware of the influence of regional socioeconomic and cultural factors on the spectrum of child abuse. (French abstract) (34 ref).

409. Kaestner, Elisabeth; Rosen, Linda & Appel, Philip. (1977). **Patterns of drug abuse: Relationships with ethnicity, sensation seeking, and anxiety.** *Journal of Consulting & Clinical Psychology,* 45(3), 462-468.
Administered the Sensation-Seeking Scale (SSS) and the State-Trait Anxiety Inventory (STAI) to 30 White, 30 Black, and 30 Hispanic male narcotic drug abusers in residential treatment. Individual drug abuse histories were assessed in semistructured interviews. Results are as follows: (a) White Ss scored significantly higher on the 5 SSS subtests than did either Black or Hispanic Ss. No significant differences were obtained between ethnic groups on the STAI. (b) Even though the prevalence of the use of alcohol, cannabis, street methadone, and cocaine was similar in the 3 ethnic groups, significantly more White Ss had used amphetamines, barbiturates, tranquilizers, methaqualone, inhalants, and psychedelics. (c) SSS scores and anxiety correlated significantly with the number of different drugs used by Whites, although the measures were virtually unrelated to drug use among non-Whites. The frequency of use of stimulant, depressant, or hallucinogenic drugs was unrelated to the user's level of sensation seeking or anxiety.

410. Kail, Barbara L. & Lukoff, Irving F. (1984). **The Black female addict's career options: A typology and theory.** *American Journal of Drug & Alcohol Abuse,* 10(1), 39-52.
Studied Black men and women (aged 18+ yrs) entering an inner-city methadone-maintenance treatment program to determine how Black women differ from Black men in their heroin-using careers and to examine differences among Black women in their integration of drug use and lifestyle. Two structured interviews were conducted with each S at intake. Gender-related differences were evident in the ties respondents maintained while engaged in heroin use: Women were more likely to establish their marriages prior to addiction and to be living with spouse and/or children upon entering treatment, while men were more likely to have been employed regularly while addicted and to have worked a greater number of months in the year prior to entering treatment. Women were more likely to begin using heroin at an older age and to report contact with a family member who used heroin, while men were more likely to be involved with crime. Both age and sex may be important factors in limiting access to different lifestyles. Treatment of women as a monolithic group obscures both the differences among women and their similarities to men. The fact that female addicts are not a monolithic group should sensitize service providers and decision makers. It is recommended that future programs and policies take this into account in formulating treatment modalities and that future studies examine the relative merits of single-sex vs heterosexual treatment programs. (37 ref).

411. Kapsis, Robert E. (1978). **Residental succession and deliquency: A test of Shaw and McKay's theory of cultural transmission.** *Criminology: An Interdisciplinary Journal,* 15(4), 459–486.
Examined the impact of neighborhood cultural and institutional life on rates of delinquency among Black male adolescents. Focusing on 3 adjacent Black neighborhoods at varying levels of Black population change, this study tested 3 corollaries derived from a causal model adapted from C. R. Shaw and H. D. McKay's cultural transmission theory of delinquency; Ss were 5,545 students, a stratified probability sample of 1,479 Black males, 2,126 non-Black males, 1,076 Black females, and 864 non-Black females. The preliminary results are compatible with the model: The level of delinquency was higher in a racially changing than in 2 more racially stable neighborhoods. Other findings, however, fail to support the cultural transmission interpretation of these results. Contrary to Shaw and McKay, delinquency was lowest in the area where criminal influences were the most pronounced. This anomaly is discussed and interpreted in a manner consistent with M. L. DeFleur and R. Quinney's (1966) reformulation of differential association theory. (33 ref).

412. Kashani, J. H.; Horwitz, E. & Daniel, A. E. (1982). **Diagnostic classification of 120 delinquent boys.** *Bulletin of the American Academy of Psychiatry & the Law,* 10(1), 51–60.
Investigated the diagnostic classification, demographic characteristics, and intellectual abilities of 120 delinquents (aged 13–18 yrs) in a prospective manner. Within 48 hrs of admission to the training school, Ss were interviewed and a DSM—II classification made. For each variable examined, the primary analyses consisted of comparisons of the aggressive and nonaggressive groups and the socialized and undersocialized groups. 74% of Ss were classified as socialized, 26% as undersocialized. 71% were classified as aggressive, 29% as nonaggressive. 71% of aggressive and 81% of nonaggressive Ss fell into the socialized category. Blacks (41% of the total sample) were mostly classified as aggressive (90%), while only 57% of Whites were so classified. Socialized Ss obtained significantly higher scores on the IQ measures (especially in verbal ability) than did the undersocialized Ss. Although the majority of both groups came from urban communities, a higher proportion of the socialized Ss came from rural communities, suggesting that interpersonal bonds are more likely to develop in small, closely knit rural communities than in cities. In summary, it was found that the undersocialized came mostly from cities, had less developed IQs, and were predominantly Black in comparison to the socialized, who were more likely to come from a rural community, have developed some bonding, and were predominantly White. (12 ref).

413. Kirk, Alton R. & Zucker, Robert A. (1979). **Some sociopsychological factors in attempted suicide among urban Black males.** *Suicide & Life-Threatening Behavior,* 9(2), 76–86.
Tested the hypothesis that Black consciousness and group cohesiveness will be lower and depression will be higher among suicide attempters than among a group of nonattempters matched for age, marital status, and level of education. 20 inner-city, young adult Black males with a suicide attempt in the last 6 mo, and 20 matched controls were examined. 67% of the suicide attempters and 80% of the controls completed a personal opinion questionnaire that included the MMPI Depression scale and the Multiple Affect Adjective Checklist (MAACL) to assess demographic data, Black consciousness, anomie, group cohesiveness, and depression. Results show that suicide attempters had significantly lower Black consciousness and greater anomie than controls. Mean MMPI *D* scale differences were significant in the predicted direction, but MAACL differences were not significant. The validity of the theory of Black self-hatred as the basic cause of suicidal behavior among Blacks is questioned. A 2-factor

theory of suicide, focusing on forces moving the person away from suicide toward positive subgroup ties, is proposed. (19 ref).

414. Kosten, Thomas R.; Rounsaville, Bruce J. & Kleber, Herbert D. (1985). **Ethnic and gender differences among opiate addicts.** *International Journal of the Addictions,* 20(8), 1143–1162.
Compared the clinical characteristics of and treatment implications for 5 groups of addicts—Black and White males and females and Hispanic males. Results indicate that among the 522 addicts (aged 18–65 yrs), the 60 Puerto Ricans had the most frequent unemployment, the least education, the most polydrug abuse and violent crimes, the highest rate of schizophrenic or anxiety disorders, and more neurotic and depressive symptoms than the other male Ss. The 126 female Ss had frequent unemployment, high rates of depression and anxiety disorders, and more severe medical problems than men. Some differences between Black and White males in drug use were also found between Black and White females. The 177 White males had a high rate of antisocial personality and polydrug abuse but had fairly good economic functioning. The 159 Black males had poor occupational functioning but relatively little psychopathology. (35 ref).

415. Leung, Kwok & Drasgow, Fritz. (1986). **Relation between self-esteem and delinquent behavior in three ethnic groups: An application of item response theory.** *Journal of Cross-Cultural Psychology,* 17(2), 151–167.
Examined the hypothesis that low levels of self-esteem are related to high frequencies of delinquent behaviors in 3 ethnic groups of males in the US (consisting of 1,241 Blacks, 2,690 Whites, and 678 Hispanics). Ss were part of a nationwide longitudinal survey of youths (aged 14–21 yrs) who were interviewed in 1979 and 1980. Item response theory was first used to assess the measurement equivalence of a 10-item self-esteem scale and a 7-item delinquent behavior scale across the 3 groups. Regression analyses showed that the proposed hypothesis may hold for Whites but not for Blacks and Hispanics. Whites and Blacks reported similar levels of self-esteem; Hispanics reported lower levels. Methodological and substantive implications of the results are discussed.

416. Lewandowski, Nancy G.; Saccuzzo, Dennis P. & Lewandowski, Denis G. (1977). **The WISC as a measure of personality types.** *Journal of Clinical Psychology,* 33(1), 285–291.
Attempted to provide evidence for the utility of the WISC to identify a specific group of individuals. 80 incarcerated juvenile offenders in the 70–79 IQ range were separated according to race and sex and their differential WISC patterns studied. Results focus on the efficiency of each of Wechler's hypotheses for the adolescent sociopath. Post-hoc analysis provided tentative additional signs by which to identify juvenile offenders in the 70–79 IQ range. Consistencies between results of the present analysis and previous studies are noted. The clear pattern that emerged strongly supports the potential of the WISC as a measure of personality types.

417. Lewis, Collins E.; Cloninger, C. Robert & Pais, John. (1983). **Alcoholism, antisocial personality and drug use in a criminal population.** *Alcohol & Alcoholism,* 18(1), 53–60.
Administered structured interviews to 309 males (237 Whites, 72 Blacks) on probation or parole and elicited information concerning antisocial behavior, alcohol and drug use, military history, and family structure. Additional psychosocial and criminal information was obtained from Ss' probation and parole records. Findings show that the prevalence of antisocial personality was similar for Whites and Blacks (72 and 67%, respectively). Within both racial groups, antisocial Ss tended to be younger, have a lower educational level, and experience more illicit drug use than non-antisocials. White antisocials had a significantly higher prevalence of alcoholism

than their Black counterparts. This risk of alcoholism in Ss with alcohol abuse was also higher in White antisocials than in Black ones. White, but not Black, antisocials had a significantly higher prevalence of alcoholism than their non-antisocial counterparts. White antisocials with drug abuse and dependence (DAD) had significantly higher rates of alcoholism than their Black counterparts. White antisocials with DAD had significantly higher rates of alcoholism than White non-antisocials with DAD and White antisocials without DAD. However, White antisocials without DAD had comparable prevalence to their non-antisocial counterparts. Comparable analyses of Blacks revealed no significant differences. (22 ref).

418. Lewis, Collins E.; Robins, Lee N. & Rice, John. (1985). **Association of alcoholism with antisocial personality in urban men.** *Journal of Nervous & Mental Disease,* 173(3), 166–174.
119 antisocial (mean age 32.8 yrs) and 103 nonantisocial (mean age 32.8 yrs) Black urban males were followed up and administered a structured evaluation of psychiatric, psychosocial, medical, and family history variables. Psychiatric diagnoses were based on the clinical interview and record material. Results indicate that Ss with antisocial personalities had a higher rate of alcoholism than those without antisocial personality. A family history of problem drinking, low educational level, and excessive irritability were also closely associated with alcoholism. Clinical, genetic, and neurophysiological implications of these findings are discussed. (50 ref).

419. Liska, Allen E. & Reed, Mark D. (1985). **Ties to conventional institutions and delinquency: Estimating reciprocal effects.** *American Sociological Review,* 50(4), 547–560.
Examined the relationship between juvenile delinquency, school attachment, and parental attachment, using data from 1,886 male 10th and 11th graders classified as upper or lower class and as Black or White. Ss completed self-reports assessing these variables. Present results indicate a negative effect of attachment on delinquency. Except for a small subsample of Black Ss, 3 major causal effects were found to underlie the relationship between delinquency and attachment. Parental attachment affected delinquency, which affected school attachment, which in turn affected parental attachment. Results are discussed in terms of social control theory. The recursiveness assumption is questioned, and it is asserted that delinquency is as likely to affect attachment as attachment is to affect delinquency. A nonrecursive model using ordinary least-squares crosslag and simultaneous equation methodology is estimated. Findings suggest that the effects of attachment and delinquency are reciprocal and contingent on social status, thus casting doubt on the validity of extant research as a test of social control theory. (38 ref).

420. Lorefice, Laurence; Steer, Robert A.; Fine, Eric W. & Schut, Jacob. (1976). **Personality traits and moods of alcoholics and heroin addicts.** *Journal of Studies on Alcohol,* 37(5), 687–689.
Administered the Eysenck Personality Inventory (Form A) and the Profile of Mood States to 50 Black males, 25 alcoholics, and 25 addicts. Only the Neuroticism-Stability scale scores were significantly different: The alcoholics were more neurotic than the narcotic addicts.

421. Martin, William T. (1984). **Religiosity and United States suicide rates, 1972–1978.** *Journal of Clinical Psychology,* 40(5), 1166–1169.
Analyzed official suicide statistics and data on religious involvement from the General Social Surveys (National Opinion Research Center, 1981) for representative subpopulations of the US. Variations in the suicide rates of White males, Black males, White females, and Black females from 1972–1978 were significantly inversely correlated with variations in the church attendance of the respective subpopulations during this period. No significant differences were found between the

correlations for White and Black females and for White and Black males or between those for Black females and males and for White females and males. Findings support the general hypothesis that religiosity deters suicide. It is suggested that the sociological explanation for effectiveness of religious involvement is that it enhances group cohesiveness. Psychologically, it may be effective because it enhances psychic cohesiveness, the integration of the conscious mind with the unconscious. (16 ref).

422. McCreary, Charles & Padilla, Eligio. (1977). **MMPI differences among Black, Mexican-American, and White male offenders.** *Journal of Clinical Psychology,* 33(1), 171–177.
Compared MMPI scores of 40 Black, 36 Mexican-American, and 267 White male offenders (mean ages, 33.6, 31.9, and 31.8 yrs, respectively). Comparisons were performed on unmatched and matched (education and occupation) groups that utilized all profiles or valid ones only and examined both trait (individual scales) and type differences. Black–White differences on the *Ma, K,* and *Hy* scales appeared to reflect cultural factors, while differences on *Mf* and alcoholism seemed to be accounted for by socioeconomic differences. Cultural factors seemed to be related to differences between Mexican-Americans and Whites on the *L, K,* and Overcontrolled Hostility scales, while socioeconomic factors appeared to explain differences on the *Hs* scale. Type differences were not apparent except that Mexican-Americans were classified more often as psychiatric, while Whites and Blacks scored well into the sociopathic range. (16 ref).

423. Murray, Leslie; Heritage, Jeannette & Holmes, William. (1976). **Black–White comparisons on the MMPI Mini-Mult.** *Southern Journal of Educational Research,* 10(2), 105–114.
Compared Mini-Mult performance of 40 White and 40 Black 12–15 yr old male delinquents selected on the basis of similar IQ, socioeconomic level, domestic status, and grade level. There was no significant difference between the performance of Black and White Ss on any scale of the Mini-Mult.

424. Nurco, David N.; Cisin, Ira H. & Ball, John C. (1986). **Use of nonnarcotic drugs by narcotic addicts.** Proceedings of the 47th Annual Scientific Meeting of the Committee on Problems of Drug Dependence: Problems of drug dependence, 1985 (1985, Baltimore, Maryland). *National Institute on Drug Abuse: Research Monograph Series,* 67, 295–299.
Investigated the popularity and intensity of nonnarcotic drug use among 195 Black and 159 White male narcotic addicts (mean age 34.1 yrs). Data from interviews indicate that for most Ss, periods of addiction included the use of various nonnarcotic drugs, especially marihuana and cocaine. Thus, what appears to be the consequences of narcotic use may be exacerbated by an interactive or catalytic effect of narcotic and nonnarcotic drugs. In addition, most Ss were seldom completely drug free. Even during periods when they were not addicted to narcotic drugs, Ss used other drugs, particularly marihuana. Drug use patterns of Black and White Ss during both addictive and nonaddictive periods were also compared.

425. Nurco, David N.; Cisin, Ira H. & Ball, John C. (1985). **Crime as a source of income for narcotic addicts.** *Journal of Substance Abuse Treatment,* 2(2), 113–115.
Conducted confidential interviews with 165 Black and 153 White male narcotic addicts (mean age 34.1 yrs) to determine their criminal activity while addicted and not addicted. During periods of addiction, Black and White Ss derived a mean of 71.8% and 64.4%, respectively, of their income from illegal sources. During periods of nonaddiction, the respective mean percentages were 28.1 and 16.8. Implications for assignment of drug abusers to various treatment programs are discussed. (6 ref).

426. Nurco, David N.; Cisin, Ira H. & Balter, Mitchell B. (1982). **Trends in the age of onset of narcotic addiction.** *Chemical Dependencies: Behavioral & Biomedical Issues,* 4(3), 221–228.
Attempted to determine age at 1st use of alcohol, narcotics, and other drugs, with emphasis on the onset of narcotic addiction. The present study differed in design from previous research in that it attempted to investigate a community-wide population of narcotic users, together with any changes that may have taken place, not only with respect to the type of person who entered addiction, but also in the nature of the addictive process over time. 252 Ss were selected from a police roster of male narcotic abusers between 1952 and 1971. The sample consisted of 10 Whites and 10 Blacks in each of the 1st 15 yrs of the study and 5 Whites and 5 Blacks in each of the last 5 yrs of the study. 244 of the Ss reported using alcohol; Whites were approximately 2 yrs younger than Blacks at the time of their 1st drink. The average age among Whites for 1st alcohol use declined over the years from 15 to 11 yrs of age. Blacks began at age 15 and declined only to age 14. Prevalent age for onset of addiction (under or over 18 yrs) shifted back and forth over the years. Results show that a disproportionately large number of the Ss became addicted during the 1955–1959 period, the majority of them being under 18 yrs. It is suggested that a loosening of moral and social standards associated with rapidly changing world events may have increased the risk for this population and may have made them more vulnerable to a career with drugs when exposed early to narcotics. (6 ref).

427. Pallone, Nathaniel J. & Hennessey, James J. (1977). **Some correlates of recidivism among misdemeanants and minor felons: A 12-month follow-up.** *Journal of Social Psychology,* 101(2), 321–322.
Examined correlates of recidivism among 160 White, Black, and Puerto Rican male ex-offenders. No significant relationships were observed between recidivism and race or ethnicity, religious group membership, alcohol use history, socioeconomic status associated with Ss' usual occupation, level of formal education, age at first recorded arrest, or number of prior convictions.

428. Panella, Deborah & Henggeler, Scott W. (1986). **Peer interactions of conduct-disordered, anxious-withdrawn, and well-adjusted Black adolescents.** *Journal of Abnormal Child Psychology,* 14(1), 1–11.
Examined the relationship between behavior problems and adolescent peer relations in 30 lower-class, inner-city Black male adolescents (aged 15–18 yrs) divided into 3 equal-sized groups based on teacher ratings of individual psychosocial functioning (conduct-disordered, anxious-withdrawn, well-adjusted). Groups were matched on age, IQ (Weschler Adult Intelligence Scale [WAIS] Vocabulary scores), and father absence. An observational method was used to evaluate dominance, conflict, affect, and social competence manifested with a friend and with a well-adjusted stranger (1 of 30 male adolescent controls of similar demographic makeup). Results indicate that conduct-disordered and anxious-withdrawn Ss displayed less social competence and less positive affect than well-adjusted Ss when interacting with both friends and strangers. Anxious-withdrawn Ss evidenced more personal apprehension than their well-adjusted counterparts. All groups showed greater leadership ability, talked more, and showed less personal apprehension with friends than with strangers. Findings support the role of peer relations in the maintenance and exacerbation of adolescent psychosocial difficulties. (36 ref).

429. Patalano, Frank. (1977). **Height on the Draw-A-Person: Comparison of figure drawings of Black and White male drug abusers.** *Perceptual & Motor Skills,* 44(3, Pt 2), 1187–1190.
Administered the Draw-A-Person test to 30 Black and 30 White 14–25 yr old male drug abusers in a residential therapeutic community. Mean height and mean area of the female figures drawn by Black Ss were greater than the mean height and mean area of the female figures drawn by White Ss. More Black Ss drew the female figure taller than the male figure. Data are discussed in regard to family background and sociocultural considerations.

430. Penk, W. E. et al. (1981). **MMPI differences of male Hispanic-American, Black, and White heroin addicts.** *Journal of Consulting & Clinical Psychology,* 49(3), 488–490.
Tested 2 hypotheses: (a) that Hispanic-American heroin addicts are better adjusted than White (majority group) addicts and (b) that Hispanics characteristically are less open about expressing psychological symptoms and are more masculine in their interests. All Ss were given the MMPI. Both hypotheses were confirmed in MANOVAs and analyses of covariance among 41 Hispanic-American, 161 White, and 268 Black heroin addicts, with age (mean age of Ss 30.13 yrs), education, and socioeconomic status serving as covariates. (8 ref).

431. Penk, W. E. et al. (1981). **Visual memory for Black and White male heroin and nonheroin drug users.** *Journal of Abnormal Psychology,* 90(5), 486–489.
Compared levels of intellectual functioning, as measured by the Raven Progressive Matrices (RPM), with expected levels of visual memory, as measured by the Benton Revised Visual Retention Test (BVRT). Whereas substance abusers scored within the average range of intelligence on the RPM, on the BVRT the means of both 467 heroin addicts and 310 polydrug abusers were 2 standard deviations below expected performance. Significant differences found in analysis of covariance and multiple regression models were not attributable to either demographic factors (age, education, socioeconomic status) or personality differences (as measured by MMPI scales). Like polydrug abusers, heroin addicts evidenced interference in immediate, short-term memory, confirming earlier findings of marked perceptual disturbances among detoxified addicts. Unlike earlier findings, results reveal significant ethnic differences. A need for establishing Black norms is indicated for the BVRT and perhaps for other neuropsychological assessment procedures that lack ethnic norms. (9 ref).

432. Poklis, Alphonse. (1982). **Pentazocine/tripelennamine (T's and Blues) abuse: A five year survey of St. Louis, Missouri.** *Drug & Alcohol Dependence,* 10(2–3), 257–267.
Presents data concerning the continuous increase in the iv use of pentazocine/tripelennamine combination in St. Louis, Missouri, from 1977–1981. Initial popularity of the illegal drugs was related to the decline in the quality of street heroin. Serious adverse reactions include clonic-tonic seizures and pulmonary foreign body granulomatosis. Addicts are usually Black males, 20–30 yrs old, from poor areas of the city. (30 ref).

433. Robins, Lee N. & Wish, Eric. (1977). **Childhood deviance as a developmental process: A study of 223 urban Black men from birth to 18.** *Social Forces,* 56(2), 448–473.
Explored whether or not deviance can be viewed as a developmental process in which one type of deviant act leads to another. Criteria that would need to be met if such a process exists are proposed. These criteria are applied to data from records and interviews with 223 Black men concerning the ages at which 13 kinds of childhood behaviors began. Results appear consistent with both a quantitative and a qualitative developmental process.

434. Robins, Lee N.; West, Patricia A. & Murphy, George E. (1977). **The high rate of suicide in older White men: A study testing ten hypotheses.** *Social Psychiatry,* 12(1), 1–20.

A persistent finding in the epidemiology of suicide is the high rate in older White men in the US. The relationship of beliefs and behaviors to suicidal thoughts and attempts in 104 lower-class male psychiatric and medical patients, composed equally of Blacks and Whites, in the age range of high risk (45–64) was investigated, drawing upon 10 hypotheses about suicide from sociological and neuropsychiatric literature. Variables found associated with suicidal thoughts or acts in both Black and White patients were then explored in a group of normal Black and White males of the same ages and social class. When the hypothesized behaviors or attitudes were more frequent both in suicidal patients in both races and in the general sample of Whites, the hypothesis was viewed as a possible explanation for the excess suicides in older White men. Six variables were found both to describe suicidal as compared with nonsuicidal patients and to distinguish normal White from Black men: social integration, differential association, attitudes toward aging, secular attitudes, brain damage from alcohol, and depressive illness. (36 ref).

435. Savitz, Leonard; Rosen, Lawrence & Lalli, Michael. (1980). **Delinquency and gang membership as related to victimization.** *Victimology*, 5(2–4), 152–160.
Investigated the manner in which officially recorded delinquency and membership in a combative gang may be associated with subjective estimates of future criminal victimizations (fear of crime) and with overt victimization experiences. Using data from 532 Black and 502 White 14-yr-old males, it was determined that a police or court record of delinquency did not influence measured fear levels, but was positively associated with the chances of being the victim of a criminal act. Gang membership within a fighting gang was associated with lower levels of a real fear and less fear of (subsequent) victimization; it was, however, associated with slightly higher chances of actual victimization. It is concluded that having a delinquency record of being a combative gang member was only slightly related to articulated fear of crime or to victimization experiences.

436. Schaefer, Charles E. (1975). **The three wishes and future ambitions of emotionally disturbed boys.** *Devereux Forum*, 10(1), 1–5.
Discusses the answers of 50 Black, lower-class delinquent boys 7–13 yrs old, prior to residential treatment, to the "Three Wishes" and "Future Ambitions" questions. Results were not significantly different from those obtained from normal children of comparable age.

437. Shaffer, John W.; Nurco, David N.; Ball, John C. & Kinlock, Timothy W. (1985). **The frequency of nonnarcotic drug use and its relationship to criminal activity among narcotic addicts.** *Comprehensive Psychiatry*, 26(6), 558–566.
Investigated the frequency with which various nonnarcotic drugs were used and the relationship of such use to the commission of different types of crime using confidential interview data obtained from 354 male narcotic addicts (mean age 34.1 yrs). Frequency, type of nonnarcotic drugs used, and the relationship of such use to the commission of different types of crime were found to be a joint function of race (Black/White) and current narcotic addiction status (addicted/not addicted). Members of both races tended to use more nonnarcotic drugs during periods of active addiction to narcotics than during periods of nonaddiction. Analyses provided evidence that higher rates of use of certain nonnarcotic drugs were associated with higher rates of commission of certain types of crime; however, a cause and effect relationship could not be proven. Findings indicate that cocaine use appears to be associated with increased criminal activity among Blacks but not among Whites. (12 ref).

438. Shaffer, John W.; Nurco, David N.; Ball, John C. & Kinlock, Timothy W. (1986). **Patterns of non-narcotic drug use among male narcotic addicts.** *Journal of Drug Issues*, 16(3), 435–442.
Interviewed 195 Black and 159 White male narcotic addicts (mean age 34.1 yrs) concerning their use of nonnarcotic drugs during periods of active addiction to narcotics (principally heroin) and during nonaddiction. 12 types of nonnarcotic substances were found to be in use. The types, amounts, and patterns in which nonnarcotic drugs were used were found to be a joint function of race and narcotic addiction status. Factor analysis showed 3 patterns of nonnarcotic use during periods of narcotic addiction and 3 during nonaddiction among Blacks, and 4 patterns of nonnarcotic use during addiction and 5 during nonaddiction in Whites. Cluster analysis identified 4 addict types.

439. Shaffer, John W.; Wegner, Norma; Kinlock, Timothy W. & Nurco, David N. (1983). **An empirical typology of narcotic addicts.** *International Journal of the Addictions*, 18(2), 183–194.
On the basis of structured interview data concerning their life-styles, behaviors, circumstances, and activities during their most recent periods of addiction, 230 Black and 230 White male narcotic addicts (mean age 28.7 yrs) were empirically classified, or "typed," using factor and cluster analytic techniques in a multistage process. Mean factor score profiles for each of 8 types derived are presented in terms of sociability, deviancy, income, living conditions, and employment. (21 ref).

440. Siomopoulos, V. (1978). **Psychiatric diagnosis and criminality.** *Psychological Reports*, 42(2), 559–562.
Examined the distribution of various offenses among various psychiatric diagnoses in a sample of 342 Black and 109 White male indicted felons who were adjudicated unfit to stand trial. Armed robbery was the leading offense among the total sample and also among those 347 Ss diagnosed as schizophrenic and among the 39 Ss with personality disorders. Schizophrenia was the leading psychiatric diagnosis among the total population as well as among the accused for each and every type of offense except arson. Organic brain syndromes were associated exclusively with crimes of high degree of violence, whereas mental retardation was found primarily among those accused of minor crimes.

441. Spaights, Ernest & Simpson, Gloria. (1986). **Some unique causes of Black suicide.** *Psychology: A Quarterly Journal of Human Behavior*, 23(1), 1–5.
Suggests that suicide among Blacks is increasing at an alarming rate, especially among young Black males between 20–23 yrs of age. Black teenagers are also highly vulnerable. While many factors in suicidal behavior are present in both White and Black populations—anger, low self-esteem, depression, an inability to express feelings, and difficulties in family structure—some aspects are unique to the Black population and must be explored. Among these are effects of upward mobility and Black cultural expectations for males, which include repression of feelings and strict obedience to parents and elders. Some Blacks may also find it difficult to identify with their race. Gangs and drug abuse also contribute to the problem. Poverty and racism can cause depression, a known factor in suicidal behavior. (12 ref).

442. Steer, Robert A.; Shaw, Brian F.; Beck, Aaron T. & Fine, Eric W. (1977). **Structure of depression in Black alcoholic men.** *Psychological Reports*, 41(3, Pt 2), 1235–1241.
Administered the Beck Depression Inventory to 103 Black men (mean age 39.28 yrs) receiving outpatient treatment for alcoholism, and subjected the scores to factor analyses using a maximum-likelihood solution. Three meaningful oblique dimensions were identified as Cognitive-Affective Impairment, Retarded Depression, and Escapism. The factor structure of

the Black alcoholic men was descriptively compared to those previously reported for racially heterogeneous alcoholic patients and for primarily depressed patients; the factors of depression for the Black alcoholic men were comparable to those described for the other 2 clinical samples. (22 ref).

443. Terrell, Francis & Taylor, Jerome. (1980). **Self concept of juveniles who commit Black on Black crimes.** *Corrective & Social Psychiatry & Journal of Behavior Technology, Methods & Therapy,* 26(3), 107–109.
Ss were 30 lower-class, Black male youths. Half were detained as suspects for committing a crime involving the property of another Black (Group 1); the other half (Group 2) were detained as suspects for committing a crime involving the physical injury of another Black. Three assessment techniques were used: (a) F. Terrell and J. Taylor's Black Ideology Scale; (b) the Tennessee Self-Concept Scale; and (c) a background questionnaire. Results support the hypothesis that Blacks who commit crimes against property (Group 1) have a higher global level of self-esteem as well as a higher level of ethnic identification than Blacks who commit crimes against persons (Group 2). Results do not permit the conclusion that self-concept mediates Black-on-Black crime. (8 ref).

444. Thompson, William E. & Dodder, Richard A. (1986). **Containment theory and juvenile delinquency: A reevaluation through factor analysis.** *Adolescence,* 21(82), 365–376.
Attempted to operationalize 7 components of containment theory (W. C. Reckless, 1967) and to examine the relationship between delinquency and the containment variables among categories of race (Black vs White) and sex. Containment variables investigated included self-perception, goal orientation, frustration tolerance, retention of norms, internalization of rules, available meaningful roles, and group reinforcement. Data were collected from 677 adolescents in a variety of high schools and correction institutions and were divided into categories by race and sex. Factor analysis indicated that the structure of the relationships among the 7 containment variables and delinquency was noticeably similar across race and sex categories, with the exception of Black females. Data provide support for containment theory in explaining juvenile delinquency across 3 of the race and sex categories, with strongest support demonstrated for White males. Scales of the 7 containment variables by items are appended. (11 ref).

445. Thornton, Carolyn I. & Carter, James H. (1986). **Treatment considerations with Black incestuous families.** 88th Annual Convention and Scientific Assembly of the National Medical Association (1983, Chicago, Illinois). *Journal of the National Medical Association,* 78(1), 49–53.
Contends that society does not hold sexual misconduct among Blacks to be of an equal degree of magnitude as that of Whites. Rather, when incest is reported in Black families, it is often minimized or disregarded by agencies assigned to investigate and treat the problem. A conceptual model for the development of incest is presented; this model includes such factors as boundary and role confusion and poor impulse control. It is argued that these factors create an environment in which all social and emotional needs, including sexual ones, are met within the family. Characterological problems or psychosis, mental retardation, and alcohol and drug abuse are frequently viewed as contributing to the loss of control. Additional stressful occurrences that increase the probability of incest are financial setbacks, job loss, death, and extended absence of the mother from the home. Three case vignettes are presented to illustrate some general problems that influence the identification and treatment of father–daughter incest in Black families and the scarcity of law enforcement involvement in such cases. Psychological manifestations of incest victims are delineated, and treatment concerns are noted. (27 ref).

446. Thorsell, Bernard A. & Chambers, Robert. (1974). **The adjudication process and self-conception.** *Personality & Social Psychology Bulletin,* 1(1), 327–329.
Data from 82 male 11–17 yr old White, Black, and Chicano delinquents and 75 typical White junior high school students support the hypotheses that (a) juvenile offenders, having experienced the adjudication process, would exhibit self-conceptions that are significantly more negative than those of nonoffenders, and (b) degree of negativeness of self-conception would be significantly related to ethnic background. White offenders showed the highest degree of negativeness of self-conception, followed by Chicanos and Blacks, in that order.

Learning Disorders & Mental Retardation

447. Elliott, Stephen N. et al. (1985). **Three-year stability of WISC—R IQs for handicapped children from three racial/ethnic groups.** *Journal of Psychoeducational Assessment,* 3(3), 233–244.
Investigated the long-term stability of Wechsler Intelligence Scale for Children—Revised (WISC—R) IQs (Full Scale, Verbal, and Performance) for male and female Ss from 3 racial or ethnic groups (115 male and 60 female Anglos, 39 male and 28 female Mexican-Americans, and 100 male and 40 female Blacks). The 3-yr stability coefficients for the Ss compared well with those established with a 3-wk interval during the standardization of the WISC—R. Specific findings indicated that Anglo Ss' IQs were significantly more stable than those of Blacks on all 3 IQ scales and also more stable than those of Mexican-Americans on the Performance and Full Scales. Sex of the S had minimal influence on test score stability; only females' Verbal performances resulted in significantly larger stability coefficients than those of males. These and other results are discussed from educational, developmental, and psychometric perspectives. (21 ref).

448. Terrell, Francis; Terrell, Sandra L. & Taylor, Jerome. (1981). **Effects of type of reinforcement on the intelligence test performance of retarded Black children.** *Psychology in the Schools,* 18(2), 225–227.
Examined the effects of reinforcement on 100 Black male 9–11 yr olds who had been diagnosed as being mildly mentally retarded, using the WISC—R. After each correct response, Ss were given no reinforcement, a candy reward, traditional social reinforcement, or culturally relevant social reinforcement. Ss given tangible or culturally relevant rewards obtained significantly higher scores that did Ss given either no reinforcement or traditional social reinforcement. (3 ref).

449. Weiss, Elizabeth. (1984). **Learning disabled children's understanding of social interactions of peers.** *Journal of Learning Disabilities,* 17(10), 612–615.
Judgments of children who manifested social problems—physically aggressive and learning disabled (LD) males—were compared with judgments of children whose behavior was more appropriate. 111 Black, inner-city 11–15 yr olds were divided into 4 groups—nonaggressive learners in a mainstream setting, aggressive learners in classes for the emotionally disturbed (ED) or in day treatment, nonaggressive LD Ss in classes for the LD or resource rooms, and aggressive LD Ss in classes for LD/ED or in day treatment—and either viewed videotapes of similar children engaging in friendly, fighting, or horseplay interactions or heard verbal descriptions of the same events. No differences were found between aggressive and nonaggressive Ss, suggesting that aggressive perceivers do not necessarily "project" their own characteristics onto others. However, LD Ss, both aggressive and nonaggressive, found all scenes more unfriendly. Differences in responses to videotapes and to verbal descriptions alone suggest that conclusions about social perceptions obtained from one mode of

stimulus presentation may not generalize to other modes or to life situations. (12 ref).

Physical & Psychosomatic Disorders

450. Beresford, Thomas P.; Blow, Frederic C. & Hall, Richard C. (1986). **AIDS encephalitis mimicking alcohol dementia and depression.** *Biological Psychiatry,* 21(4), 394–397.
Reports the case of a 29-yr-old Black male admitted to a Veterans Administration psychiatric service, with encephalitis occurring in a setting consistent with acquired immune deficiency syndrome (AIDS). It is noted that AIDS and its complications can mimic psychiatric syndromes, including depression and dementia, or delirium related to illnesses such as alcoholism. Acting out behavior, seen in the present case, may also be mistaken as a symptom of sociopathy. (7 ref).

451. Drexler, Corinne. (1975). **A four-year-old boy experiences surgery for a genital defect.** *Maternal-Child Nursing Journal,* 4(3), 197–205.
Describes the experiences of a 4-yr-old Black male who underwent surgery to repair a genital defect, focusing on his preparation for hopitalization and surgery, the major sources of anxiety he encountered, and the behaviors he demonstrated in his efforts to deal with his experiences.

452. Loeb, Roger C. & Sarigiani, Pamela. (1986). **The impact of hearing impairment on self-perceptions of children.** *Volta Review,* 88(2), 89–100.
Examined how 64 children with varying degrees of hearing impairment differed from 74 visually impaired children and 112 children with no major sensory impairments. Ss (aged 8–15 yrs) were 132 females and 118 males, and 108 Blacks and 142 Whites. Assessment included the Children's Locus of Control Scale and the Piers-Harris Children's Self Concept Scale (The Way I Feel About Myself). Hearing-impaired Ss were found to have lower self-esteem and related problems in self-confidence, peer and family relations, and academics. Communication barriers often appeared to be a source of the problems. Sex, race, severity of handicap, and age of onset had a substantial impact.

453. Robinson, Paul & Andersen, Arnold E. (1985). **Anorexia nervosa in American Blacks.** Conference on Anorexia Nervosa and Related Disorders (1984, Swansea, Wales). *Journal of Psychiatric Research,* 19(2–3), 183–188.
Investigated 5 cases of anorexia nervosa in Black American patients, aged 14–34 yrs. All had lost parents by death or divorce. Three had a family history of obesity and of a physical illness related to obesity. Two were male, and both of these had a previous history of serious psychiatric disturbance. Three Ss had a 1st- or 2nd-degree relative with affective disorder. Two Ss showed a primary lack of sexual interest, and 1 male was bisexual. Four of the Ss came from Social Classes 3–5. (10 ref).

454. Schoenberg, Bruce S.; Anderson, Dallas W. & Haerer, Armin F. (1985). **Severe dementia: Prevalence and clinical features in a biracial US population.** *Archives of Neurology,* 42(8), 740–743.
In a Mississippi county containing 49.1% Black and 50.1% White residents, 80 of 23,842 residents were identified with severe dementia (i.e., requiring constant supervision). Although no striking differences were found between groups in incidence, age-adjusted prevalence rates were higher for Blacks and for females. Prevalence is a function of both incidence and survival. In a screening of 5,489 40–64 yr old residents, 3 Ss were identified with severe dementia, 1 of whom had primary chronic progressive dementia. (10 ref).

455. Yakulis, Irene M. (1975). **Changing concepts of death in a child with sickle cell disease.** *Maternal-Child Nursing Journal,* 4(2), 117–120.

Observed the progression of an 8-yr-old Black male's understanding of death and his concomitant fears. During repeated hospital admissions, the S manifested acute separation anxiety. He viewed death as a threatening force or as a "personification" that could overwhelm him. Following the death of his father, however, the S began verbalizing his concerns about death and asked questions regarding the cause of death. It is suggested that the awareness of his own diagnosis (sickle cell anemia) and the death of his father resulted in the S's development of 2 concepts of death—causation and irreversible separation.

TREATMENT AND PREVENTION

456. Arnold, L. Eugene; Strobl, Donald & Weisenberg, Allen. (1972). **Hyperkinetic adult: Study of the "paradoxical" amphetamine response.** *JAMA: Journal of the American Medical Association,* 222(6), 693–694.
Found a form of the hyperkinetic syndrome, assumed to be a juvenile condition, in a 22-yr-old Black male with a previously undiagnosed condition. S showed the pathognomonic paradoxical calming of the hyperkinetic by amphetamine. Further evidence was obtained from quantitative self-estimations of mood following double-blind administrations of d-amphetamine sulfate and placebo. Compared to his response to placebo, S not only showed externally visible calming and depression, but also subjectively reported decreased anxiety, increased depression, and increased concentration, with no change in self-esteem.

457. Barton, Gail M. & Jacisin, John J. (1973). **Being Black: A help or hindrance to getting psychiatric treatment.** *Psychiatric Opinion,* 10(6), 35–42.
Reports the case of a Black male psychiatric patient with many psychiatric hospitalizations and bizarre behavior, to illustrate how different segments of the psychiatric system react to a Black patient and how being Black both helps and hinders getting psychiatric treatment. Blackness was a definite help for the patient in attending a prestigious university, obtaining financial assistance, being accepted into a hospital, getting legal help, and being remembered by staff. However, being Black was a hindrance equally as often; it left the patient ill-prepared for the academic bureaucracy and lifestyle and for middle-class methods of understanding or handling illness. It conjured up stereotypes in the minds of those he dealt with so that they reacted to a caricature rather than to him. Suggestions for changing the psychiatric system to make it more functional for Blacks are made.

458. Carter, James H. & Jordan, Barbara M. (1972). **Inpatient therapy for Black paranoid men.** *Hospital & Community Psychiatry,* 23(6), 180–182.
Examined the applicability of traditional treatment methods to the Black patient in a study with 16 21–35 yr old Black male paranoid schizophrenics. Ss were treated by a Black psychiatrist in reality-oriented group therapy sessions aimed at solving current problems and developing positive concepts of self and the group. Although considered incorrigible at the beginning of the program, over half the patients were discharged after 6 mo of therapy. Others, who were ready for discharge, could not be placed. Problems associated with being Black and a psychiatric patient are briefly noted. Questions concerning the use of all Black groups led by a Black therapist, the problems of mixed racial groups, and the cultural and social values of Blacks are considered.

459. Chipman, Abram. (1978). **Psychogenic impotence and the Black man's burden.** *American Journal of Psychotherapy,* 32(4), 603–612.
Presents clinical material on a single case of impotence in a middle-aged Black man. The symbolic meanings of the symp-

tom in terms of the patient's aggression, feelings about his racial self-image, and the options that allow for male identity are discussed, along with some aspects of an interracial treatment situation in these changing times. (12 ref).

460. Clark, Carl G. & Miller, Howard L. (1971). **Validation of Gilberstadt and Duker's 8-6 profile type on a Black sample.** *Psychological Reports,* 29(1), 259–264.
Replicated the procedure employed by H. Gilberstadt and J. Duker (see PA, Vol 40:1589) with a midwestern sample to determine the characteristics of the 8-6 MMPI profile type with a southeastern Black sample of 10 male patients. The cardinal features of paranoid schizophrenia seemed remarkably similar in both groups, but significant differences were found in traits, symptoms, and MMPI scale scores. In general, the southeastern Black sample showed a somewhat greater surface manifestation of pathological traits and admitted to more experiences that are viewed in the White culture as odd and bizarre. The differences are interpreted as probably reflecting different base-line personality characteristics between southeastern Blacks and midwestern Whites. The more apparently pathological symptoms and traits in the Black population are interpreted as a manifestation of truly adaptive behavior for this subgroup in an aversive social environment.

461. Cohn, Cal K.; Wright, James R. & DeVaul, Richard A. (1977). **Post head trauma syndrome in an adolescent treated with lithium carbonate: Case report.** *Journal of Clinical Psychiatry,* 38(8), 630–631.
Presents the case of a 12-yr-old Black male who sustained closed head trauma, following which he developed agitated hypomanic behavior. After his failure to respond to several treatment modalities, he was begun on lithium carbonate for 6 mo, at which time the medication was discontinued without recurrence of pathological behavior.

462. Crouch, Linda. (1972). **Disturbance in language and thought.** *Journal of Psychiatric Nursing & Mental Health Services,* 10(3), 5–9.
Presents and discusses theories concerning the schizophrenic's disturbed language and thought processes with particular reference to the work of S. Arieti. Therapeutic nursing intervention with such patients is described and illustrated with data from a 19-yr-old hospitalized Negro male. (22 ref).

463. Epstein, Leonard H. & Hersen, Michel. (1974). **Behavioral control of hysterical gagging.** *Journal of Clinical Psychology,* 30(1), 102–104.
Application of a simple reinforcement technique resulted in the rapid control of a long-standing, debilitating gagging disorder that appeared refractory to medical intervention in a 26-yr-old Black male. While inpatient treatment required external reinforcement to motivate the S to control his disorder, maintenance of gains during follow-up suggests that he was then able to generate self-control over his behavior. Moreover, corroboration of follow-up data by the S's wife negates the possible interpretation that he had only modified his report of gagging. Results provide clinical support for the instigation of procedures that teach patients to manage their own behavior.

464. Hersen, Michel; Matherne, Paula M.; Gullick, Eugenia L. & Harbert, Terry L. (1972). **Instructions and reinforcement in the modification of a conversion reaction.** *Psychological Reports,* 31(3), 719–722.
Sequentially examined the effects of 2 variables, instructions and social reinforcement, on a 19-yr-old unmarried, Black male with a conversion reaction. Reinforcement in the form of praise resulted in an increase in S's ability to walk. When reinforcement was removed, other variables including instructions, expectancy, social reinforcement from other patients, and self-reinforcement may have contributed to unexpected improvements in walking. However, reinstitution of reinforcement led to the most dramatic increases in walking.

465. Hopkins, Thomas J. (1972). **The role of community agencies as viewed by Black fathers.** *American Journal of Orthopsychiatry,* 42(3), 508–516.
Reports that discussions with Black fathers in a family center indicate that far too little attention has been paid to their views, feelings, and concerns about social agencies. Experiences provided by agencies which affirm or negate black fatherhood are discussed. Guiding principles are proposed for the development of an enhancing agency milieu wherein Black fathers can maintain their masculinity and become the leading and motivating force in their community.

466. Jensen, Peter S. (1984). **Case report of conversion catatonia: Indication for hypnosis.** *American Journal of Psychotherapy,* 38(4), 566–570.
Describes the successful hypnotic treatment of a 25-yr-old Black male who displayed symptoms of suicidal ideation, insomnia, and feelings of depression alternating with emptiness and boredom that led to an acute catatonic reaction. S met DSM-III criteria for borderline personality disorder. It is contended that since conversion mechanisms may underlie some presentations of catatonia, hypnosis may assist clinicians in the differential diagnosis of acute catatonic conditions. (15 ref).

467. Kirk, Alton R. (1986). **Destructive behaviors among members of the Black community with a special focus on males: Causes and methods of intervention.** Special Issue: The Black male: Critical counseling, developmental, and therapeutic issues: III. *Journal of Multicultural Counseling & Development,* 14(1), 3–9.
Discusses the relationship between stress, depression, homicide, and suicide within the psychosocial context of an ethnic minority group. The relationship between mental health and destructive behavior among Blacks and methods of intervention and prevention are discussed. It is contended that stress is significantly related to the degree and amount of power perceived by an individual within the societal context and that, consequently, Blacks experience a great deal of stress. (12 ref).

468. Kroeker, L. L. (1974). **Pretesting as a confounding variable in evaluating an encounter group.** *Journal of Counseling Psychology,* 21(6), 548–552.
Evaluated the effectiveness of an encounter group designed to enhance relationships between 3 groups of 68 15–21 yr old Black inner-city males and 3 groups of 38 White and 2 Black policemen and the interaction between pretesting and treatment and its effects on outcome. There were 3 experimental and 3 control groups which either did or did not participate in the pretest and treatment portions of the study; all groups completed the posttest. The 2 evaluation measures were the Alienation Index Inventory and a specially developed projective device; these were administered by White and Black experimenters to same-race groups. Results indicate that the proportion of variance contributed by pretesting is influenced by group membership, treatment, and outcome criterion and is largely unpredictable. It is suggested that such variance be controlled in each experiment. (16 ref).

469. Lake, C. Raymond & Fann, William E. (1973). **Possible potentiation of haloperidol neurotoxicity in acute hyperthyroidism.** *British Journal of Psychiatry,* 123(576), 523–525.
Reports the case of a 54-yr-old Negro male demonstrating increased neurotoxic rigidity apparently due to haloperidol.

470. Levine, David G.; Levin, Donald B.; Sloan, Ira H. & Chappel, John N. (1972). **Personality correlates of success in a methadone maintenance program.** *American Journal of Psychiatry,* 129(4), 456–460.

Compared degree of success in a methadone maintenance program with the psychiatric diagnosis, disability, and manifestations of anxiety, depression and paranoia, object relatedness, and compliance of 30 Black male heroin addicts. Groups were evenly divided into (a) stepped-up group (drug-free at least 6 mo and helping other patients in the clinic), (b) voluntary reenrollment group (previous drop-outs), and (c) drop-out group. Descriptive psychiatric diagnoses and degree of paranoia were of no value in differentiating among the 3 groups; levels of anxiety and depression were inversely related. Stepped-up Ss were the most anxious and least depressed, the drop-outs the least anxious and most depressed; the stepped-up Ss also had the highest scores in compliance. The possible reasons for the various differences among groups in anxiety and depression and the treatment implications are discussed.

471. Mayercak, Susan. (1981). **The integration of developmental theory and kinesthetic sensitivity in the treatment of a schizophrenic adolescent.** *Pratt Institute Creative Arts Therapy Review,* 2, 1–6.
Presents the case of a Black 15-yr-old schizophrenic to illustrate how movement therapy can be used to facilitate progression through early developmental stages. Therapy included the following stages: (1) therapist observing S and being observed, (2) therapist reflecting facial and body expressions, (3) using complementary efforts and an awareness of S's kinespheric preferences to foster the growth of the therapeutic relationship, (4) "shadowing" and "darting" behavior of the S, and (5) allowing S to "call the shots" in terms of use of space. 10 mo after initial therapy, S established relationships with certain peers and teachers. (9 ref).

472. Meyers, Edna O. (1971). **"Pride and Prejudice."** *Journal of Contemporary Psychotherapy,* 3(2), 105–110.
Discusses the pride of the Black man in the face of a history of humiliation and the prejudice of therapists despite their devotion to objectivity. The tendency of those in the helping professions to quickly diagnose pathology, to generalize about disinterest in learning, and to deplore certain housing and kinship patterns is discussed. It is concluded that "the Black man is not White, and there is no reason in the world, therefore, why he should be judged, evaluated, assessed and categorized as if he ought to be White."

473. Nail, Richard L.; Gunderson, Eric & Arthur, Ransom J. (1974). **Black–White differences in social background and military drug abuse patterns.** *American Journal of Psychiatry,* 131(10), 1097–1102.
Studied drug-abuse patterns and social backgrounds of 833 US Navy enlisted men (764 White and 69 Black) admitted to a drug rehabilitation center. Black Ss reported better school adjustment, less delinquency, and fewer difficulties in their home lives than did Whites. They had used heroin more frequently than Whites but were less involved with hallucinogenic drugs. It is suggested that different cultural patterns may underlie the drug-abuse behaviors of the 2 groups. White users seem to be expressing new varieties of delinquent or antisocial behavior, while Blacks are following long-established subcultural patterns of drug use. (25 ref).

474. Pugh, Thomas J. & Mudd, Emily H. (1971). **Attitudes of Black women and men toward using community services.** *Journal of Religion & Health,* 10(3), 256–277.
A standardized interview was administered to 102 Black people, 81 women following childbirth, and 21 men. The results were tabulated in the form of percentages, and their responses to "felt difficulties" were rank ordered. Male and female Ss had similar concerns, including worry about employment, education, amount of income, marital relations, sex, crowded housing, and birth control. Nearly 30% of both groups went to their mothers first for personal help.

475. Reardon, James P.; Tosi, Donald J. & Gwynne, Peter H. (1977). **The treatment of depression through Rational Stage Directed Hypnotherapy (RSDH): A case study.** *Psychotherapy: Theory, Research & Practice,* 14(1), 95–103.
Describes the treatment by RSDH of a 45-yr-old Black male with a schizophrenic disorder of the depressed type. Criterion measures included objective test results (MMPI, Tennessee Self-Concept Scale, Multiple Affect Adjective Checklist) and behavioral data. Following treatment, the client's thought processes were intact and rational, his anxiety was considerably diminished, and his mood disturbance was more controlled.

476. Small, Maurice M. (1975). **Treatment of stuttering: A case history.** *Perceptual & Motor Skills,* 41(3), 812.
Describes successful treatment of a 19-yr-old Black male which involved (a) behavioral analysis, (b) regulated breathing, (c) progress through a hierarchy of successive approximations of fluent speech with verbal reinforcement and punishment for fluency and dysfluency, and (d) initiation of conversations in increasingly difficult social situations outside the treatment room.

477. Sovner, Robert. (1975). **Case report of the Boston State Hospital, Dorchester, Massachusetts: LVI. The diagnosis and treatment of manic depressive illness in childhood and adolescence.** *Psychiatric Opinion,* 12(9), 37–42.
Presents the case of a 19-yr-old single Black male with a history of increasing difficulties, including psychiatric hospitalizations for withdrawn, antisocial, bizarre, and disorganized behavior. Placed on lithium carbonate after a tentative diagnosis of mania, he showed an immediate, rapid, and positive response. This patient's history and response to treatment suggest that children and adolescents may suffer from depression and mania.

478. Stoudenmire, John. (1973). **Behavioral treatment of voyeurism and possible symptom substitution.** *Psychotherapy: Theory, Research & Practice,* 10(4), 328–330.
Presents a case study that describes the relatively successful treatment of voyeuristic behaviors using behavioral techniques. A 44-yr-old Black male had been a peeping tom since the age of 13. He was of borderline mental retardation with an IQ of 77. He and his wife were asked to keep a record of his peeping urges and fantasies and from this they were encouraged to have intercourse or, if not feasible, for him to masturbate at these times. Assertive training for the patient was also initiated. Nine therapy sessions occurred over 15 mo. As these symptoms subsided, old ones recurred; namely, alcoholic excess and jealousies about an earlier and brief marriage of his wife. These were dealt with and resolved somewhat. The possibility of symptom substitution is discussed.

479. Uomoto, Jay M. (1986). **Examination of psychological distress in ethnic minorities from a learned helplessness framework.** *Professional Psychology: Research and Practice,* 17(5), 448–453.
Outlines L. Y. Abramson and colleague's (see PA, Vol 61:305) reformulated model of learned helplessness, in which behavioral deficits result from a noncontingency between response and outcome. The helplessness sequence is illustrated in a case of a 55-yr-old Black male whose deficits were attributed to events involving racial discrimination. Locus of control and attributional styles are discussed in the context of minority mental health issues. An attributional style grid is proposed as a way in which the clinician can identify appropriate clinical and community interventions on the basis of the particular salient attributions operating for the patient. In this grid, problems such as a patient's lack of skills, employer prejudice, or the state of the economy are classified as being global or specific, stable or unstable, and internal or external. The value of cognitive therapy, exposure to a controlling type

of experience, remediation of specific skills deficits, and social advocacy are discussed. (36 ref).

480. Weber, Dudley L.; Ruvolo, Charles & Cashin, Patrick. (1973). **Sudden death following electroconvulsive therapy.** *New York State Journal of Medicine,* 73(8), 1000–1001.
Reports a case of sudden death caused by massive pulmonary embolism following electroconvulsive therapy (ECT). A 59-yr-old Black male with chief complaint of depression of 1-wk duration was treated with chlorpromazine for 12 days without improvement. ECT was administered on the 13th and 14th days. He died 2 hrs after the 2nd treatment. Autopsy revealed emboli in both main branches of the pulmonary arteries. The role of ECT in embolism formation is discussed.

481. Weems, Luther B. & Wolowitz, Howard M. (1969). **The relevance of power theme's among male, Negro and White, paranoid and non-paranoid schizophrenics.** *International Journal of Social Psychiatry,* 15(3), 189–196.
Hypothesized and confirmed that (a) "Negro male paranoids have greater power concerns than Negro male nonparanoids; (b) White male paranoids have greater power concerns than White male nonparanoids; (c) male paranoids, regardless of race, have greater power concerns than male nonparanoids; (d) Negro males have greater power concerns than White males regardless of psychopathology; and (e) Negro male paranoids have greater power concerns than White male paranoids." Ss were 32 20–35 yr old male institutionalized patients, 8 from each group. The Shorkey-Wolowitz manual for scoring power themes in TAT stories was used. (24 ref).

Psychotherapy & Psychotherapeutic Counseling

482. Baumgartner, Dena D. (1986). **Sociodrama and the Vietnam combat veteran: A therapeutic release for a wartime experience.** *Journal of Group Psychotherapy, Psychodrama and Sociometry,* 39(1), 31–39.
Discusses the use of sociodrama in the treatment of Vietnam veterans with posttraumatic stress disorder. A pilot project involving sociodrama was implemented at a veterans outreach center. Black male veterans met for 8 weekly sessions, and pre- and posttreatment scores on a stress test were compared with those of a control group of veterans. Evaluations of the group were highly positive. It is suggested that sociodrama gave Ss a look at their role in society, provided structure to sessions, and increased group cohesion.

483. Evans, Leonard A.; Acosta, Frank X.; Yamamoto, Joe & Hurwicz, Margo-Lea. (1986). **Patient requests: Correlates and therapeutic implications for Hispanic, Black, and Caucasian patients.** *Journal of Clinical Psychology,* 42(1), 213–221.
States that a patient's reason for coming to a psychiatric outpatient clinic (his/her request for service) should be the focal point while the therapist develops an appropriate therapeutic plan for that patient. Data were collected on 81 male (mean age 31.4 yrs) and 92 female (mean age 34.4 yrs) Hispanic, Black, and White patients with regard to their reasons for coming to the clinic and selected demographic and process/outcome variables. Factor analysis generated 3 conceptual factors, which accounted for 13 reasons for coming to the clinic, such as reality contact, clarification, and social intervention. The relationship of these factors with selected demographic and therapy outcome variables was tested statistically, and implications for therapy with low-income and minority patients are discussed. (13 ref).

484. Gunnings, Thomas S. & Lipscomb, Wanda D. (1986). **Psychotherapy for Black men: A systemic approach.** Special Issue: The Black male: Critical counseling, developmental, and therapeutic issues: III. *Journal of Multicultural Counseling & Development,* 14(1), 17–24.

Suggests that a systemic approach to counseling (one that focuses on the environment as the key factor in determining attitudes, values, and behaviors) should be used in providing services to Black men. The model allows a view of clients' problems in the context of the systems that affect them on a daily basis. The model requires the counselor and the client to be provocative and proactive. (17 ref).

485. Hobbs, Sharon R. (1985). **Issues in psychotherapy with Black male adolescents in the inner city: A Black clinician's perspective.** Special Issue: The Black male: Critical counseling, developmental, and therapeutic issues: I. *Journal of Non-White Concerns in Personnel & Guidance,* 13(2), 79–87.
Considers that the adolescent is at a developmental period in which characteristics that make for easy involvement in a therapeutic relationship are most conflictual. The Black male adolescent living in an inner city reflects all of the conflicts of this period. Clinical work with adolescents often triggers intense countertransference in the therapist. For Black therapists working with Black male adolescents, countertransference can result in severe stress to the therapeutic relationship and premature termination if the therapist has not worked it through in his/her own analysis. Impoverished Black male adolescents usually present several problems that require involvement with various agencies and institutions, and it is easy to spend the better part of a therapy session helping the youngster juggle appointments and plan strategies for dealing with these interested parties. A major concern of Black male adolescents is the label given or implied by referral to a psychiatric clinic. Case reports of a Black 12-yr-old male and a Black 15-yr-old male are presented. (11 ref).

486. Jones, Billy E. & Gray, Beverly A. (1984). **Similarities and differences in Black men and women in psychotherapy.** *Journal of the National Medical Association,* 76(1), 21–27.
A survey of 93 psychiatrists (17 Black and 8 White females, and 34 Black and 34 White males) concerning the psychotherapy of Black men and women indicated that there were more similarities than differences between the men and women. Black male patients aged 31–40 yrs and Black women aged 26–30 yrs and 31–40 yrs were most frequently seen for treatment. The patients were usually married and employed in technical or semiprofessional occupations. Both men and women had depression as the most frequent presenting problem, with work-related and family problems the next most frequent presenting problems. Black men were most often diagnosed as having affective (nonpsychotic) disorders, with anxiety disorders the 2nd most frequent diagnosis. The reverse was true for women. Black men had aggression/passivity as the most frequent unconscious conflict and high/low self-esteem as the second. Again, the order of frequency was reversed for women. For both the men and women, the psychiatrists felt racism was an important issue to consider in the treatment process and found that rage was related to racism. (9 ref).

487. Jones, Billy E.; Gray, Beverly A. & Jospitre, Jacques. (1982). **Survey of psychotherapy with Black men.** *American Journal of Psychiatry,* 139(9), 1174–1177.
Surveyed 51 Black and 42 White psychiatrists regarding psychotherapy with Black patients. 99% of Black Ss and 48% of White Ss were currently treating Black patients. Their Black male patients were typically married, were 31–40 yrs old, had technical or semiprofessional occupations and some college education, sought treatment for depression or work-related problems, and remained in psychotherapy 13 wks or more. Aggression/passivity was the most frequent unconscious conflict among Black male patients, and developing new coping mechanisms was the most difficult treatment stage. Racism was often a causative factor in their pathology or was expressed as a symptom. (11 ref).

488. Jones, Billy E. & Gray, Beverly A. (1983). **Black males and psychotherapy: Theoretical issues.** *American Journal of Psychotherapy,* 37(1), 77–85.
Discusses events that would precipitate a Black male's need for psychotherapy, where he would seek treatment, and conflicts presented in treatment. The role of racism, both in relation to intrapsychic conflicts and external stress, is discussed. Four major conflict areas from which problems may arise during psychotherapy are self-esteem, sex, aggression, and dependency. (14 ref).

489. Juni, Samuel. (1982). **On the conceptualization and treatment of catatonia.** *American Journal of Psychoanalysis,* 42(4), 327–334.
Suggests that all psychopathology, including schizophrenia, represents a tactical reorganization of behavior, cognition, and affect initiated by the ego's self-preservation drive. The conceptualization of catatonia is accepted as a defensive reaction; catatonic schizophrenia includes a physical impediment of psychic origin that affects motility and behavioral expression and that absolves the ego from devising other means of containing the threatening material intrapsychically. Reaction formation is the primary dynamic in hysteria and catatonia. Compulsion and conversion reaction differ only in the domain of this implicit defense. Although the threatening affect is bereft of insight in both conditions, there is a clear dichotomy between compulsion and conversion with respect to insight of the implicit defense. Conversion reaction is established as a particular subcategory of catatonia, insofar as defensive dynamics are concerned. Whereas the ego strengths of the conversion patient confine the deliberate disorganization induced to block the behavior expression of a specific threatening affect, such insulation is not feasible in catatonia, where total mobility arrest is the ego response to affective expression threat. For an intervention perspective, one must capitalize on the organization/disorganization constellation of the pathological syndrome and mobilize the theoretically static cognitive energy for therapeutic purposes. (22 ref).

490. Krakenberg, Susan J. (1981). **An application of American Sign Language to the psychiatric setting.** *American Journal of Orthopsychiatry,* 51(4), 715–718.
Discusses theoretical dimensions of the use of American Sign Language with hearing individuals. The case of a 9-yr-old Black male is presented to illustrate the use of signs with an emotionally disturbed child as a form of clinical intervention to foster language and reading development and behavioral controls. (21 ref).

491. Lange, Gusty. (1980). **Sexually provocative behavior of older male, acting-out adolescents within a multi-media group setting.** *Pratt Institute Creative Arts Therapy Review,* 1, 18–24.
A White female therapist describes her field assignment at a special education school where she worked with a group of 6 Black males (17–20 yrs old) referred to the school for various emotional, behavioral, and adaptive problems. The focus is on sexually provocative behavior as manifested in the therapeutic relationship and in the use of multimedia and expressive modalities. (13 ref).

492. Larrabee, Marva J. (1986). **Helping reluctant Black males: An affirmation approach.** Special Issue: The Black male: Critical counseling, developmental, and therapeutic issues: III. *Journal of Multicultural Counseling & Development,* 14(1), 25–38.
Contends that the affirmation approach to counseling (AAC) provides a framework in which to work effectively with Black, male clients and presents a case example of a 14-yr-old Black, male student with repeated fighting behavior. It is suggested that the AAC offers counselors a flexible set of verbal skills that permit the building of rapport with reluctant, Black, male clients while avoiding the potential damage to self-esteem that occurs when these clients are persuaded to change by counselor-influencing techniques. (46 ref).

493. Minrath, Marilyn. (1985). **Breaking the race barrier: The White therapist in interracial psychotherapy.** *Journal of Psychosocial Nursing & Mental Health Services,* 23(8), 19–24.
Argues that racial and ethnic stereotyping is a defensive maneuver used by patient and therapist to cope with the anxiety aroused by the interracial nature of the relationship. It is noted that through the reflective process of analyzing his/her feelings and reactions to the ethnic minority patient, the White therapist can develop an inner clarity that serves as a resource for coping with the unique conflicts presented in interracial psychotherapy. It is also suggested that exploring the patient's cultural background and inquiring about customs, lifestyle, language, and the use of idioms express the therapist's desire to learn about and understand the sociocultural world of the patient and communicate a genuine interest while nurturing the development of empathy. The case histories of 2 Black males (aged 16 and 28 yrs), a 35-yr-old Black female, and a 24-yr-old Puerto Rican female are presented to illustrate the importance of accepting the patient's individuality in the development of the interracial therapeutic relationship. (13 ref).

494. Pope, Bonita R. (1986). **Black men in interracial relationships: Psychological and therapeutic issues.** Special Issue: The Black male: Critical counseling, developmental, and therapeutic issues: III. *Journal of Multicultural Counseling & Development,* 14(1), 10–16.
Discusses the possible counseling needs of a Black man involved in an interracial relationship. It is suggested that needs will depend on motivations for developing such a relationship. It is concluded that the aim of therapy for the Black man is to help him understand value and cultural conflicts and to foster greater knowledge of self, self-confidence, and racial dignity. (15 ref).

495. Wesson, K. Alan. (1975). **The Black man's burden: The White clinician.** *Black Scholar,* 6(10), 13–18.
Discusses the problems White clinicians have understanding the life and culture of their Black patients. A dialogue between a White psychiatrist and a Black patient is presented to illustrate these problems.

Behavior Therapy & Behavior Modification

496. Braud, Lendell W.; Lupin, Mimi N. & Braud, William G. (1975). **The use of electromyographic biofeedback in the control of hyperactivity.** *Journal of Learning Disabilities,* 8(7), 420–425.
Discusses the case of a 6.5-yr-old Black hyperactive male who was taught to reduce his muscular activity and tension through the use of electromyographic biofeedback for 11 sessions. The S was instructed to turn off a tone which signaled the presence of muscular tension. Muscular tension and activity decreased both within and across sessions. A follow-up session after a 7-mo interval indicated that he continued to be able to control hyperactivity. Improvement was seen in the S's behavior in class and at home as long as he continued to practice and use, both at home and at school, the techniques he had learned in the laboratory. The S also improved by a range of 25–56 mo on 4 subtests of the Illinois Test of Psycholinguistic Abilities. Improvement also occurred on a group-administered achievement test at school. These gains indicate that pretest scores were depressed by hyperactivity and poor attention. There was also improvement in the S's self-confidence and self-concept.

497. Fantuzzo, John; Harrell, Kathy & McLeod, Mary. (1979). **Across-subject generalization of attending behavior as a function of self-regulation training.** *Child Behavior Therapy,* 1(4), 313–321.
Examined the effect of a target child's self-regulation of attentive behavior on the attentive behavior of a nonreinforced adjacent peer. Ss were 2 Black male 3rd graders. The target S received training in self-regulation of attentive behavior; the peer received no training. An ABAB withdrawal design was used to assess the degree of generalization of treatment effect across Ss. During the treatment phase, the target S gave himself points contingent on his attentiveness, which were exchanged for back-up reinforcers. Results show that increases in attentive behavior by the target S were paralleled in the nontargeted peer. (31 ref).

498. Goldenberg, Edward E. & DeNinno, John. (1977). **A weight-loss program using self-control techniques in a correctional facility: An experimental case study.** *Offender Rehabilitation,* 1(3), 283–290.
The S of this study was a 27-yr-old Black male of average intelligence, with a severe eating disorder. He was 5 ft 8 in tall and weighed 280 lbs and was incarcerated at the Wisconsin Correctional Institute. Treatment, resulting in a 40-lb weight loss, consisted of 25 weekly sessions with 4 distinct phases: (a) treatment, 3 mo; (b) reversal, 1 mo; (c) treatment, 3 mo; and (d) follow-up, 7 mo later. Follow-up indicated weight stabilization. Significant factors in achieving this result were the S's drive, the therapist's insistence, and constant reminders. The caution is expressed, however, that data from case studies do not necessarily generalize. (16 ref).

Health Care Services

499. Brennan, Thomas P.; Gedrich, Amy E.; Jacoby, Susan E.; Tardy, Michael J. et al. (1986). **Forensic social work: Practice and vision.** *Social Casework,* 67(6), 340–350.
Presents a conceptual paradigm for forensic social work by describing theoretical and clinical aspects as drawn from work in Cook County, Illinois. The forensic social worker has both social work and law enforcement functions. Providing treatment and protecting the community are aspects of integrating the goals of criminal justice and mental health; the individual forensic social worker implements a practical link between the mental health and criminal justice systems. Case examples illustrate the types of clients referred to forensic social workers and the issues of assessment and treatment. The forensic social worker frequently deals with clients with problems that are too difficult for the social service programs. In the future, a more assertive approach to crisis intervention is planned for the social service department.

500. Carter, James H. (1984). **Providing clinical services for the unserved and underserved populations: The Black patient.** Fifth Annual Cross-Cultural Conference: Crises, changes, and a holistic approach to survival (1983, Myrtle Beach, SC). *Psychiatric Forum,* 12(2), 32–37.
Discusses the provision of services for special Black populations—the elderly, young males, and Vietnam veterans. A starting point for effective mental health intervention with elderly Blacks is independent cultural education by the therapist. This must include recognition of the traumatization of racism. While there are limited opportunities for elderly Blacks to participate in the American dream of social and economic advancement, many Blacks achieve a satisfaction with age. Black men represent special problems because they are one of the most powerless groups in America. Strongly related to the issue of masculinity are problems encountered in achieving manhood. These problems have complex causes that involve the stereotype of the castrating Black mother and high rates of unemployment, crime involvement, and substance abuse. During the Vietnam era, Black draftees represented the more educated and socially adjusted members of their communities, and their postwar failures to readjust to society have helped to diminish the Black communities' strengths. (13 ref).

501. Hendricks, Leo E. (1980). **Unwed adolescent fathers: Problems they face and their sources of social support.** *Adolescence,* 15(60), 861–869.
In a pilot study, interviews were held with 20 Black, adolescent, unwed fathers. No dominant theme presented itself among the problems presented by the Ss; problems ranged from inadequate income to "disadvantage to be young and try to raise a kid in a proper way." Findings in regard to sources of social support were more clear-cut. When asked, "Who would you go to first with a problem?" 95% of Ss indicated their family. 75% of the time the person providing support was either the mother or father of the S. Peers as a source of social support were strongly rejected, as were clergymen and school teachers. None of the Ss indicated that they would seek out a social service agency for help. However, when asked, "If a teenage parenting agency offered services to unwed fathers, would you be interested in receiving such services?" 95% of Ss gave a positive answer. Based on analysis of the problems faced by Ss, parenting agencies might offer services in such areas as parenting education, vocational guidance, and psychosocial counseling. (8 ref).

502. Hendricks, Leo E. (1983). **Suggestions for reaching unmarried Black adolescent fathers.** *Child Welfare,* 62(2), 141–146.
Reported a study of 95 unwed Black adolescent fathers. Results indicate that 49% of the Ss had had their first coital experiences with a girl by the time they were 12 yrs old. 54% of the Ss were 17 yrs or younger when they became a father, 65% were likely to have come from a family with 5 or more children, and 60% were likely to have come from families where fathers were present in the home. When asked how they considered the relationship between themselves and the young mothers, both before and after the pregnancy, 60% of the fathers said that it was one of love. With regard to their children, 98% expressed an interest in their children's future. It is suggested that human service workers should offer practical help to these fathers in serving them and that the use of peer counselors may be advisable in opening up communication among the fathers so that information concerning such matters as fathers' rights, sex education, the role of a father, and consumer education can be discussed freely. (6 ref).

503. Hilliard, Asa G. (1985). **A framework for focused counseling on the African-American man.** Special Issue: The Black male: Critical counseling, developmental, and therapeutic issues: I. *Journal of Non-White Concerns in Personnel & Guidance,* 13(2), 72–78.
Considers that the counselor of male African-Americans must remember that their environment is characterized by unique cultural and socio-political forces that must be understood, and in some cases, used by the therapist, in providing needed assistance. A critical review of models of meanings in counseling and psychotherapy, goals for counseling and psychotherapy, historical and cultural background, and changes in training for therapists are required. Although there are some special differences in treatment received by the African-American man and the African-American woman, at the basic level their situations are the same. Conceptually, what matters is that African-Americans be seen as a people with all the similarities and diversities typical of any people. It is the people as a whole who experience general conditions that call for unique approaches to counseling and psychotherapy. (15 ref).

504. Jones, Yolanda E. (1985). **The double-whammy.** *Emotional First Aid: A Journal of Crisis Intervention,* 2(4), 39–41.

Addresses the issue of crisis intervention with the hearing-impaired person (deaf or hard-of-hearing) by persons who work in a mental health facility and who have little or no knowledge of deafness or sign language skills. The case of a deaf 19-yr-old Black male who had no communication skills is presented. (2 ref).

505. June, Lee N. (1986). **Enhancing the delivery of mental health and counseling services to Black males: Critical agency and provider responsibilities.** Special Issue: The Black male: Critical counseling, developmental, and therapeutic issues: III. *Journal of Multicultural Counseling & Development,* 14(1), 39–45.
Addresses the issue of the responsibility of agencies and providers to create effective delivery of counseling services to Black males. It is suggested that as agencies become open to a seeking mode of service delivery, have diverse staff members, use an aggressive outreach approach, destigmatize the counseling process, become knowledgeable of Black psychology and other conceptual approaches, and develop relationships with agencies of high visibility in the Black community, more innovative ways of counseling Black men will result. (25 ref).

506. Lovitt, Robert. (1984). **Rorschach interpretation in a multidisciplinary hospital setting.** *Professional Psychology: Research and Practice,* 15(2), 244–250.
Presents a case study that illustrates the use of the Rorschach to provide information used in resolving an acute behavioral conflict between an 18-yr-old Black male patient and medical personnel in a hospital setting. The S was perceived as "obnoxious" rather than as emotionally dysfunctional because of a clash between his style of responding to an illness and the pattern of medical care administered. Rorschach interpretation was used to reorient the medical staff about the nature of their medical care and to provide a more accurate understanding of the S's psychological distress. (8 ref).

507. Marohn, Richard C.; Offer, Daniel; Ostrov, Eric & Trujillo, Jaime. (1979). **Four psychodynamic types of hospitalized juvenile delinquents.** *Adolescent Psychiatry,* 7, 466–483.
Reports on data obtained in a 1969–1974 study of 30 male and 25 female Black (18 Ss) and White (38 Ss) juvenile delinquents hospitalized at a state psychiatric institute and engaged in a comprehensive individual, family, group, and milieu therapy program. Factor analysis of psychometric and demographic data yielded 4 psychodynamic types of delinquents: impulsive, narcissistic, depressed, and borderline. Case illustrations are included. (24 ref).

508. McKenzie, V. Michael. (1986). **Ethnographic findings on West Indian-American clients.** *Journal of Counseling & Development,* 65(1), 40–44.
Collected ethnographic data on 9 8–13 yr old Black, English-speaking, West-Indian males by observing and interacting with the Ss for 6 mo. Analyses of the data provided themes and guides for collection of a 2nd set of data obtained during quasi-structured interviews with the original 9 Ss, an additional 6 Black male 15–17 yr old high school students with West-Indian backgrounds, and 11 counselors. The culturally relevant factors that were extricated from the interviews were organized into 3 categories: family orientations, family and peer group relationships, and adolescents' personal development. Findings indicate that West-Indian students have strong taboos against seeking counseling. Also, their cultural background affects their career choices, and their biculturalism induces conflict within their families. (17 ref).

509. Morycz, Richard K. (1985). **Caregiving strain and the desire to institutionalize family members with Alzheimer's disease: Possible predictors and model development.** *Research on Aging,* 7(3), 329–361.
Determined whether the strain experienced by caregivers of relatives with Alzheimer's disease is strongly related to the desire of families to institutionalize their older members. Data were collected from structured interviews and a telephone follow-up survey of 80 families caring for Alzheimer patients (average patient age 78 yrs; average caregiver age 55 yrs). Extent of family burden, stressors such as functional deficits and incapacities of the patient, environmental factors, family strain, and vigilance/disruptiveness were assessed. The desire of a caregiver to institutionalize a patient with Alzheimer's disease was found to be greater when the caregiver experienced increased strain or burden, when a patient was widowed, when more physical labor was involved in caregiving tasks, and when the patient lived alone. Intensity of family strain (or felt stress) could be best predicted by the availability to the caregiver of social support: Less support implied more strain. However, for male caregiving groups and for all Black caregivers, strain did not play a significant role in predicting the desire to institutionalize. (4 p ref).

510. Newton, Patricia A. (1983). **An evaluation of the cost effectiveness of day hospitalization for Black male schizophrenics.** *Journal of the National Medical Association,* 75(3), 273–285.
Compared the relative cost effectiveness of day hospitalization to inpatient treatment in a group of 28 18–24 yr old Black schizophrenic males who were assigned to the inpatient control group or to the day hospital experimental group. Global Assessment Scale scores were measured upon intake, at the time of discharge, and at the 3-mo follow-up to determine the level of patient functioning for each treatment group. Cost outcome measures were made for each program and a side-by-side cost effective analysis was conducted between the two. Results reveal evidence that day treatment was superior to inpatient care at a lower cost for a longer period of time. (21 ref).

511. Proctor, Enola K. & Rosen, Aaron. (1981). **Expectations and preferences for counselor race and their relation to intermediate treatment outcomes.** *Journal of Counseling Psychology,* 28(1), 40–46.
The expectations and preferences of 26 White and 8 Black male veterans for the race of their counselor were investigated at the time the clients entered treatment in a midwestern outpatient mental health clinic. In addition, Ss' satisfaction with treatment, measured by a 3-factor self-rating scale and dropout status, were analyzed in relation to Ss' expectations and preferences for counselor race and the racial makeup of the treatment dyad. Results indicate that White and Black clients alike expected their counselor to be White. About half of the White Ss and half of the Blacks indicated that they had no preferences. However, the significant association between race and S preference for counselor race suggests that Ss expressing preferences preferred counselors of their own race. Dropout and satisfaction with treatment were not related to the nature of Ss' racial expectations and preferences or to the racial makeup of the treatment dyads. (35 ref).

512. Ralston, Penny A. & Griggs, Mildred B. (1985). **Factors affecting utilization of senior centers: Race, sex, and socioeconomic differences.** *Journal of Gerontological Social Work,* 9(1), 99–111.
Interviews with 110 older adults (mean age 71 yrs; 46% Black, 52% female, 54% from white-collar backgrounds, and 53% married) revealed that Blacks were significantly more committed than Whites to attending senior center programs. Males received significantly more encouragement from their spouses to attend than did females. White-collar Black females received significantly more encouragement to attend from confidants and children than any other group. "Lack of interesting activities" was a major obstacle to senior center utilization for white-collar respondents. (18 ref).

513. Rau, John H. & Kaye, Nanci. (1977). **Joint hospitalization of mother and child: Evaluation in vivo.** *Bulletin of the Menninger Clinic,* 41(4), 385–394.
Describes the effects of joint hospitalization of a male 10-mo-old and his 17-yr-old unwed Black mother, diagnosed as suffering from an adjustment reaction of adolescence with depression. Implications for wider use of joint psychiatric hospitalization for mothers and young children or infants are discussed. (17 ref).

514. Schaefer, Charles E.; Kelsey, John W. & Fridovich, Joel M. (1977). **A comparison of racial ethnic preferences among boys in residential treatment.** *Devereux Forum,* 12(1), 46–49.
Compared racial and ethnic group preferences of 142 Black, White, and Latin males (ages 7–14 yrs) in 2 living units of a residential treatment center for emotionally disturbed boys. Sociometric data were obtained as measures of group cohesiveness among children with differing racial and ethnic characteristics. Results indicate that when one group was dominant in numbers, the Black children chose disproportionately more Black children than White children as those with whom they wanted to sit during a bus trip. However, when no one group had a clear majority in numbers, better integration resulted among children of differing racial and ethnic backgrounds.

515. Sladen, Bernard J. (1982). **Effects of race and socioeconomic status on the perception of process variables in counseling.** *Journal of Counseling Psychology,* 29(6), 560–566.
Analyzed the effects of race and socioeconomic status (SES) on the perception of process variables in counseling, including judged counselor empathy, judged counselor–client cognitive similarity, and attraction. The study used a 2 by 12 by 2 by 6 design (race of S, tape order, SES of client, race of counselor and client) with repeated measures on the SES of client variable and the race of counselor and client variable. Following empathy training, 12 Black and 12 White undergraduate middle-class males listened to 12 specially prepared counselor–client taped dialogs and rated the counselor and client on each tape on the process variables being researched. All hypotheses were confirmed. Both Black and White Ss gave highest counselor empathy ratings, client–counselor attraction and cognitive similarity ratings, and client improvement ratings to matchings in which the counselor and client were similar over race and social class, and they gave lowest ratings when the counselor and client were dissimilar over race and social class. Effects of client accent were generally not significant. (26 ref).

516. Terrell, Francis & Terrell, Sandra. (1984). **Race of counselor, client sex, cultural mistrust level, and premature termination from counseling among Black clients.** *Journal of Counseling Psychology,* 31(3), 371–375.
Administered an inventory designed to assess the extent to which they trusted White people to 135 27–41 yr old Black clients as they visited a community mental health center for the 1st time. Equal numbers of Ss were assigned to a Black and White counselor for an intake interview. Analyses of counselor's race, mistrust level, and Ss' sex in relationship to premature termination of counseling showed that significant percentages of shared variance were found for counselors' race and trust level. It is suggested that Black clients who are distrustful of White people should be seen by a Black counselor, at least initially. (14 ref).

517. Thomas, Charles W. (1985). **A view from counseling of adult Afro-American males.** Special Issue: The Black male: Critical counseling, developmental, and therapeutic issues: I. *Journal of Non-White Concerns in Personnel & Guidance,* 13(2), 43–53.
Discusses counseling implications of the psychological characteristics of the adult Black male. It is argued that recent efforts to improve the welfare of Black Americans have not had much impact, largely because there has been little change in conceptual frameworks. Enhancement of the human condition requires a network of political, psychological concepts that are used to direct beneficial responses in society. Human services for Afro-Americans must be comprehensive if they are to be useful in correcting the ills that come from individual victimization and group dehumanization. Of particular concern is the adult Afro-American male, who is a high-risk victim of the inequities in society. Counseling can be useful when certain conditions place the helping relationship in the context of a shared partnership. This assumes that the counselor is not only technically skilled but is competent and secure in interpersonal relationships. It also assumes that the counselor is well-grounded in Afrocentric values and understands how socioeconomic issues are used to affect the behavior of Afro-American males. (39 ref).

518. Walco, Gary A. & Dampier, Carlton D. (1987). **Chronic pain in adolescent patients.** *Journal of Pediatric Psychology,* 12(2), 215–225.
Suggests that present methods of pain treatment are based on models of acute and chronic pain. The interface between these 2 models is discussed in relation to treating chronically ill adolescents who cope poorly with pain and are overly dependent on the medical system. Case material, involving 2 Black males (aged 20 and 16 yrs) with sickle-cell anemia is presented, and developmental issues (cognitive, independence and mastery, peer relations, and positive coping) are described to highlight the apparent key factors in the development and perpetuation of the problem. Treatment strategies and suggestions for future research are offered.

519. Warfield, John L. & Marion, Robert L. (1985). **Counseling the Black male.** Special Issue: The Black male: Critical counseling, developmental, and therapeutic issues: I. *Journal of Non-White Concerns in Personnel & Guidance,* 13(2), 54–71.
Argues that counseling the Black male within the context of US society is not an easy task for the helping professional. The counselor who seeks to intervene in the lives of Black males will face a population operating basically under 2 propositions: Proposition 1 holds that many of their problems have been imposed upon them by a racist society; Proposition 2 holds that established support systems have failed to ameliorate the problems of the Black male. Successful counselors will appreciate the importance of religion in the lives of Black people and will recognize that some Black concepts are culture bound and others are universal. The Black man, frequently troubled by problems of racism, discrimination, and poverty, is hard-pressed to maintain a quality of life that will sustain him in a state of positive mental health in American society. (49 ref).

Rehabilitation & Penology

520. Blank, Ronald J. (1981). **The partial transsexual.** *American Journal of Psychotherapy,* 35(1), 107–112.
The partial transsexual is described as a person who has begun the surgical and hormonal process of sex change but, for varying reasons, has failed to complete the process and is therefore neither male nor female. The case history of a 21-yr-old Black transsexual male is presented to demonstrate the difficulty of society and its institutions to cope with changes in sociocultural values predicated on scientific breakthroughs. (9 ref).

521. Brunswick, Ann F. & Messeri, Peter A. (1986). **Pathways to heroin abstinence: A longitudinal study of urban Black youth.** *Advances in Alcohol & Substance Abuse,* 5(3), 111–135.
Studied the effectiveness of treatment in reducing the duration of heroin careers, with special focus on gender differ-

ences. The sample consisted of 43 male and 26 female urban Black youth, aged 18–23 yrs. Simple hazard probability analysis confirmed that males and females did not differ significantly in their cumulative probabilities of abstinence from heroin. The more elaborated event-history model demonstrated, however, that treatment played a significantly different role among men and women in attaining abstinence. While a man's likelihood of abstinence was only marginally greater with treatment than without it, women's likelihood of abstinence was significantly increased by entering treatment.

522. Cellini, H. R. & Lorenz, Jerome R. (1983). **Job Club group training with unemployed offenders.** *Federal Probation,* 46(3), 46–50.
65 Black male offenders (aged 16–26 yrs) who participated in Job Club Training were administered the Sensation Seeking Scale (SSS) and the Vocabulary subtest of the California Achievement Test (CAT) 4 wks posttraining. Scores were compared for employed and unemployed Ss. No significant difference was found for CAT scores. SSS scores, however, indicated significant differences between employed and unemployed Ss: More high sensation seekers were found in the employed than in the nonemployed group. Since 46% of Ss reported being employed full time 1 mo after completing the program, the program was considered effective. However, this employment rate was significantly lower than in previous research (other Job Club success rates varied between 87 and 100% employment). (12 ref).

523. Copemann, Chester D. & Shaw, Paula L. (1975). **The effect of therapeutic intervention on the assessment scores of narcotic addicts.** *International Journal of the Addictions,* 10(5), 921–926.
Administered the WISC, the Lazarus Assertiveness Questionnaire, and the Eysenck Personality Inventory to 6 male and 8 female (mean age, 22.5 yrs) Black narcotics addicts in a behaviorally oriented halfway house. Pre- and posttreatment scores were compared. Results show that there were significant increases in WISC Full Scale, Verbal, and Performance IQs. A significant increase in assertiveness was also observed. There were no changes in extraversion or neuroticism. Results support previous studies of psychological test performance of addicts and suggest that at the time of addiction, drug users may not be functioning at their full intellectual capacities.

524. Friedman, C. Jack & Mann, Fredrica. (1976). **Recidivism: The fallacy of prediction.** *International Journal of Offender Therapy & Comparative Criminology,* 20(2), 153–164.
Conducted a 2-yr follow up study to assess the accuracy of staff member predictions of recidivism rates for 137 Black and 99 White court-adjudicated male adolescents from 3 residential correctional institutions. Administrators at each institution had an appropriate staff member complete a follow-up Institution Evaluation Questionnaire (assessing future recidivism probability) for each S. Four measures of the extent of illegal criminal acts committed by Ss during the follow-up were used as recidivism criteria: (a) the Sellin-Wolfgang score, (b) the global recidivism score, (c) the nonviolent recidivism score, and (d) the violent recidivism score. Four other measures were also examined in relation to predictions of recidivism: (a) the total weighted offenses score, (b) the most serious offense measure, (c) the total self-reported delinquency, and (d) the staff's feeling toward the youth. Data analyses revealed statistically significant correlations between staff predictions and police records on 3 out of 4 measures; no significant difference among the 3 staffs' accuracy of predictions; and (c) a significant negative correlation between staff predictions of recidivism and liking of Ss. Since the staff's overall recidivism predictions were only slightly better than chance, findings are interpreted as evidence of the fallibility of human judgment and the need for

better means of determining youth's readiness for discharge from correction institutions.

525. Haber, Gilda M. (1983). **The realization of potential by Lorton, D.C. inmates with UDC college education compared to those without UDC education.** *Journal of Offender Counseling, Services & Rehabilitation,* 7(3–4), 37–55.
Identified the differences between 56 Black male prison inmates enrolled in college classes through the University of the District of Columbia (UDC) and 62 age- and sex-matched inmates not enrolled in UDC classes (Groups 1 and 2, respectively), using interviews by trained fellow inmates and scores on the Personal Orientation Inventory (POI). Group 1 Ss came from families where the father was significantly more often present and where the father, mother or wife often had some college education. They were significantly more satisfied with their educational program (college) than were Group 2 Ss (who were enrolled in high school equivalency or vocational courses). More Group 1 Ss were 1st offenders, but they also were charged with more violent crimes than those in Group 2. Ss in Group 1 had fewer "street" and more incarcerated friends. On the POI, Ss in Group 2 scored lower than Ss in Group 1, indicating that they used time less fruitfully, lacked confidence in own judgments, had low valuation of own potential, showed low level of trust in men, and could not cope with apparent dichotomies such as good–evil and carnal–spiritual. High scores of Ss in Group 1 suggested flexibility, sensitivity to own needs, spontaneous action, acceptance of self (including own aggressiveness and anger), and capacity for intimate relations. (7 ref).

526. Johnson, Sally & Edinger, Jack D. (1981). **Treating the multiple problem exhibitionist fantasies in a restrictive setting.** *Corrective & Social Psychiatry & Journal of Behavior Technology, Methods & Therapy,* 27(2), 100–104.
Describes the successful treatment of a 36-yr-old Black male exhibitionist in a prison setting using nonaversive behavior techniques. The case is considered unique due to the treatment setting, treatment method, and the existence of multiple diagnoses in the S. The described method may be particularly applicable to exhibitionists suffering from other psychiatric and medical problems. (15 ref).

527. Levi, Mario et al. (1977). **The study of intellectual ability and scholastic achievement of institutionalized men drug addicts belonging to three different racial-ethnic groups.** *International Journal of the Addictions,* 12(4), 451–457.
Administered the Raven Progressive Matrices and the Comprehensive Test of Basic Skills tests to 364 institutionalized male drug addicts. In addition, information was collected on racial-ethnic background (White, Black, Mexican-American), school grade completed, and years away from school of all the Ss. Means, standard deviations, *F*-analysis of variances, and *t* tests between ethnic racial groups were calculated. Results indicate that in spite of overlap, White Ss always received significantly higher mean scores than the other 2 groups. White and Black Ss dropped out of school practically at the same grade level (between 10th and 11th), while Mexican-Americans dropped out of school earlier (at the 9th grade).

528. Ollendick, Thomas H.; Elliott, William & Matson, Johnny L. (1980). **Locus of control as related to effectiveness in a behavior modification program for juvenile delinquents.** *Journal of Behavior Therapy & Experimental Psychiatry,* 11(4), 259–262.
Employed a fixed token economy and a flexible behavioral contracting system in a treatment program for 24 Black and 66 White male juvenile delinquents (mean age 14.6 yrs). The Nowicki-Strickland Locus of Control Scale was administered, and its relationship to program effectiveness was assessed. Results indicate that internally oriented Ss committed fewer offenses and evidenced lower recidivism rates than did externally oriented Ss. Results are viewed to affirm the basic

principles underlying the social learning approach to treatment—namely, that behavior is learned and maintained through a reciprocal interaction between the person and his environment. (17 ref).

529. Rosenblatt, Arthur I. & Pritchard, David A. (1978). **Moderators of racial differences on the MMPI.** *Journal of Consulting & Clinical Psychology,* 46(6), 1572–1573.
In a study with 104 Black and 191 White male prison inmates, multiple discriminant analysis of MMPI scores between high-IQ White, high-IQ Black, low-IQ White, and low-IQ Black Ss yielded 2 significant canonical variates. Results suggest that racial differences on the MMPI do not occur in all racial comparisons but instead are restricted to low-IQ groups. (8 ref).

530. Simpson, D. Dwayne & Savage, L. James. (1980). **Drug abuse treatment readmissions and outcomes: Three-year follow-up of DARP patients.** *Archives of General Psychiatry,* 37(8), 896–901.
Obtained data from 2,178 Black and White males selected from a national follow-up sample of persons admitted to treatment in the Drug Abuse Reporting Program (DARP) during 1969–1972. Follow-up treatment modes included methadone maintenance, residence in a therapeutic community, outpatient drug-free treatment, outpatient detoxification treatment, and a comparison group whose members completed intake only and did not return for treatment in the DARP. Treatment readmission patterns were examined in relation to outcome measures for illicit drug use, alcohol use, employment, and criminality over time. Findings show that there were strong, reliable associations between readmission patterns and posttreatment outcomes, which suggested there were beneficial effects (including impressive behavioral improvements) of drug abuse treatment. (26 ref).

PROFESSIONAL PERSONNEL AND PROFESSIONAL ISSUES

531. Berman, Judith. (1979). **Counseling skills used by Black and White male and female counselors.** *Journal of Counseling Psychology,* 26(1), 81–84.
A videotape of culturally varied client vignettes was viewed by Black and White males and females, all of whom had at least some counselor-related training. Participants responded in writing to the question, "What would you say to this person?" The data were coded according to a counseling skills scoring system. Black males and females tended to use the more active expression skills (e.g., directions, expressions of content, and interpretations) with greater frequency than did Whites. White males and females tended to use a high percentage of attending skills. In particular, White females used reflections of feeling frequently, and White males tended to respond with questions. While race appeared as a source of strong effect, one of the major implications of this study was the relative absence of significant sex differences. Discussion focuses on cultural variation in counseling styles, implications for training, and promotion of diversity among professionals. (10 ref).

532. Berman, Judith. (1979). **Individual versus societal focus: Problem diagnoses of Black and White male and female counselors.** *Journal of Cross-Cultural Psychology,* 10(4), 497–507.
Analyzed the problem diagnoses given by 81 US Black and White male and female counselors (average age 27 yrs) to determine whether they were individually or societally focused. After viewing a videotape of culturally varied client vignettes, the participating counselors responded in writing to the question, "What do you think is the problem?" The data were scored according to an individual–societal continuum.

Race appeared as a strong source of difference: Black males and females tended to use a societal focus more frequently than did the White males and females. However, while the Whites' diagnoses were almost exclusively individual, the Blacks employed more equal distribution of individually and societally focused responses. A major finding of this study is the relatively weak significance of sex differences. (33 ref).

533. Bowman, Marjorie A. (1986). **Specialty choice of Black physicians.** *Journal of the National Medical Association,* 78(1), 13–15.
Analyzed data on 2,168 male and 1,375 female Black residents and 53,826 male and 17,337 female non-Black residents in medical schools in 1984 to examine the representation of Blacks in various medical fields. It was found that Black females, relative to non-Black females, are overrepresented in family practice; non-Black females, relative to Black females, are overrepresented in neonatal/perinatal medicine. Black females, compared to Black males, are overrepresented in family practice, nuclear radiology, urology, and transitional year; Black males are overrepresented in general surgery. Compared to their non-Black counterparts, both Black males and females are overrepresented in primary care but underrepresented in surgery and the other specialties. Racial and sex differences in medical specialties are attributed to desire to serve Black patient populations, perceived and real discrimination by other physicians and by patients, and specific factors related to medical schools. (5 ref).

EDUCATIONAL PSYCHOLOGY

534. Abramson, Edward E. (1971). **Levels of aspiration of Negro 9th grade males in integrated and segregated schools.** *Psychological Reports,* 29(1), 258.
Compared the levels of aspiration of 22 Negro 9th-grade males attending an integrated school with an equal number of Negro youth attending a segregated school. The integrated Ss had significantly higher levels of aspiration as measured by a 15-trial digit-letter substitution test. The correlation between achievement and aspiration was significant for segregated Ss but insignificant for integrated Ss.

535. Ansell, Edgar M. & Hansen, James C. (1971). **Patterns in vocational development of urban youth.** *Journal of Counseling Psychology,* 18(6), 505–508.
Investigated the vocational maturity of 375 lower- and middle-class 8th–12th grade boys. Mean scores on the Readiness for Vocational Planning Scale showed that the lower-class Ss were slower in developing vocational maturity. A univariate analysis of covariance indicated a significant difference among the groups, and Scheffe post hoc comparisons found the differences to be in Grades 10, 11, and 12 between lower- and middle-class Ss without regard to race. Lower-class Black and White Ss did not differ significantly in their vocational maturity throughout the 5 grades.

536. Backman, Margaret E. (1971). **Patterns of mental abilities of adolescent males and females from different ethnic and socioeconomic backgrounds.** *Proceedings of the Annual Convention of the American Psychological Association,* 6(Pt 2), 511–512.
Examined patterns of mental abilities, composed of group means of 6 factors. The sample, consisting of 2,925 12th graders from the nationwide study Project TALENT, included Jewish-Whites, non-Jewish-Whites, Negroes, and Orientals from 2 socioeconomic status (SES) levels. The statistical model was an analysis of variance. Ss exhibited patterns of mental abilities characteristic of their sex; these patterns were somewhat modified by ethnic background. Sex accounted for 69% of the total variance and ethnicity for 13%. Differences

related to SES accounted for only 2% of the total variance and were considered unimportant.

537. Brown, Joe H.; Frankel, Arthur; Birkimer, John C. & Gamboa, Anthony M. (1976). **The effects of a classroom management workshop on the reduction of children's problematic behaviors.** *Corrective & Social Psychiatry & Journal of Behavior Technology, Methods & Therapy,* 22(2), 39–41.
Measured (a) the comparative effectiveness of a workshop to teach behavior-change techniques vs teacher observation alone and (b) teacher attitudes before and after the workshop toward specified children and the relationship of these attitudes to student behavior change. The 25 experimental and 16 control Ss were mainly Black males with a median grade level of 3. Data included observations by the teachers and the School Behavior Checklists (L. C. Miller, 1972). Results suggest that teachers can be taught to produce significant changes in children's problematic behaviors through a large group or workshop format.

538. Bruininks, Robert H. (1970). **Teaching word recognition to disadvantaged boys.** *Journal of Learning Disabilities,* 3(1), 28–37.
Examined whether the use of teaching approaches consistent with the auditory or visual perceptual strengths of economically disadvantaged boys would facilitate their ability to learn and retain a list of unknown words. 105 economically disadvantaged Negro boys with a mean age of 8.7 yrs served as Ss. In a previous study 20 Ss had revealed visual strength and auditory weakness and 20 Ss the opposite perceptual pattern. Ss were taught to recognize 15 words by a visual or sight-word approach and another set of 15 words by an auditory or phonic teaching method. Findings failed to support the predicted interaction between perceptual aptitudes and teaching methods. Results did reveal a trend toward more efficient learning under the visual teaching method. This finding is related to other recent studies that suggest that disadvantaged children may learn more efficiently from a visual presentation of verbal material than from an auditory teaching method. (26 ref).

539. Bryson, Seymour; Bardo, Harold & Johnson, Constance. (1975). **Black female counselor and the Black male client.** *Journal of Non-White Concerns in Personnel & Guidance,* 3(2), 53–58.
Reviews and summarizes the literature discussing the effect of sex on Black counselor–client interaction. The psychological needs of Black males and the historical role of the Black female are considered. The importance of Black female counselors not stereotyping the Black male in the same manner as do Whites is stressed. Sex is viewed to be as important a factor as race in intraracial interactions between Black counselors and their clients.

540. Caplan, Paula J. (1973). **Sex differences in determinants of antisocial behavior.** *Proceedings of the 81st Annual Convention of the American Psychological Association, Montreal, Canada,* 8, 715–716.
Investigated the possibility that schools impose different standards for end of year promotion on boys and girls. An examination of report card marks for behavior of promoted and unpromoted Black children, 40 boys and 40 girls matched for report card grades in academic subjects, showed that disruptive classroom conduct was a factor in determining which girls should repeat but not which boys should repeat. The result is discussed in the light of sex behavior stereotypes.

541. Childers, Perry R. (1971). **Snow White and the Seven Dwarfs.** *Journal of Experimental Education,* 40(2), 5–8.
Describes an experiment in which the effectiveness of tape-recorded spelling lessons was assessed with 2 groups of 25 Black male homogeneous ability-grouped 4th graders. All Ss were given pre- and posttests of the Iowa Tests of Basic Skills and a spelling test. Experimental Ss were taught by a series of 8 15–20 min tape-recorded sessions followed by a 5-min discussion period with the teacher; controls received the standard lecture-discussion method. Results indicate that the recorder-assisted group (a) exceeded controls in spelling achievement and (b) responded favorably to the method of instruction, as measured by a postexperimental attitude questionnaire. It is concluded that taped lessons served as an effective teaching device in the present application.

542. Crowl, Thomas K. & MacGinitie, Walter H. (1970). **White teachers' evaluations of oral responses given by White and Negro ninth-grade males.** *Proceedings of the Annual Convention of the American Psychological Association,* 5(Pt 2), 635–636.
62 White teachers evaluated the content of tape-recorded answers given by 6 White and 6 Negro 9th-grade males in response to 2 questions. Responses containing the same wording were rated significantly lower when given by Negroes than when given by Whites. There were significant differences among individual teachers' ratings but no significant interaction between individual teachers and students' race. Bias scores for individual teachers were quite unreliable, and probably for this reason, these scores were not associated with teachers' sex or age, years of teaching experience, grade levels taught, or the percentage of Negro students previously taught.

543. Crowl, Thomas K. & MacGinitie, Walter H. (1974). **The influence of students' speech characteristics on teachers' evaluations of oral answers.** *Journal of Educational Psychology,* 66(3), 304–308.
Tape recordings were made of 6 White and 6 Black 9th-grade boys speaking identically worded answers to typical school questions. Significantly higher grades were assigned by 62 experienced White teachers to the recorded answers when spoken by White students than when spoken by Black students. Teachers who were most susceptible to vocal stereotyping could not be differentiated on the basis of sex, age, years of teaching experience, most frequently taught grade level, or the percentage of Black students most frequently taught.

544. Dales, Ruth J. & Keller, James F. (1972). **Self-concept scores among Black and White culturally deprived adolescent males.** *Journal of Negro Education,* 41(1), 31–34.
Administered the Bill's Index to Adjustment and Values instrument over a 3-yr period to 762 Black and White culturally deprived adolescent males. These self-concept scores for each year showed no clear trend for Whites but indicated higher scores in the later year of high school for Black youth. From Grades 9 to 12 the mean scores of Blacks were higher than Whites, and in the 9th and 12th grades the scores were significantly higher for Blacks.

545. Drash, Philip W. (1972). **Habilitation of the retarded child: A remedial program.** *Journal of Special Education,* 6(2), 149–159.
Utilized operant procedures with a 4.5-yr-old Negro male with a diagnosis of mild mental retardation and delayed speech. The child's father learned reinforcement techniques and conducted sessions at home in addition to weekly sessions conducted by the experimenter. After 1 yr of language development training, the program was modified to include arithmetic skills, concept development, memory skills, and other behavioral requirements tested by the WISC and Stanford-Binet. After 2 yrs, the S was progressing normally and had an IQ in the average range. He was promoted from 1st to 2nd grade and on follow-up was still doing well. It is concluded that training in speech, language, and other cognitive skills may be helpful in developing normal behaviors in children diagnosed as retarded.

546. Feshbach, Norma D. & Feshbach, Seymour. (1972). **Imitation of teacher preferences in a field setting.** *Developmental Psychology,* 7(1), 84.
Presented 34 White and 23 Black male 9–12 yr olds with 10 animal pictures for rank ordering of preferences. Four middle preference pictures were selected and displayed in the classrooms for a 1-wk period. The White female teacher of 21 White and 9 Black Ss made prearranged positive and negative statements about the pictures during that period. No comment was made by the White female teacher of the control class. Retesting on animal preferences indicated significant changes by the experimental as compared to the control group and by the Black Ss as compared to the Black controls. Results indicate that short expressions of opinion by a teacher can have a significant influence on students.

547. Hager, Paul C. & Elton, Charles F. (1971). **The vocational interests of Black males.** *Journal of Vocational Behavior,* 1(2), 153–158.
Compared the inventoried vocational interests of Black and White male freshmen. It was hypothesized that Blacks, more than Whites, would show interest in social service occupations on the Strong Vocational Interest Blank. A statistically significant difference existed between both groups, supporting the research hypothesis.

548. Hall, John A. & Wiant, Harry V. (1973). **Does school desegregation change occupational goals of Negro males?** *Journal of Vocational Behavior,* 3(2), 175–179.
Administered instruments designed to assess values affecting motivation to work and aspiration levels to over 600 Negro male seniors in Texas high schools. Results indicate that the degree and duration of school desegregation that Ss had experienced, ranging from less than 1 to more than 5 yrs, had had little effect on work and occupational aspirations.

549. Henderson, George. (1967). **Role models for lower class Negro boys.** *Personnel & Guidance Journal,* 46(1), 6–10.
Providing middle-class role models for these students is one technique that is usually recommended but seldom discussed analytically. The popular practice of providing only Negro adult role models to Negro children is challenged as being an activity that impedes the movement of lower-class Negroes into the mainstream of American life.

550. Henderson, Norman B.; Goffeney, Barbara; Butler, Bruce V. & Clarkson, Quentin D. (1971). **Differential rates of school promotion from first grade for White and Negro, male and female 7-year olds.** *Psychology in the Schools,* 8(2), 101–109.
Studied the retention policy of schools in the Portland, Oregon, area. The sample represented all children (901 Ss) who had completed a 7-yr examination and were part of the Oregon Collaborative Study. Promotion-retention rates were analyzed by race, sex, standardized test performance, and socioeconomic level. Chi-square analysis of the data indicated that Whites were retained more frequently than Blacks and boys more frequently than girls. It is suggested that this differential promotion rate appears to result from both a higher incidence of extremely poor reading achievement (especially for White boys) and a more liberal promotion policy in the lower socioeconomic schools.

551. Holowinsky, Ivan Z. & Pascale, Pietro J. (1972). **Performance on selected WISC subtests of subjects referred for psychological evaluation because of educational difficulties.** *Journal of Special Education,* 6(3), 231–235.
Investigated race and sex differences in the WISC performance of 50 male and 27 female Black children and 39 male and 18 female White children referred for psychological evaluation. Ss had a mean IQ of 79.55, a standard deviation of 12.52, and an IQ range of 57–129. Significant race differences occurred on only the Vocabulary subtest, with White children performing better than Black children. Boys performed significantly better than girls on the Picture Completion, Information, Vocabulary, and Block Design subtests. The smallest F ratio for race differences occurred on the Block Design subtest. Ss performed better on the Picture Completion subtest than on any other subtest. Findings do not support the hypothesis of racial differences in intelligence.

552. Jackson, Jacquelyne J. & Harris, Larry C. (1977). **"You may be normal when you come here, but you won't be normal when you leave," or Herman the pushout.** *Black Scholar,* 8(6), 2–11.
Personal contact, interviews, and test data with Herman, a prototype of a young Black male pushed out of desegregated schools, provide the basis for this discussion of the problems of public school desegregation. The locality, the event precipitating Herman's pushout, and his social and psychological profiles are described, and implications of the story are suggested.

553. Johnson, Douglas F. & Mihal, William L. (1973). **Performance of Blacks and Whites in computerized versus manual testing environments.** *American Psychologist,* 28(8), 694–699.
Discusses the problems of research on race and IQ and describes a study that compared the results of manual and computer testing in judging the performance of Blacks and Whites. Ss were 10 White and 10 Black male high school students. Performance by Whites was the same under both procedures. Blacks performed significantly lower in manual tests, but in computerized tests their performance improved and was indistinguishable from that of Whites. Theoretical reasons for these findings are discussed. It is felt that the computerized testing procedure circumvents many problems of earlier research. (15 ref).

554. Kapel, David E. (1970). **Environmental factors, student variables, and employment adjustment of male Negroes.** *Journal of Negro Education,* 39(4), 333–340.
Assessed the effects on 2 selected student variables of the following environmental variables: (a) percentage of Negroes in the high schools, (b) type of community, and (c) geographical regions. 466 male Negroes who were part of the respondents and nonrespondents from the Grade 12 class of 1960 in the original Project TALENT survey served as Ss. Ss were put in categories according to the regions where they attended school and further subdivided as to the character of the community where the school was located. Further subdivision was made according to Negro density. The 2 student variables were the Socio-Economic Environment Index and the General Academic Aptitude Composite. Post high school employment adjustment variables were developed. It is concluded that a function based on socially valued traits is more powerful than an earning-power function in discrimination.

555. Karweit, Nancy. (1977). **Patterns of educational activities: Discontinuities and sequences.** *Center for Social Organization of Schools Report, Johns Hopkins U.,* (Serial No. 222).
Using a retrospective life history sample (LHS), the educational activities of 851 White (all non-Blacks including Orientals, Mexican-Americans, and Puerto Ricans) and 738 Black men from age 14–30 are described. Educational attainments are detailed by race, age, and type of activity. Data on dates, incidents, and duration of part-time education and other continuing education patterns are presented. A lack of association of family background characteristics with resumption of schooling activities after labor force entry was found for both Blacks and Whites. Attainment level was related to the likelihood of resuming schooling: Black and White men with little educational attainment were unlikely to resume schooling. Ability differences between those continuing and not continuing were found for Blacks, but not consistently for Whites. Finally, the educational career patterns of the LHS are de-

scribed in relation to labor force and educational activities. (15 ref).

556. King, Charles E.; Mayer, Robert R. & Borders-Patterson, Anne. (1973). **Differential responses to Black and White males by female teachers in a southern city.** *Sociology & Social Research,* 57(4), 482–494.
Discusses the impact of a far-reaching school desegregation plan on teacher–pupil interaction at the classroom level. White males were most skillful in teacher interaction and Black males were least skillful of the 4 race–sex groups. All students interacted more with teachers in an integrated than in the all-Black school. Data are reported in terms of interactions.

557. Knight, Octavia B. (1972). **Occupational aspirations of the educable mentally retarded.** *Training School Bulletin,* 69(2), 54–57.
Investigated whether 40 Negro and 43 Caucasian 12-yr-old educable mentally retarded boys in special classes were realistic in their occupational conceptualization and interest. Results of a simple questionnaire reveal that both groups expressed realistic expectations with respect to future occupations.

558. Knight, Octavia B. (1969). **The self concept of Negro and White educable mentally retarded boys.** *Journal of Negro Education,* 38(2), 143–146.
Investigated differences in self-concepts of 40 educable mentally retarded (EMR) Negro boys and 43 EMR White boys in special classes matched for IQ, MA, CA, and socioeconomic status. Ss stated 3 things they liked best, 3 things they did not like about themselves, and how well they liked themselves. Responses did not reveal any significance. Analysis of the variables of the mothers' and fathers' education and fathers' occupation did not reach significance. Societal expectations as a factor accounting for the results are discussed.

559. Kohn, Martin & Rosman, Bernice L. (1974). **Social-emotional, cognitive, and demographic determinants of poor school achievement: Implications for a strategy of intervention.** *Journal of Educational Psychology,* 66(2), 267–276.
Investigated the effect of 3 classes of variables (preschool cognitive functioning, preschool social-emotional functioning, and background-demographic variables) on early elementary school achievement. 209 Black and White boys from lower- and middle-class backgrounds were evaluated during the preschool period and received achievement tests during the 2nd yr of elementary school. Each of the 3 classes of variables accounted for a significant proportion of the variance of the criterion measures (e.g., Kohn Social Competence Scale, Kohn Problem Checklist, Stanford-Binet Intelligence Scale, and the Metropolitan Achievement Test). When the classes of variables were examined using a hierarchical regression technique, the social-emotional and cognitive variables yielded the most information for programs of psychological intervention. Intervention directed at the social-emotional components of cognitive performance is discussed. (20 ref).

560. Kuvlesky, William P. & Thomas, Katheryn A. (1971). **Social ambitions of Negro boys and girls from a metropolitan ghetto.** *Journal of Vocational Behavior,* 1(2), 177–187.
Provides findings from an analysis of the frames of aspirational reference of 281 sophomores from an all-Negro high school located in a low-income ward of Houston, Texas. The concept of the frame of aspirational reference was operationalized to include indicators of goal levels of occupation, income, education, and place of residence and an indicator of hierarchical goal importance. Findings show that male and female Ss maintained (a) a consistently high-level frame of reference and (b) identical hierarchies of goal importance. It was also observed that males tended to hold slightly

higher educational and income goals than females and demonstrated a higher level of consistency across goal level.

561. Labov, William & Robins, Clarence. (1969). **A note on the relation of reading failure to peer-group status in urban ghettos.** *Record,* 70(5), 395–405.
43 members of Harlem Negro boys' groups showed no appreciable correlation between reading ability and school grade, whereas 32 nonmembers did in a preliminary study. This "confirms indirect evidence that teachers in the city schools have little ability to reward or punish members of the street culture, or to motivate learning by any means. We do not believe that the present college-educated staff, Negro or White, has the specific knowledge of the street culture to solve this problem. We propose a cultural intermediary be introduced into the classroom in the person of a young Negro man, 16–25 yrs old, with high school level reading skills, but not a college graduate" to perform certain functions.

562. Linder, Ronald & Fillmer, Henry T. (1970). **Auditory and visual performance of slow readers.** *Reading Teacher,* 24(1), 17–22.
Attempted to determine the comparative effectiveness of auditory, visual, and simultaneous auditory–visual presentations in 2nd-grade Negro boys who were poor readers. A rotation design was devised that balanced all combinations and sequences of task, modality, and subject. Individual children in this study did demonstrate a preference for one modality over another. Not all pupils may be expected to learn more effectively from a single type of presentation to the exclusion of another.

563. Lindholm, Byron W.; Touliatos, John & Rich, Amy. (1977). **A canonical correlation analysis of behavior problems and school achievement for different grades, sexes, and races.** *Journal of Educational Research,* 70(6), 340–342.
Examined the relation between behavior problems and school achievement. 971 Black and White children in Grades 3–6 were given the Behavior Problem Checklist and the California Achievement Tests. Results of statistical analysis indicate a generally negative correlation between the measures that varied with grade, sex, and race and that were felt to provide a framework for interpreting other research in the area. (23 ref).

564. Mann, Philip H. (1969). **Modifying the behavior of Negro educable mentally retarded boys through group counseling procedures.** *Journal of Negro Education,* 38(2), 135–142.
Examined the effect of group counseling on the self-concept, anxiety, academic performance, deportment, and attendance of educable mentally handicapped boys with attention to the variables of age, IQ, and race. 36 9.5–14 yr old boys, 12 White and 24 Negro, with IQs of 56–80 were tested with the Children's Self-Concept (CSC) Scale, the Way I Feel About Myself (WIFAM) scale, the Children's Manifest Anxiety Scale, and the WISC and were rated on academic performance, attendance, and deportment by their teachers. 18 Ss were divided into 3 racially mixed subgroups for 12 1-hr counseling sessions, while the control group had a study session. Results show (a) improved self-concept on the CSC but not on the WIFAM, (b) reduction of anxiety, (c) improvement in deportment, (d) academic improvement, and (e) no significant difference in attendance. Age and IQ were not significant. Negroes showed greater gains than Whites in reading, attendance, and reduction of anxiety. It appears that early counseling of Negro children might reduce the number of placements in special classes. (23 ref).

565. Maynard, Peter E. & Hansen, James C. (1970). **Vocational maturity among inner-city youths.** *Journal of Counseling Psychology,* 17(5, Pt 1), 400–404.
Investigated the efficacy of the Vocational Development Inventory (VDI) in measuring the vocational maturity of inner-

city boys. The VDI was administered to 180 White and 180 Black inner-city boys and 90 White suburban boys. Intelligence test results were obtained and converted to standardized T scores. The mean vocational maturity scores indicated large differences among the samples. However, when intelligence was controlled by analysis of covariance, the differences were erased. It is concluded that researchers and counselors account for a variety of intellectual and social variables when working with the vocational maturity of inner-city youth. (20 ref).

566. Meeker, Mary & Meeker, Robert. (1973). **Strategies for assessing intellectual patterns in Black, Anglo, and Mexican-American boys—or any other children—and implications for education.** *Journal of School Psychology,* 11(4), 341–350.
Used a technique derived from Guilford's Structure of Intellect (SOI) model to analyze Stanford-Binet item responses of 245 4–5 and 7–9 yr old Mexican-American, Anglo-American, and Afro-American boys from lower socioeconomic backgrounds. The SOI model conceptualizes 3 dimensions of intellectual abilities in terms of operations, content, and processes. Each of the major SOI dimensions' interactive effects were analyzed for each S group. Results are discussed in terms of specific abilities (e.g., figural intelligence) emphasized in the SOI model. It is suggested that intellectual ability can be taught provided appropriate curriculums are available and that SOI ability assessments are more valuable than traditional IQ scores. (17 ref).

567. Michel, Donald E. & Farrell, Dorothea M. (1973). **Music and self-esteem: Disadvantaged problem boys in an all-Black elementary school.** *Journal of Research in Music Education,* 21(1), 80–84.
14 10–12 yr old Black boys, referred to psychological services because of learning and behavioral problems, were given 15 biweekly 20–30 min ukulele lessons and reinforced for good behavior with candy and points counting toward earning the ukuleles. Comparison with a noncontact control group in the school's special education group showed no significant changes, although apparently there was some individual improvement. A follow-up one month later also showed no significant change in attention in classroom behavior.

568. Musgrove, Walter J. & Whitesides, Mary G. (1973). **A study of Negro and White low socio-economic class children on the variables of race, sex and kindergarten attendance and on general social adjustment.** *Florida Journal of Educational Research,* 15, 10–17.
Administered the Stanford Achievement Test (SAT) to 92 2nd graders who had had kindergarten experience and 68 2nd-grade controls who had not attended kindergarten. All Ss were from low socioeconomic backgrounds. Teacher ratings of the general social adjustment of each child were also obtained. Results show that (a) girls performed significantly better than boys on 5 of the 6 subtests of the SAT; (b) a Sex by Kindergarten Attendance interaction was significant, showing that boys with and girls without kindergarten experience performed better than boys without and girls with that experience; (c) race, kindergarten attendance, and Race by Sex and Race by Kindergarten Attendance interactions had no effects on performance; and (d) nonkindergarten girls were rated as significantly better socially adjusted than nonkindergarten boys. It is suggested that the greatest differences in academic achievement can be traced to sex differences.

569. Pinchot, Nancy; Riccio, Anthony C. & Peters, Herman J. (1975). **Elementary school students' and their parents' preferences for counselors.** *Counselor Education & Supervision,* 15(1), 28–33.
180 Northern White, Afro-American Black, and Appalachian White male and female 6th graders and 90 of their parents stated their preferences for 1 of 6 videotapes of different counselors in an interview situation, completed demographic questionnaires, and took the California Test of Personality (students only). 26 hypotheses relating to sex, race, and cultural background variables in Ss' preferences for different types of counselors were tested. Overall results suggest that for girls, the sex of the counselor was a major variable in counselor preference, but not for boys. Black and White students most preferred counselors of their own races, and both White and Black Ss least preferred the male counselor of each race. No personality variables were significant. Black and White parents also preferred counselors of the same race. Implications for the profession are noted.

570. Portuges, Stephen H. & Feshbach, Norma D. (1972). **The influence of sex and socioethnic factors upon imitation of teachers by elementary schoolchildren.** *Child Development,* 43(3), 981–989.
Presented 2 4-min films to 48 White advantaged and 48 Black disadvantaged 3rd and 4th graders. Each film depicted a teacher presenting a geography lesson. The teachers were distinctively dressed, used different incidental gestures and remarks, and employed contrasting reinforcement techniques, one positive and the other negative. After observing the films, Ss assumed the role of teachers. A control group of 24 Ss who had not seen the films was also included. Significantly greater imitation of the teacher model's incidental behaviors was observed among advantaged Ss, among girls, and in response to the positive reinforcing teacher.

571. Riccio, Anthony C. & Barnes, Keith D. (1973). **Counselor preferences of senior high school students.** *Counselor Education & Supervision,* 13(1), 36–40.
Studied the effects of race (Black or White), subculture (Appalachian or northern White), and sex on counselor preferences of 30 male and 30 female Black, Appalachian White, and northern White 10–12th graders (180 Ss). Ss viewed videotapes of 6 counselors, a male and female from each of the 3 racial and subcultural groups. Black Ss expressed a significantly greater preference for Black counselors, specifically a Black male counselor. White Ss generally preferred White counselors, although the trend was not significant. The Black male counselor was the 2nd choice (next to the Appalachian female) of all White students. Significantly different preferences based on sex were found only for Black Ss; 42 of the 60 Black Ss selected a male counselor. Implications for counseling and administrative processes are discussed.

572. Sappington, Andrew & Grizzard, Robert. (1975). **Self-discrimination responses in Black school children.** *Journal of Personality & Social Psychology,* 31(2), 224–231.
Previous studies have found that the performance of Blacks on intellectual tasks decreases in the presence of Whites. The present study attempted to determine whether this performance decrement still exists by administering 3 trials of a digit symbol task (the WAIS Digit Symbol subscale) to 40 Black male 7th and 8th graders in the presence of either White or Negro counselors. The digit symbol task was labeled as either intellectual or motor skill. In addition, tests (e.g., the MMPI) were used to measure expectancy, incentive, anxiety, hostility, defensiveness, and task satisfaction. It was found that the students performed better in the presence of Whites and that this was a function of task complexity and task labeling. Of several theories considered, K. W. Spence's (1958) analysis of the relationship of drive level to performance can best explain the data. No source for the increased drive in the presence of Whites was found.

573. Shaw, Marvin E. (1974). **The self-image of Black and White pupils in an integrated school.** *Journal of Personality,* 42(1), 12–22.
Administered the Harvey Self-Image Scale to 346 Blacks and 745 Whites in the fall and again in the spring during 2 successive school years in recently integrated elementary

schools. Data show that (a) boys saw themselves as significantly less sociable but more independent than did girls; (b) Blacks perceived themselves as being significantly more independent and hostile than did Whites; (c) sociability generally increased whereas achievement orientation decreased as a function of grade level; (d) Blacks either decreased in sociability or showed no change, whereas Whites either showed no change or increased in sociability during the school year; and (e) during the school year, Ss in Grades 2 and 3 decreased in hostility, those in Grades 4 and 5 showed no change, and Ss in Grade 6 increased in perceived hostility. Differences between the self-perceptions of boys and girls are consistent with cultural sex roles. Findings with regard to Blacks vs Whites indicate that emphasis on the positivity–negativity dimension of self-perceptions may be misplaced; emphasis should be directed to the particular characteristics attributed to self by Blacks and Whites. Data also question the hypothesis that the self-concepts of Blacks become less positive in an integrated school.

574. Smith, Trina P. & Ribordy, Sheila C. (1980). **Correlates of reflection-impulsivity in kindergarten males: Intelligence, socioeconomic status, race, fathers' absence, and teachers' ratings.** *Psychological Reports,* 47(3, Pt 2), 1187–1191.
Assessed 72 kindergarten males for reflection-impulsivity with the Matching Familiar Figures Test. Cognitive style on this test was examined in relation to intelligence, socioeconomic status, race, fathers' absence, and teachers' ratings of impulsivity. Findings show that Ss whose fathers were absent from the home made more errors on the test than Ss whose fathers were present. Teachers rated more intelligent Ss as more impulsive; these ratings were positively correlated with errors but not latencies. No significant differences in cognitive style were found for race or socioeconomic groups. (14 ref).

575. Stroup, Atlee L. & Robins, Lee N. (1972). **Elementary school predictors of high school dropout among Black males.** *Sociology of Education,* 45(2), 212–222.
Analyzed elementary school predictors of high school dropout for a sample of 223 Black urban males. Of 13 original variables, 6 produced a multiple R with dropout of .637. School retardation, truancy, early drinking activity, parental social status, and number of elementary schools attended were most clearly associated with high school dropout.

576. Sullivan, Allen R. (1972). **The influence of social processes on the learning abilities of Afro-American school children: Some educational implications.** *Journal of Negro Education,* 41(2), 127–136.
Assigned 120 Afro-American males, selected from a larger pool of 290 enrolled in kindergarten and 3rd and 6th grades, to 3 levels of socioeconomic status and 2 stimulus conditions on a paired-associate task: (a) concrete dialectic where actual objects were presented and (b) abstract dialetic where pictures of objects were presented. The Deprivation Index was used as a measure of social process. Results of an analysis of variance indicated significant differences in favor of Grade 6, high social process, and the concrete task. It is concluded that educational programming should include the variables identified in this study.

577. Tatham, Clifford B. & Tatham, Elaine L. (1974). **Academic predictors for Black students.** *Educational & Psychological Measurement,* 34(2), 371–374.
Designated 45 Black males and 28 Black females as either academically successful (graduation, or grade point average of at least 1.0) or academically unsuccessful. A 2-way (Sex by Academic Success) multivariate analysis of variance indicated that with respect to standard scores on the Scholastic Aptitude Test, Verbal and Mathematical, and on the High School Readiness Test, males differed significantly from females. The successful males differed from the unsuccessful males with respect to these 3 variables, but no such difference

was found for females. It is concluded that measures used in academic achievement should not be the only measures used in selecting Black students for admittance to college; others, such as motivation and socioeconomic background, also need to be considered.

578. Van den Daele, Leland D. (1970). **Preschool intervention through social learning for disadvantaged children.** *Journal of Negro Education,* 39(4), 296–304.
Designed an intervention program to provide the disadvantaged male with a competent model, a set of appropriate roles, and an opportunity for positive, role-derived interaction. 16 3–4 yr old children from low-income families were used. Ss were divided into 2 groups and a male model, 1 Negro and 1 White, assigned to each group. Ss were taken through an array of role play procedures. There was also positive verbal and physical interaction with the child in the context of imitative play. The program continued for 25 wks during which each model interacted with his group 2 hrs/day, 3 days/wk. The models changed groups after 12 wks. The Peabody Picture Vocabulary Test, selected cards from the Children's Apperception Test, and the Decision-Making Interview were administered to the children at 5-wk intervals. Results show significant cognitive, affective, and ego gains.

579. Wasserman, Herbert L. (1972). **A comparative study of school performance among boys from broken and intact Black families.** *Journal of Negro Education,* 41(2), 137–141.
Studied a sample of 117 Black families living in a low income housing development, including at least 1 son between 10 and 16 yrs. 48 families had a father present, 43 had a father absent, and 26 had an unclear status and were called mixed. A school achievement index was used based on marks in major subjects and whether the student was in an appropriate grade for his age. No differences among groups were found. No statistical significance tests are reported.

580. Weber, George H. & Motz, Annabelle B. (1968). **School as perceived by the dropout.** *Journal of Negro Education,* 37(2), 127–134.
16 disadvantaged male Negro school dropouts were interviewed to determine perceptions of school personnel: the principal, teachers, counselors, and school policemen. The staff and classroom experience was generally defined in negative terms and indicated a great deal of school distance between staff and students. Indifference and punitive attitudes combined with academic boredom, constant failure, and inability to alter the situation produced "classroom" dropouts and later "school" dropouts.

581. Weiss, Mark H. & McKenzie, Donald H. (1972). **The effects of videotape focused feedback on facilitative genuineness in interracial encounters.** *Comparative Group Studies,* 3(2), 247–259.
Selected 7 school counselors (Black and White, male and female) from among 19 participating in a 2-wk conference on cross-racial counseling. Ss were given 10 hrs of group experience using videotape focused feedback in addition to the regular program. Experimental Ss did not differ from controls in facilitative genuineness as rated by trained judges, though they were selected more frequently by the total group as individuals of greatest impact. (16 ref).

582. Whetstone, Robert D. & Hayles, V. Robert. (1975). **The SVIB and Black college men.** *Measurement & Evaluation in Guidance,* 8(2), 105–109.
Examined the relative usefulness of the Strong Vocational Interest Blank (SVIB) for 69 Black and 75 White male college students. The study provided evidence that the SVIB can be relevant for Black students without applying different norms. Significant differences in interest patterns and the corresponding relationships of those patterns and specific scale scores with intended college majors were explored. Explana-

tions of the results are given with special emphasis on the backgrounds of the Ss and the current cultural situation. Areas where there may be a cultural bias in the SVIB or its interpretation are mentioned. Results point to several important counseling suggestions when using the SVIB with Black college males.

Curriculum & Programs & Teaching Methods

583. Chester, Nia L. (1983). **Sex differentiation in two high school environments: Implications for career development among Black adolescent females.** *Journal of Social Issues,* 39(3), 29–40.
Compared 127 Black male and female 9th–12th graders on career-related variables at 2 high schools, one a predominantly White liberal arts high school and the other a racially more integrated vocational high school. Based on a review of the literature regarding institutional and racial differences in attitudes toward career development in women, it was hypothesized that more sex differences would exist among the Black Ss at the liberal arts school than at the vocational school, and that these differences would favor the males. The hypotheses were confirmed. While females attending the liberal arts high school had lower aspirations, less vocationally relevant self-concepts, and lower self esteem than their male counterparts, they were also less likely to perceive events as the result of either internal forces or of external forces. It is concluded that Black females may experience environments differently than do Black males, due to the combined and independent effects of racism and sexism. It is concluded that studies involving the effects of different settings on minority group behavior should examine relationships separately by gender. (37 ref).

584. Edgar, Rose & Clement, Paul W. (1980). **Teacher-controlled and self-controlled reinforcement with underachieving Black children.** *Child Behavior Therapy,* 2(4), 33–56.
Four academically underachieving Black male 4th graders aged 9–10 yrs (WISC-R Full Scale IQs 88, 100, 105, and 90, respectively) served in a set of single-S, intensive studies on the comparative effects of teacher-controlled (TCR) and self-controlled reinforcement (SCR). They attended a 1-hr tutoring class 3 days/wk for 14 wks. Four academic behaviors and 4 indices of academic achievement constituted the measures of outcome. Each S participated in at least 2 baseline phases, 2 TCR phases, and 2 SCR phases, each lasting 2 wks. The order of presenting the active treatment conditions was counterbalanced across Ss. Within- and across-Ss analyses were made. Both types of analysis showed SCR to be more effective than TCR in increasing academic behaviors. This difference in effectiveness did not appear consistently on the nontreated academic behaviors, but the achievement data did demonstrate generalized differential effects favoring SCR. (35 ref).

585. Huey, Wayne C. & Rank, Richard C. (1984). **Effects of counselor and peer-led group assertive training on Black adolescent aggression.** *Journal of Counseling Psychology,* 31(1), 95–98.
48 8th–9th grade Black males, selected for their aggressive classroom behavior, were randomly assigned to professional or peer counselor assertive training groups, professional or peer counselor discussion groups, and a no-treatment control group. All Ss were administered a pretest and posttest battery measuring assertive skill level, anger level, a projective assessment of aggression, and classroom aggressive behavior. Results suggest that professional counselors and peer counselors are equally effective in teaching assertive skills and that Ss who learn assertive responses will exhibit significantly less aggressive behavior. (14 ref).

586. Kerlin, Marcella A. & Latham, William L. (1977). **Intervention effects of a crisis-resource program.** *Exceptional Children,* 44(1), 32–34.
21 8.3–12.6 yr old low socioeconomic Black males exhibiting problem behaviors were randomly assigned to 1 of 3 groups (2 experimental and 1 control). Pre- and postcrisis resource intervention scores on observed classroom behavior and the Walker Problem Behavior Identification Checklist showed significant differences in social behavior among Ss in the experimental groups.

587. Marrett, Cora B. & Gates, Harold. (1983). **Male-female enrollment across mathematics tracks in predominantly Black high schools.** *Journal for Research in Mathematics Education,* 14(2), 113–118.
Examined sex differences in enrollment across mathematics tracks for 6 predominantly Black senior high schools in a large city. The schools each served Grades 10–12; 3 were 99% Black; and school size ranged from 1,200 to 2,700 students. The aggregate data for the schools showed only slight variation in the male-female ratio across the 2 tracks: Females were about half of the students in each track. There were differences among the schools, however, in the tracking patterns for female students and in the way that the female and male enrollees were divided between the tracks. In most of the schools, relatively few students of either sex were taking the higher track courses. The findings suggest that participation in higher level mathematics courses might reflect important characteristics of and conditions within schools. (5 ref).

588. Pentecoste, Joseph. (1983). **Male-female differences in a labor market orientation program.** *College Student Journal,* 17(4), 378–380.
Compared male-female differences on gain scores for 2 achievement measures, the Wide Range Achievement Test and a world of work questionnaire, that were used in a labor market orientation training program for 125 Black 11th and 12th graders. No significant differences were found between females and males. It was hypothesized that levels of teacher and employer expectation might have been one source of differences in past studies. (8 ref).

589. Stevenson, Howard C. & Fantuzzo, John W. (1984). **Application of the "generalization map" to a self-control intervention with school-aged children.** *Journal of Applied Behavior Analysis,* 17(2), 203–212.
Assessed the ability of a comprehensive self-control intervention to increase the mathematics performance of a 5th-grade Black male in a regular classroom setting; another underachieving 5th-grade Black male from the same classroom served as the untreated control. The intervention incorporated a number of self-management skills. All possible classes of generalization as outlined by R. S. Drabman et al (1979) were assessed. An ABAB design with follow-up was used to determine the effectiveness of the intervention for the treated S's mathematics performance in the school setting as well as the degree of generalization across the following untreated dimensions: behavior (disruptiveness), setting (home), S (classmate), and time period (follow-up). The effective intervention produced the following generalizations: S, behavior, S/behavior, setting, S/setting, behavior/setting, S/behavior/setting, time, S/time, setting/time, S/setting/time, and S/behavior/setting/time. Features of this intervention that may have promoted generalization are discussed. (33 ref).

590. Thomson-Rountree, Phyllis & Woodruff, Ann E. (1982). **An examination of Project AWARE: The effects on children's attitudes toward themselves, others, and school.** *Journal of School Psychology,* 20(1), 20–31.
80 5th and 6th graders were administered the California Test of Personality, the School Sentiment Index, and a locus of control scale. Control and experimental (i.e., participating in Project AWARE) Ss were sex- and race-matched. Results

show that experimental Ss achieved greater personal adjustment and accepted responsibility for negative outcomes in social situations. White Ss scored higher in personal and social adjustment. Black Ss evidenced more positive attitudes toward school. Females scored significantly higher than males on social adjustment and attitudes toward peers. Black Ss in the control group had less positive attitudes toward teachers than White Ss in the experimental group. (23 ref).

591. Wolter, Carl F.; Pigott, H. Edmund; Fantuzzo, John W. & Clement, Paul W. (1984). **Student-administered group-oriented contingencies: The application of self-regulation techniques in the context of a group to increase academic productivity.** *Techniques,* 1(1), 14–22.
Student-administered group-oriented contingencies were piloted as a behavioral intervention for increasing the arithmetic performance of school-age children. Three underachieving 5th-grade Black males were formally assessed for arithmetic output performance (the Comprehensive Test of Basic Skills) and disruptive behavior in a classroomlike setting at a child outpatient clinic. The effectiveness of this intervention was assessed with an ABAB withdrawal design. Findings indicate that the contingencies were effective in increasing arithmetic performance and reducing disruptive behavior with all 3 Ss. Additional benefits of the intervention and implications of this treatment strategy are discussed. (38 ref).

Academic Learning & Achievement

592. Abbott, Ann A. (1981). **Factors related to third grade achievement: Self-perception, classroom composition, sex, and race.** *Contemporary Educational Psychology,* 6(2), 167–179.
Investigated the relationship between self-perception and academic achievement among 116 3rd-grade Black and White disadvantaged children. Race, sex, IQ, self-perception, and student's perception of their teacher's perceptions were examined as sources of variance in academic achievement. A stepwise multiple regression analysis revealed that self-perceptions accounted for more variance in academic achievement for Ss who are of the same sex and race as the teacher than for those who are not. It was also found that self-perceptions of Black Ss in all-Black classrooms accounted for more variance in respect to achievement than did self-perceptions of Blacks in integrated classrooms. (32 ref).

593. Allen, Walter R. (1978). **Race, family setting, and adolescent achievement orientation.** *Journal of Negro Education,* 47(3), 230–243.
Studied 245 White and Black working- and middle-class 2-parent Chicago families, each of which included at least one son, aged 14–18. Both parents and sons completed a questionnaire on individual and family characteristics during 2-hr individualized interviews. Data were analyzed using ANOVA and product-moment correlations. Results indicate that White families differed significantly from Black families in socioeconomic status. White sons were found to have significantly higher self-esteem than Black sons; however, results do not indicate a negative self-concept among Blacks. The aspirations of both Black and White adolescents were significantly related to the occupation of their fathers. In addition, significant relationships were found between the education and the family income of the fathers of the White adolescents. Aspirations of Black sons were significantly correlated with their mothers' expectations; the aspirations of White adolescents were strongly correlated to their fathers' aspirations.

594. Bing, Eric G. & Morris, William N. (1985). **The effects of direct and vicarious task feedback on the achievement expectations of Black and White children.** *Merrill-Palmer Quarterly,* 31(3), 301–314.

Conducted 2 experiments to determine how initial task experiences of success and failure combine with observation of task outcomes of same-age, same-sex peers to affect the achievement expectations of 2nd and 3rd graders. Ss were randomly assigned to 1 of 3 conditions: The problems were solvable (success) or unsolvable (failure), or there were no problems (no feedback). Results of both experiments, the 1st with 75 lower-class urban Black children, and the 2nd with 75 middle-class rural White children, show that Ss' expectations were increased by their own success and the observed success of peers and were lowered by both direct and vicarious failure. However, Black and White Ss differed in their response to conditions that were designed to determine the relative influence of Black vs White comparison others. Lower-class Black Ss were more influenced by same-race comparison others only after a relatively unexpected initial outcome (failure for boys and success for girls), whereas middle-class White Ss showed a tendency to be more influenced by same-race others, regardless of their prior task experience. Achievement motivation and differential familiarity with other-race children are offered as possible explanations for this difference. (31 ref).

595. Bridgeman, Brent & Burbach, Harold J. (1976). **Effects of Black vs. White peer models on academic expectations and actual performance of fifth grade students.** *Journal of Experimental Education,* 45(1), 9-12.
274 Black and White 5th graders of both sexes were shown 1 of 2 videotapes of 12 other students working on an academic task (reading a paragraph and answering questions about it). On one tape, 2 Black students were congratulated by the teacher for having gotten the best score, while on the other tape 2 White students were congratulated. Comparisons indicated that Black males who viewed the videotape of Blacks succeeding expected to, and actually did, score higher than Black males who observed White students succeeding. All other comparisons were not significant.

596. Covin, Theron M. & Hatch, Gary L. (1976). **Intellectual differences in Black and White southern low achievers.** *Psychological Reports,* 39(3, Pt 2), 1269–1270.
Compared the WISC IQs of 15 male and 15 female Whites and 15 male and 15 female Blacks. Mean IQs on the Verbal, Performance, and Full Scale for Blacks were 69.68, 69.92, and 66.91, respectively; these were significantly lower than the respective averages of 79.80, 79.80, and 79.50, for Whites. Means, standard deviations, and t scores for stratified samples by sex and race are also reported.

597. DeBord, Larry W. (1977). **The achievement syndrome in lower-class boys.** *Social Psychology Quarterly,* 40(2), 190–196.
Among the limitations of previous studies of need for achievement are their small samples of predominantly White, middle-class Ss and the treatment of achievement orientation as a unidimensional concept. The present research addressed these issues by employing both fantasy and questionnaire measures of the achievement syndrome in a lower-class sample of 48 Black and 45 White male 4th–6th graders. Reading-grade placement, controlling for mental ability, served as the criterion of actual achievement. Some evidence for an achievement syndrome appeared among Blacks, but the evidence was less clear among Whites. (24 ref).

598. Fowler, Patrick C. & Richards, Herbert C. (1978). **Father absence, educational preparedness, and academic achievement: A test of the confluence model.** *Journal of Educational Psychology,* 70(4), 595–601.
Investigated predictions of academic deficits due to early and continuing parental absence, as derived from R. Zajonc and G. Markus's (see PA, Vol 53:9290) and Zajonc's (see PA, Vol 56:589) confluence model. To test these predictions, equal numbers of father-present and father-absent lower-class Black

kindergartners (60 of each sex) were assessed on 12 educational preparedness measures. Two years later, they were tested for reading, mathematics, and language arts achievement. A Father by Absence by Sex analysis of covariance (with social class controlled) of preparedness factor scores revealed no significant effects. Similar multivariate analysis of the achievement criteria revealed main (favoring father-present Ss) and interaction effects on the mathematics test. Pair-wise comparisons suggested that father presence facilitated the mathematics performance of girls more than boys. Results only partially support the confluence model predictions. (23 ref).

599. Hall, Vernon C.; Huppertz, John W. & Levi, Alan. (1977). **Attention and achievement exhibited by middle- and lower-class Black and White elementary school boys.** *Journal of Educational Psychology,* 69(2), 115–120.
In-class behaviors of 80 7–8 yr old boys equally divided by race (Black and White) and social class (middle and lower) were recorded. Ss were administered the Peabody Picture Vocabulary Test, the Raven Coloured Progressive Matrices, and the Test of Basic Experience. The 3 observers compiled and used a list of behaviors judged to be all-inclusive of what occurs in normal classroom activity. No differences were found between groups in percentage of time attending. Although there were social class and race differences in achievement and intelligence test scores, no relationship was found between attending and these variables. Finally, there was a significant correlation between the intelligence and achievement test scores but no evidence that the relationship was different for the different groups.

600. Hall, Vernon C.; Merkel, Steven; Howe, Anne & Lederman, Norman. (1986). **Behavior, motivation, and achievement in desegregated junior high school science classes.** *Journal of Educational Psychology,* 78(2), 108–115.
To locate possible antecedents for racial differences in science achievement, measures of mathematics and reading achievement, causal attribution, attitude toward school success, and in-class behavior were acquired from 40 Black and 40 White junior high school students, both groups evenly divided between males and females. Significant group differences were limited to mean achievement test scores and science grades. Achievement scores were significantly related to grades, but classroom behaviors also accounted for a significant and unique portion of the variance. There were no significant relationships between behaviors and other student measures. Teacher ratings of effort, ability, course difficulty, and environment were also acquired. Teachers rated Whites as smarter and believed that Black females exerted the greatest effort and Black males the least. As a secondary interest, number and type of student interactions were recorded. Few hostile interracial encounters were observed, and interactions were predominately within race. (18 ref).

601. Jantz, Richard K. & Sciara, Frank J. (1975). **Does living with a female head-of-household affect the arithmetic achievement of Black fourth-grade pupils?** *Psychology in the Schools,* 12(4), 468–472.
Studied the records of 1,073 Black 4th graders, of whom 300 were living with a female head-of-household and 773 with a male head-of-household. No significant differences were found in mean scores between male and female Ss on the Metropolitan Achievement Test. Significant differences were found favoring those Ss living with male heads-of-household, particularly for females and for Ss with Lorge-Thorndike IQs over 100. It is noted that findings should not be considered as simple cause and effect relationships but rather as indicative of potential difficulty for some pupils. (1 p ref).

602. Jordan, Theresa J. (1981). **Self-concepts, motivation, and academic achievement of Black adolescents.** *Journal of Educational Psychology,* 73(4), 509–517.

Investigated the unique and common contributions made by global self-concept, academic self-concept, and need for academic competence to the variance in academic achievement of inner city Black adolescents. Data on these variables were collected from 328 8th-grade students attending a New York City public junior high school. Results of commonality procedures indicate that academic self-concept and need for academic competence each accounted for significant proportions of criterion variance, whereas global self-concept did not. Explanations of variance in academic achievement were better for males than for females after the possible confounding effects of verbal ability had been partialled out. Directions for intervention strategies aimed at enhancing academic achievement are suggested for the 2 sexes. (53 ref).

603. Kerckhoff, Alan C. & Campbell, Richard T. (1977). **Black-White differences in the educational attainment process.** *Sociology of Education,* 50(1), 15–27.
Of 390 White and 113 Black males originally studied as 9th graders in 1969, 324 White and 79 Black Ss were recontacted in 1974 to obtain information about high school performance and educational attainment. Comparisons between Blacks and Whites were made. As in previous research the Wisconsin model of status attainment proved less powerful in explaining Black than White attainments, socioeconomic status of origin having practically no explanatory power for Blacks. However, ambition and a measure of disciplinary difficulties in junior high school were more effective in explaining high school performance for Blacks than Whites, and high school performance was a stronger prediction of attainment for Blacks than Whites. As a result, the full model explains Blacks' attainments as fully as those of Whites.

604. Mangieri, John N. & Olsen, Henry D. (1977). **Self-concept-of-achievement ability and reading proficiency of Black and White males in an adult education course.** *Journal of Negro Education,* 46(4), 456–461.
Examined the relationship between reading ability and self-concept of academic ability. 188 males (101 Blacks and 87 Whites) enrolled in an adult basic education program in rural Ohio completed the Nelson-Denny Reading Test (Form B) and the Michigan State Self-Concept of Academic Ability Scale (SCOAA). Results indicate that Ss (Black or White, analyzed separately or together) reading above grade level had a more favorable self-concept of academic ability than did Ss reading below grade level. All Black participants, regardless of reading scores, had higher self-concepts than White participants. Blacks reading above grade level had a higher self-concept of ability than Whites with the same level of reading proficiency; however, no such difference was found between Black and White Ss reading below grade level. Results confirm similar studies conducted in the 1960's.

605. Pugh, M. D. (1976). **Statistical assumptions and social reality: A critical analysis of achievement models.** *Sociology of Education,* 49(1), 34–40.
The statistical assumptions of asymmetry and linearity in path models of academic achievement are critically examined using data from 724 Black and White high school seniors. Analysis suggests that student self-evaluations of academic capability and school performance may be reciprocally related and that academic achievement may be more resistant to change among poor than among average students. Both findings would be masked in simple recursive path models. Data are consistent with the conclusion of J. S. Coleman et al (*Equality of Educational Opportunity Report,* 1966) that different predispositional factors affect achievement among Blacks and Whites. (22 ref).

606. Reid, Pamela T. & Robinson, W. LaVome. (1985). **Professional Black men and women: Attainment of terminal academic degrees.** *Psychological Reports,* 56(2), 547–555.

Examined the family backgrounds and personality characteristics of Black professionals who held doctorates for possible commonalities and sex differences. 30 Black men and 34 Black women from a variety of professional fields participated in a mail survey, which included demographic items and personality scales (e.g., the California F Scale). Most Ss had educated mothers who were employed during their childhood. Ss held traditional religious affiliations, had small numbers of children, and had spouses who typically were college graduates. Ss were highly motivated and self-oriented individuals who were tolerant of differences in moral and personal values. Women were less conventional than men, were likely to be unmarried and childless, and had parents with more education. In general, however, few sex differences on personality measures were found. (21 ref).

607. Scheinfeld, Daniel R. (1983). **Family relationships and school achievement among boys of lower-income urban Black families.** *American Journal of Orthopsychiatry,* 53(1), 127–143.
Studied 33 poor Black urban mothers' views of the ideal relationship between their sons and the world to the sons' academic achievement. Ss were interviewed and their responses were coded on 9 dimensions: purposeful agent, trust-selectivity, social connectedness, exchange with the environment beyond the home, competence-gaining activity, dominance vs exchange, concern with child's emotional needs, adaptation to threat, and meaning of adaptation. Factor analysis yielded a single factor: Active Engagement vs Defensive Isolation. There was a significant correlation between mothers' factor scores and boys' achievement factor scores. Mothers of high achievers expressed ideals for their sons that emphasized self-motivated, active, learning engagement with the world; mothers of low achievers expressed ideals that emphasized constraint, isolation, and adult control. Findings suggest that there are personality characteristics that differentiate high and how achievers in lower-income Black elementary school populations. Data also suggest that there are 2 interlocking issues in the relationship of mother–son interactions: (1) the adaptive aim of the mother—appetitive or aversive; and (2) the tendency of the mother to endorse or negate the child's expression of his effectance motivation. (25 ref).

608. Scott, Ralph. (1985). **Sex and race achievement profiles in a desegregated high school in the deep South.** *Mankind Quarterly,* 25(3), 291–302.
Examined test scores in 133 Black and 210 White high school students (161 males) who attended desegregated schools throughout their school years. Ss' California Achievement Test (CAT) scores, obtained during 10th grade, showed that males scored higher on language (mechanics) and females on spelling. Whites scored significantly higher in all CAT categories; however, the magnitude of the racial gap varied considerably, being narrowest in spelling and mathematics and widest in reading. It is also noted that Black males outperformed Black females in reading and language (expression), whereas Black females did better in spelling and language (mechanics). (17 ref).

609. Thomas, Gail E. & Gordon, Samuel A. (1983). **Evaluating the payoffs of college investments for Black, White, and Hispanic students.** *Center for Social Organization of Schools Report, Johns Hopkins U.,* (Serial No. 344).
Examined how attending a 2-yr vocational college vs a 4-yr college, and pursuing a college major in the technical sciences vs education and the social sciences, affected the subsequent educational and occupational attainment of a national sample of White, Black, and Hispanic undergraduates. It was hypothesized that the type of colleges that Ss attend and their college major would have a significant effect on educational and occupational attainment. The main and interaction effects of college type, college major, and race and sex were examined. Both college type and college major had a signifi-

cant effect on educational attainment. College type also exerted a small but significant main effect on occupational attainment for the total sample of 2- and 4-yr Ss. Interactions of college type with race and sex were also found. Educational attainment was the major determinant of occupational attainment for Blacks and Whites, while sex and educational expectations were the most important determinants for Hispanics. (50 ref).

Classroom Dynamics & Student Adjustment & Attitudes

610. Bromberg, Matthew. (1984). **A kind of equal.** *Child & Adolescent Social Work Journal,* 1(2), 71–73.
The author describes his experience of being the sole White participant on an all Black high school basketball team and his frustrated attempts to become an equal and accepted team member. Topics of discussion include the author's feeling that he must assimilate to be accepted; his assumption of an ingratiating, subservient role; and the resulting loss of self-esteem. The author concludes that, for a short time, he experienced what Blacks face in a predominantly White society.

611. Burbach, Harold J. & Bridgeman, Brent. (1976). **Relationship between self-esteem and locus of control in Black and White fifth-grade students.** *Child Study Journal,* 6(1), 33–37.
Examined the relationship between Coopersmith's Self Esteem Inventory (CSEI) and the Intellectual Achievement Responsibility Questionnaire (IAR). A sample of 274 5th graders was subdivided by sex and race, and a low positive relationship between these 2 scales persisted across all groups. When the total Intellectual score was separated into its Intellectual-Success and Intellectual-Failure and components and correlated with the CSEI, it was discovered that for females and Black males, self-esteem was significantly related to taking personal credit for academic success. High self-esteem among White males was significantly related to accepting blame for academic failure.

612. Clark, Maxine L.; Windley, Linda; Jones, Linda & Ellis, Steve. (1986). **Dating patterns of Black students on White Southern campuses.** *Journal of Multicultural Counseling & Development,* 14(2), 85–93.
In a survey of 34 female and 44 male Black unmarried college students attending 2 largely White Southern universities, it was hypothesized that Black men would engage in interracial dating more frequently than Black women and that students who preferred to date Blacks would have more favorable perceptions of Blacks than students who preferred to date both Blacks and Whites. Responses to a dating survey and the Adjective Checklist showed that more Black males preferred to date interracially than Black women but were not currently doing so. The 2nd hypothesis was not confirmed. Overall, most Ss, regardless of sex, seriously and casually dated within their race. (16 ref).

613. Coffield, K. E. & Buckalew, L. W. (1985). **University student apathy: Sex, race, and academic class variables.** *Psychological Record,* 35(4), 459–463.
Examined student apathy among 112 female and 88 male Black undergraduates using the Purpose in Life Test. Comparisons of data with those of a heterogeneous university sample by K. E. Coffield (see PA, Vol 67:2060) showed that both groups had similar apathy levels. In applying sex–race dichotomies, however, Black males showed significantly less apathy than Black females or heterogeneous university males. Black juniors and incoming heterogeneous freshmen displayed greater apathy behaviors than did other academic classes. Potential explanations are offered for the differential behavior noted. (7 ref).

614. Crew, James C. (1982). **An assessment of needs among Black business majors.** *Psychology: A Quarterly Journal of Human Behavior,* 19(1), 18–22.
Tested the hypothesis that there is no difference in need for achievement, power, or affiliation between Black male and female business majors. 42 Black graduate and undergraduate business students were administered a modification of the TAT. Findings indicate no significant differences in these needs between males and females. Results are inconsistent with recent research results indicating that the need structure of the contemporary Black woman may place her at a disadvantage in the management profession, relative to her male colleague. (19 ref).

615. Dillard, John M. (1976). **Relationship between career maturity and self-concepts of suburban and urban middle- and urban lower-class preadolescent Black males.** *Journal of Vocational Behavior,* 9(3), 311–320.
Investigated the relationship between career maturity and self-concepts of 252 6th-grade Black males. Student samples were drawn from (a) the suburban middle class, (b) the urban middle class, and (c) the urban lower class in 42 schools in 3 New York state counties. The Attitude scale of the Career Maturity Inventory and the Coopersmith Self-Esteem Inventory were used to assess the association of career maturity and self-concepts. Results indicate relatively weak positive relationships between career maturity and self-concepts. Significant career maturity differences were found; however, self-concepts of the 3 groups were not significantly different. Of the set of independent variables predicting and estimating variance accounted for (socioeconomic status, family intactness, place of residence, and reading), socioeconomic status had strongest predictive effect on career maturity. It is suggested that researchers examine elementary school Black students' career development in view of the group with whom they identify most. (25 ref).

616. Downing, Leslie L. & Bothwell, Kenneth H. (1979). **Open-space schools: Anticipation of peer interaction and development of cooperative interdependence.** *Journal of Educational Psychology,* 71(4), 478–484.
42 same-sex pairs of varied racial composition were randomly selected from 8th graders in each of 2 matched schools, with open- vs closed-space architectural styles. Open-space Ss were more likely to develop cooperative interdependence in a mixed-motive game (a decomposed prisoner's dilemma) and were more inclined to make proximal seating choices indicative of anticipated peer interaction. A Sex by Race by Trial Blocks interaction effect reflected different patterns of responding for males and females. Females of either race learned to cooperate in same-race pairs and to compete in mixed-race pairs. White males learned to cooperate and Black males to compete independent of their partner's race. External scores on Rotter's Internal–External Locus of Control Scale were not related to schools but were, as expected, higher for Black than for White students. (14 ref).

617. Gilroy, Faith D. & Desai, Harsha B. (1986). **Computer anxiety: Sex, race and age.** *International Journal of Man-Machine Studies,* 25(6), 711–719.
Describes 2 studies with 614 undergraduate and graduate college students that (1) examined antecedents of computer anxiety, and (2) exposed 2 groups of Ss who had no previous experience with computers to 2 treatments designed to lower the anxiety. Results indicate that for those persons with high anxiety in an English composition course, treatment in which Ss used word processing as a tool was more effective than was a course in computer programming in reducing computer anxiety. The programming course, however, was significantly more effective in reducing anxiety than was no treatment. Women were represented more often than men in the high anxiety conditions. Results are discussed in relation to training techniques in educational and workplace environments.

618. Grevious, Carole. (1985). **A comparison of occupational aspirations of urban Black college students.** *Journal of Negro Education,* 54(1), 35–42.
Questionnaire results on occupational aspirations, education, and family background obtained from 127 male and 132 female Black undergraduates show that males' aspirations were significantly more prestigious than those of females. There were sex differences in choice of field, and when males and females aspired to the same general fields, they selected different areas of specialization. Implications for career guidance are noted. (21 ref).

619. Hunt, Janet G. & Hunt, Larry L. (1977). **Racial inequality and self-image: Identity maintenance as identity diffusion.** *Sociology & Social Research,* 61(4), 539–559.
Examined "interpersonal mediation" interpretations of self-image maintenance in low-status circumstances. In a secondary analysis of data collected by M. Rosenberg and R. G. Simmons (1972) on 690 male 5th–12th graders, it was found that Black males held higher levels of self-regard in terms of esteem and sex-role identification than their White counterparts, but had lower senses of personal efficacy in the early (but not later) school years. While the self-attitudes of Black males were relatively positive and seemed to be held in connection with predominantly conventional value orientations, these attitudes were not intercorrelated or firmly grounded in more specific terms of self-description in a manner comparable to those of the White males. Controls for racial composition of schools (integrated or segregated) and personal attachment to school showed self-attitudes of Black males to be more positive in segregated schools and where school attachment was low. (26 ref).

620. Irvine, Jacqueline J. (1985). **Teacher communication patterns as related to the race and sex of the student.** *Journal of Educational Research,* 78(6), 338–345.
Summarizes previous research of teacher communication patterns related to student race and sex and examined 61 White and 6 Black teachers' verbal communications in the natural classroom as a function of the race and sex of the student. 494 White male, 342 White female, 316 Black male, and 298 Black female kindergarten through 7th graders from 67 classrooms in 10 schools in 4 school systems were observed in a dyadic interaction system, and teachers' verbal feedback was recorded and analyzed according to 14 categories, including praise academic, positive academic, negative procedure, no response, and total communication. Results reveal 2 significant main effects for race, 5 main effects for sex, and 3 significant race/sex interactions. Black students received more negative behavioral feedback and more positive–negative feedback than did White students. Females received significantly less total communication, less praise, less negative behavior feedback, less neutral procedure feedback, and less nonacademic feedback than males. The significant race/sex interactions emphasized the White female's infrequent communications with teachers, with White females receiving significantly less total communication than the other 3 sex/race groups. White females also received less neutral behavioral feedback and less academic feedback than did White males. (79 ref).

621. Irvine, Russell W. (1979). **Structure of school, personality and high school dropouts.** *Journal of Negro Education,* 48(1), 67–72.
Compared 40 high school dropouts with 31 high school graduates on a measure of their perception of the school as a "feminine" institution. Ss were Black males 18–20 yrs old, and the groups were matched on age, family integrity, and socioeconomic status. Parts of the California Personality Inventory were administered; the interest of the study focused on the Femininity subscale, but other subscales were included to insure S naivete. A Likert-type schedule was designed that included 50 statements (e.g., "Male/female teachers favor girls

over boys or boys over girls in certain situations"). Results support Hypothesis 1, that Black dropouts will show more masculinity than graduates. Hypothesis 2, that Black dropouts perceive, more than graduates, that school is a "feminine" institution, was not supported; no significant differences between the groups in this regard were found. (10 ref).

622. Jarman, Charles. (1976). **Education as a dimension of status incongruence between parents and the self perceptions of college students.** *Sociology of Education,* 49(3), 218–222.
Examined the relationship between maternal dominance (relative educational status of parents) and attrition rates in 262 Black males who entered a predominantly Black college in the South in 1963. Ss responded to questionnaires and measures of self-esteem, self-evaluation, and locus of control (Rotter's Internal–External Control Scale) upon college entry. On 1 dimension of self-perception (rejection of self-derogatory images) Ss who had come from families in which the mother's level of educational attainment was higher than that of the father's evaluated themselves significantly higher than other Ss. Other relationships involving internal control, attrition rate, acceptance of the Protestant ethic, and, to some extent, a positive self-evaluation, were not significantly related to status incongruence of parents.

623. Kelly, Paul K. & Wingrove, C. Ray. (1975). **Educational and occupational choices of Black and White, male and female students in a rural Georgia community.** *Journal of Research & Development in Education,* 9(1), 45–56.
Questionnaires administered to 1,705 students in Grades 9–12 showed that educational expectations were not lower for upper grades. Black males were consistently below Whites and Black females in educational expectations, whereas Black females were equal to or above Whites in expectations. Disproportionate numbers of both Blacks and Whites aspired to either professional or managerial positions. The gap between occupational aspirations and expectations was greater for Blacks than Whites. Female occupational choices tended to equal or to exceed those of males. (18 ref).

624. Lee, Courtland C. (1983). **An investigation of the athletic career expectations of high school student athletes.** *Personnel & Guidance Journal,* 61(9), 544–547.
Questionnaire data from 215 White and 171 Black male high school athletes indicated that 36% of the Black Ss who started on their teams expected a career in sports, compared to 14% of the White starters, 11% of the Black nonstarters, and 8% of the White nonstarters. Parental influence and academic performance did not significantly affect athletic expectations, although expectations were related to coaches' encouragement. Since less than 2% of high school athletes will ever make it to the professional level, such an apparent lack of reality in career planning may mean disappointment and frustration for many high school athletes. It is recommended that career counselors, coaches, and parents work together to present the student athlete with a range of career options and emphasize the important relationship between academic and athletic goals. (24 ref).

625. Littig, Lawrence W. & Reynolds, Carolyn D. (1984). **Effects of sex ratios on occupational prestige and desirability among Black and White university students.** *Social Behavior & Personality,* 12(2), 115–119.
Attempted to replicate J. C. Touhey's (1974; see also PA, Vol 52:895) research on the effect of increased proportion of women incumbents on the prestige and desirability of 6 high-status occupations. 200 Black and White college students, divided equally by race and sex, rated these occupations under instructions that they were either low and stable or high and increasing in proportion of women. The proportion of women did not affect the prestige ratings of the occupations for any of the S groups. Proportion of women affected occupational desirability for men and women and for Blacks

and Whites. In each instance, the effect was to increase desirability for one group and to decrease it for the other. (9 ref).

626. Parker, Woodrow M.; Berieda, Martha & Sloan, Delories. (1984). **Exploring male–female relations among Black college students: A survey.** *Journal of Non-White Concerns in Personnel & Guidance,* 12(2), 40–47.
Investigated Black students' experiences in male–female relations at the University of Florida. 55 Black upper division students (25 males and 30 females) participated in the study. Ss were randomly selected from fraternities, sororities, and other student organizations. The survey instrument consisted of an open-ended questionnaire that asked Ss to describe 3 of the most critical problems they thought existed between Black men and women on their campus. The most critical problems listed were the lack of social skills (62.25% males and 47.42% females). Specifically cited were the lack of respect, trust, honesty, appreciation, communication, and understanding. The 2nd most critical category was negative emotions (13.75% males and 14.43% females). Frequently listed negative emotions were hostility, jealousy, negative competition, and ego problems. Other problem areas were sex role difficulties, faculty values, external forces, and lack of career goals. (7 ref).

627. Picou, J. Steven; Cosby, Arthur G.; Curry, Evans W. & Wells, Richard H. (1977). **Race and the formation of academic self concept: A casual analysis.** *Southern Journal of Educational Research,* 11(2), 57–70.
Isolates a component of the self related to the school learning experience—academic self-concept. Previous theoretical and empirical research provides the basis for specifying a causal model which outlines the process of acacemic self-concept formation. The model is subjected to a path analytic solution for data gathered by the 3rd author et al (1975) from a sample of 80 Black and 99 White male high school youth residing in a large midwestern metropolitan area. Results reveal the existence of differential variable effects, by race, for the causal model. (21 ref).

628. Pliner, Judith E. & Brown, Duane. (1985). **Projections of reactions to stress and preference for helpers among students from four ethnic groups.** *Journal of College Student Personnel,* 26(2), 147–151.
64 White, 50 Black, 53 Hispanic, and 62 Asian-American undergraduates (123 females and 106 males) at a Texas university were surveyed for their expected reactions to stressful events and preferences for 17 sources of help. Ss estimated how stressful events would be if they occurred in the future in 4 domains: academic, financial, family, and personal. Results show that in the academic domain, older Blacks and Hispanics perceived events as potentially more stressful than did older Asian-Americans, and Hispanics had significantly higher stress ratings than Whites. The scores of older Blacks were not higher than those of Whites. Black males perceived that they would experience more stress in the personal domain than did Black females. Younger White females had higher stress scores than older White females. Blacks and Hispanics perceived events in the financial domain as more stressful than Whites or Asian-Americans. Stated preferences for a formal source of help were related positively to age and negatively to SES. Implications for financial-aid programs and counseling are noted. (19 ref).

629. Reiff, Judith C. (1985). **What are the reading preferences of *your* children?** *Journal of Instructional Psychology,* 12(2), 93–97.

Administered the Carbo Reading Style Inventory to 350 kindergartners through 5th graders. Responses were classified according to the reading approach most appropriate to Ss' preferences. Self-selected materials and language experience were the most frequent choices; programmed materials and basal readers were the least favorite approaches when analyzed by sex and race. (8 ref).

630. Sagar, H. Andrew; Schofield, Janet W. & Snyder, Howard N. (1983). **Race and gender barriers: Preadolescent peer behavior in academic classrooms.** *Child Development,* 54(4), 1032–1040.
Observed the classroom behavior of 48 Black (24 male, 24 female) and 44 White (23 male, 21 female) 6th graders in an urban desegregated school. Observations were made once a week in each classroom during a full semester using a time sampling method. In addition to noting the race and sex of the S being observed, as well as that of his/her interactants, observers also coded the source of the interaction (S, interactant, or both) and its task orientation (whether the behavior was related to academic tasks). As predicted, Ss interacted primarily with others of their own race and sex, although gender aggregation was less pronounced for Blacks than Whites. Also, as predicted, boys interacted more across racial lines than girls. Blacks were almost twice as likely as Whites to be the source of cross-race interactions. No race effects were apparent in Ss' own task orientation, but peer behaviors were more likely to be task-related when directed toward White rather than Black interactants. A parallel study of sociometric choice conducted in the same school reinforced most of these findings. (25 ref).

631. Schab, Fred. (1979). **Adolescence in the South: A comparison of Blacks and Whites not prepared for the world of work.** *Adolescence,* 14(55), 599–605.
Presented a questionnaire to 1,248 Black and White Georgia high school students on their attitudes toward working (i.e., need for freedom or independence in work, working conditions, general work philosophy, and rewards for working). Responses were analyzed by sex, race, and whether the S was in a college prep or a general curriculum. It was found that (a) Black and White males and Black females were equally concerned with job independence (e.g., "I would prefer to work for myself") and college prep White females were least concerned; (b) college prep Ss were less likely to agree to working on an assembly line; (c) females were more likely to prefer a shorter work week; and (d) Black males did not wish to work for a woman boss. All Ss agreed that a good job was important for men, but there were mixed responses to the statement that marriage was most important for women.

632. Shapiro, H. Jack & Stern, Louis W. (1977). **Importance of Maslow-type needs to business college seniors: Blacks, Whites, males, females.** *Psychological Reports,* 40(3, Pt 2), 1227–1235.
Examined the importance of various hierarchical needs, as described by A. Maslow, to Black and White, male and female business college seniors. Data show that hierarchical needs are more universal for all cultures than are superficial behaviors or desires. The cultural differences between the races begin to be manifest in the magnitude of the individual needs. Data indicate that the Black Ss placed greater importance on most of the needs studied than did the 249 Whites regardless of sex. (23 ref).

633. Slaney, Robert B. & Brown, Michael T. (1983). **Effects of race and socioeconomic status on career choice variables among college men.** *Journal of Vocational Behavior,* 23(3), 257–269.
Compared 48 Black and 48 White undergraduate males who were matched using O. D. Duncan's (1961) socioeconomic indicator (SEI) ratings and divided into upper and lower socioeconomic groups. This methodology avoided confounding race and SES and permitted study of their interaction. Variables relevant to the career choice process were chosen as outcome measures. Ss were administered a battery of tests that included the Vocational Preference Inventory (VPI) and Career Decision Scale. No group differences on age or educational level were found. Z tests of the distributions of Ss by VPI types indicated race, SEI, and race × SEI differences in preference for artistic, realistic, and investigative occupations, respectively. ANOVAs indicated a racial difference on one measure of career indecision, and SEI differences on a 2nd measure of career indecision and on the relationship between the Ss' VPI types and college major. Z tests of the distribution of the most important factors listed as career goal impediments indicated race × SEI differences. (41 ref).

634. Spaights, Ernest; Dixon, Harold E. & Nickolai, Susanne. (1985). **Attitude of Black collegians toward Jews and economic matters.** *College Student Journal,* 19(2), 118–122.
Examined the attitudes of 60 male and 116 female Black college students toward stereotypical notions of Jews with regard to economic matters. Ss completed a Likert-type scale, and responses were analyzed by sex using a 2 × 2 Chi-square test of independence. Results suggest that Blacks continue to harbor negative attitudes toward Jews and that Black males are more inclined to express negative perceptions toward Jews than Black females. (9 ref).

635. Steinberg, Jane A. & Hall, Vernon C. (1981). **Effects of social behavior on interracial acceptance.** *Journal of Educational Psychology,* 73(1), 51–56.
To test children's use of race and social behavior as cues in social acceptance, 128 Black and White male kindergartners and 1st graders rated 6 unknown videotaped target children for likability. Targets varied factorially on race (Black or White) and exhibited either positive, negative, or neutral classroom social behavior. Across age, socioeconomic status, and race, Ss used behavior as a cue, accounting for 50% of likability variance. Positive targets were liked equivalently, but Black neutral and negative targets were liked less than White counterparts. Racial but not socioeconomic status differences in the use of behaviors as social cues were found. Negative targets were liked more by Blacks than Whites and neutral targets were liked more by Whites than Blacks. (9 ref).

636. Thirer, Joel & Wieczorek, Philip J. (1984). **On and off field social interaction patterns of Black and White high school athletes.** *Journal of Sport Behavior,* 7(3), 105–114.
53 Black and 64 White male varsity high school athletes completed a questionnaire assessing their attitudes toward and their involvement in interracial interactions. Both Whites and Blacks expressed a preference for desegregated schools and a desire for more friends of a different race. However, about a third of both groups reported no interactions with players of a different race during practice or games. In addition, 62.5% of Whites reported no interaction with Blacks outside of sports, and 49% of Blacks had no interactions with Whites except for sports. Findings suggest that interracial social interaction habits may be firmly established at the high school level or earlier. (French abstract) (19 ref).

637. Thomas, Mark J. (1976). **Realism and socioeconomic status (SES) of occupational plans of low SES Black and White male adolescents.** *Journal of Counseling Psychology,* 23(1), 46–49.
Studied 118 low SES Black and White male high school students to clarify certain definitional problems related to the assessment of the occupational plans of low SES youth (using the Vocational Choice Inventory). Vocational choice realism was defined by the extent to which intelligence (Science Research Associates Pictorial Reasoning Test) corresponded to the intelligence level recommended in the *Dictionary of Occupational Titles* (1965). It was demonstrated that when given the opportunity, the students were able to distinguish between

their aspirations and expectations. Further, low SES Blacks were not significantly more unrealistic than Whites in their occupational expectations, and both Blacks and Whites aspired to, preferred, and expected to enter occupations at similar SES levels. Especially with respect to low SES Ss, the importance of distinguishing among different levels of vocational plans on a fantasy-reality continuum is stressed. (23 ref).

638. Tucker, M. Belinda & Yates, J. Frank. (1976). **Success expectations and preferences for individual and collaborative learning among Black and White college students.** *Journal of Negro Education,* 45(3), 295–305.
Gave 26 Black and 28 White male students part of the French Test of Insight (as an index of motive to achieve) and part of the Mandler-Sarason Test Anxiety Questionnaire (as a measure of need to avoid failure). In what was described as an unrelated experiment, Ss were told they were to solve a problem that was correctly solved 50% of the time by others, asked whether they would rather solve the problem alone, in a group, or in a group with an expert, and to estimate (zero to 10) their chances of solving the problem under each condition. Both Black and White students estimated their chances of solving the problem as best when an expert was present, and they did not differ significantly in degree of overall confidence in being able to solve the problem. However, in the work-alone condition, Whites rated their chances of success significantly better than did Blacks. Results of an analysis using scores on the 2 personality measures as a means of understanding why Blacks, who expected to do better in group settings, did not choose to work in group settings more imply that Black Ss may have been relatively more concerned with the satisfaction of ego needs than with objective gains. Practical implications for education are noted. (17 ref).

639. Verna, Gary B. & Runion, Keith B. (1985). **The effects of contextual dissonance on the self-concept of youth from a high versus low socially valued group.** *Journal of Social Psychology,* 125(4), 449–458.
Examined the self-concept of students from either a high or low socially valued group who were immersed in a contextually dissonant school setting. Ss were 315 7th- and 8th-grade Black and White males and females. Of this group, 54 Ss were bused to a school where their group was in the minority (dissonant context). The remaining Ss stayed in the school where their group was in the majority (consonant context). Results support the contextual dissonance theory for Ss from the lower socially valued group but not for those from the higher socially valued group. A significant interaction for the former group of Ss involving Dissonant vs Consonant Context by Male and Female by Fall vs Spring Semester showed that the number of negative attributes ascribed to the self was higher for Ss bused into a dissonant context than for those remaining in a consonant context; this difference was significant for the fall testing only. Change in self-concept from fall to spring semester differed depending on whether Ss were male or female as well as on whether or not they were bused into a dissonant context. (17 ref).

640. Wen, Shih-Sung & McCoy, Rose E. (1976). **Personal concerns and manifest anxiety in Black students.** *Journal of Clinical Psychology,* 32(1), 64–66.
Investigated the areas and magnitude of personal problems and their relationships with manifest anxiety in 154 male and 202 female Black undergraduates in a predominantly Black state university in the South. Ss were administered the Mooney Problem Check List and The Taylor Manifest Anxiety Scale. Both males and females were highly concerned with problems in college work, finance, living conditions, and employment, social and recreational activities and curriculum and teaching procedure. Significant positive correlations were found between the number of problems and anxiety scores in

9 areas for males and in all 11 areas for females. Two problem areas that did not correlate significantly with anxiety scores for males were social and recreational activities and home and family.

641. Williams, James H. & Haynes, Norris M. (1983). **Black junior high school students' perceptions of the role and effectiveness of counselors.** *Journal of Non-White Concerns in Personnel & Guidance,* 11(4), 152–156.
185 Black males and 212 Black females in Grades 7, 8, and 9 completed a questionnaire assessing their perception of the role and effectiveness of the school counselor. Chi-square analyses were used to examine the relationship between grade level, sex, and age (13–16 yrs) and the perception of the role and effectiveness of the counselor. Results suggest that neither the grade level nor the sex of Ss influenced their perception of the role of the counselor. Ss' age, however, did have an influence: 14- and 16-yr-olds judged the counselor's role more positively than did 13- and 15-yr-olds. A number of Ss in all age groups were uncertain about what the counselor's role was supposed to be. Seventh and 8th graders rated the effectiveness of the counselor higher than did 9th graders. A possible explanation for this finding may be that 9th graders are in a transition phase and have greater psychological and emotional needs that may not be adequately met by the counselor whose duties are varied and demanding. (8 ref).

642. Wolfstetter-Kausch, Heidi & Gaier, Eugene L. (1981). **Alienation among Black adolescents.** *Adolescence,* 16(62), 471–485.
With reference to the notion of alienation, it is assumed that the social conditions experienced by Black adolescents in American society induce feelings of disenfranchisement from society as a whole and from school as its representative. Based on the assumption of "matriarchy" in the Black lower class, it was hypothesized that the privileged and dominant position of the female would cause female adolescents to feel less alienated than male adolescents. A study of 32 females and 26 male Black high school students was conducted, using a questionnaire based on a multifactor concept of alienation. Results revealed that alienation among Ss was pervasive (i.e., Ss were alienated from both society and school). The hypothesis of a lower degree of feelings of alienation among females was not supported, indicating the need to reevaluate the assumption of "matriarchy." (30 ref).

Special & Remedial Education

643. Gresham, Frank M. & Reschly, Daniel J. (1987). **Sociometric differences between mildly handicapped and nonhandicapped Black and White students.** *Journal of Educational Psychology,* 79(2), 195–197.
We investigated sociometric differences between mainstreamed mildly handicapped and nonhandicapped Black and White students in a factorial design by using three indexes of peer acceptance. Results indicated differential patterns of peer acceptance between Black and White mildly handicapped children. We noted no main effects for race or sex; there was, however, a significant multivariate Sample × Race interaction effect. Race accounted for little variance in the sociometric status of mildly handicapped and nonhandicapped students. We discuss the implications of this study in terms of the degree of disparity between White and Black mildly handicapped and nonhandicapped students.

644. Low, Benson P. & Clement, Paul W. (1982). **Relationships of race and socioeconomic status to classroom behavior, academic achievement, and referral for special education.** *Journal of School Psychology,* 20(2), 103–112.
109 4th-grade boys from varying racial (Anglo, Black, and Hispanic) and socioeconomic status (SES) backgrounds were observed systematically on 4 occasions for 12 behaviors. Data

also were collected on academic achievement (as measured by the Comprehensive Test of Basic Skills) and special education referral. Multivariate analyses indicate no race-related differences in observed behavior and only 1 SES-related difference. Black and Hispanic Ss did not differ reliably, but both were lower than Anglo Ss in achievement. A nonstepwise discriminant function analysis utilizing race, SES, and observational data as predictors of referral for special education failed to make statistically reliable predictions. The relative unimportance of race and SES as predictors challenges the validity of alleged "institutional racism" in referrals for special education. (31 ref).

645. McIntyre, Lonnie D. & Pernell, Eugene. (1985). **The impact of race on teacher recommendations for special education placement.** Special Issue: The Black male: Critical counseling, developmental, and therapeutic issues: II. *Journal of Multicultural Counseling & Development,* 13(3), 112–120. Reviews the literature regarding the overrepresentation of Black male students in special education programs. In studies in which the findings did not clearly suggest race as a significant factor in teacher referral, there was an evident trend of referring students dissimilar from one's own background. It is argued that provisions must be made to provide educators with new knowledge regarding the lifestyles, learning styles, and behavior styles of Black male students. Recommendations are made to strengthen the knowledge base needed to prevent the continued disproportionate placement of Black males in special education classes. (22 ref).

646. Wright, Loyd S. (1974). **Conduct problem or learning disability?** *Journal of Special Education,* 8(4), 331–336. 47 3rd grade males identified by their teacher as having conduct problems were administered a battery of tests (e.g., the Wepman Auditory Discrimination Test, the Illinois Test of Psycholinguistic Abilities, and the WISC Vocabulary subtest) to determine (a) how many had reading problems and central processing dysfunctions; and (b) the correlations between their reading performance and central information-processing abilities, race, social class, and maternal employment. 24 Ss had both reading problems and central processing dysfunctions; however, factors related to the family and community were more closely related to reading performance than to measures of specific central information-processing abilities, per se. Results suggest that remediation for this type of child should consider not only factors within the child but the family and community as well.

Counseling & Measurement

647. Alston, Herbert L. & Doughtie, Eugene B. (1975). **Correspondence of constructs measured by the Kindergarten Screening Inventory by sex and ethnic group.** *Psychology in the Schools,* 12(4), 428–429. Investigated whether the constructs measured by the Kindergarten Screening Inventory (KSI) were the same for males and females and for Anglo-American, Negro-American, and Mexican-American groups. Ss were 1,527 kindergartners. The factor-relating procedure proposed by H. F. Kaiser et al (1969) to determine the extent to which the same constructs were measured with different groups was used. The correspondence between the constructs measured by the KSI for males and females and for the Anglo-American and Negro-American and Mexican-American groups was very similar. Findings indicate that substantially the same constructs are being measured by the KSI for both sexes and all ethnic groups.

648. Brown, John A. (1984). **Group work with low-income Black youths.** *Social Work with Groups,* 7(3), 111–124. Low-income Black youths face problems that negatively affect their self-concepts and educational achievement. Without an education, their opportunities for social mobility are severely decreased. The small group is suggested as a medium of intervention in the public schools by which large numbers of low-income Black youths can be reached. W. Schwartz's (1977) reciprocal model of social group work and the theoretical perspective of symbolic interactionism can provide the basis of such groups. The operation of a group involving Black junior high school males is discussed, and the applicability of some of the insights gained from this group to group work with Blacks in general is considered. (26 ref).

649. Dong, Hei-ki; Sung, Yong H. & Dohm, Thomas E. (1985). **The validity of the Ball Aptitude Battery (BAB): I. Relationship to high school academic success.** *Educational & Psychological Measurement,* 45(3), 627–637. Administered the BAB to 545 female and 464 male high school seniors in Illinois and Texas, representing 3 ethnic groups (Black, Hispanic, and White). In addition to the collection of the BAB test data, criterion data—total grade point average, grades in 9 academic courses, and ACT Assessment Program scores—were obtained for 801 students. Results show that BAB tests adequately predicted academic success in 10 areas of study and ACT scores, even though certain level differences were found in mean scores on the BAB. The findings of few significant differential validities for sex and ethnic groups suggest that the same battery of ability tests can serve for different ethnic and sex groups for purposes of career planning. (11 ref).

650. Drasgow, Fritz. (1987). **Study of the measurement bias of two standardized psychological tests.** *Journal of Applied Psychology,* 72(1), 19–29. Psychological tests are subject to two distinct forms of bias. The first form, measurement bias, occurs when individuals with equal standing on the trait measured by the test, but sampled from different subpopulations, have different expected test scores. Relational bias, the second type of bias, exists with respect to a second variable if a measure of bivariate association differs across groups. Empirical studies have found little evidence of relational bias. Two recent court cases, however, seem to have been more influenced by considerations of measurement bias than the literature concerning relational bias. Unfortunately, a consequence of both court cases is that the respective test makers must select items for future tests on the basis of a statistic (proportion correct) that is inappropriate for evaluating measurement bias. More sophisticated approaches may also suffer from methodological difficulties unless special precautions are taken. In this article, tests of English and Mathematics Usage are analyzed by measurement bias methods in which several steps are taken to reduce methodological artifacts. Many items are found to be biased. Nonetheless, the sizes of these effects are very small and no cumulative bias across items is found. (27 ref).

651. Gilsdorf, Dale L. (1978). **Counselor preference of Mexican-American, Black, and White community college students.** *Journal of Non-White Concerns in Personnel & Guidance,* 6(4), 162–168. Examined the counselor preferences of a sample of 60 male students in community college in the Southwest, 20 students each from the ethnic groups Mexican-American, Black, and White. Students preferred counselors of their own race. Implications for counseling are discussed. (16 ref).

652. Glutting, Joseph J.; Barker, William F. & Gelardo, Mark S. (1983). **Effects of student attributes on kindergarten scores across product and process tests.** *Journal of Psychoeducational Assessment,* 1(3), 261–271. Administered the Draw-A-Man Test (DAMT), the Cooperative Preschool Inventory—Revised Edition (PI), and the Goodman Lock Box (GLB) to 558 kindergartners categorized by age (5 yrs to 5 yrs 5 mo, 5 yrs 6 mo to 5 yrs 11 mo, and 6 yrs to 6 yrs 5 mo), ethnicity, sex, SES, and language background to determine the effects of these attributes on test scores. There were 116 Anglo females, 144 Anglo males, 45 Black females, 53 Black males, 95 Puerto Rican females, and 105 Puerto Rican males comprising the S population. Results show that all 3 tests were influenced by at least 2 of the student variables. Age increments were found for only 3 of 5 processes on the GLB. Sex modified DAMT scores. SES effect was greatest on the verbal product of the PI. Language modified DAMT and PI scores, but only the Organization scale of the GLB was modified by language. It is suggested that process variables are less influenced by the factors than product instrument scores (DAMT and PI) and that the GLB is nondiscriminatory against minority children. (51 ref).

653. Hobbs, Steven A. & Walle, Dennis L. (1985). **Validation of the Children's Assertive Behavior Scale.** *Journal of Psychopathology & Behavioral Assessment,* 7(2), 145–153.
Examined the validity of L. Michelson and R. Wood's (1982) Children's Assertive Behavior Scale (CABS) in 88 female and 72 male 3rd, 4th, and 5th graders. 82 Ss were Black, and 78 were White. Ss indicated their 3 best friends and the 3 children whom they would most wish to be like and completed the CABS. Ss who obtained either high or low scores on peer nominations of friendship and admiration were compared on CABS passive, aggressive, and assertive scores. Results indicate that Ss who scored high on positive peer nominations responded in a significantly less aggressive manner than Ss who received low scores on such nominations. These effects were observed for the CABS format that consisted of stimulus situations involving adults but not for the form involving peers. There was a significant interaction between race and aggressive scores regarding responses toward adults and peers and between sex and sociometric status regarding responses toward peers. Findings support the CABS as a measure of social skill that discriminates between children of differing sociometric status. (21 ref).

654. Hoover, H. D. & Kolen, Michael J. (1984). **The reliability of six item bias indices.** *Applied Psychological Measurement,* 8(2), 173–181.
Investigated the reliabilities of 6 item-bias indices for each of the 11 tests of the Iowa Tests of Basic Skills, using random samples of 5th-graders. Data consisted of item responses of 200 Black males, 200 Black females, 200 White males, and 200 White females. The reliability of an index was defined as its stability from one randomly equivalent group to another, and both racial and sexual bias were considered. In addition, correlations among bias indices were investigated. Results indicate that the item-bias indices investigated were fairly unreliable when based on sample sizes of 200 minority and 200 majority Ss. Findings suggest that, with sample sizes of about 200, the use of item bias indices to screen achievement test items cannot result in consistent decisions regarding which items are biased. (17 ref).

655. Lopez, Thomas & Kliman, Gilbert W. (1980). **The cornerstone treatment of a preschool boy from an extremely impoverished environment.** *Psychoanalytic Study of the Child,* 35, 341–375.
The Cornerstone method, described by the 2nd author (1968–1978), is an attempt, within the context of a community clinic, to integrate psychoanalytic therapy with the therapeutic nursery education of preschool children in order to more fully exploit the properties of each. The psychoanalyst treats the children individually in the classroom 3 or more times weekly, and the teachers simultaneously conduct a therapeutic nursery program with affection, example, limit setting, guidance, and stimulation. The successful treatment of a profoundly developmentally delayed Black child from the age of 2 to 6 yrs is given in detail. (47 ref).

656. Lothstein, Leslie. (1985). **Group therapy for latency age Black males: Unplanned interventions, setting, and racial transferences as catalysts for change.** *International Journal of Group Psychotherapy,* 35(4), 603–623.
Discusses the special problems and processes encountered in organizing and running a group therapy program for Black, latency-age, male children within an urban school setting. The group chosen for intervention consisted of 5 boys (aged 11–13 yrs) and was formed at the request of the school's psychiatric consultant, who found that many of the boys who were evaluated could not tolerate the demands of an individual therapy session and often acted out of control once they returned to their classrooms. The group leaders were 2 White clinical psychology interns (a man and a woman). In the course of the group, several important issues emerged that served as catalysts for change: unplanned interventions, setting effects, co-therapy issues, and racial transferences. The findings and follow-up suggest that a modified expressive group psychotherapy approach can be successful in treating inner-city Black children. (33 ref).

657. Marlowe, Roy H. et al. (1978). **Severe classroom behavior problems: Teachers or counsellors.** *Journal of Applied Behavior Analysis,* 11(1), 53–66.
Determined the relative effectiveness of teacher and counseling approaches in the reduction of disruptive or inappropriate classroom behavior in 12 academically low achieving, 7th-grade, Black male students. Three groups, with nearly equal mean inappropriate behaviors, were randomly assigned to 1 of 3 treatment conditions: behavioral, client-centered, or no counseling. Each experimental group received 15 30-min counseling sessions, at a rate of 2–3 times/wk. In addition to counseling, all Ss subsequently received teacher approval in the classroom. Results indicate that the teacher was able to reduce inappropriate behavior more than any counseling group. There were also indications that behavioral counseling, but not client-centered counseling, was moderately helpful in reducing inappropriate classroom behavior. (35 ref).

658. Miller, Janice & Eller, Ben F. (1985). **An examination of the effect of tangible and social reinforcers on intelligence test performance of middle school students.** *Social Behavior & Personality,* 13(2), 147–157.
Studied whether intelligence quotient mean test scores on the Otis–Lennon Mental Ability Test could be significantly increased through the use of tangible and intangible rewards of money and praise in 135 middle school students. Ss, identified as lower and middle socioeconomic class Whites and lower socioeconomic Blacks, were randomly assigned to 3 groups. The stratified groups, 2 experimental and 1 control, contained approximately the same number of males and females. Results indicate that (1) significant increases in the test scores of lower class Blacks were dependent on monetary reward; (2) significant increases in the test scores of middle and lower class Whites occurred when spoken verbal praise was administered; and (3) the sequencing of money first and praise second led to significant increases in the scores of lower and middle class White females and middle class males. (6 ref).

659. Minatoya, Lydia Y. & Sedlacek, William E. (1984). **Assessing attitudes of White university students toward Blacks in a changing context.** *Journal of Non-White Concerns in Personnel & Guidance,* 12(2), 69–79.
Administered a revised version of a situational attitude scale (SAS) developed by W. E. Sedlacek and G. C. Brooks (see PA, Vol 45:9830) to 259 (144 male and 115 female) White university freshmen to determine their attitudes toward Black individuals. The SAS employs semantic differential items. Form A describes situations with no mention of race, and Form B uses the same situations but includes the word Black. Ss were not aware that 2 forms of the instrument existed, and forms were randomly assigned to them. Results were analyzed

by 2-way analysis of variance (ANOVA) for each of the 100 items, with sex and form as main effects. 59 of the 100 items showed significant differences between the neutral and race explicit forms, thereby providing evidence for the validity of the instrument. 25 items were significantly different by sex of the S, and 3 items showed significant differences on the interaction form and sex. Results generally indicate that White students tended to react more negatively to situations where the word Black was inserted than they did where race was unspecified. (14 ref).

660. Payne, Beverly D.; Smith, Janet E. & Payne, David A. (1983). **Sex and ethnic differences in relationships of test anxiety to performance in science examinations by fourth and eighth grade students: Implications for valid interpretations of achievement test scores.** *Educational & Psychological Measurement,* 43(1), 267–270.
Scores from a 15-item measure of test anxiety were correlated with performances on a science achievement test. Samples of 171 4th-grade and 187 8th-grade students were subdivided by sex and race. A tendency was noted for the magnitude of correlations to be (a) higher in Grade 8 than in Grade 4, (b) positive for Blacks but negative for Whites, and (c) suggest that test anxiety operates differentially for Black and White students. (6 ref).

661. Perry, Joyce L. & Locke, Don C. (1985). **Career development of Black men: Implications for school guidance services.** Special Issue: The Black male: Critical counseling, developmental, and therapeutic issues: II. *Journal of Multicultural Counseling & Development,* 13(3), 106–111.
Identifies various systemic forces—sociological, cultural, and economic—that differentially affect the vocational development of Black males. It is suggested that because of these processes, Black male career awareness, exploration, and planning is qualitatively different from groups in the American mainstream. School guidance programs that can effectively address the career-development needs of Black males are characterized by advocacy, proactive services, outreach, and differential use of counseling tools. (15 ref).

662. Ponterotto, Joseph G.; Anderson, William H. & Grieger, Ingrid Z. (1986). **Black students' attitudes toward counseling as a function of racial identity.** *Journal of Multicultural Counseling & Development,* 14(2), 50–59.
Examined the attitudes of 69 female and 38 male Black 17–46 yr old students at a medium-sized, predominantly White public university toward counseling, their preferences for a counselor of the same race, and preferences for mental health resources. Ss completed a 75-item questionnaire containing a demographic inventory, a racial identity scale, an attitudes toward seeking professional psychological help scale, questions pertaining to preferences for a racially similar counselor or psychologist, and rankings of sources of help for a personal problem (e.g., clergy, faculty member, dean, parent, friend, counselor, psychiatrist). Results show that the main effects of sex and racial identity were not significant but that the sex × racial identity interaction was significant: Women in the internalization stage of racial identity development had the most favorable attitudes toward counseling. Attitudes between women and men within the encounter stage of identity development did not differ. Internalized males and females and encounter-stage females ranked friends and parents as preferred sources of help. No significant effects for counselor variables (age, sex, ethnicity, or degree) were found. It is concluded that for this population, attitudes toward counseling were not solely a function of sex or racial identity development per se but were a product of their interaction. Limitations of the survey and possible effects of the predominantly White institution on the Ss' attitudes are suggested. (24 ref).

663. Porché, Lisa M. & Banikiotes, Paul G. (1982). **Racial and attitudinal factors affecting the perceptions of counselors by Black adolescents.** *Journal of Counseling Psychology,* 29(2), 169–174.
Presented to 247 Black male and female high school students racial and attitudinal information about a hypothetical male or female counselor and asked them to express their perceptions of the counselor. Attitudinal information about a counselor had a stronger effect than racial information on Ss' perception of the counselor: Counselors portrayed as attitudinally similar were rated significantly higher in attractiveness, trustworthiness, expertness, and social attraction than those portrayed as attitudinally dissimilar. Racial information also influenced perceived attractiveness: White counselors were rated higher than Black ones in attractiveness, although there was no difference in ratings of trustworthiness or expertise. White female counselors were perceived as more expert than their Black female counterparts, whereas the ratings of male counselors were not influenced by the racial variable. Implications for counselor–client relationships and the development of mental health services for minority populations are discussed. (33 ref).

664. Powers, Stephen & Jones, Patricia B. (1984). **Factorial stability of the California Achievement Test.** *Educational & Psychological Research,* 4(4), 221–224.
Administered the California Achievement Test to 3,743 5th-grade pupils and 3,718 7th-grade students. Separate factor analyses for Black males, Black females, Hispanic males, Hispanic females, White males, and White females in the 5th and 7th grades indicated the presence of a single achievement factor in each group. Factor structures for each group were compared across grades using coefficients of congruence. Results indicate that the California Achievement Test was essentially stable across grades and race-sex combinations. (6 ref).

665. Powers, Stephen & Jones, Patricia B. (1984). **Factorial invariance of the California Achievement Tests across race and sex.** *Educational & Psychological Measurement,* 44(4), 967–970.
Administered 6 subtests of the California Achievement Tests (CAT)—Form C to 3,742 5th graders (100 Black males [BMs], 125 Black females (BFs), 601 Hispanic males [HMs], 595 Hispanic females [HFs], 1,183 White males [WMs], and 1,138 White females [WFs]) and to 3,718 7th graders (103 BMs, 112 BFs, 523 HMs, 495 HFs, 1,269 WMs, and 1,216 WFs). Results were factor analyzed separately for each race and sex group combination. One factor best described the factor structure of the test for each group. The structures of each group were compared using coefficients of congruence. Findings indicate that the CAT is essentially invariant with regard to race and sex. (5 ref).

666. Powers, Stephen; Thompson, Douglas; Azevedo, Barbara & Schaad, Olivia. (1983). **The predictive validity of the Stanford Mathematics Test across race and sex.** *Educational & Psychological Measurement,* 43(2), 645–649.
426 Black and White pupils were administered either the intermediate Stanford Mathematics Test (SMT; 6th graders), the advanced SMT (8th graders), or the California Achievement Test (Mathematics; 8th and 9th graders). Results of regression analyses and ANOVA showed no significant differences in mean residuals by race. Differences of small magnitude occurred by sex in one group, which indicated underprediction for females and overprediction for males. (10 ref).

667. Reynolds, Cecil R. (1979). **The invariance of the factorial validity of the Metropolitan Readiness Tests for Blacks, Whites, males, and females.** *Educational & Psychological Measurement,* 39(4), 1047–1052.
The 6 subtests comprising the Metropolitan Readiness Tests (MRT) were factor analyzed separately for 90 White female, 86 White male, 73 Black female, and 73 Black male 1st

graders. A single factor best described the structure of the test for each group. Coefficients of congruence for the factor between each pair of groups always exceeded .92. Thus, the factor structure of the MRT is essentially invariant with regard to race and sex variables. (25 ref).

668. Reynolds, Cecil R. (1980). **Differential construct validity of a preschool battery for Blacks, Whites, males, and females.** *Journal of School Psychology,* 18(2), 112–125.
Administered 7 major preschool tests (e.g., Metropolitan Readiness Test) to 90 White female, 86 White male, 73 Black female, and 73 Black male kindergartners. Scaled scores from the instruments were submitted to principal factoring, with iterations for the total sample and separately by race/sex groupings. The average intercorrelation of the pretests was similar across race and sex. A 2-factor solution of the battery was derived for the total group and for each of the 4 subgroups. The 2-factor solution was highly similar across race and sex, as indicated by the large coefficients of congruence obtained between factors derived within each group, thus supporting the equivalence of internal psychometric properties of the battery across race and sex. No evidence was determined to support sexual or racial dimorphism in the early structure of cognitive abilities. (39 ref).

669. Reynolds, Cecil R. (1980). **An examination for bias in a preschool test battery across race and sex.** *Journal of Educational Measurement,* 17(2), 137–146.
Evaluated the predictive validity of a battery of preschool tests (e.g., McCarthy Drawing Tests, Lee-Clark Reading Readiness Test, Metropolitan Readiness Test) over a 12-mo period using 322 preschoolers (90 White females, 86 White males, 73 Black females, 73 Black males). The battery was administered at the end of kindergarten and the Metropolitan Achievement Test at the end of 1st grade. A regression equation was determined using all preschool measures to predict achievement scores. Predictions were also made for each individual test, and residual terms calculated. No significant differences occurred in mean residuals between any pair of groups, indicating an absence of bias in prediction across race and sex with the large battery. When subsets of the larger battery were examined, sex bias in prediction was seen, indicating significant underprediction of female performance in some achievement areas. However, the magnitude of the effect was small. (26 ref).

670. Scott, Ralph. (1981). **FM: Clinically meaningful Rorschach index with minority children?** *Psychology in the Schools,* 18(4), 429–433.
Examined the possibility that the FM (animal movement) index may serve as a forerunner of abstract thinking, which is best illustrated by M (human activity) in Rorschach theory with older Ss; the hypothesis was studied using a Black male aged 3 yrs 4 mo. Results support the major finding that FM may enable educational diagnosticians to more accurately estimate the intellectual capabilities of some preschool minority and other culturally disadvantaged children. (17 ref).

671. Sewell, Trevor E. & Martin, Roy P. (1976). **Racial differences in patterns of occupational choice in adolescents.** *Psychology in the Schools,* 13(3), 326–333.
Investigated patterns of occupational choice and correlates of these patterns for 97 Black male inner-city high school juniors and seniors. The pattern of occupational choice was distinctly different from that of the middle-class, White normative sample of the occupational scale and other select samples in that the present Ss demonstrated more interest in artistic, health, and welfare fields. Locus of control correlated significantly with only one occupational category (interest in mechanical occupations), but generally was not a reliable correlate of occupational choice. Grade level was strongly related to positive choices. Implications for vocational counseling are discussed. (16 ref).

672. Starkman, Stanley; Butkovich, Catherine & Murray, Terrence. (1976). **The relationship among measures of cognitive development, learning proficiency, academic achievement, and IQ for seventh grade, low socioeconomic status Black males.** *Journal of Experimental Education,* 45(2), 52–56.
Examined the degree of relationship among measures of learning proficiency; cognitive development (following Piaget); school achievement in reading, mathematics, and spelling; and IQ among 79 low socioeconomic status Black males attending the 7th grade in an inner-city school. The following hypotheses were tested: (a) There would be a positive and significant relationship between measures of learning proficiency or cognitive growth and school achievement; (b) learning and cognitive variables would fall into a common factorial domain; and (c) the latter 2 variables would hold a reciprocal relationship within that domain. Hypothesis (a) was not supported, while (b) and (c) were supported. The latter 2 results support A. R. Jensen's (see PA, Vol 43:9740) 2-level theory of learning. These findings and between-pupil differences in cognitive development are discussed.

673. Stevens, Gwendolyn. (1981). **Bias in the attribution of hyperkinetic behavior as a function of ethnic identification and socioeconomic status.** *Psychology in the Schools,* 18(1), 99–106.
75 school psychologists, parents, and elementary teachers observed films of an Afro-American, a Mexican-American, and an Anglo-American 8-yr-old boy and assessed each child for hyperkinesis, using a behavioral rating scale developed for this study. The hypothesis that the perceived socioeconomic status and ethnic identification of assessees would influence assessors' attributions of hyperkinetic behavior was tested and supported. Lower socioeconomic status children and ethnic minority children were rated as more hyperkinetic than were middle socioeconomic status or Anglo-American children. Findings are explained in terms of attribution theory. (15 ref).

674. Stricker, Lawrence J. (1984). **The stability of a partial correlation index for identifying items that perform differentially in subgroups.** *Educational & Psychological Measurement,* 44(4), 831–837.
Evaluated the stability of a partial correlation index and 2 other methods—comparisons of item characteristic curves and the comparisons of item difficulties—in assessing race (White vs Black) and sex differences in the performance of verbal items on the Graduate Record Examination. Test data of 1,222 White males, 1,471 White females, 284 Black males, and 626 Black females were used. Results show that, in general, the partial correlation index, like the other indexes, exhibited substantial consistency in identifying the same items in different samples from the same populations and displayed congruence in its values. However, indexes had a general instability in the analyses of sex differences for Blacks, probably stemming from the small samples of Blacks involved. It is suggested that indexes be restricted to samples of at least 1,500 Ss with no fewer than 300 in the smallest subgroup. (15 ref).

675. Thompson, Ron A. & Cimbolic, Peter. (1978). **Black students' counselor preference and attitudes toward counseling center use.** *Journal of Counseling Psychology,* 25(6), 570–575.
Surveyed 42 female and 33 male Black college students to determine factors related to Black student use of the university counseling center. Counselor preference, sex of client, sex of counselor, race of counselor, and type of problem were analyzed as to their effects on counseling center use. Results indicate that Black clients preferred Black counselors and that the likelihood of taking a problem to the counseling center increased as counselor preference increased. Also, the likelihood of taking a problem to the center was significantly greater if the counselor to be seen was Black rather than White. Client and counselor sex, and type of problem (personal or educational-vocational) had no effect on potential counseling center usage. (20 ref).

676. Tidwell, Romeria & Bachus, Vickie A. (1977). **Group counseling for aggressive school children.** *Elementary School Guidance & Counseling,* 12(1), 2–7.
Examined the effects of group counseling on the fighting behavior of 24 Black males enrolled in Grades 4–6 of an urban elementary school. Ss met in groups of 6 for 8 bi-monthly hour-long sessions focusing on (a) helping behavior, (b) decision making, (c) empathy, and (d) aggression. In a follow-up role-playing exercise, the majority of Ss exhibited a preference for discussion rather than physical fighting as a means of resolving interpersonal disputes. Results suggest that group counseling emphasizing value teaching and decision making may be applied by counselors, teachers, and parents as a useful technique for dealing with disruptive pupil behavior.

677. Tomlinson, Jerry R.; Acker, Nancy; Canter, Andrea & Lindborg, Sherrie. (1977). **Minority status, sex, and school psychological services.** *Psychology in the Schools,* 14(4), 456–460.
The sex and minority status of 355 students referred for psychological services from a random sample of elementary, junior high, and senior high schools in an urban school system were examined in relation to the frequency of referral, type of problem, and the nature of subsequent psychological services. Minority Ss were identified as 127 Black Americans, 42 Native Americans, and 5 Orientals. A significantly higher percentage of both minority students (48%) and males (68%) were referred for psychological services; males were referred approximately twice as often as females. When referral problems were characterized as either academic or behavior problems, there were no differences between majority and minority students nor between males and females on percentage referred for each type of problem. Parent contacts were made significantly more often for majority students and for females, and recommendations to parents of majority students were more varied than those made to parents of minority students. Special Education resource services were recommended significantly more often for minority students. Possible reasons and implications of these findings are discussed.

APPLIED PSYCHOLOGY

678. Austin, David L. (1972). **The case of Donald A.: To hire or not to hire.** *Personnel & Guidance Journal,* 50(5), 392–394.
Considers the personal, educational, and work experience of an unemployed Black male seeking vocational counseling from 2 viewpoints, and indicates how the same data can be interpreted in such a way that a person appears either not worth hiring or deserving of an opportunity.

679. Barry, John R. (1971). **Motivation of the disadvantaged.** *Rehabilitation Research & Practice Review,* 3(1), 21–28.
Discusses the motivations of young, Black, urban males between 18 and 24 yrs of age who are not regularly employed. Rather than attributing a lack of drive to this group, different motives characteristic of this group are considered. Preliminary attempts to motivate the disadvantaged are described along with some experimental approaches to combat and/or redirect dependencies. (28 ref).

680. Brief, Arthur P. & Aldag, Ramon J. (1975). **Male-female differences in occupational attitudes within minority groups.** *Journal of Vocational Behavior,* 6(3), 305–314.
Administered a questionnaire about job preferences and outcomes and perceived instrumentality of performance to 31 female and 33 male Black participants in a pre-employability program associated with a high school in a large southern city (Group A) and 38 female and 55 male Black participants (Group B) in a similar New York City pre-employability

program (mean ages 17.5 and 18.7 yrs, respectively). Preferences were operationalized in terms of the valences of 2nd-level outcomes associated with the job which S aspired to after training. No significant differences were found between mean scores of males and females on any of the 11 valence and 11 instrumentality items for Group A. For Group B, only mean scores for the valence of the social interaction item were significantly different for males and females. Contrary to previous studies, however, it was males for whom the valence of social interaction was most important. Rankings of instrumentalities and valences were remarkably similar between sexes. (37 ref).

681. Coleman, James S.; Blum, Zahava D.; Sorensen, Aage B. & Rossi, Peter H. (1972). **White and Black careers during the first decade of labor force experience: I. Occupational status.** *Center for Social Organization of Schools Report, Johns Hopkins U.,* (Serial No. 44).
Used retrospective life history data in an analysis of the processes which lead to differential levels of occupational success. Data were collected from cohorts of 738 Black and 851 White 30–39 yr old men in 1968. Educational level far outweighed other individual characteristics in determining the occupational status of 1st jobs. The value of education for Whites was about twice that for Blacks. 58.3% of the status difference between Blacks and Whites was due to the different levels of background resources brought to the labor market, 32.5% to differences in efficacy of these resources, and the remaining 9.2% to unexplained differences. The initial status difference between the 2 groups was 5.59 status units and widened to 10.95 units by the end of 10 yrs. Approximately half the differences in status changes were due to original levels of resources and approximately half to the differential efficacy of the same resources and activities. The efficacy of intervening events (primarily part-time education and on-the-job training) was just as great for Blacks as for Whites.

682. Enneis, William H. (1970). **The Black man in the world of work: Minority employment barriers from the EEOC viewpoint.** *Professional Psychology,* 1(5), 435–439.
The equal employment opportunity commission has advocated that hiring standards or qualifications be systematically validated against employee job performance, and that applicant screening methods and cut-off scores be altered when selection methods have not demonstrated validity for a specific job. Arguments for using ethnic groups as a moderator variable in validation of predictors are cited. It is noted that statistical validity may be confused with relevance concerning employee performance. The changing patterns of minority recruiting and selection instruments with past validity are seen to emphasize the need for differential validation.

683. Greenhaus, Jeffrey H. & Gavin, James F. (1972). **The relationship between expectancies and job behavior for White and Black employees.** *Personnel Psychology,* 25(3), 449–455.
Investigated the relationship between effort-reward expectancy and job performance for Whites and Blacks. Ss were 390 White and 81 Black male, blue collar employees of a major airline. A Survey of Employee Opinions was administered to all Ss, and a supervisory rating form was used to measure job performance. Results indicate that the relationship between expectancy and work motivation criteria was low for both samples.

684. Hill, Walter A. & Hughes, David. (1974). **Variations in leader behavior as a function of task type.** *Organizational Behavior & Human Performance,* 11(1), 83–96.
Studied the flexibility of leader behavior with 48 Black and 48 White male undergraduate Ss. 12 Black and 12 White older Ss were selected as leaders, while the remaining Ss were assigned randomly as members of 12 Black, 12 White, and 12 mixed dyads. Results indicate that leader behavior as mea-

sured by the Interaction Process Analysis changed as the group performed different tasks. There were no behavior differences as a function of leader's race, although an interaction was found in the directive categories between task and dyad composition. (33 ref).

685. James, Sherman A.; LaCroix, Andrea Z.; Kleinbaum, David G. & Strogatz, David S. (1984). **John Henryism and blood pressure differences among Black men: II. The role of occupational stressors.** *Journal of Behavioral Medicine,* 7(3), 259–275.
In a continuation of a study by the 1st author and colleagues (see PA, Vol 71:9545) of "John Henryism," a cultural pattern through which Black Americans attempt to control their environment through hard work, the effects of psychosocial job stressors on the resting blood pressure (BP) of 112 Black male workers (aged 17–60 yrs) were examined. Job stressors included unemployment, lack of job security, lack of job success, the perception of inhibited anger about unfair wages, and the perception that being Black had hindered chances for achieving job success. The influence of on-the-job social support and John Henryism on several of these relationships was also examined. For systolic BP, a main effect was observed for job security, and an interaction effect was observed for employment status and time of day of interview. For diastolic BP, significant interactions were observed for job success and John Henryism, and for job success and the perception that being Black had hindered chances for achieving job success. Findings further clarify under what conditions John Henryism may be associated with higher BPs in Black men and also shed light on the emotional pathways through which selected job stressors may influence resting BP. (24 ref).

686. Katzell, Raymond A.; Ewen, Robert & Korman, Abraham K. (1974). **Job attitudes of Black and White workers: Male blue-collar workers in six companies.** *Journal of Vocational Behavior,* 4(3), 365–376.
Administered a 74-item attitude questionnaire in 6 companies to 101 Black and 87 White male blue-collar employees holding similar jobs in the same company. Differences between the 2 racial groups were not marked, both in terms of job satisfaction and in other respects. Where there were differences, results for the Black workers were usually slightly more favorable. Results were not uniform across the different companies. (23 ref).

687. Leigh, Duane E. (1976). **The occupational mobility of young men, 1965–1970.** *Industrial & Labor Relations Review,* 30(1), 68–78.
Data from the 1970 census were used to identify some of the important determinants of job advancement among 25–34 yr old Black and White males. A major finding of the study is that mobility was positively related to length of schooling, with a racial differential favoring Whites explainable in terms of the observed racial differences in educational endowments.

688. Milutinovich, Jugoslav S. (1977). **Black–White differences in job satisfaction, group cohesiveness and leadership style.** *Human Relations,* 30(12), 1079–1087.
Data from 3 organizations (N = 460) were used to compare the job satisfaction, group cohesiveness, and perception of leadership style of Black and White, blue-collar and white-collar, male and female workers in a stratified matched sample. Results suggest some differences in work attitudes between Black and White workers. The most dissatisfied group of workers were the Black white-collar females when compared with their White counterparts. However, for some occupational classes differences in work attitudes seemed minimal. (36 ref).

689. Nafziger, Dean H.; Holland, John L.; Helms, Samuel T. & McPartland, James M. (1972). **Applying an occupational classification to a national representation sample of work histories of young men and women.** *Center for Social Organization of Schools Report, Johns Hopkins U.,* (Serial No. 13).
Tested the usefulness of J. Holland's (see PA, Vol. 34:6165) occupational classifications for ordering work histories. National representation work histories were obtained from samples of 2,142 White and 716 Black 14-24 yr old females and 2,570 White and 914 Black 14–24 yr. old males. Females were interviewed once in 1968. Males were interviewed in 1966, 1967, and 1968. Analysis of occupational change and stability was performed by assigning scores to different occupational categories according to their psychological relatedness to one another. Analyses, performed by organizing and reorganizing work histories or occupations into 6 by 6 tables according to Holland's classification and then testing selected hypotheses from his theory of vocational behavior, were applied to work histories, consistency of codes, occupational aspirations, and family relationships. The theoretical implications of classification tests and theory are discussed. It is suggested that generally positive outcomes obtained with national representative samples should be supplemented by the use of unrepresentative samples in which more analytic tests are possible. (20 ref).

690. Parsons, George E. & Wigtil, James V. (1974). **Occupational mobility as measured by Holland's theory of career selection.** *Journal of Vocational Behavior,* 5(3), 321–330.
Examined the occupational mobility of men aged 45–59 yrs as measured by J. L. Holland's (1966) theory of career selection and its relationship to men in the work force. Ss were a total of 5,030 Black and White US men in 235 sample areas comprising 485 counties and independent cities, representing every state and the District of Columbia. Stability was discussed in 2 distinct ways, within a job and in the kind of work a man does over a career. In his research, Holland concluded that Realistic and Investigative personality types would change personality type less often and have more stable job choices in comparison to other personality types. Results of this study support these findings to some extent. However, it is concluded that stability in a personality type was strongly influenced by the number of jobs available in a particular personality type and the structure of the labor market demand. Results also show that psychological concepts seem to be more important in changing jobs than in selecting initial jobs.

691. Picou, J. Steven. (1978). **Race, athletic achievement and educational aspiration.** *Sociological Quarterly,* 19(3), 429–438.
Explored the relationship between athletic achievement and educational aspiration for 299 Black and 1,207 White male high school seniors. Results indicate that athletic behavior facilitates the association of White athletes with a college-oriented peer group, producing an indirect influence on aspiration. In contrast, athletic behavior for Black athletes is unmediated, indicating that other intervening social-psychological factors may be relevant. The theoretical significance of these results is discussed and suggestions are provided for future research on the consequences of interscholastic athletics for educational aspiration. (32 ref).

692. Sandefur, Gary D. & Scott, Wilbur J. (1983). **Minority group status and the wages of Indian and Black males.** *Social Science Research,* 12(1), 44–68.
Data from the 1976 Survey of Income and Education were used to examine the differences in wages among 6,447 White and 2,014 Black, and 597 Indian males (aged 20–54 yrs). Differences in characteristics such as cultural identification and education between Indians and Whites largely accounted for the difference in the average wage of these 2 groups. On the other hand, minority status, as well as characteristics, was

important in understanding the differences in the average wage of Blacks and Whites. It is suggested that Blacks experience more discrimination than do Indians and that this accounts for the larger impact of minority status for Blacks. (38 ref).

693. Sapolsky, Barry S. (1980). **The effect of spectator disposition and suspense on the enjoyment of sport contests.** *International Journal of Sport Psychology,* 11(1), 1–10.
94 Black and White male undergraduates viewed portions of a close or lopsided basketball game that was won by either an all-Black or an all-White team and rated their enjoyment of the final 18 baskets scored. Black Ss enjoyed baskets by Black athletes more than did White Ss. Counter to expectations, White Ss did not express any greater enjoyment with baskets by White athletes than did Black Ss. The effect of suspense on enjoyment was negligible. (French, Spanish, Italian, & German abstracts) (10 ref).

694. Schenkel, K. F. & Hudson, R. H. (1970). **The Black man in the world of work: Reclaiming the hard-core unemployed through training.** *Professional Psychology,* 1(5), 439–443.
Describes a training program established by Lockheed-Georgia company in 1967 to evaluate the feasibility of motivating and developing disadvantaged persons into productive citizens. Criteria for candidate selection and psychological tests used are described, including the MMPI, Wide Range Achievement Test, the US Employment Service General Aptitude Test Battery, the Environmental Participation Index, and the Kuder Preference Record. Phases of training included (a) orientation, (b) basic shop phase, (c) fabrication and assembly, and (d) skills and services, each phase leading to greater specialization. Plans were made to investigate relationships between test scores, scores and training performance, and scores and on-the-job performance. Projected follow-up studies are described which will compare trainee graduates with new employees and with a sample of all-Black new employees.

695. Schmitt, Neal & Hill, Thomas E. (1977). **Sex and race composition of assessment center groups as a determinant of peer and assessor ratings.** *Journal of Applied Psychology,* 62(3), 261–264.
Evaluated the effects of sex and race composition of assessment center groups on assessment center ratings for 54 racially and sexually mixed groups. Results indicate that there were minimal effects as a result of the race–sex composition of the group, but some assessment ratings for Black females were negatively and significantly correlated with the number of White males in the assessment group. The ratings of White males tended to be higher when the number of White males in the assessment group increased. (16 ref).

696. Sherman, Martin F.; Smith, Robert J. & Sherman, Nancy C. (1983). **Racial and gender differences in perceptions of fairness: When race is involved in a job promotion.** *Perceptual & Motor Skills,* 57(3, Pt 1), 719–728.
Examined 106 Black and 69 White undergraduates' (82 males and 93 females) perceptions of fairness in a fictitious ambiguous situation where 1 stimulus person (a male employee) was described as promoted over another and race was the only manipulated variable. The 2 (race of S) × 2 (sex of S) × 2 (race of promoted employee) × 2 (race of nonpromoted employee) factorial ANOVA indicated that not only did race of the evaluator influence perceptions of fairness, but it also interacted with race of the stimulus persons. Blacks perceived more unfairness operating in the situations than Whites, and they saw the promoted employee as less qualified than Whites did. Blacks perceived the White employee's promotion over the Black employee as the most unfair, while Whites saw no difference among the situations. An expected sex difference was found: Females were more likely than males to perceive

the company's decision as unfair. Blacks were more favorable to the use of quotas than Whites, and Blacks believed there had been more discrimination and less progress in the last decade. (27 ref).

697. Valecha, Gopal K. (1972). **Construct validation of internal–external locus of reinforcement related to work-related variables.** *Proceedings of the Annual Convention of the American Psychological Association,* 7(Pt. 1), 455–456.
Administered an abbreviated 11-item scale of internal–external locus of reinforcement to a national probability sample of 4,330 males of 16–26 yr old in 1968. Eight hypotheses were tested. Data are separately analyzed for Whites and Blacks. There were generally significant results obtained for Whites but not for Blacks. The internal–external construct as measured by the 11-item scale appears to have a much better construct validity for Whites than Blacks.

698. Watson, John & Williams, John. (1977). **Relationship between managerial values and managerial success of Black and White managers.** *Journal of Applied Psychology,* 62(2), 203–207.
Recent research has shown a relationship between personal values and the success of managers. The present study attempted to determine if a relationship exists between the managerial success of Black managers and their personal values. 64 Black male and 64 White male managers from a variety of business organizations completed the Personal Values Questionnaire developed in 1967 by G. W. England. The managerial success index was a measure of pay relative to age. For Whites results were similar in direction and magnitude to findings in previous research. For Blacks results were similar in direction but not quite so strong as the previous data collected on White samples. Thus, results of the present study do not refute the basic thesis that personal values can be used in the selection and placement process. Additional research is needed, however, to firmly establish this point.

699. Wilson, Kenneth L. & Butler, John S. (1978). **Race and job satisfaction in the military.** *Sociological Quarterly,* 19(4), 626–638.
Past studies of job satisfaction for minority groups relegated the racial issue to the initial determinant of status attainment deficiencies that indirectly influence job satisfaction. In a sample of over 9,000 military men, including almost 1,500 Blacks, 3 questions were examined: (a) Do past findings on job satisfaction apply to the military setting? (b) Are the conditions contributing to job satisfaction for Blacks qualitatively different from those for Whites? (c) What are the implications of the emergence of separatist attitudes among Blacks for work experiences in an integrated setting? The Black–White differences uncovered were traced to the historical development in race relations in America, pivoting on the racial experience of the 1960s. Implications for other minority groups are discussed. (31 ref).

700. Wright, Sonia. (1975). **Work response to income maintenance: Economic, sociological, and cultural perspectives.** *Social Forces,* 53(4), 552–562.
Studied the validity of the assumption that income maintenance creates disincentives to work in the context of economic, sociological, and cultural perspectives on work among the poor. This idea was tested with data from the New Jersey Negative Income Tax (NIT) Experiment. Contrary to predictions derived from economic theory and culture of poverty speculations, data from Black, White, and Puerto Rican male heads of households in poverty tracts in New Jersey and Pennsylvania who received at least 1 quarterly interview during the 2nd and 3rd yrs of the study ($n = 1,119$ and 993, respectively) show: (a) no such disincentive effects among male heads of households; (b) consistent and significant effects on work activity of prior labor force history and extent of par-

ticipation, age, health, family structure, education, and welfare status; and (c) that even those who exhibited a variety of allegedly detrimental personality traits, as described by the culture of poverty thesis, and those least integrated into the work ethic still showed no work reduction as a result of NIT. (47 ref).

Occupational Attitudes & Interests & Guidance

701. Braddock, Jomills H. & McPartland, James M. (1983). **More evidence on social-psychological processes that perpetuate minority segregation: The relationship of school desegregation and employment desegregation.** *Center for Social Organization of Schools Report, Johns Hopkins U.,* (Serial No. 338).
Used data from the Black subsample of the National Longitudinal Surveys Youth Cohort to investigate the effects of school desegregation on subsequent employment desegregation. Analysis is based on 472 female and 602 male Blacks who reported being employed either full- or part-time at the time of the 1980 survey. It was found that in the North, Blacks from desegregated schools were more likely to be located in desegregated occupational work groups. Moreover, Blacks from desegregated school backgrounds made fewer racial distinctions about the friendliness of their co-workers or about the competence of their employment supervisors. In contrast, Blacks from segregated schools tended to find desegregated co-workers to be less friendly and White supervisors to be less competent. Evidence suggests that both early school desegregation experiences and current community desegregation patterns promote desegregation in work environments, with school desegregation showing a greater impact, particularly among northern Blacks. Thus, it appears that the inferred social-psychological processes that perpetuate minority segregation across institutional settings are not artifactual, but are outcomes of cross-race experiences in the varied institutional settings. Results also suggest that early desegregated experiences create a different attitudinal basis among Blacks that, in part, produces or sustains desegregation in adulthood. (18 ref).

702. Brenner, O. C. & Tomkiewicz, Joseph. (1982). **Job orientation of Black and White college graduates in business.** *Personnel Psychology,* 35(1), 89–103.
Examined differences in job orientation between Black and White male and female business college graduates. Of the 104 Black Ss, 51 were male and 53 female; of the 238 Whites, 121 were male and 117 females. Significant race differences were found on 10 of 25 job characteristics, Blacks rating 9 of these more important than Whites. Significant Race by Sex interactions existed on 4 characteristics, while sex differences were found on 9. Factor analysis indicated that Blacks valued long-range career objectives and structure considerably more than Whites, while their preference for intrinsic and extrinsic factors was less pronounced. Methods by which organizations can satisfy the greater importance placed on many job characteristics by Blacks are explored. (28 ref).

703. Cosby, Arthur G.; Thomas, John K. & Falk, William W. (1976). **Patterns of early adult status attainment and attitudes in the nonmetropolitan South.** *Sociology of Work & Occupations,* 3(4), 411–428.
Uses data from a study of Southern, nonmetropolitan youth to report the patterns of congruency and deflection in occupational and educational attitudes and attainment. Descriptive comparisons of status aspiration, expectations and attainment were made for 427 White and 268 Black males from 6 Deep South states. Aspirations and expectation levels for future occupational and educational attainment were apparently "unrealistic" in terms of available opportunities and also appeared to be only marginally related to present attainment. Although White levels of these variables somewhat exceeded

comparable levels for Blacks, both groups generally had unrealistic and optimistic attitudes. It is hypothesized that in a success-oriented society, unrealistic future orientations allow those who are not succeeding to deny failure by projecting future achievements. (18 ref).

704. Daniels, Stacey. (1986). **Relationship of employment status to mental health and family variables in Black men from single-parent families.** *Journal of Applied Psychology,* 71(3), 386–391.
Reinterviewed, at a 6-yr follow-up, 90 Black males (mean age 23 yrs) reared in female-headed, single-parent households and initially interviewed at ages 16 and 17 yrs (C. B. Wilkerson and W. A. O'Connor, 1977). At interview Ss completed the SCL-90, the Life Experiences Survey, a social adjustment scale, and an ecologic assessment record. They were grouped in employment categories of superachievers, average, underemployed, and unemployed. Employment status was related to social adjustment and current life experiences ratings. Superachievers felt more competent, had higher aspirations, and were more satisfied with their lives than members of other groups. Longer father presence in the home was associated with more successful employment, as was a highly educated mother. Socioeconomic differences between the groups were slight and did not account for any direct or indirect effects. Strongest predictors of employment status were high school grades and length of father presence. Age, mother's age, and family income during the preschool and high school years also entered into the predictive equation. (25 ref).

705. Dillard, John M. (1976). **Socioeconomic background and the career maturity of Black youths.** *Vocational Guidance Quarterly,* 25(1), 65–70.
Studied the relationship of career maturity to reading achievement and socioeconomic status (SES). Ss were 252 6th-grade suburban and urban Black males in New York State. Hollingshead's Two Factor Index of Social Position determined middle or lower SES; the Career Maturity Inventory–Attitude Scale (CMI) assessed career maturity; and the Stanford Achievement Test, the Metropolitan Achievement Test, and the Iowa Test of Basic Skills measured reading skill levels. Statistical analyses, including simple correlations, analysis of variance, and analysis of covariance, showed (a) a low positive correlation overall between SES and CMI, (b) significantly higher reading levels for Ss of middle than of lower SES, and (c) a significant relationship between SES and career maturity even when CMI scores were controlled for reading ability levels. Overall, reading achievement appears less related to career maturity than SES variables such as cultural and socialization factors. Counselors should help students explore attitudes and values before the end of high school and should develop career programs that involve students' families.

706. Dillard, John M. & Campbell, N. Jo. (1982). **Career values and aspirations of adult female and male Puerto Ricans, Blacks, and Anglos.** *Journal of Employment Counseling,* 19(4), 163–170.
Hypothesized that there would be no significant sex or ethnic-group differences between the career values and aspirations of Blacks, Puerto Ricans, and Whites. 154 Blacks (105 women, 49 men), 99 Whites (57 women, 42 men), and 51 Puerto Ricans (32 women, 19 men) completed measures of SES, work values, and career aspirations. Findings show significant differences (1) among the career values of the 3 ethnic groups; (2) among Black, Puerto Rican, and White males' career aspirations; (3) between Black males' and females' career values; (4) in median values of activity preference (AP) and attitudes toward earnings (ATE) for Black, Puerto Rican, and White females; (5) between AP and ATE measures for Black males and females; and (6) between ATE and pride in work for White males and females. Findings indicate that the

levels of career values among both Puerto Rican and Black women and men are more similar than the levels of career values among White men and women and are discussed in relation to situational determinants. (12 ref).

707. Gottfredson, Linda S. (1978). **Race and sex differences in occupational aspirations: Their development and consequences for occupational segregation.** *Center for Social Organization of Schools Report, Johns Hopkins U.,* (Serial No. 254).
Data from the National Assessment of Educational Progress regarding occupational aspirations, values, and self-reported competencies of 13- and 17-yr-olds and adults aged 26–35 yrs were used to examine race and sex differences in orientation to particular types of occupations. Data indicate that (a) society-wide stereotypes about good jobs are mirrored in the occupational aspirations of children, (b) the stereotypes about the occupations appropriate for men are different from those for women, (c) these stereotypes are largely the same for all racial and ethnic groups, (d) as children go through adolescence their aspirations become more realistic, and (e) the races and sexes adjust their aspirations toward different sets of occupations. It is suggested that strategies to decrease occupational segregation by decreasing educational handicaps will not eradicate all important differences in what the races and sexes bring to the labor market. (3 p ref).

708. Gurin, Patricia. (1981). **Labor market experiences and expectancies.** *Sex Roles,* 7(11), 1079–1092.
Compared labor market experiences of 850 White males, 79 Black males, 542 White females, and 100 Black females. Results indicate that while women had "invested in their human capital" nearly as often as men, they had tried job training or job changes less often and had acquired additional schooling more often. Compared to White men, both groups of women expressed lower work-related expectancies. Part of the White male expectancy edge can be attributed to differences in past investment strategies. Black and White women who had tried to make work changes did not differ from White men in present expectancies. Results suggest that adult socialization in the labor market is a potentially important area of research on women's employment. (16 ref).

709. Kerckhoff, Alan C. & Jackson, Robert A. (1982). **Types of education and the occupational attainments of young men.** *Social Forces,* 61(1), 24–45.
Examined the effects of high school curriculum and vocational training on occupational outcomes among 989 White and 242 Black males when they were aged 25–29 and 29–33 yrs. Findings suggest that (a) the usual status attainment model has inadequately specified the relationship between educational and occupational attainment, (b) the common conclusion that Black occupational outcomes are less predictable than those of Whites is unwarranted, and (c) curriculum and vocational training have strong effects for Blacks because they help move Blacks into people-oriented and data-processing occupations. (17 ref).

710. Leonard, Patricia Y. (1985). **Vocational theory and the vocational behavior of Black males: An analysis.** Special Issue: The Black male: Critical counseling, developmental, and therapeutic issues: II. *Journal of Multicultural Counseling & Development,* 13(3), 91–105.
Examines both process- and personality-based theories of career choices in terms of their applicability to the Black male. Selected indicators of the current status of Blacks and research on their vocational maturity, occupational aspirations, personality, and self-concept are reviewed. The degree to which key assumptions of these current theories are useful in predicting career choices and describing the career development process for young Black men is analyzed. Implications for career education and vocational counseling and guidance with this group are discussed. (49 ref).

711. Littig, Lawrence W. (1979). **Motivational correlates of real to ideal occupational aspiration shifts among Black and White men and women.** *Bulletin of the Psychonomic Society,* 13(4), 227–229.
Shifts from traditionally "open real" to traditionally "closed ideal" occupational aspirations were examined among 140 Black and 70 White men and 200 Blacks and 100 White women students in either traditionally Black or White US colleges as functions of social class and achievement, affiliation, and power motivations. It was hypothesized that achievement and power, but not affiliation and motivations would manifest an effect in fantasized ideal closed aspirations. In general, women shifted, men did not. Middle-class White women shifted regardless of motive type or strength. Among middle- and working-class Black women, the predominant trend for the 3 motives was for the low-motivation group to shift and the high-motivation group not to shift, contrary to the hypothesis. Results suggest that strong motivation results in a correspondence between real and ideal occupational aspirations in Black women but not in White women. (5 ref).

712. Littig, Lawrence W. (1975). **Personality, race, and social class determinants of occupational goals.** *International Mental Health Research Newsletter,* 17(2), 2–6,.
Reviews the author's research on occupational goal determinants for Black and White American and English youth of college age. Examining effects of needs for achievement, affiliation, and power on aspirations to enter traditionally closed occupations (upward mobility), the investigations revealed the following: (a) For women, no identifiable relationship appeared between occupational aspirations and the motivational variables, race, and social class. (b) For working-class Black men, achievement needs were linked to aspiration to closed occupations. (c) For middle-class men overall, affiliation needs were related to closed-occupation aspiration. Since the American occupational structure is moving toward sponsored mobility, which favors affiliation motivation, the future is uncertain for achievement-oriented working-class people. (35 ref).

713. O'Brien, William F. & Walsh, W. Bruce. (1976). **Concurrent validity of Holland's theory for non-college degreed Black working men.** *Journal of Vocational Behavior,* 8(2), 239–246.
Explored 2 areas: the concurrent validity of J. L. Holland's (1973) theory for employed noncollege degreed Black men using 2 different definitions of vocational orientation; and the relationships among same scales across the 2 inventories. Concurrent validity was studied by administering the Vocational Preference Inventory (VPI) and the Self Directed Search (SDS) to 121 17–68 yr old men workers in occupational environments consistent with Holland's 6 vocational environments. The VPI and the SDS scales tended to effectively discriminate among the occupational groups consistent with Holland's theoretical notions. Results tend to suggest that Holland's theory is meaningful for employed noncollege degreed Black men.

714. Rotberg, Heidi L.; Brown, Duane & Ware, William B. (1987). **Career self-efficacy expectations and perceived range of career options in community college students.** *Journal of Counseling Psychology,* 34(2), 164–170.
The first purpose of the present study was to explore the relation of socioeconomic status (SES), race, gender, career self-efficacy, career interests, and sex role orientation to career-choice range in female–male, and non-gender-dominated careers. The second purpose was to determine the relation of SES, race, sex role orientation, gender, and career interests to career self-efficacy. Results indicated that career interest and career self-efficacy expectations significantly predicted range of perceived career options above and beyond the contributions of the other dependent variables. Similarly,

career interest and sex role orientation predicted self-efficacy expectations. Recommendations for future investigations of the career self-efficacy model of occupational choice as well as some possible applications of the findings to career counseling are made.

715. Thomas, Michele B. & Neal, Patricia A. (1978). **Collaborating careers: The differential effects of race.** *Journal of Vocational Behavior,* 12(1), 33–42.
Conducted a study with 165 female and 105 male Black undergraduates enrolled in introductory psychology or human development courses at a predominantly Black university. Ss responded to 5 stories about married Black physicians whose total income was greatest, respectively, when the husband cared for the children (Story 1), the wife cared for the children (Story 2), either spouse cared for them (Story 3), the wife earned more than the husband (Story 4), or the husband earned more than the wife (Story 5). In contrast to the results of a study completed at a predominantly White university by C. Peterson and J. Peterson (see PA, Vol 55:11080), Black females favored maternal child care even when, as a result, the family income was reduced and had significantly less of a preference for higher relative salary for the wife than did females in the study at a predominantly White university. Although Black males preferred maternal child care in Story 2 and Story 3, the preference was significantly less than that of males in the study at a predominantly White university. Results are discussed in terms of their relevance to collaborating career patterns among middle-class Black families.

716. Walsh, W. Bruce; Bingham, Rosie P. & Sheffey, Marie A. (1986). **Holland's theory and college educated working Black men and women.** *Journal of Vocational Behavior,* 29(2), 194–200.
Investigated differences between college-educated working men and women employed in traditional occupations who took the Vocational Preference Inventory (VPI) and the Self Directed Search: A Guide to Educational and Vocational Planning (SDS). The VPI and the SDS were administered to 44 female and 64 male Black college-educated workers in 3 of J. L. Holland's (1978, 1985) environmental categories (realistic, investigative, and enterprising). In general, the findings for the 3 VPI and SDS scales and for these occupational groups indicate that Black women, when compared to Black men in the same occupation, tend to report similar mean raw scores. Black men and women in the same occupation seem to be far more similar than different. (11 ref).

Personnel Selection & Training

717. Becker, Brian E. & Krzystofiak, Frank J. (1982). **The influence of labor market discrimination on locus of control.** *Journal of Vocational Behavior,* 21(1), 60–70.
Hypothesized that direct victims of labor market discrimination would be more external than Blacks who did not recognize discrimination but who, in turn, would be more external than those who recognized but had not experienced discrimination. Prior research has established the existence of racial differences in locus of control as well as a relationship between labor market experience and locus of control. Drawing on a national probability sample of 2,857 young men (769 Blacks), multiple regression analysis was used to estimate the effect of labor market discrimination (over 2 yrs) on subsequent locus of control. Ss completed a version of Rotter's Internal–External Locus of Control Scale and answered questions on discrimination. Results indicate that perceptions of employment discrimination influenced the level of externality among Blacks, over and above racial identification. Blacks who viewed themselves as victims of employment discrimination experienced twice the increase in externality as Blacks reporting no awareness of discrimination. (20 ref).

718. Landis, Dan et al. (1976). **Can a Black "culture assimilator" increase racial understanding?** *Journal of Social Issues,* 32(2), 169–183.
A programmed instruction approach to race relations training in the US Army involved developing the technique (culture assimilator) and testing it in the field. In the development phase 65 Black officers, 90 Black enlisted men, 65 White officers, and 90 White enlisted men participated. In the field test 84 White and 85 Black junior grade officers participated. Major results are as follows: (a) The problems used in the assimilator represented events far more familiar to Black officers than to White officers. (b) Blacks obtained higher scores than Whites on the assimilator, indicating greater knowledge of the Black perspective on race relations in the Army. (c) Significant evidence of learning of acculturative materials by White officers was obtained. (d) There was significant improvement on an independent test of intercultural understanding. (18 ref).

Environmental Psychology & Environmental Issues

719. Rodin, Judith. (1976). **Density, perceived choice, and response to controllable and uncontrollable outcomes.** *Journal of Experimental Social Psychology,* 12(6), 564–578.
Conducted 2 experiments to consider the effects of chronic high residential density on responses to choice and controllable and uncontrollable outcomes. In Study 1, 32 Black 6–9 yr old males responded to obtain candy as reinforcement and, during certain phases of the procedure, were able to select a schedule which allowed them to pick their own candy rather than having the experimenter select candy for them. Ss who lived in high residential density were significantly less likely than Ss from less dense homes to try to control the administration of available outcomes. In Study 2, with 172 7th and 8th graders, Ss were preexposed to a solvable or unsolvable cognitive learning task and tested for how well they subsequently learned a solvable problem. Ss from high density homes did significantly more poorly than less crowded Ss when the 1st problem was unsolvable. It is suggested that chronic density limits prediction and control in the home environment and consequently leads to the development of decreased expectancies for contingency between response and outcome in other control-relevant situations. (30 ref).

Section II. Selected Citations to Other Relevant Journal Articles on Black Males in the United States

This section contains selective citations to journal articles that focus primarily on gender and racial differences between Black males in the United States and other groups. References were retrieved from the PsycINFO database by searching for the concept of *Black males* (or synonyms) in the abstract as well as in the title, descriptor, and identifier fields. Entries are organized alphabetically within the major/minor classification categories used by *Psychological Abstracts* and the PsycINFO database.

PSYCHOMETRICS

720. Bart, William M.; Rothen, Wolfgang & Read, Sherry. (1986). **An ordering-analytic approach to the study of group differences in intelligence.** *Educational & Psychological Measurement,* 46(4), 799–810.

721. Butler-Omololu, Cynthia; Doster, Joseph A. & Lahey, Benjamin. (1984). **Some implications for intelligence test construction and administration with children of different racial groups.** *Journal of Black Psychology,* 10(2), 63–75.

722. Humphreys, Lloyd G.; Fleishman, Allen I. & Lin Pang-chieh. (1977). **Causes of racial and socioeconomic differences in cognitive tests.** *Journal of Research in Personality,* 11(2), 191–208.

Test Construction & Validation

723. Hanley, Jerome H. & Barclay, Allan G. (1979). **Sensitivity of the WISC and WISC-R to subject and examiner variables.** *Journal of Black Psychology,* 5(2), 79–84.

724. Holcomb, William R.; Adams, Nicholas A. & Ponder, Howard M. (1984). **Are separate Black and White MMPI norms needed? An IQ-controlled comparison of accused murderers.** *Journal of Clinical Psychology,* 40(1), 189–193.

725. Kass, Richard A.; Mitchell, Karen J.; Grafton, Frances C. & Wing, Hilda. (1983). **Factorial validity of the Armed Services Vocational Aptitude Battery (ASVAB), Forms 8, 9 and 10: 1981 Army applicant sample.** *Educational & Psychological Measurement,* 43(4), 1077–1087.

726. Katzenmeyer, W. G. & Stenner, A. Jackson. (1977). **Estimation of the invariance of factor structures across sex and race with implications for hypothesis testing.** *Educational & Psychological Measurement,* 37(1), 111–119.

727. Knuckle, Essie P. & Asbury, Charles A. (1986). **WISC-R discrepancy score directions and gender as reflected in neuropsychological test performance of Black adolescents.** *Journal of Research & Development in Education,* 20(1), 44–51.

728. Lachar, David; Butkus, Michael & Hryhorczuk, Linda. (1978). **Objective personality assessment of children: An exploratory study of the Personality Inventory for Children (PIC) in a child psychiatric setting.** *Journal of Personality Assessment,* 42(5), 529–537.

729. McLoughlin, Caven S. & Koh, Tong-he. (1982). **Testing intelligence: A decision suitable for the psychologist?** *Bulletin of the British Psychological Society,* 35, 308–311.

730. Miele, Frank. (1979). **Cultural bias in the WISC.** *Intelligence,* 3(2), 149–164.

731. Munford, Paul R. (1978). **A comparison of the WISC and WISC-R on Black child psychiatric outpatients.** *Journal of Clinical Psychology,* 34(4), 938–943.

732. Nelson, W. M.; Edinger, Jack D. & Wallace, John. (1978). **The utility of two Wechsler Adult Intelligence Scale short forms with prisoners.** *Journal of Personality Assessment,* 42(3), 302–311.

733. Patalano, Frank. (1980). **MMPI two-point code-type frequencies of drug abusers in a therapeutic community.** *Psychological Reports,* 46(3, Pt 1), 1019–1022.

734. Reynolds, Cecil R. & Paget, Kathleen D. (1983). **National normative and reliability data for the revised Children's Manifest Anxiety Scale.** *School Psychology Review,* 12(3), 324–336.

735. Reynolds, Cecil R.; Willson, Victor L. & Chatman, Steve. (1984). **Relationships between age and raw score increases on the Kaufman-Assessment Battery for Children.** *Psychology in the Schools,* 21(1), 19–24.

736. Shih-sung Wen & An-yen Liu. (1976). **The validity of each of the four scales of the Survey of Study Habits and Attitudes (SSHA) for each of two samples of college students and under each of two treatment conditions involving use of released class time.** *Educational & Psychological Measurement,* 36(2), 565–568.

737. Snyder, Douglas K.; Kline, Rex B. & Podany, Edward C. (1985). **Comparison of external correlates of MMPI substance abuse scales across sex and race.** *Journal of Consulting & Clinical Psychology,* 53(4), 520–525.

738. Vance, Hubert B. & Engin, Ann W. (1978). **Analysis of cognitive abilities of Black children's performance on WISC-R.** *Journal of Clinical Psychology,* 34(2), 452–456.

739. Vance, Hubert B.; Hankins, Norman & McGee, Harold. (1979). **A preliminary study of Black and White differences on the Revised Wechsler Intelligence Scale for Children.** *Journal of Clinical Psychology,* 35(4), 815–819.

740. Witt, Philip H. & Gynther, Malcolm D. (1975). **Another explanation for Black-White MMPI differences.** *Journal of Clinical Psychology,* 31(1), 69–70.

EXPERIMENTAL PSYCHOLOGY (HUMAN)

741. France, Kenneth. (1973). **Effects of "White" and of "Black" examiner voices on IQ scores of children.** *Developmental Psychology,* 8(1), 144.

742. Goldstein, Harris S. & Peck, Rosalind. (1973). **Maternal differentiation, father absence and cognitive differentiation in children.** *Archives of General Psychiatry,* 29(3), 370–373.

743. Pargman, David. (1977). **Perceptual cognitive ability as a function of race, sex and academic achievement in college athletes.** *International Journal of Sport Psychology,* 8(2), 79–91.

PHYSIOLOGICAL PSYCHOLOGY

744. Bridge, T. Peter et al. (1985). **Platelet monoamine oxidase activity: Demographic characteristics contribute to enzyme activity variability.** *Journal of Gerontology,* 40(1), 23–28.

745. Lester, David. (1976). **Age, sex and racial differences in morphology.** *Psychological Reports,* 38(1), 106.

746. Myers, Hector F.; Bastien, Rochelle T. & Miles, Ralph E. (1983). **Life stress, health, and blood pressure in Black college students.** *Journal of Black Psychology,* 9(2), 1–25.

COMMUNICATION SYSTEMS

747. Baptiste, David A. (1986). **The image of the Black family portrayed by television: A critical comment.** *Marriage & Family Review,* 10(1), 41–65.

748. Barry, Thomas E. & Hansen, Richard W. (1973). **How race affects children's TV commercials.** *Journal of Advertising Research,* 13(5), 63–67.

749. Darden, Betty J. & Bayton, James A. (1977). **Self-concept and Blacks' assessment of Black leading roles in motion pictures and television.** *Journal of Applied Psychology,* 62(5), 620–623.

750. Entwisle, Doris R. & Garvey, Catherine. (1972). **Verbal productivity and adjective usage.** *Language & Speech,* 15(3), 288–298.

751. Hudson, Amelia I. & Holbrook, Anthony. (1981). **A study of the reading fundamental vocal frequency of young Black adults.** *Journal of Speech & Hearing Research,* 24(2), 197–201.

752. La France, Marianne. (1974). **Nonverbal cues to conversational turn taking between Black speakers.** *Personality & Social Psychology Bulletin,* 1(1), 240–242.

753. Poussaint, Alvin F. (1974). **Blaxploitation movies: Cheap thrills that degrade Blacks.** *Psychology Today,* 7(9), 22–32,.

DEVELOPMENTAL PSYCHOLOGY

754. Baron, Reuben M. & Ganz, Richard L. (1972). **Effects of locus of control and type of feedback on the task performance of lower-class Black children.** *Journal of Personality & Social Psychology,* 21(1), 124–130.

755. Bernstein, Martin E. & Di Vesta, Francis J. (1971). **The formation and reversal of an attitude as functions of assumed self-concept, race, and socioeconomic class.** *Child Development,* 42(5), 1417–1431.

756. Bloom, Richard. (1970). **Dimensions of mental health in adolescent boys.** *Journal of Clinical Psychology,* 26(1), 35–38.

757. Breyer, Norman L. & May, Jack G. (1970). **Effect of sex and race of the observer and model on imitation learning.** *Psychological Reports,* 27(2), 639–646.

758. Cross, John F. & Cross, Jane. (1971). **Age, sex, race, and the perception of facial beauty.** *Developmental Psychology,* 5(3), 433–439.

759. Cross, John F.; Cross, Jane & Daly, James. (1971). **Sex, race, age, and beauty as factors in recognition of faces.** *Perception & Psychophysics,* 10(6), 393–396.

760. Doke, Larry A. & Risley, Todd R. (1972). **Some discriminative properties of race and sex for children from an all Negro neighborhood.** *Child Development,* 43(2), 677–681.

761. Eiland, Rebecca & Richardson, Don. (1976). **The influence of race, sex and age on judgments of emotion portrayed in photographs.** *Communication Monographs,* 43(3), 167–175.

762. Garrett, Aline M. & Willoughby, R. H. (1972). **Personal orientation and reactions to success and failure in urban Black children.** *Developmental Psychology,* 7(1), 92.

763. Graves, Avis J. (1972). **Attainment of conservation of mass, weight, and volume in minimally educated adults.** *Developmental Psychology,* 7(2), 223.

764. Greenberger, Ellen; Campbell, Paul; Sorensen, Aage B. & O'Connor, Jeanne. (1971). **Toward the measurement of psychosocial maturity.** *Center for Social Organization of Schools Report, Johns Hopkins U.,* (Serial No. 110),

765. Griffing, Penelope. (1974). **Sociodramatic play among young Black children.** *Theory into Practice,* 13(4), 257–265.

766. Hansley, Clementine & Busse, Thomas V. (1969). **Perceptual exploration in Negro children.** *Developmental Psychology,* 1(4), 446.

767. Hayes, Edward D. & Hambright, Jerold E. (1984). **Moral judgment among Black adolescents and White adolescents from different socioeconomic levels.** *Journal of Negro Education,* 53(4), 418–423.

768. Heider, Eleanor R. (1971). **Style and accuracy of verbal communications within and between social classes.** *Journal of Personality & Social Psychology,* 18(1), 33–47.

769. Jackson, James S.; Bacon, John D. & Peterson, John. (1978). **Life satisfaction among Black urban elderly.** *International Journal of Aging & Human Development,* 8(2), 169–179.

770. Katz, Phyllis A. (1967). **Verbal discrimination performance of disadvantaged children: Stimulus and subject variables.** *Child Development,* 38(1), 233–242.

771. Kolsin, Sandra; Koslim, Bertram; Pargament, Richard & Bird, Henry. (1971). **Children's social distance constructs: A developmental study.** *Proceedings of the Annual Convention of the American Psychological Association,* 6(Pt. 1), 151–152.

772. Laurence, Ronald & Sutton-Smith, Brian. (1968). **Novel responses to toys: A replication.** *Merrill-Palmer Quarterly,* 14(2), 159–160.

773. Miller, Thomas W. (1975). **Effects of maternal age, education, and employment status on the self-esteem of the child.** *Journal of Social Psychology,* 95(1), 141–142.

774. Nicholas, Karen B.; Mccarter, Robert E. & Heckel, Robert V. (1971). **The effects of race and sex on the imitation of television models.** *Journal of Social Psychology,* 85(2), 315–316.

775. Oberle, Wayne H. (1974). **Role models of Black and White rural youth at two stages of adolescence.** *Journal of Negro Education,* 43(2), 234–244.

776. Olmsted, Patricia P. & Sigel, Irving E. (1970). **The generality of color-form preference as a function of materials and task requirements among lower-class Negro children.** *Child Development,* 41(4), 1025–1032.

777. Seegmiller, Bonni R. & King, William L. (1975). Relations between behavioral characteristics of infants, their mothers' behaviors, and performance on the Bayley Mental and Motor Scales. *Journal of Psychology,* 90(1), 99–111.

778. Thompson, Norman L., Jr. & McCandless, Boyd R. (1970). It score variations by instructional style. *Child Development,* 41(2), 425–436.

779. Turner, Charles. (1971). Effects of race of tester and need for approval on childrens' learning. *Journal of Educational Psychology,* 62(3), 240–244.

780. Wohlford, Paul; Santrock, John W.; Berger, Stephen E. & Liberman, David. (1971). Older brothers' influence on sex-typed, aggressive, and dependent behavior in father-absent children. *Developmental Psychology,* 4(2), 124–134.

781. Zytkoskee, Adrian; Strickland, Bonnie R. & Watson, James. (1971). Delay of gratification and internal versus external control among adolescents of low socioeconomic status. *Developmental Psychology,* 4(1, Pt. 1), 93–98.

Cognitive & Perceptual Development

782. Atkin, Robert et al. (1977). Ability factor differentiation, Grades 5 through 11. *Applied Psychological Measurement,* 1(1), 65–76.

783. Capute, Arnold J. et al. (1985). Normal gross motor development: The influences of race, sex and socio-economic status. *Developmental Medicine & Child Neurology,* 27(5), 635–643.

784. Costantino, Giuseppe & Malgady, Robert G. (1983). Verbal fluency of Hispanic, Black and White children on TAT and TEMAS, a new thematic apperception test. *Hispanic Journal of Behavioral Sciences,* 5(2), 199–206.

785. Goldstein, David; Meyer, William J. & Egeland, Byron. (1978). Cognitive performance and competence characteristics of lower- and middle-class preschool children. *Journal of Genetic Psychology,* 132(2), 177–183.

786. Perney, Violet H. (1976). Effects of race and sex on field dependence-independence in children. *Perceptual & Motor Skills,* 42(3, Pt 1), 975–980.

787. Vance, Hubert B. & Gaynor, Patricia E. (1976). A note on cultural difference as reflected in the Wechsler Intelligence Scale for Children. *Journal of Genetic Psychology,* 129(1), 171–172.

Psychosocial & Personality Development

788. Billingham, Robert E. & Walters, James. (1978). Relationship between parent preference and peer preference among preadolescents. *Journal of Genetic Psychology,* 133(2), 163–169.

789. Billy, John O. & Udry, J. Richard. (1985). Patterns of adolescent friendship and effects on sexual behavior. *Social Psychology Quarterly,* 48(1), 27–41.

790. Brunswick, Ann F. & Messeri, Peter A. (1984). Origins of cigarette smoking in academic achievement, stress and social expectations: Does gender make a difference? *Journal of Early Adolescence,* 4(4), 353–370.

791. Cantor, Gordon N. (1978). Race and sex effects in the conformity behavior of children. *Augustana College Library Occasional Paper,* (Serial No. 14).

792. Dancy, Barbara L. & Handal, Paul J. (1981). Effect of gender and age on family climate scores of Black adolescents and preliminary norms. *Psychological Reports,* 48(3), 755–757.

793. Dillard, John M. & Campbell, N. Jo. (1981). Influences of Puerto Rican, Black, and Anglo parents' career behavior on their adolescent children's career development. *Vocational Guidance Quarterly,* 30(2), 139–148.

794. Finkel, Madelon L. & Finkel, David J. (1983). Male adolescent sexual behavior, the forgotten partner: A review. *Journal of School Health,* 53(9), 544–547.

795. Hendrix, Beverly L. (1980). The effects of locus of control on the self-esteem of Black and White youth. *Journal of Social Psychology,* 112(2), 301–302.

796. Henry, Susan E.; Medway, Frederic J. & Scarbro, Harold A. (1979). Sex and locus of control as determinants of children's responses to peer versus adult praise. *Journal of Educational Psychology,* 71(5), 604–612.

797. Houston, Lawrence N. (1981). Romanticism and eroticism among Black and White college students. *Adolescence,* 16(62), 263–272.

798. Lee, Courtland C. (1984). Work values of rural Black, White, and Native American adolescents: Implications for contemporary rural school counselors. *Counseling & Values,* 28(2), 63–71.

799. Lee, Courtland C. (1984). An investigation of the psychosocial variables in the occupational aspirations and expectations of rural Black and White adolescents: Implications for vocational education. *Journal of Research & Development in Education,* 17(3), 28–34.

800. Mitchell, Jim; Wilson, Kenneth; Revicki, Dennis & Parker, Leslie. (1985). Children's perceptions of aging: A multidimensional approach to differences by age, sex, and race. *Gerontologist,* 25(2), 182–187.

801. Moore, Carolyn D. & Handal, Paul J. (1980). Adolescents' MMPI performance, cynicism, estrangement, and personal adjustment as a function of race and sex. *Journal of Clinical Psychology,* 36(4), 932–936.

802. Moore, Clifford L. (1978). Racial preference and intelligence. *Journal of Psychology,* 100(1), 39–43.

803. Moore, J. William; Hauck, William E. & Denne, Thomas C. (1984). Racial prejudice, interracial contact, and personality variables. *Journal of Experimental Education,* 52(3), 168–173.

804. Osborne, W. Larry & LeGette, Helen R. (1982). Sex, race, grade level, and social class differences in self-concept. *Measurement & Evaluation in Guidance,* 14(4), 195–201.

805. Richman, Charles L.; Clark, M. L. & Brown, Kathryn P. (1985). General and specific self-esteem in late adolescent students: Race × gender × SES effects. *Adolescence,* 20(79), 555–566.

806. Rust, James O. & McCraw, Anne. (1984). Influence of masculinity-femininity on adolescent self-esteem and peer acceptance. *Adolescence,* 19(74), 359–366.

807. Samuels, Douglas D. & Griffore, Robert J. (1978). The relationship between maternal anxiety and self-esteem of preschool-aged children. *Child Study Journal,* 8(2), 93–99.

808. Sanders, James F.; Poole, Thomas E. & Rivero, W. T. (1980). Death anxiety among the elderly. *Psychological Reports,* 46(1), 53–54.

809. Short, Geoffrey A. (1981). **Racial attitudes among Caucasian children: An empirical study of Allport's "total rejection" hypothesis.** *Educational Studies,* 7(3), 197–204.

810. Speelman, Diana & Hoffman, Charles D. (1980). **Personal space assessment of the development of racial attitudes in integrated and segregated schools.** *Journal of Genetic Psychology,* 136(2), 307–308.

811. Vaughan, Sandra L.; Stabler, John R. & Clance, Pauline R. (1981). **Children's monetary evaluations of body parts as a function of sex, race, and school grade.** *Journal of Psychology,* 107(2), 203–209.

812. Verna, Gary B. (1982). **A study of the nature of children's race preferences using a modified conflict paradigm.** *Child Development,* 53(2), 437–445.

813. Weigel, Ronald M. (1985). **Demographic factors affecting assertive and defensive behavior in preschool children: An ethological study.** *Aggressive Behavior,* 11(1), 27–40.

814. Weisfeld, Glenn E.; Weisfeld, Carol C. & Callaghan, John W. (1984). **Peer and self perceptions in Hopi and Afro-American third- and sixth-graders.** *Ethos,* 12(1), 64–84.

815. Westney, Ouida E.; Cole, O. Jackson & Munford, Theodosia L. (1986). **Adolescent unwed prospective fathers: Readiness for fatherhood and behaviors toward the mother and the expected infant.** *Adolescence,* 21(84), 901–911.

816. Wilcox, Steven & Udry, J. Richard. (1986). **Autism and accuracy in adolescent perceptions of friends' sexual attitudes and behavior.** *Journal of Applied Social Psychology,* 16(4), 361–374.

817. Willis, Frank N. & Reeves, Dennis L. (1976). **Touch interactions in junior high students in relation to sex and race.** *Developmental Psychology,* 12(1), 91–92.

SOCIAL PROCESSES AND SOCIAL ISSUES

818. Alston, Jon P.; Peek, Charles W. & Wingrove, C. Ray. (1972). **Religiosity and Black militancy: A reappraisal.** *Journal for the Scientific Study of Religion,* 11(3), 252–261.

819. Bayton, James A. & Muldrow, Tressie W. (1968). **Interacting variables in the perception of racial personality traits.** *Journal of Experimental Research in Personality,* 3(1), 39–44.

820. Brigham, John C. & Richardson, Curtis B. (1979). **Race, sex, and helping in the marketplace.** *Journal of Applied Social Psychology,* 9(4), 314–322.

821. Brown, Thomas E. (1969). **Sex education and life in the Black ghetto.** *Religious Education,* 64(6), 450–458.

822. Burns, Alice. (1970). **Blackman and Whiteman in a mother–child symbiotic unit.** *Voices: The Art & Science of Psychotherapy,* 6(2), 62–64.

823. Cameron, Paul. (1969). **Valued aspects of religion to Negroes and Whites.** *Proceedings of the 77th Annual Convention of the American Psychological Association,* 4(Pt. 2), 741–742.

824. Chambers, Carl D.; Moffett, Arthur D. & Cuskey, Walter R. (1971). **Five patterns of Darvon abuse.** *International Journal of the Addictions,* 6(1), 173–189.

825. Donagher, Patricia C.; Poulos, Rita W.; Liebert, Robert M. & Davidson, Emily S. (1975). **Race, sex and social example: An analysis of character portrayals on inter-racial television entertainment.** *Psychological Reports,* 37(3, Pt 2), 1023–1034.

826. Duncan, Beverly & Duncan, Otis D. (1969). **Family stability and occupational success.** *Social Problems,* 16(3), 273–285.

827. Foley, Linda A. (1977). **Personality characteristics and interracial contact as determinants of Black prejudice toward Whites.** *Human Relations,* 30(8), 709–720.

828. Franklin, Raymond S. (1969). **The political economy of Black Power.** *Social Problems,* 16(3), 286–301.

829. Frazier, Arthur & Roberts, Virgil. (1969). **A discourse on Black nationalism.** *American Behavioral Scientist,* 12(4), 50–56.

830. Friedman, Neil. (1969). **Africa and the Afro-American: The changing Negro identity.** *Psychiatry,* 32(2), 127–136.

831. Geerken, Michael & Gove, Walter R. (1974). **Race, sex, and marital status: Their effect on mortality.** *Social Problems,* 21(4), 567–580.

832. Gitter, A. George & O'Connell, Stephen M. (1970). **Racial appearance of ideal Blacks.** *CRC Report, Boston U.,* (Serial No. 48).

833. Green, Paul E. (1973). **Multivariate procedures in the study of attitudes and status impressions.** *Social Science Research,* 2(4), 353–369.

834. Grupp, Stanley E. (1972). **Multiple drug use in a sample of experienced marijuana smokers.** *International Journal of the Addictions,* 7(3), 481–491.

835. Jones, Stanley E. (1971). **A comparative proxemics analysis of dyadic interaction in selected subcultures of New York City.** *Journal of Social Psychology,* 84(1), 35–44.

836. Katz, Irwin; Henchy, Thomas & Allen, Harvey. (1968). **Effects of race of tester, approval–disapproval, and need on Negro children's learning.** *Journal of Personality & Social Psychology,* 8(1, Pt. 1), 38–42.

837. King, Karl. (1967). **A comparison of the Negro and White family power structure in low income families.** *Child & Family,* 6(2), 65–74.

838. King, Karl. (1969). **Adolescent perception of power structure in the Negro family.** *Journal of Marriage & the Family,* 31(4), 751–755.

839. Lerner, Richard M. & Karson, Michael. (1973). **Racial stereotypes of early adolescent White children.** *Psychological Reports,* 32(2), 381–382.

840. Littig, Lawrence W. (1968). **Negro personality correlates of aspiration to traditionally open and closed occupations.** *Journal of Negro Education,* 37(1), 31–36.

841. Lowinger, Paul; Darrow, Charlotte & Huige, Frida. (1969). **Case study of the Detroit uprising: The troops and the leaders.** *Archives of General Psychiatry,* 21(1), 33–38.

842. Massey, Robert F. (1972). **Meta-subjectivity: A model for interracial understanding.** *International Journal of Group Tensions,* 2(4), 71–85.

843. McMillen, David L. (1974). **Confidence in stereotypes concerning ethnic groups.** *Journal of Social Psychology,* 93(2), 203–210.

844. Peretti, Peter O. & Keller, Helga. (1980). **Status position, upward mobility, and attitude change among Blacks: A comparative approach.** *Journal of Psychological Researches,* 24(1–2), 34–42.

845. Rice, Audrey S.; Ruiz, Rene A. & Padilla, A. M. (1974). **Person perception, self-identity, and ethnic group preference in Anglo, Black, and Chicano preschool and third-grade children.** *Journal of Cross-Cultural Psychology,* 5(1), 100–108.

846. Sattler, Jerome M.; Skenderian, Daniel & Passen, Andrew J. (1972). **Examiners' race and subjects' responses to an attitude scale.** *Journal of Social Psychology,* 87(2), 321–322.

847. Shelibow, Barbara. (1973). **An investigation into the relationship between self-esteem and skin color among Hispanic children.** *Graduate Research in Education & Related Disciplines,* 7(1), 64–82.

848. Sutker, Patricia & Gilliard, Rickie S. (1970). **Personal sexual attitudes and behavior in Blacks and Whites.** *Psychological Reports,* 27(3), 753–754.

849. Sutker, Patricia B. & Kilpatrick, Dean G. (1973). **Personality, biographical, and racial correlates of sexual attitudes and behavior.** *Proceedings of the 81st Annual Convention of the American Psychological Association, Montreal, Canada,* 8, 261–262.

850. Teahan, John E. & Podany, Edward C. (1974). **Some effects of films of successful Blacks on racial self-concept.** *International Journal of Social Psychiatry,* 20(3–4), 274–280.

851. Throne, John M. (1972). **An operant interpretation of Black rage.** *Psychotherapy: Theory, Research & Practice,* 9(1), 36–39.

852. Zelnik, Melvin. (1968). **The census and Selective Service.** *Eugenics Quarterly,* 15(3), 173–176.

853. Zweigenhaft, Richard L. (1985). **Race, sex, and nuclear war.** *Genetic, Social & General Psychology Monographs,* 111(3), 283–301.

Social Structure & Social Roles

854. Ehrlich, Ira F. (1975). **The aged Black in America: The forgotten person.** *Journal of Negro Education,* 44(1), 12–23.

855. Kutza, Elizabeth A. (1986). **A policy analyst's response.** *Gerontologist,* 26(2), 147–149.

856. Teahan, John E. (1975). **A longitudinal study of attitude shifts among Black and White police officers.** *Journal of Social Issues,* 31(1), 47–56.

Culture & Ethnology & Religion

857. Colquit, Jesse L. (1976). **The Black student's quest for identity and self determination.** *College Student Journal,* 10(2), 103–106.

858. Dovidio, John F. & Gaertner, Samuel L. (1981). **The effects of race, status, and ability on helping behavior.** *Social Psychology Quarterly,* 44(3), 192–203.

859. Giambra, Leonard M. (1982). **Daydreaming: A Black–White comparison for 17–34-year-olds.** *Journal of Personality & Social Psychology,* 42(6), 1146–1156.

860. Mare, Robert D. & Winship, Christopher. (1984). **The paradox of lessening racial inequality and joblessness among Black youth: Enrollment, enlistment, and employment, 1964–1981.** *American Sociological Review,* 49(1), 39–55.

861. McConahay, John B. (1983). **Modern racism and modern discrimination: The effects of race, racial attitudes, and context on simulated hiring decisions.** *Personality & Social Psychology Bulletin,* 9(4), 551–558.

862. Sciara, Frank J. (1983). **Skin color and college student prejudice.** *College Student Journal,* 17(4), 390–394.

Marriage & Family

863. Dressler, William W. (1985). **Extended family relationships, social support, and mental health in a southern Black community.** *Journal of Health & Social Behavior,* 26(1), 39–48.

864. Joesting, Joan & Joesting, Robert. (1975). **Birth order and desired family size: A replication.** *Journal of Individual Psychology,* 31(2), 211–212.

865. Melton, Willie & Thomas, Darwin L. (1976). **Instrumental and expressive values in mate selection of Black and White college students.** *Journal of Marriage & the Family,* 38(3), 509–517.

866. Pope, Hallowell & Mueller, Charles W. (1976). **The intergenerational transmission of marital instability: Comparisons by race and sex.** *Journal of Social Issues,* 32(1), 49–66.

867. Thompson, Kenrick S. (1980). **A comparison of Black and White adolescents' beliefs about having children.** *Journal of Marriage & the Family,* 42(1), 133–139.

Political & Legal Processes

868. Buckhout, Robert. (1984). **Double mistaken identifications in Dallas: Texas v. Lenell Geter and Anthony Williams.** *Social Action & the Law,* 10(1), 3–11.

869. Ctr for Responsive Psychology. (1985). **Admissibility of defense expert testimony.** *Social Action & the Law,* 10(3), 81–82.

870. Fontaine, Patricia A. (1985). **The case dispositions of temporarily trial-incompetent criminal defendants.** *Journal of Psychiatry & Law,* 13(3–4), 435–448.

871. Hart, Roland J. (1979). **Crime and punishment in the army.** *US Army Research Institute for the Behavioral & Social Sciences,* (Technical Report No. 383).

872. Pryor, Bert & Buchanan, Raymond W. (1984). **The effects of a defendant's demeanor on juror perceptions of credibility and guilt.** *Journal of Communication,* 34(3), 92–99.

873. Sigelman, Lee & Welch, Susan. (1984). **Race, gender, and opinion toward Black and female presidential candidates.** *Public Opinion Quarterly,* 48(2), 467–475.

874. Weiner, Kenneth; Chelst, Kenneth & Hart, William. (1984). **Stinging the Detroit criminal: A total system perspective.** *Journal of Criminal Justice,* 12(3), 289–302.

Psychosexual Behavior & Sex Roles

875. Belcastro, Philip A. (1985). **Sexual behavior differences between Black and White students.** *Journal of Sex Research,* 21(1), 56–67.

876. Bell, Margaret E. (1979). **Attitudes toward changing economic roles for women.** *Journal of Instructional Psychology,* 6(3), 38–40.

877. Bieber, Irving & Bieber, Toby B. (1979). **Male homosexuality.** *Canadian Journal of Psychiatry,* 24(5), 409–421.

878. Christensen, Harold T. & Johnson, Leanor B. (1978). **Premarital coitus and the southern Black: A comparative view.** *Journal of Marriage & the Family,* 40(4), 721–732.

879. Crovitz, Elaine & Steinmann, Anne. (1980). **A decade later: Black–White attitudes toward women's familial role.** *Psychology of Women Quarterly,* 5(2), 170–176.

880. Finkel, Madelon L. & Finkel, David J. (1978). **Male adolescent contraceptive utilization.** *Adolescence,* 13(51), 443–451.

881. Henry, Wilma J. & Piercy, Fred P. (1984). **Assertive/aggressive ratings of women as a function of the raters' race and sex.** *Journal of Non-White Concerns in Personnel & Guidance,* 12(3), 85–98.

882. Johnson, Miriam M. (1977). **Androgyny and the maternal principle.** *School Review,* 86(1), 50–69.

883. Price, James H. & Miller, Patricia A. (1984). **Sexual fantasies of Black and of White college students.** *Psychological Reports,* 54(3), 1007–1014.

884. Ransford, H. Edward & Miller, Jon. (1983). **Race, sex, and feminist outlooks.** *American Sociological Review,* 48(1), 46–59.

885. Staples, Robert. (1978). **Race, liberalism-conservatism and premarital sexual permissiveness: A bi-racial comparison.** *Journal of Marriage & the Family,* 40(4), 733–742.

Drug & Alcohol Usage

886. Caetano, Raul. (1984). **Ethnicity and drinking in northern California: A comparison among Whites, Blacks and Hispanics.** *Alcohol & Alcoholism,* 19(1), 31–44.

887. Humphrey, John A.; Stephens, Virginia & Allen, Donald F. (1983). **Race, sex, marihuana use and alcohol intoxication in college students.** *Journal of Studies on Alcohol,* 44(4), 733–738.

888. Zinberg, Norman E.; Harding, Wayne M. & Winkeller, Miriam. (1977). **A study of social regulatory mechanisms in controlled illicit drug users.** *Journal of Drug Issues,* 7(2), 117–133.

EXPERIMENTAL SOCIAL PSYCHOLOGY

889. Bradley, Larry; Snyder, C. R. & Katahn, Martin. (1972). **The effects of subject race and sex and experimenter race upon classroom-related risk-taking behavior.** *Psychonomic Science,* 28(6), 362–364.

890. Cantor, Gordon N. (1972). **Effects of familiarization on children's ratings of pictures of Whites and Blacks.** *Child Development,* 43(4), 1219–1229.

891. Cohen, Robert & Murray, Edward J. (1972). **Censure of vicarious aggression as an instigation to subsequent aggression.** *Journal of Consulting & Clinical Psychology,* 39(3), 473–477.

892. Dertke, Max C.; Penner, Louis A. & Ulrich, Kathleen. (1974). **Observer's reporting of shoplifting as a function of thief's race and sex.** *Journal of Social Psychology,* 94(2), 213–221.

893. Fromkin, Howard L.; Klimoski, Richard J. & Flanagan, Michael F. (1972). **Race and competence as determinants of acceptance of newcomers in success and failure work groups.** *Organizational Behavior & Human Performance,* 7(1), 25–42.

894. Gaertner, Samuel & Bickman, Leonard. (1971). **Effects of race on the elicitation of helping behavior: The wrong number technique.** *Journal of Personality & Social Psychology,* 20(2), 218–222.

895. Gitter, A. George & Black, Harvey. (1968). **Expression and perception of emotion: Race and sex.** *CRC Report, Boston U.,* (Serial No. 19).

896. Harris, Mary B. (1977). **Sex-role stereotypes, models' race, and imitation.** *Psychological Reports,* 41(3, Pt 1), 875–885.

897. Kane, Thomas R. & Tedeschi, James T. (1973). **Impressions created by conforming and independent persons.** *Journal of Social Psychology,* 91(1), 109–116.

898. Maddock, Richard C. & Kenny, Charles T. (1973). **Impression formation as a function of age, sex, and race.** *Journal of Social Psychology,* 89(2), 233–243.

899. Malpass, Roy S. & Kravitz, Jerome. (1969). **Recognition for faces of own and other race.** *Journal of Personality & Social Psychology,* 13(4), 330–334.

900. Mastroianni, Mike & Khatena, Joe. (1972). **The attitudes of Black and White high school seniors toward integration.** *Sociology & Social Research,* 56(2), 221–227.

901. Neely, J. J.; Heckel, R. V. & Leichtman, H. M. (1973). **The effect of race of model and response consequences to the model on imitation in children.** *Journal of Social Psychology,* 89(2), 225–231.

902. Parrott, George L. & Coleman, Georgetta. (1971). **Sexual appeal: In Black and White.** *Proceedings of the Annual Convention of the American Psychological Association,* 6(Pt. 1), 321–322.

903. Parrott, George L. & Saiia, Steve. (1972). **Heterosexual perception: In Black and White.** *Proceedings of the Annual Convention of the American Psychological Association,* 7(Pt. 1), 289–290.

904. Rokeach, Milton; Miller, Martin G. & Snyder, John A. (1971). **The value gap between police and policed.** *Journal of Social Issues,* 27(2), 155–171.

905. Sherif, Carolyn W. (1973). **Social distance as categorization of intergroup interaction.** *Journal of Personality & Social Psychology,* 25(3), 327–334.

906. Thayer, Stephen. (1973). **Lend me your ears: Racial and sexual factors in helping the deaf.** *Journal of Personality & Social Psychology,* 28(1), 8–11.

907. Vander Kolk, Charles J. (1978). **Physiological reactions of Black, Puerto Rican, and White students in suggested ethnic encounters.** *Journal of Social Psychology,* 104(1), 107–114.

Group & Interpersonal Processes

908. Adams, Kathrynn A. (1980). **Who has the final word? Sex, race, and dominance behavior.** *Journal of Personality & Social Psychology,* 38(1), 1–8.

909. Adams, Kathrynn A. (1983). **Aspects of social context as determinants of Black women's resistance to challenges.** *Journal of Social Issues,* 39(3), 69–78.

910. Feinman, Saul & Gill, George W. (1978). **Sex differences in physical attractiveness preferences.** *Journal of Social Psychology,* 105(1), 43–52.

911. Ickes, William. (1984). **Compositions in Black and White: Determinants of interaction in interracial dyads.** *Journal of Personality & Social Psychology,* 47(2), 330–341.

912. Smith, David E.; Willis, Frank N. & Gier, Joseph A. (1980). **Success and interpersonal touch in a competitive setting.** *Journal of Nonverbal Behavior,* 5(1), 26–34.

Social Perception & Motivation

913. Brigham, John C.; Maass, Anne; Snyder, Larry D. & Spaulding, Kenneth. (1982). **Accuracy of eyewitness identification in a field setting.** *Journal of Personality & Social Psychology,* 42(4), 673–681.

914. Cash, Thomas F. & Duncan, Nancy C. (1984). **Physical attractiveness stereotyping among Black American college students.** *Journal of Social Psychology,* 122(1), 71–77.

915. Derlega, Valerian J.; McAnulty, Michael; Strout, Sally & Reavis, Charles A. (1980). **Pygmalion effects among Blacks: When and how expectancies occur.** *Journal of Applied Social Psychology,* 10(3), 260–271.

916. Leventhal, Gloria & Krate, Ronald. (1977). **Physical attractiveness and severity of sentencing.** *Psychological Reports,* 40(1), 315–318.

917. Malpass, Roy S. (1974). **Racial bias in eyewitness identification.** *Personality & Social Psychology Bulletin,* 1(1), 42–44.

918. McGlynn, Richard P.; Megas, James C. & Benson, Daniel H. (1976). **Sex and race as factors affecting the attribution of insanity in a murder trial.** *Journal of Psychology,* 93(1), 93–99.

919. Rollman, Steven A. (1978). **The sensitivity of Black and White Americans to nonverbal cues of prejudice.** *Journal of Social Psychology,* 105(1), 73–77.

920. Smith, Lynette E. & Millham, Jim. (1979). **Sex role stereotypes among Blacks and Whites.** *Journal of Black Psychology,* 6(1), 1–6.

921. Sunnafrank, Michael & Fontes, Norman E. (1983). **General and crime related racial stereotypes and influence on juridic decisions.** *Cornell Journal of Social Relations,* 17(1), 1–15.

922. Turner, Barbara F. & Turner, Castellano B. (1975). **Race, sex, and perception of the occupational opportunity structure among college students.** *Sociological Quarterly,* 16(3), 345–360.

923. Ugwuegbu, Denis C. (1976). **Black jurors' personality trait attribution to a rape case defendant.** *Social Behavior & Personality,* 4(2), 193–201.

924. Wasserman, Juli; Wiggins, Nancy; Jones, Lawrence & Itkin, Stuart. (1974). **A cross-cultural study of the attribution of personological characteristics as a function of facial perception.** *Personality & Social Psychology Bulletin,* 1(1), 45–47.

925. Yarkin, Kerry L.; Town, Jerri P. & Wallston, Barbara S. (1982). **Blacks and women must try harder: Stimulus persons' race and sex attributions of causality.** *Personality & Social Psychology Bulletin,* 8(1), 21–24.

926. Zweigenhaft, Richard L. (1977). **The other side of unusual first names.** *Journal of Social Psychology,* 103(2), 291–302.

PERSONALITY

927. Bradbury, Paul J.; Wright, Shelle D.; Walker, C. Eugene & Ross, Jack M. (1975). **Performance on the WISC as a function of sex of E, sex of S, and age of S.** *Journal of Psychology,* 90(1), 51–55.

928. Corsino, Louis. (1982). **Malcolm X and the Black Muslim Movement: A social psychology of charisma.** *Psychohistory Review,* 10(3–4), 165–184.

929. Cross, Donald T.; Barclay, Allan & Burger, Gary K. (1978). **Differential effects of ethnic membership, sex, and occupation on the California Psychological Inventory.** *Journal of Personality Assessment,* 42(6), 597–603.

930. Davis, Stephen F.; Martin, Dan A.; Wilee, Cean T. & Voorhees, James W. (1978). **Relationship of fear of death and level of self-esteem in college students.** *Psychological Reports,* 42(2), 419–422.

931. Fisher, Gary. (1967). **The performance of male prisoners on the Marlowe-Crowne Social Desirability Scale: II. Differences as a function of race and crime.** *Journal of Clinical Psychology,* 23(4), 473–475.

932. Frankel, A. Steven & Barrett, James. (1971). **Variations in personal space as a function of authoritarianism, self-esteem, and racial characteristics of a stimulus situation.** *Journal of Consulting & Clinical Psychology,* 37(1), 95–98.

933. Freeman, Harvey R.; Schockett, Melanie R. & Freeman, Evelyn B. (1975). **Effects of gender and race on sex-role preferences of fifth-grade children.** *Journal of Social Psychology,* 95(1), 105–108.

934. Gentry, W. Doyle et al. (1983). **The relation of demographic attributes and habitual anger-coping styles.** *Journal of Social Psychology,* 121(1), 45–50.

935. Gynther, Macolm D. & Ullom, Jeanne. (1976). **Objections to MMPI items as a function of interpersonal trust, race, and sex.** *Journal of Consulting & Clinical Psychology,* 44(6), 1020.

936. Ivancevich, John M.; Matteson, Michael T. & Gamble, George O. (1987). **Birth order and the Type A coronary behavior pattern.** *Individual Psychology: Journal of Adlerian Theory, Research & Practice,* 43(1), 42–49.

937. Kahoe, Richard D. (1974). **A Negro-White difference in psychological meaning of job incentives.** *Journal of Social Psychology,* 92(1), 157–158.

938. Kaplan, H. B. (1973). **Self-derogation and social position: Interaction effects of sex, race, education, and age.** *Social Psychiatry,* 8(2), 92–99.

939. Keane, Terence M. et al. (1983). **Blacks' perceptions of assertive behavior: An empirical evaluation.** *Behavior Modification,* 7(1), 97–111.

940. Kindall, Luther M. & McClain, Edwin W. (1973). **The Southern Black college student as adolescent: A psychohistorical study.** *Journal of Negro Education,* 42(1), 5–10.

941. Kurtz, James P. & Zuckerman, Marvin. (1978). **Race and sex differences on the Sensation Seeking Scales.** *Psychological Reports,* 43(2), 529–530.

942. Lachman, Sheldon J. & Waters, Thomas F. (1969). **Psychosocial profile of riot arrestees.** *Psychological Reports,* 24(1), 171–181.

943. Lao, Rosina C. (1970). **Internal-external control and competent and innovative behavior among Negro college students.** *Journal of Personality & Social Psychology,* 14(3), 263–270.

944. Levinson, Boris M. (1966). **A comparative study of Northern and Southern Negro homeless men.** *Journal of Negro Education,* 35(2), 144–150.

945. Levinson, Boris M. (1970). **The New York City skid row Negro: Some research findings.** *Mental Hygiene,* 54(4), 548–552.

946. McNamara, J. R.; Porterfield, C. L. & Miller, L. E. (1969). **The relationship of the Wechsler Preschool and Primary Scale of Intelligence with the Coloured Progressive Matrices (1956) and the Bender Gestalt Test.** *Journal of Clinical Psychology,* 25(1), 65–68.

947. Murray, Saundra R. & Mednick, Martha T. (1975). **Perceiving the causes of success and failure in achievement: Sex, race, and motivational comparisons.** *Journal of Consulting & Clinical Psychology,* 43(6), 881–885.

948. Nisan, Mordecai. (1973). **Perception of time in lower-class Black students.** *International Journal of Psychology,* 8(2), 109–116.

949. Olivier, K. & Barclay A. (1967). **Stanford-Binet and Goodenough-Harris Test performances of Head Start children.** *Psychological Reports,* 20(3, PT. 2), 1175–1179.

950. Shade, Barbara J. (1976). **The modal personality of urban Black middle-class elementary school children.** *Journal of Psychology,* 92(2), 267–275.

951. Snortum, John R. & Ashear, Victor H. (1972). **Prejudice, punitiveness, and personality.** *Journal of Personality Assessment,* 36(3), 291–296.

952. Turner, Castellano B. & Turner, Barbara F. (1982). **Gender, race, social class, and self-evaluations among college students.** *Sociological Quarterly,* 23(4), 491–507.

953. Zuckerman, Diana M. (1980). **Self-esteem, self-concept, and the life goals and sex-role attitudes of college students.** *Journal of Personality,* 48(2), 149–162.

PHYSICAL AND PSYCHOLOGICAL DISORDERS

954. Allon, Richard. (1971). **Sex, race, socioeconomic status, social mobility, and process-reactive ratings of schizophrenics.** *Journal of Nervous & Mental Disease,* 153(5), 343–350.

955. Aronson, Stanley M. & Aronson, Betty E. (1969). **Clinical neuropathological conference.** *Diseases of the Nervous System,* 30(5), 345–352.

956. Aronson, Stanley M. & Aronson, Betty E. (1970). **Clinical neuropathological conference.** *Diseases of the Nervous System,* 31(7), 497–503.

957. Broman, Sarah H.; Nichols, Paul L. & Kennedy, Wallace A. (1972). **Precursors of low IQ in young children.** *Proceedings of the Annual Convention of the American Psychological Association,* 7(Pt. 1), 77–78.

958. Cohen, Elliot S.; Harbin, Henry T. & Wright, M. J. (1975). **Some considerations in the formulation of psychiatric diagnoses.** *Journal of Nervous & Mental Disease,* 160(6), 422–427.

959. Curran, J. Roger & Wetmore, Stephen J. (1972). **Alcoholic myopathy.** *Diseases of the Nervous System,* 33(1), 19–22.

960. Doll, Richard E.; Rubin, Robert T. & Gunderson, E. K. (1969). **Life stress and illness patterns in the US Navy: II. Demographic variables and illness onset in an attack carrier's crew.** *Archives of Environmental Health,* 19, 748–752.

961. DuPont, Robert L. (1971). **Profile of a heroin-addiction epidemic.** *New England Journal of Medicine,* 285(6), 320–324.

962. Eysenck, Sybil B. & Eysenck, Hans J. (1971). **A comparative study of criminals and matched controls on three dimensions of personality.** *British Journal of Social & Clinical Psychology,* 10(4), 362–366.

963. Gilmore, Karen; Rudden, Marie & Kalman, Thomas P. (1980). **Psychiatric manifestations of sarcoidosis.** *Canadian Journal of Psychiatry,* 25(4), 329–331.

964. Hendin, Herbert. (1974). **Students on heroin.** *Journal of Nervous & Mental Disease,* 158(4), 240–255.

965. Henning, John J. & Levy, Russell H. (1967). **Verbal-Performance IQ differences of White and Negro delinquents on the WISC and WAIS.** *Journal of Clinical Psychology,* 23(2), 164–168.

966. Landers, William F.; Ball, Steven E. & Halcomb, Charles G. (1972). **Digital skin temperature as a physiological correlate of attention in nonretarded and retarded children.** *American Journal of Mental Deficiency,* 76(5), 550–554.

967. Leith, William R. & Timmons, Jack L. (1983). **The stutterer's reaction to the telephone as a speaking situation.** *Journal of Fluency Disorders,* 8(3), 233–243.

968. Maas, Jeannette P. (1967). **Incidence and treatment variations between Negroes and Caucasians in mental illness.** *Community Mental Health Journal,* 3(1), 61–65.

969. Madanes, Cloe; Dukes, Joyce & Harbin, Henry. (1980). **Family ties of heroin addicts.** *Archives of General Psychiatry,* 37(8), 889–894.

970. Miller, Jerome S.; Sensenig, John; Stocker, Robert B. & Campbell, Richard. (1973). **Value patterns of drug addicts as a function of race and sex.** *International Journal of the Addictions,* 8(4), 589–598.

971. Morris, Jeffrey B.; Kovacs, Maria; Beck, Aaron T. & Wolffe, Andrew. (1974). **Notes toward an epidemiology of urban suicide.** *Comprehensive Psychiatry,* 15(6), 537–547.

972. Naditch, M. P. (1974). **Locus of control, relative discontent and hypertension.** *Social Psychiatry,* 9(3), 111–117.

973. Panda, Kailash C. & Lynch, William W. (1974). **Effects of race and sex on attribution of intellectual achievement: Responsibility for success and failure situations among educable mentally retarded children.** *Indian Journal of Mental Retardation,* 7(2), 72–80.

974. Raskin, Allen; Crook, Thomas H. & Herman, Kenneth D. (1975). **Psychiatric history and symptom differences in black and white depressed patients.** *Journal of Consulting & Clinical Psychology,* 43(1), 73–80.

975. Seiden, Richard H. (1970). **We're driving young Blacks to suicide.** *Psychology Today,* 4(3), 24–28.

976. Silverman, Ira J. & Dinitz, Simon. (1974). **Compulsive masculinity and delinquency: An empirical investigation.** *Criminology: An Interdisciplinary Journal,* 11(4), 498–515.

977. Stein, Marvin; Levy, Michael T. & Glasberg, H. Mark. (1974). **Separations in Black and White suicide attempters.** *Archives of General Psychiatry,* 31(6), 815–821.

978. Unkovic, C. M. & Ducsay, W. J. (1969). **An application of configurational analysis to the recidivism of juvenile delinquent behavior.** *Journal of Criminal Law, Criminology & Police Science,* 60(3), 340–344.

Mental Disorders

979. Allen, Irving M. (1986). **Posttraumatic stress disorder among Black Vietnam veterans.** *Hospital & Community Psychiatry,* 37(1), 55–61.

980. Amen, Daniel G. (1985). **Post-Vietnam stress disorder: A metaphor for current and past life events.** *American Journal of Psychotherapy,* 39(4), 580–586.

981. Anthony, Nicholas. (1976). **Malingering as role taking.** *Journal of Clinical Psychology,* 32(1), 32–41.

982. Martin, Ronald L.; Cloninger, C. Robert; Guze, Samuel B. & Clayton, Paula J. (1985). **Mortality in a follow-up of 500 psychiatric outpatients: I. Total mortality.** *Archives of General Psychiatry,* 42(1), 47–54.

983. Steele, Robert E. (1978). **Relationship of race, sex, social class, and social mobility to depression in normal adults.** *Journal of Social Psychology,* 104(1), 37–47.

Behavior Disorders & Antisocial Behavior

984. Baker, F. M. (1984). **Black suicide attempters in 1980: A preventive focus.** *General Hospital Psychiatry,* 6(2), 131–137.

985. Bell, Carl C. et al. (1986). **Misdiagnosis of alcohol-related organic brain syndromes: Implications for treatment.** Special Issue: Treatment of Black alcoholics. *Alcoholism Treatment Quarterly,* 2(3–4), 45–65.

986. Bettes, Barbara A. & Walker, Elaine. (1986). **Symptoms associated with suicidal behavior in childhood and adolescence.** *Journal of Abnormal Child Psychology,* 14(4), 591–604.

987. Bush, James A. (1976). **Suicide and Blacks: A conceptual framework.** *Suicide: A Quarterly Journal of Life-Threatening Behavior,* 6(4), 216–222.

988. Combs-Orme, Terri; Taylor, John R.; Scott, Ellen B. & Holmes, Sandra J. (1983). **Violent deaths among alcoholics: A descriptive study.** *Journal of Studies on Alcohol,* 44(6), 938–949.

989. Davis, Robert. (1979). **Black suicide in the seventies: Current trends.** *Suicide & Life-Threatening Behavior,* 9(3), 131–140.

990. Farnworth, Margaret. (1984). **Family structure, family attributes, and delinquency in a sample of low-income, minority males and females.** *Journal of Youth & Adolescence,* 13(4), 349–364.

991. Garey, Richard E.; Daul, George C.; Samuels, Monroe S. & Egan, Raymond R. (1983). **Medical and sociological aspects of T's and Blues abuse in New Orleans.** *American Journal of Drug & Alcohol Abuse,* 9(2), 171–182.

992. Green, Pamela D. & Galbraith, Gary G. (1986). **Associative responses to double entendre drug words: A study of drug addicts and college students.** *Personality & Social Psychology Bulletin,* 12(1), 31–39.

993. Heacock, Don R. (1976). **The Black slum child and the problem of aggression.** *American Journal of Psychoanalysis,* 36(3), 219–226.

994. Kercher, Glen A. & McShane, Marilyn. (1984). **The prevalence of child sexual abuse victimization in an adult sample of Texas residents.** *Child Abuse & Neglect,* 8(4), 495–501.

995. LaFree, Gary D. (1982). **Male power and female victimization: Toward a theory of interracial rape.** *American Journal of Sociology,* 88(2), 311–328.

996. Manning, Frederick J. et al. (1983). **Drug "overdoses" among U.S. soldiers in Europe, 1978–1979: II. Psychological autopsies following deaths and near-deaths.** *International Journal of the Addictions,* 18(2), 153–166.

997. Nurco, David N. & DuPont, Robert L. (1977). **A preliminary report on crime and addiction within a community-wide population of narcotic addicts.** *Drug & Alcohol Dependence,* 2(2), 109–121.

998. Poussaint, Alvin F. (1983). **Black-on-Black homicide: A psychological-political perspective.** Second International Institute Proceedings on Victimology: Victimology: International perspectives (1982, Bellagio, Italy). *Victimology,* 8(3–4), 161–169.

999. Ryan, Joseph J. & Blom, Bernhard E. (1979). **WAIS characteristics and violent behavior: Failure to generalize versus failure to replicate.** *Journal of Consulting & Clinical Psychology,* 47(3), 581–582.

1000. Singer, Simon I. (1986). **Victims of serious violence and their criminal behavior: Subcultural theory and beyond.** *Violence & Victims,* 1(1), 61–70.

1001. Steer, Robert A. (1978). **Moods and biorhythms of heroin addicts.** *Psychological Reports,* 43(3, Pt 1), 829–830.

1002. Steer, Robert A.; McElroy, Margo G. & Beck, Aaron T. (1982). **Structure of depression in alcoholic men: A partial replication.** *Psychological Reports,* 50(3, Pt 1), 723–728.

1003. Stephens, Richard C.; Levine, Stephen & Ross, Wesley. (1976). **Street addict values: A factor analytic study.** *Journal of Social Psychology,* 99(2), 273–281.

1004. True, William R. & Pevnick, Jeffrey S. (1983). **Abuse of pentazocine combined with tripelennamine: An interaction of pharmacological and demographic characteristics.** *International Journal of the Addictions,* 18(8), 1063–1071.

Learning Disorders & Mental Retardation

1005. Bryan, Tanis H. & Bryan, James H. (1978). **Social interactions of learning disabled children.** *Learning Disability Quarterly,* 1(1), 33–38.

1006. Lambert, Nadine M. (1979). **Contributions of school classification, sex, and ethnic status to adaptive behavior assessment.** *Journal of School Psychology,* 17(1), 3–16.

Physical & Psychosomatic Disorders

1007. Caramazza, Alfonso; Basili, Annamaria G.; Koller, Jerry J. & Berndt, Rita S. (1981). **An investigation of repetition and language processing in a case of conduction aphasia.** *Brain & Language,* 14(2), 235–271.

1008. Dimsdale, Joel E.; Pierce, Chester; Schoenfeld, David; Brown, Anne et al. (1986). **Suppressed anger and blood pressure: The effects of race, sex, social class, obesity, and age.** *Psychosomatic Medicine,* 48(6), 430–436.

1009. Gentry, W. Doyle et al. (1982). **Habitual anger-coping styles: I. Effect on mean blood pressure and risk for essential hypertension.** *Psychosomatic Medicine,* 44(2), 195–202.

1010. Grand, Sheldon A. & Strohmer, Douglas C. (1983). Minority perceptions of the disabled. *Rehabilitation Counseling Bulletin,* 27(2), 117–119.

1011. Hall, Howard & Bell, Xyna. (1985). **Increases in cancer rates among Blacks.** *Journal of Black Psychology,* 12(1), 1–14.

1012. Jacobs, Rosevelt. (1983). **Psychological aspects of chronic pain.** *Journal of the National Medical Association,* 75(4), 387–391.

1013. Robinson, Robert G. et al. (1983). **Mood changes in stroke patients: Relationship to lesion location.** *Comprehensive Psychiatry,* 24(6), 555–566.

1014. Slavney, Phillip R. & Teitelbaum, Mark L. (1985). **Patients with medically unexplained symptoms: DSM-III diagnoses and demographic characteristics.** *General Hospital Psychiatry,* 7(1), 21–25.

1015. Varney, Nils R. & Digre, Kathleen. (1983). **Color "amnesia" without aphasia.** *Cortex,* 19(4), 545–550.

1016. Waldron, Ingrid et al. (1977). **The coronary-prone behavior pattern in employed men and women.** *Journal of Human Stress,* 3(4), 2–18.

1017. Wolf, Thomas M.; Hunter, Saundra M.; Webber, Larry S. & Berenson, Gerald S. (1981). **Self-concept, locus of control, goal blockage, and coronary-prone behavior pattern in children and adolescents: Bogalusa Heart Study.** *Journal of General Psychology,* 105(1), 13–26.

TREATMENT AND PREVENTION

1018. Aiduk, Robert & Langmeyer, Daniel. (1972). **Prediction of client success with vocational rehabilitation in a state mental hospital.** *Rehabilitation Counseling Bulletin,* 16(1), 3–10.

1019. Aledort, Stewart L. & Jones, Morgan. (1973). **The Euclid House: A therapeutic community halfway house for prisoners.** *American Journal of Psychiatry,* 130(3), 286–289.

1020. Brown, Barry S., et al. (1972). **Impact of a multimodality treatment program for heroin addicts.** *Comprehensive Psychiatry,* 13(4), 391–397.

1021. Brown, David; Winsberg, Bertrand G.; Bialer, Irv & Press, Mark. (1973). **Imipramine therapy and seizures: Three children treated for hyperactive behavior disorders.** *American Journal of Psychiatry,* 130(2), 210–212.

1022. Carkhuff, Robert R. & Berenson, Bernard G. (1972). **The utilization of Black functional professionals to reconstitute troubled families.** *Journal of Clinical Psychology,* 28(1), 92–93.

1023. Cimbolic, Peter. (1973). **T group effects on Black clients' perceptions of counselors.** *Journal of College Student Personnel,* 14(4), 296–302.

1024. Costello, Raymond M.; Fine, Harold J. & Blau, Burton I. (1973). **Racial comparisons on the Minnesota Multiphasic Personality Inventory.** *Journal of Clinical Psychology,* 29(1), 63–65.

1025. de Leon, George. (1974). **Phoenix House: Psychopathological signs among male and female drug-free residents.** *Addictive Diseases: An International Journal,* 1(2), 135–151.

1026. Fontana, Alan F. & Corey, Michel. (1969). **Patient leaders: Middlemen in a conflict of interests.** *Proceedings of the 77th Annual Convention of the American Psychological Association,* 4(Pt. 2), 529–530.

1027. Gardner, William E. (1972). **The differential effects of race, education and experience in helping.** *Journal of Clinical Psychology,* 28(1), 87–89.

1028. Goldensohn, Sidney S.; Fink, Raymond & Shapiro, Sam. (1971). **The delivery of mental health services to children in a prepaid medical care program.** *American Journal of Psychiatry,* 127(10), 1357–1362.

1029. Greenberg, L. M.; Deem, M. A. & McMahon, S. (1972). **Effects of dextroamphetamine, chlorpromazine, and hydroxyzine on behavior and performance in hyperactive children.** *American Journal of Psychiatry,* 129(5), 532–539.

1030. Hankoff, Leon D.; Rabiner, Charles J. & St. George Henry, Cecil. (1971). **Comparison of the satellite clinic and the hospital-based clinic.** *Archives of General Psychiatry,* 24(5), 474–478.

1031. Hersen, Michel; Turner, Samuel M.; Edelstein, Barry A. & Pinkston, Susan G. (1975). **Effects of phenothiazines and social skills training in a withdrawn schizophrenic.** *Journal of Clinical Psychology,* 31(4), 588–594.

1032. Hunyady, Joan & Trott, D. Merilee. (1972). **Another look at the handicapped and their approach to occupational choice.** *Michigan Personnel & Guidance Journal,* 4(1), 46–50.

1033. Krebs, Richard L. (1971). **Some effects of a white institution on black psychiatric outpatients.** *American Journal of Orthopsychiatry,* 41(4), 589–596.

1034. Lepkin, Milton. (1975). **A program of industrial consultation by a community mental health center.** *Community Mental Health Journal,* 11(1), 74–81.

1035. Luchins, Daniel J. & Goldman, Morris. (1985). **High-dose bromocriptine in a case of tardive dystonia.** *Biological Psychiatry,* 20(2), 179–181.

1036. McCabe, O. Lee; Kurland, Albert A. & Sullivan, Dorothy. (1974). **A study of methadone failures in an abstinence program.** *International Journal of the Addictions,* 9(5), 731–740.

1037. McGinnis, Nancy H.; Schwab, John J. & Warheit, George J. (1973). **Race-sex analyses of social psychiatric impairment.** *Proceedings of the 81st Annual Convention of the American Psychological Association, Montreal, Canada,* 8, 495–496.

1038. Price, Neil; Glazer, William & Morgenstern, Hal. (1985). **Demographic predictors of the use of injectable versus oral antipsychotic medications in outpatients.** 137th Annual Meeting of the American Psychiatric Association (1984, Los Angeles, California). *American Journal of Psychiatry,* 142(12), 1491–1492.

1039. Raskin, Allen & Crook, Thomas H. (1975). **Antidepressants in Black and White inpatients.** *Archives of General Psychiatry,* 32(5), 643–649.

1040. Richardson, Henry; Brooks, Jeffrey; Cohen, Mark & Kern, Joseph. (1974). **A three year follow-up study of 43 heroin addicts in a suburban community.** *Journal of Drug Education,* 4(4), 389–398.

1041. Ward, Michael E.; Saklad, Stephen R. & Ereshefsky, Larry. (1986). **Lorazepam for the treatment of psychotic agitation.** *American Journal of Psychiatry,* 143(9), 1195–1196.

Psychotherapy & Psychotherapeutic Counseling

1042. Banik, Sambhu N. & Mendelson, Martin A. (1978). **Group psychotherapy with a paraplegic group, with an emphasis on specific problems of sexuality.** *International Journal of Group Psychotherapy,* 28(1), 123–128.

1043. Forrest, Grace. (1975). **The problems of dependency and the value of art therapy as a means of treating alcoholism.** *Art Psychotherapy,* 2(1), 15–43.

1044. Jackson, Anna M.; Farley, Gordon K.; Zimet, Sara G. & Waterman, Jill M. (1978). **Race and sex as variables for children involved in treatment.** *Psychological Reports,* 43(3, Pt 1), 883–886.

1045. Jones, Billy E. & Gray, Beverly A. (1985). **Black and White psychiatrists: Therapy with Blacks.** *Journal of the National Medical Association,* 77(1), 19–25.

1046. Muñoz, John A. (1986). **Countertransference and its implementation in the treatment of a Hispanic adolescent boy.** *Psychiatry,* 49(2), 169–179.

1047. Rohrbaugh, Michael. (1984). **The strategic systems therapies: Misgivings about mixing the models.** *Journal of Strategic & Systemic Therapies,* 3(3), 28–32.

1048. Tasman, Allan. (1982). **Loss of self-cohesion in terminal illness.** *Journal of the American Academy of Psychoanalysis,* 10(4), 515–526.

1049. Wilmer, Harry A. (1982). **Vietnam and madness: Dreams of schizophrenic veterans.** *Journal of the American Academy of Psychoanalysis,* 10(1), 47–65.

1050. Wyatt, Gail E.; Strayer, Richard G. & Lobitz, W. Charles. (1976). **Issues in the treatment of sexually dysfunctioning couples of Afro-American descent.** *Psychotherapy: Theory, Research & Practice,* 13(1), 44–50.

Behavior Therapy & Behavior Modification

1051. Daniel, William H. (1982). **Management of chronic rumination with a contingent exercise procedure employing topographically dissimilar behavior.** *Journal of Behavior Therapy & Experimental Psychiatry,* 13(2), 149–152.

1052. Pigott, H. Edmund & Gonzales, Frank P. (1987). **Efficacy of videotape self-modeling in treating an electively mute child.** *Journal of Clinical Child Psychology,* 16(2), 106–110.

Health Care Services

1053. Anderson, John W. (1983). **The effects of culture and social class on client preference for counseling methods.** *Journal of Non-White Concerns in Personnel & Guidance,* 11(3), 84–88.

1054. Cole, Joan & Pilisuk, Marc. (1976). **Differences in the provision of mental health services by race.** *American Journal of Orthopsychiatry,* 46(3), 510–525.

1055. Ebmeier, Corinne. (1982). **Manifestations of guilt in an immobilized school-age child.** *Maternal-Child Nursing Journal,* 11(2), 109–115.

1056. Gift, Thomas E.; Harder, David W.; Ritzler, Barry A. & Kokes, Ronald F. (1985). **Sex and race of patients admitted for their first psychiatric hospitalization: Correlation and prognostic power.** *American Journal of Psychiatry,* 142(12), 1447–1449.

1057. Lightfoot, Orlando B. (1983). **Preventive issues and the Black elderly: A biopsychosocial perspective.** *Journal of the National Medical Association,* 75(10), 957–963.

1058. Martin, Douglas O. & Thomas, Michele B. (1982). **Black student preferences for counselors: The influence of age, sex, and type of problem.** *Journal of Non-White Concerns in Personnel & Guidance,* 10(4), 143–153.

1059. Pomales, Jay; Claiborn, Charles D. & LaFromboise, Teresa D. (1986). **Effects of Black students' racial identity on perceptions of White counselors varying in cultural sensitivity.** *Journal of Counseling Psychology,* 33(1), 57–61.

1060. Qadir, Ghulam. (1982). **Violence in an open psychiatric unit.** *Journal of Psychiatric Treatment & Evaluation,* 4(5), 409–413.

1061. Schlauch, Robert W.; Reich, Peter & Kelly, Martin J. (1979). **Leaving the hospital against medical advice.** *New England Journal of Medicine,* 300(1), 22–24.

1062. Schneider, Lawrence J.; Laury, Patrick D. & Hughes, Howard H. (1980). **Ethnic group perceptions of mental health service providers.** *Journal of Counseling Psychology,* 27(6), 589–596.

1063. Seaberg, James R. & Tolley, Eve S. (1986). **Predictors of the length of stay in foster care.** *Social Work Research & Abstracts,* 22(3), 11–17.

1064. Trappler, B.; Viswanathan, R. & Sher, J. (1986). **Alzheimer's disease in a patient on long-term hemodialysis: A case report.** *General Hospital Psychiatry,* 8(1), 57–60.

1065. Turkat, David. (1980). **Demographics of hospital recidivists.** *Psychological Reports,* 47(2), 566.

1066. Vergara, Tacie L. (1984). **Meeting the needs of sexual minority youth: One program's response.** *Journal of Social Work & Human Sexuality,* 2(2–3), 19–38.

Rehabilitation & Penology

1067. Baker, F. M. (1986). **The Black "skid row" alcoholic: Initiation of treatment in the emergency room.** Special Issue: Treatment of Black alcoholics. *Alcoholism Treatment Quarterly,* 2(3–4), 129–139.

1068. Blumstein, Alfred. (1982). **On the racial disproportionality of United States' prison populations.** *Journal of Criminal Law & Criminology,* 73(3), 1259–1281.

1069. Bracy, Sharon A. & Simpson, D. Dwayne. (1983). **Status of opioid addicts 5 years after admission to drug abuse treatment.** *American Journal of Drug & Alcohol Abuse,* 9(2), 115–127.

1070. Fernandez-Pol, Blanca; Bluestone, Harvey; Missouri, Clarence; Morales, Gertrude et al. (1986). **Drinking patterns of inner-city Black Americans and Puerto Ricans.** *Journal of Studies on Alcohol,* 47(2), 156–160.

1071. Goetting, Ann & Howsen, Roy M. (1986). **Correlates of prisoner misconduct.** *Journal of Quantitative Criminology,* 2(1), 49–67.

1072. Joe, George W.; Lloyd, Michael R.; Simpson, D. Dwayne & Singh, B. Krishna. (1983). **Recidivism among opioid addicts after drug treatment: An analysis by race and tenure in treatment.** *American Journal of Drug & Alcohol Abuse,* 9(4), 371–382.

1073. Karp-Gelernter, Elaine; Savage, Charles & McCabe, O. Lee. (1982). **Evaluation of clinic attendance schedules for LAAM and methadone: A controlled study.** *International Journal of the Addictions,* 17(5), 805–813.

1074. Kennedy, Daniel B. (1984). **A theory of suicide while in police custody.** *Journal of Police Science & Administration,* 12(2), 191–200.

1075. Lindquist, Charles A. (1983). **Screening ex-offenders for employment services: A preliminary assessment.** *Federal Probation,* 46(2), 42–48.

1076. Page, Richard C. (1978). **The social learning processes of severely disabled group counseling participants.** *Psychosocial Rehabilitation Journal,* 2(2), 28–35.

1077. Patalano, Frank. (1978). **Personality dimensions of drug abusers who enter a drug-free therapeutic community.** *Psychological Reports,* 42(3, Pt 2), 1063–1069.

1078. Pisciotta, Alexander W. (1983). **Race, sex, and rehabilitation: A study of differential treatment in the juvenile reformatory, 1825–1900.** *Crime & Delinquency,* 29(2), 254–269.

1079. Simpson, D. Dwayne; Joe, George W.; Lehman, Wayne E. & Sells, S. B. (1986). **Addiction careers: Etiology, treatment, and 12-year follow-up outcomes.** *Journal of Drug Issues,* 16(1), 107–122.

1080. Simpson, D. Dwayne & Savage, L. James. (1982). **Client types in different drug abuse treatments: Comparisons of follow-up outcomes.** *American Journal of Drug & Alcohol Abuse,* 8(4), 401–418.

1081. Wexler, Harry K. & de Leon, George. (1977). **The therapeutic community: Multivariate prediction of retention.** *American Journal of Drug & Alcohol Abuse,* 4(2), 145–151.

1082. Wurtele, Sandy K.; King, Abby C. & Drabman, Ronald S. (1984). **Treatment package to reduce SIB in a Lesch-Nyhan patient.** *Journal of Mental Deficiency Research,* 28(3), 227–234.

PROFESSIONAL PERSONNEL AND PROFESSIONAL ISSUES

1083. Sharma, Vijay. (1977). **Is racial attitude change a function of locus of control?** *Journal of Non-White Concerns in Personnel & Guidance,* 5(4), 163–167.

EDUCATIONAL PSYCHOLOGY

1084. Ammon, Paul R. & Ammon, Mary S. (1971). **Effects of training Black preschool children in vocabulary versus sentence construction.** *Journal of Educational Psychology,* 62(5), 421–426.

1085. Asbury, Charles A. (1973). **Cognitive correlates of discrepant achievement in reading.** *Journal of Negro Education,* 42(2), 123–133.

1086. Baker, Eugene A. & Owen, David R. (1969). **Negro-White personality differences in integrated classrooms.** *Proceedings of the 77th Annual Convention of the American Psychological Association,* 4(Pt. 2), 539–540.

1087. Baratz, Stephen S. & Baratz, Joan C. (1970). **Early childhood intervention: The social science base of institutional racism.** *Harvard Educational Review,* 40(1), 29–50.

1088. Biggs, Barbara E. & Felton, Gary S. (1973). **Reducing test anxiety of collegiate Black low achievers in an academic setting.** *Journal of Negro Education,* 42(1), 54–57.

1089. Boney, J. Don; Dunn, Charleta & Bass, Thomas. (1971). **An analysis of the participation of racially integrated guidance groups of culturally different children in elementary school.** *Journal of Negro Education,* 40(4), 390–393.

1090. Burrell, Leon & Rayder, Nicholas F. (1971). **Black and White students' attitudes toward White counselors.** *Journal of Negro Education,* 40(1), 48–52.

1091. Caldwell, Mark B. & Knight, David. (1970). **The effect of Negro and White examiners on Negro intelligence test performance.** *Journal of Negro Education,* 39(2), 177–179.

1092. Carter, Donald E.; DeTine, Susan L.; Spero, June & Benson, Forrest W. (1975). **Peer acceptance and school-related variables in an integrated junior high school.** *Journal of Educational Psychology,* 67(2), 267–273.

1093. Carver, Ronald P. (1968). **Evaluation of a listening comprehension test for disadvantaged junior high school boys.** *American Institutes for Research Final Report, Washington, D.C.,* (Serial No. R68-2).

1094. Croake, James W.; Keller, James F. & Catlin, Nancy. (1973). **WPPSI, Rutgers, Goodenough, Goodenough-Harris I.Q.'s for lower socioeconomic, Black, preschool children.** *Psychology,* 10(2), 58–65.

1095. Davis, Larry; Cartwright, Ramon; Freeman, Phyllis & Carter, Louis. (1982). **A qualitative look at Black female social work educators.** *Journal of Sociology & Social Welfare,* 9(1), 146–153.

1096. Dole, Arthur A. & Passons, William R. (1972). **Life goals and plan determinants reported by Black and White high school seniors.** *Journal of Vocational Behavior,* 2(3), 209–222.

1097. Edwards, Ozzie L. (1975). **Cohort and sex changes in Black educational achievement.** *Sociology & Social Research,* 59(2), 110–120.

1098. Elkind, David. (1971). **From ghetto school to college campus: Some discontinuities and continuities.** *Journal of School Psychology,* 9(3), 241–245.

1099. Epps, Edgar G.; Katz, Irwin; Perry, Aubrey & Runyon, Eugene. (1971). **Effect of race of comparison referent and motives on Negro cognitive performance.** *Journal of Educational Psychology,* 62(3), 201–208.

1100. Farver, Albert S.; Sedlacek, William E. & Brooks, Glenwood C. (1975). **Longitudinal predictions of university grades for Blacks and Whites.** *Measurement & Evaluation in Guidance,* 7(4), 243–250.

1101. Glatthorn, Allan A. (1974). **The student as person.** *Theory into Practice,* 13(5), 366–370.

1102. Goldstein, Harris S. & Peck, Rosalind. (1971). **Cognitive functions in Negro and White children in a child guidance clinic.** *Psychological Reports,* 28(2), 379–384.

1103. Harris, Edward E. (1970). **Personal and parental influences on college attendance: Some Negro-White differences.** *Journal of Negro Education,* 39(4), 305–313.

1104. Hedegard, James M. & Brown, Donald R. (1969). **Encounters of some Negro and White freshmen with a public multiversity.** *Journal of Social Issues,* 25(3), 131–144.

1105. Heffernon, Andrew & Bruehl, Dieter. (1971). **Some effects of race of inexperienced lay counselors on Black junior high school students.** *Journal of School Psychology,* 9(1), 35–37.

1106. Henderson, Norman B.; Fay, Warren H.; Lindemann, Sally J. & Clarkson, Quentin D. (1973). **Will the IQ test ban decrease the effectiveness of reading prediction?** *Journal of Educational Psychology,* 65(3), 345–355.

1107. Hodgkins, Benjamin J. & Stakenas, Robert G. (1969). **A study of self-concepts of Negro and White youth in segregated environments.** *Journal of Negro Education,* 38(4), 370–377.

1108. Katz, Irwin; Atchison, Calvin O.; Epps, Edgar G. & Roberts, S. Oliver. (1972). **Race of evaluator, race of norm, and expectancy as determinants of Black performance.** *Journal of Experimental Social Psychology,* 8(1), 1–15.

1109. Lanier, James & Wittmer, Joe. (1977). **Teacher prejudice in referral of students to EMR programs.** *School Counselor,* 24(3), 165–170.

1110. Liebler, Roberta. (1973). **Reading interests of Black and Puerto Rican, inner city, high school students.** *Graduate Research in Education & Related Disciplines,* 6(2), 23–43.

1111. Long, Barbara H. & Henderson, Edmund H. (1970). **Social schemata of school beginners: Some demographic correlates.** *Merrill-Palmer Quarterly,* 16(4), 305–324.

1112. Meredith, William V. & Coffey, Linda W. (1970). **Assessment of KELP as a treatment variable in a Headstart program.** *Florida Journal of Educational Research,* 12(1), 69–78.

1113. Miller, Harry L. (1973). **Race vs. class in teachers' expectations.** *Psychological Reports,* 32(1), 105–106.

1114. Nolle, David B. (1973). **Alternative path analytic models of student-teacher influence: The implications of different strokes for different folks.** *Sociology of Education,* 46(4), 417–426.

1115. Olsen, Henry D. (1972). **Effects of changes in academic roles on self concept of academic ability of Black and White compensatory education students.** *Journal of Negro Education,* 41(4), 365–369.

1116. Page, Willie F. (1975). **Self-esteem and internal versus external control among Black youth in a summer aviation program.** *Journal of Psychology,* 89(2), 307–311.

1117. Pallone, Nathaniel J.; Richard, Fred S. & Hurley, Robert B. (1970). **Key influences of occupational preference among Black youth.** *Journal of Counseling Psychology,* 17(6), 498–501.

1118. Parker, Harry J.; Sternlof, Richard E. & McCoy, John F. (1971). **Objective versus individual mental ability tests with former Head Start children in the first grade.** *Perceptual & Motor Skills,* 32(1), 287–292.

1119. Paschal, Billy J. & Williams, Richard H. (1970). **Some effects of participation in a summer Upward Bound program on the self-concept and attitude of the disadvantaged adolescent.** *Journal of Negro Education,* 39(1), 34–43.

1120. Pfeifer, C. Michael & Sedlacek, William E. (1971). **The validity of academic predictors for Black and White students at a predominantly White university.** *Journal of Educational Measurement,* 8(4), 253–261.

1121. Pikulski, John J. (1971). **Candy, word recognition and the "disadvantaged".** *Reading Teacher,* 25(3), 243–246.

1122. Runyon, Howard L. & Williams, Robert L. (1972). **Differentiating reinforcement priorities of junior high school students.** *Journal of Experimental Education,* 40(3), 76–80.

1123. Scott, Ralph. (1970). **Perceptual skills, general intellectual ability, race, and later reading achievement.** *Reading Teacher,* 23(7), 660–668.

1124. Seagoe, May V. (1971). **Children's play in three American subcultures.** *Journal of School Psychology,* 9(2), 167–172.

1125. Selby, James E. (1973). **Relationships existing among race, student financial aid, and persistence in college.** *Journal of College Student Personnel,* 14(1), 38-40.

1126. Thomas, Gail E. (1977). **Race and sex effects on access to college.** *Center for Social Organization of Schools Report, Johns Hopkins U.,* (Serial No. 229).

1127. Veroff, Joseph & Peele, Stanton. (1969). **Initial effects of desegregation on the achievement motivation of Negro elementary school children.** *Journal of Social Issues,* 25(3), 71–91.

1128. Washington, Valora. (1982). **Grade level differences in teacher perceptions of students by race and sex.** *Journal of Applied Developmental Psychology,* 3(1), 81–83.

1129. Watley, Donivan J. (1971). **Black and non-Black youth: Does marriage hinder college attendance?** *National Merit Scholarship Corporation, Research Reports,* 7(5), 28.

1130. Willis, Jerry. (1972). **Teaching appropriate hallway behavior to an emotionally disturbed, trainably retarded child.** *SALT: School Applications of Learning Theory,* 5(1), 11–16.

Curriculum & Programs & Teaching Methods

1131. Fantuzzo, John W. & Clement, Paul W. (1981). **Generalization of the effects of teacher- and self-administered token reinforcers to nontreated students.** *Journal of Applied Behavior Analysis,* 14(4), 435–447.

1132. Jenkins, Louis E. & Guthrie, George M. (1976). **Behavior rehearsal for high risk freshmen.** *Journal of Psychology,* 92(2), 147–154.

Academic Learning & Achievement

1133. Levine, Frederic J. (1976). **Influence of field-independence and study habits on academic performance of Black students in a predominantly White university.** *Perceptual & Motor Skills,* 42(3, Pt 2), 1101–1102.

1134. Meier, Scott T.; McCarthy, Patricia R. & Schmeck, Ronald R. (1984). **Validity of self-efficacy as a predictor of writing performance.** *Cognitive Therapy & Research,* 8(2), 107–120.

1135. Pascarella, Ernest T. (1985). **Racial differences in factors associated with bachelor's degree completion: A nine-year follow-up.** *Research in Higher Education,* 23(4), 351–373.

1136. Pedrini, Bonnie C. & Pedrini, D. T. (1978). **Multivariate assessment of ACT composite scores of disadvantaged and regular freshman.** *Education,* 99(1), 36–43.

1137. Reiff, Judith C. (1986). **Identifying perceptual preferences of elementary children to prevent learning problems.** *Psychology: A Quarterly Journal of Human Behavior,* 23(1), 47–52.

1138. Sewell, Trevor E.; Farley, Frank H.; Manni, John L. & Hunt, Portia. (1982). **Motivation, social reinforcement, and intelligence as predictors of academic achievement in Black adolescents.** *Adolescence,* 17(67), 647–656.

1139. Thomas, Charles L. (1979). **Relative effectiveness of high school grades for predicting college grades: Sex and ability level effects.** *Journal of Negro Education,* 48(1), 6–13.

1140. Thomas, Gail E. (1977). **Family status and standardized achievement tests as contingencies for Black and White college entry.** *Center for Social Organization of Schools Report, Johns Hopkins U.,* (Serial No. 239).

1141. Zimmerman, Marc L.; Goldston, John T. & Gadzella, Bernadette M. (1977). **Prediction of academic performance for college students by sex and race.** *Psychological Reports,* 41(3, Pt 2), 1183–1186.

Classroom Dynamics & Student Adjustment & Attitudes

1142. Bahr, Stephen J. & Leigh, Geoffrey K. (1978). **Family size, intelligence, and expected education.** *Journal of Marriage & the Family,* 40(2), 331–335.

1143. Black, Michael S. (1977). **Attitudes of inner-city junior high school males toward vocational education and work.** *Journal of Research & Development in Education,* 10(2), 99–115.

1144. Chen, Kathleen. (1978). **Semantic habits and attitudes of Black college students.** *Psychological Reports,* 42(3, Pt 1), 963–969.

1145. Gruber, Joseph J. (1975). **A directional analysis of peer status scores in a racially integrated residential high school for the disadvantaged.** *American Corrective Therapy Journal,* 29(5), 158–164.

1146. Harper, Frederick D. & Hawkins, Milton. (1977). **A profile of Black graduate students on the Personal Orientation Inventory.** *Journal of Non-White Concerns in Personnel & Guidance,* 5(4), 168–174.

1147. Hillman, Stephen B. & Davenport, G. Gregory. (1978). **Teacher–student interactions in desegregated schools.** *Journal of Educational Psychology,* 70(4), 545–553.

1148. Keller, John W.; Piotrowski, Chris & Sherry, Dave. (1982). **Perceptions of the college environment and campus life: The Black experience.** *Journal of Non-White Concerns in Personnel & Guidance,* 10(4), 126–132.

1149. Lietz, Jeremy J. (1977). **School deportment and student teacher sex and ethnicity.** *Psychology in the Schools,* 14(1), 72–76.

1150. Manese, Jeanne E. & Sedlacek, William E. (1985). **Changes in religious behaviors and attitudes of college students from 1973 to 1983.** Special Issue: Values and ethics in family therapy. *Counseling & Values,* 30(1), 74–77.

1151. Nichols, O. Clovis. (1983). **Five determinants of ethnic distance among Black college students.** *College Student Journal,* 17(2), 172–175.

1152. Pepinsky, Harold B. & DeStefano, Johanna S. (1983). **Interactive discourse in the classroom as organizational behavior.** *Advances in Reading/Language Research,* 2, 107–137.

1153. Schroth, Marvin L. (1976). **Sex and grade-level differences in need achievement among Black college students.** *Perceptual & Motor Skills,* 43(1), 135–140.

1154. Simpson, Adelaide W. & Erickson, Marilyn T. (1983). **Teachers' verbal and nonverbal communication patterns as a function of teacher race, student gender, and student race.** *American Educational Research Journal,* 20(2), 183–198.

1155. Stewart, Doreen & Vaux, Alan. (1986). **Social support resources, behaviors, and perceptions among Black and White college students.** *Journal of Multicultural Counseling & Development,* 14(2), 65–72.

1156. Wooldridge, Peter & Richman, Charles L. (1985). **Teachers' choice of punishment as a function of a student's gender, age, race, and IQ level.** *Journal of School Psychology,* 23(1), 19–29.

Special & Remedial Education

1157. Bice, Thomas R.; Halpin, Glennelle & Halpin, Gerald. (1986). **A comparison of the cognitive styles of typical and mildly retarded children with educational recommendations.** *Education & Training of the Mentally Retarded,* 21(2), 93–97.

1158. Morris, John D.; Kelsey, Edith & Martin, Robert A. (1980). **Comparison of WISC-R performance of urban and rural special education students.** *Psychological Reports,* 46(2), 671–677.

Counseling & Measurement

1159. Bracken, Bruce A.; Prasse, David P. & McCallum, R. Steve. (1984). **Peabody Picture Vocabulary Test—Revised: An appraisal and review.** *School Psychology Review,* 13(1), 49–60.

1160. Chase, Clinton I. (1986). **Essay test scoring: Interaction of relevant variables.** *Journal of Educational Measurement,* 23(1), 33–41.

1161. Hunter, Saundra M. et al. (1985). **Measurement assessment of the Type A coronary prone behavior pattern and hyperactivity/problem behaviors in children: Are they related? The Bogalusa Heart Study.** *Journal of Human Stress,* 11(4), 177–183.

1162. Mitchell, Karen J. & Molidor, John B. (1986). **Factor structure of the MCAT and pilot essay.** *Educational & Psychological Measurement,* 46(4), 1019–1027.

1163. Neal, Annie W. (1976). **Analysis of responses to items on the Peabody Picture Vocabulary Test according to race and sex.** *Journal of Educational Research,* 69(7), 265–267.

1164. Reynolds, Cecil R. (1978). **Teacher–psychologist interscorer reliability of the McCarthy Drawing Tests.** *Perceptual & Motor Skills,* 47(2), 538.

1165. Sapp, Gary L. & Marshall, John. (1984). **The Otis-Lennon School Ability Test: A study of validity.** *Psychological Reports,* 55(2), 539–544.

1166. Simpson, Robert G. & Eaves, Ronald C. (1983). **The concurrent validity of the Woodcock Reading Mastery Tests relative to the Peabody Individual Achievement Test among retarded adolescents.** *Educational & Psychological Measurement,* 43(1), 275–281.

1167. Stricker, Lawrence J. (1982). **Identifying test items that perform differentially in population subgroups: A partial correlation index.** *Applied Psychological Measurement,* 6(3), 261–273.

1168. Wilson, Nancy H. & Rotter, Joseph C. (1986). **Anxiety management training and study skills counseling for students on self-esteem and test anxiety and performance.** *School Counselor,* 34(1), 18–31.

APPLIED PSYCHOLOGY

1169. Adams, Edward F. (1978). **A multivariate study of subordinate perceptions of and attitudes toward minority and majority managers.** *Journal of Applied Psychology,* 63(3), 277–288.

1170. Allen, William R. & Ruhe, John A. (1976). **Verbal behavior by Black and White leaders of biracial groups in two different environments.** *Journal of Applied Psychology,* 61(4), 441–445.

1171. Feldman, Jack. (1973). **Race, economic class, and perceived outcomes of work and unemployment.** *Journal of Applied Psychology,* 58(1), 16–22.

1172. Ford, David L. (1985). **Facets of work support and employee work outcomes: An exploratory analysis.** *Journal of Management,* 11(3), 5–20,37.

1173. Gavin, J. & Ewen, R. (1974). **Racial differences in job attitudes and performance: Some theoretical considerations and empirical findings.** *Personnel Psychology,* 27(3), 455–464.

1174. Gitter, A. George; Altavela, Julie & Mostofsky, David I. (1974). **Effect of sex, religion, and ethnicity on occupational status perception.** *Journal of Applied Psychology,* 59(1), 96–98.

1175. Hamner, W. Clay; Kim, Jay S.; Baird, Lloyd & Bigoness, William J. (1974). **Race and sex as determinants of ratings by potential employers in a simulated work-sampling task.** *Journal of Applied Psychology,* 59(6), 705–711.

1176. Miner, John B. (1977). **Motivational potential for upgrading among minority and female managers.** *Journal of Applied Psychology,* 62(6), 691–697.

1177. Mobley, William H. (1982). **Supervisor and employee race and sex effects on performance appraisals: A field study of adverse impact and generalizability.** *Academy of Management Journal,* 25(3), 598–606.

1178. Natziger, Dean H. (1973). **A Markov chain analysis of the movement of young men using the Holland occupational classification.** *Center for Social Organization of Schools Report, Johns Hopkins U.,* (Serial No. 148).

1179. Palinkas, Lawrence A. (1985). **Racial differences in accidental and violent deaths among U.S. Navy personnel.** *Military Medicine,* 150(11), 587–592.

1180. Patten, Thomas H. & Dorey, Lester E. (1972). **An equal employment opportunity sensitivity workshop.** *Training & Development Journal,* 26(1), 42–53.

1181. Rodenstein, Judith M. (1982). **Follow-up and evaluation of job placement in employment and training.** *Journal of Employment Counseling,* 19(4), 171–183.

1182. Rosen, Hjalmar & Turner, John. (1971). **Effectiveness of two orientation approaches in hard-core unemployed turnover and absenteeism.** *Journal of Applied Psychology,* 55(4), 296–301.

1183. Ryan, Edward J.; Watson, John G. & Hailey, William A. (1983). **Goal constraints on Black and White managers' decision processes.** *Journal of Psychology,* 113(2), 231–235.

1184. Wing, Hilda. (1981). **Estimation of the adverse impact of a police promotion examination.** *Personnel Psychology,* 34(3), 503–510.

Occupational Attitudes & Interests & Guidance

1185. Berman, Gerald S. & Haug, Marie R. (1975). **Occupational and educational goals and expectations: The effects of race and sex.** *Social Problems,* 23(2), 166–181.

1186. Esposito, Ronald P. (1977). **The relationship between the motive to avoid success and vocational choice.** *Journal of Vocational Behavior,* 10(3), 347–357.

1187. Lawrence, William & Brown, Duane. (1976). **An investigation of intelligence, self-concept, socioeconomic status, race, and sex as predictors of career maturity.** *Journal of Vocational Behavior,* 9(1), 43–52.

1188. Pelham, Judy P. & Fretz, Bruce R. (1982). **Racial differences and attributes of career choice unrealism.** *Vocational Guidance Quarterly,* 31(1), 36–42.

1189. Pound, Ronald E. (1978). **Using self-concept subscales in predicting career maturity for race, and sex subgroups.** *Vocational Guidance Quarterly,* 27(1), 61–70.

1190. Schab, Fred. (1978). **Work ethic of gifted Black adolescents.** *Journal of Youth & Adolescence,* 7(3), 295–299.

Personnel Selection & Training

1191. Braddock, Jomills H.; Crain, Robert L.; McPartland, James M. & Dawkins, Russell L. (1985). **How race affects job placement decisions: Results of a vignette experiment with a national sample of employers.** *Center for Social Organization of Schools Report, Johns Hopkins U.,* (Serial No. 359).

1192. Grove, David A. (1981). **A behavioral consistency approach to decision making in employment selection.** *Personnel Psychology,* 34(1), 55–64.

1193. Landis, Dan et al. (1978). **Use of a Black "culture assimilator" to increase racial understanding.** *US Army Research Institute for the Behavioral & Social Sciences,* (Technical Report No. 310).

1194. Matarazzo, Joseph D. & Wiens, Arthur N. (1977). **Black Intelligence Test of Cultural Homogeneity and Wechsler Adult Intelligence Scale scores of Black and White police applicants.** *Journal of Applied Psychology,* 62(1), 57–63.

1195. Tzeng, Oliver C. & Landis, Dan. (1979). **Relationship between intercultural awareness and personality variables in interracial encounters.** *US Army Research Institute for the Behavioral & Social Sciences,* (Technical Report No. 422).

Section III. Selected Citations to the Dissertation Literature on Black Males in the United States

This section contains citations to the dissertation literature on Black males in the United States. References, which are covered in *Dissertation Abstracts International* (formerly *Dissertation Abstracts*), were retrieved from the PsycINFO database by searching for the concept of *Black males* (or synonyms) in the title, descriptor, and identifier fields. Entries are organized alphabetically within the major/minor classification categories used by *Psychological Abstracts* and the PsycINFO database.

PSYCHOMETRICS

1196. Moore, Clifford L. (1973). **The effect of the examiner's race on Wechsler Preschool and Primary Scale of Intelligence I.Q.'s and Black children's racial preference.** 34(6-B), 2904.

1197. Selters, Rex R. (1974). **An investigation of the relationship between ethnic origin and reactions to the MMPI.** 34(10-B), 5210.

Test Construction & Validation

1198. Bush, Robbie W. (1986). **A comparative study of the performance of Black and White males on the WAIS—R intelligence test.** 46(10-A), 2966.

1199. Carlton, Betty B. (1980). **Canonical analysis of the relationship between the study of values and the differential value profile.** 40(8-A), 4483.

1200. Carr, Lucy M. (1984). **Constancy of Performance subtest and IQ scores of the WISC and WISC-R as an indicator of innate intellectual ability in exceptional children.** 44(8-A), 2435–2436.

1201. DuRant, Margaret B. (1975). **The effect of examiner familiarity on two subtests of the Illinois Test of Psycholinguistic Abilities.** 36(6-A), 3503–3504.

1202. Farnum, Mary K. (1981). **Social interest in children.** 42(4-A), 1487.

1203. Glixman, Marika R. (1977). **Cognitive functioning on the Rorschach as a diagnostic tool.** 37(7-B), 3607–3608.

1204. Johnson, David L. (1984). **A Black apperceptive method: Experimental form, a pilot study.** 45(6-A), 1691.

1205. MacCornack, Frederick A. (1977). **The effects of response bias on the reliability and validity of data in a survey of adolescent males.** 38(4-A), 2339.

1206. Murdock, Louis J. (1975). **Utilizing Smith's Inventory to investigate Black male and female differences in identity structure.** 35(12-B, Pt 1), 6078.

1207. Schecter, Jerry S. (1981). **Impulsivity: Its assessment by psychometric, clinical-psychomotor and situational measures in a behavior disorder population.** 41(11-A), 4661.

1208. Sheffey, Marie A. (1982). **Holland's theory: Concurrent validity for college educated Black males.** 43(6-A), 1952.

1209. Terrell, Francis. (1976). **The development of an inventory to measure aspects of Black nationalism ideology.** 36(7-B), 3631.

1210. Terrell, Sandra L. (1979). **Performance of Black and White children on the Peabody Picture Vocabulary Test as a function of race of examiner and type of social reinforcer administered.** 39(8-B), 3783.

1211. Walters, Glenn D. (1983). **Racial variations on the MacAndrew Alcoholism Scale of the MMPI.** 43(8-B), 2720.

EXPERIMENTAL PSYCHOLOGY (HUMAN)

1212. Bayless, Vaurice G. (1980). **Selected research studies and professional literature dealing with physiological, socioeconomic, psychological, and cultural differences between Black and White males with reference to the performance of athletic skills.** 41(4-A), 1472.

1213. Bushell, Robert D. (1974). **A comparative test of the competency and perceived similarity theories of imitation.** 34(10-B), 5162.

1214. Coleman, Mary L. (1976). **The effects of theoretical information on transfer with Black sixth grade students: A comparison with Henrickson and Schroeder.** 36(7-A), 4341.

1215. Hamby, John V. (1974). **Accuracy of responding in extinction following errorless discrimination training with continuous and intermittent reinforcement.** 35(2-A), 888.

1216. Mattox, Joe A. (1979). **The effects of race and counterbalancing on facial recognition and eyewitness identification.** 40(4-B), 1930–1931.

1217. Perlman, Gerald S. (1972). **The ameliorative effects of humor on induced anxiety in a Black and White population.** 33(4-B), 1803–1804.

1218. Stukalin, Joel J. (1973). **A study of disadvantaged eleven-year olds' risk-assumption as related to locus of control flexible thinking and demographic factors.** 34(4-B), 1762-1763.

1219. Terrell, Hilton P. (1972). **Some subject variables in cross-modal transfer.** 33(4-B), 1774.

PHYSIOLOGICAL PSYCHOLOGY

1220. Davis, Adrienne C. (1985). **Cardiovascular reactivity, anger management and personality traits among young Black males.** 45(11-B), 3653.

1221. Gonzales, Luis C. (1977). **Physiological reactions of Black and White men to simulated interracial encounters.** 37(12-B, Pt 1), 6303.

COMMUNICATION SYSTEMS

1222. Ellingson, David J. (1975). **Effects of dialect vocabulary differences between Black and White boys on free recall measures.** 35(7-A), 4247.

1223. Hennigan, Charles T. (1968). **An inquiry into the oral communication patterns of eight disadvantaged pre-school Negro boys in Houston, Texas, 1966.** 28(7-A), 2485.

1224. Hudson, Barbara H. (1984). **A descriptive study of male and female speech stereotypes on selected television shows with predominantly Black characteristics.** 44(10-A), 3049.

1225. St. Martin, Gail M. (1976). **Male/female differential encoding and intercultural differential decoding of nonverbal affective communication.** 37(5-A), 2499–2500.

DEVELOPMENTAL PSYCHOLOGY

1226. Barnard, Caroline G. (1972). **Psychological and interpersonal correlates of personality integration in fifth-grade boys of different race and social class.** 33(4-B), 1778–1779.

1227. Bradshaw, Jo A. (1970). **Situational variables in verbal conditioning with children using a paired-associate paradigm.** 3(5-B), 2952.

1228. Chronister, Mary R. (1974). **The effects of reward magnitude on young boys' delay behavior.** 34(9-B), 4655-4656.

1229. Currier, Joseph R. (1972). **Relationship of race-image of Negro males to figure-ground perception in a black-white perceptual field.** 32(10-B), 6044.

1230. Ducote, Charlotte A. (1983). **A study of the reading and speaking fundamental vocal frequency of aging Black adults.** 44(4-B), 1080–1081.

1231. Evans, Dorothy A. (1969). **The effects of instructional set on expectancy change and expectancy generalization in inner city children.** 29(10-B), 3910.

1232. Feeley, Joan T. (1972). **Interest patterns and media preferences of boys and girls in grades four and five.** 33(1-A), 190.

1233. Freeman, Hazel J. (1974). **The operative effect of common variables on the early development of the success potential for successful Black adult American males.** 34(9-A, Pt 1), 5476-5477.

1234. Goldstein, Lynn M. (1986). **Linguistic variation in English as a second language as a function of contact versus identification.** 47(3-A), 887.

1235. Grimmett, Sadie A. (1970). **Problem solving on the game Twenty Questions by males of four ethnocultural groups at two grade levels.** 30(10-A), 4274.

1236. Harris, Helena. (1967). **The development of moral attitudes in White and Negro boys.** 28(6-B), 2624.

1237. Helwig, Loren D. (1980). **A study of certain significant educational variables in two Black cultures.** 40(7-A), 3892.

1238. Jenkins-Monroe, Valata. (1979). **A phenomenological approach to the study of cognitive styles in problem-solving of Black children.** 39(7-B), 3520.

1239. Jones, Randel R. (1973). **The effects of interpersonal and developmental variables on competitive behavior in low socioeconomic Black male children.** 33(8-B), 3943.

1240. Lavinson, Norman B. (1970). **Father's presence, nurturance, and alternate responding as related to transgression in young Negro boys.** 30(11-B), 5223-5224.

1241. Lewis, Cheri L. (1970). **Ethnic and social class differences in values related to effective coping behavior.** 30(7-B), 3374.

1242. Lipoff, Dennis A. (1973). **An investigation of competition in children.** 33(8-B), 3950.

1243. Mackenzie, Carolyn S. (1970). **Motor inhibition and capacity for delay of gratification in two classes of Negro boys.** 31(2-A), 665.

1244. Maruyama, Yoshio. (1969). **The sense of competence in middle adolescent boys.** 30(5-B), 2405-2406.

1245. Masingale, Eula M. (1972). **Father-absence as related to parental role-play behavior.** 32(12-B), 7294.

1246. Minetos, Peter. (1971). **Influence of male intervention figure upon sex-role identification of certain preschool children.** 31(10-A), 5208.

1247. Murray, Mary M. (1983). **The middle years of life of middle class Black men: An exploratory study.** 43(11-B), 3753.

1248. Phillips, Judith. (1967). **Performance of father-present and father-absent southern Negro boys on a simple operant task as a function of the race and sex of the experimenter and the type of social reinforcement.** 28(1-B), 366.

1249. Piercy, Patricia A. (1976). **The relationship of cognitive functioning to the development of sex role in Black male children ages four to ten.** 37(4-B), 1974.

1250. Ratcliff, Kathryn S. (1977). **In their thirties: A study of the young adult outcomes in a sample of urban Black males.** 38(6-A), 3744-3745.

1251. Vaughan, Peter B. (1977). **A developmental study of race-esteem and self-esteem of Black boys and girls in third and seventh grades.** 38(6-A), 3735.

1252. Ward, Joan G. (1974). **Locus of control, social reinforcement, and task performance of Black and Spanish-surnamed children.** 34(7-B), 3479.

1253. Wilkinson, Robert J. (1971). **An analysis of the relationship between psycholinguistic abilities and articulatory abilities of Negro and white first grade boys.** 31(9-B), 5695.

1254. Williams, Nancy G. (1973). **The acquisition of syntax by middle-class and culturally different Black children in grades one, two, three, five, six and eight.** 33(9-A), 4959–4960.

1255. Zaffy, Donna J. (1970). **Help-seeking behavior in second, fourth, and sixth grade Negro boys of low and middle socioeconomic status.** 31(2-B), 908.

Cognitive & Perceptual Development

1256. Baker, Bailey B. (1981). **An investigation of the communicative competence of teenage boys in a northern urban warren.** 42(5-A), 1848.

1257. Bondy, Andrew S. (1976). **The effects of manipulating objects in modeling films on imitative response topographies.** 37(3-B), 1456.

1258. Keane, William M. (1976). **Black mothers and their sons: Correlates and predictors of cognitive development from the second to the sixth year of life.** 37(6-B), 3081.

1259. Rector, Madelynne T. (1984). **The study of rotations and spatial displacements of certain Bender Gestalt figures by Black children.** 45(6-B), 1935.

1260. Rosenbaum, Dave. (1974). **Assessment of divergent thinking in children: Effects of task context, race, and socioeconomic status.** 34(7-B), 3507-3508.

1261. Schaefer, William M. (1977). **Factors associated with intellectual development: Birth order and family size effects for a select population.** 38(4-A), 2009-2010.

1262. Siegel, Ronald J. (1983). **Effects of preschool intervention, socioeconomic status and acquisition of perceptual skills on subsequent verbal test performance: Longitudinal analyses.** 43(11-B), 3754.

1263. Worthy, Phyllis D. (1984). **An analysis of fundamental motor skills of urban Black and urban White children of middle childhood age.** 45(1-A), 120.

Psychosocial & Personality Development

1264. Alexander, Sharon J. (1977). **Locus of control and sex role expectations in Black and White, female and male children.** 38(2-B), 957.

1265. Cisneros-Solis, Maria G. (1983). **The relationship between coping and self-esteem: A tri-ethnic longitudinal study.** 43(7-B), 2366.

1266. Curtis-Boles, Harriet A. (1985). **Life satisfaction in the later years: A cross-cultural investigation.** 45(9-B), 3065.

1267. Dailey, Lige. (1986). **Playing the dozens: A psycho-historical examination of an African American ritual.** 46(9-A), 2822.

1268. Dancy, Barbara L. (1982). **Black male and female adolescents' perception of family climate, psychological adjustment, peer relationships, and grade point average: A function of parental marital status, chronological age, sex, or perceived family conflict.** 43(5-B), 1595.

1269. Fineberg, Emanuel. (1976). **The sensitivity of children to adult attitudes expressed in body postures.** 36(9-A), 5942-5943.

1270. Griffing, Penelope S. (1975). **The relationship between socioeconomic status and sociodramatic play among Black kindergarten students.** 35(11-B), 5617.

1271. Grodsky, Alicia. (1986). **White children's information-seeking and racial beliefs about Blacks and Orientals.** 46(8-B), 2836.

1272. Harris, Joseph D. (1979). **The development of moral judgment and a sense of experienced injustice among urban Black children.** 40(5-B), 2436.

1273. Harris, Mollie R. (1974). **Developmental patterns of student attitudes toward the world of work and relationships between selected correlates.** 34(7-A), 4104.

1274. Herbert, James I. (1986). **Adult psychosocial development: The evolution of the individual life structure of Black male entrepreneurs.** 47(5-B), 2196.

1275. Jenkins, Robert C. (1986). **Correlates of the social networks of young Black men.** 47(1-B), 377.

1276. Kaner, Harriette. (1982). **Adolescent reactions to race and sex of professional television newscasters.** 43(2-A), 298.

1277. Kersey, Katharine C. (1973). **The effects of male absence on impulsivity and self control in preschool children.** 34(4-A), 1704.

1278. Klein, Richard A. (1975). **Racial similarities versus prestige roles as determinants of identification in Black and White male children.** 36(1-A), 189-190.

1279. Looney, Jacqueline. (1985). **The relationship of ego development and identity formation in Black males and females.** 46(3-B), 999-1000.

1280. Mastenbrook, John L. (1980). **Child, environmental, and cultural characteristics as correlates of adaptive behavior in normal children.** 41(4-B), 1540.

1281. Matthews, Graham P. (1976). **Father-absence and the development of masculine identification in Black preschool males.** 37(3-A), 1458.

1282. McDonald, Ozzie H. (1981). **Stereotypical daydreams and their relationship to personal role preferences across different races.** 42(2-B), 777-778.

1283. McGrew, John M. (1977). **Class, ethnic, and age effects on the sensitvity to facial and vocal cues.** 38(4-A), 2004.

1284. Morse, Roberta N. (1975). **Some factors influencing the masculinity of urban Black male high school seniors.** 35(11-B), 5699.

1285. Munoz, Millie C. (1982). **An exploratory study of the effects of young children's color biases, racial attitudes, and racial preferences on their sharing behavior.** 42(8-A), 3487.

1286. Nall, Hiram A. (1983). **Just like brothers: An ethnographic approach to the friendship ties of an urban group of elderly Black men.** 43(7-A), 2390.

1287. Pennington, Gregory. (1985). **Inhibited power motivation, locus of control, active coping style, and blood pressure differences among Black male adolescents.** 46(2-B), 655.

1288. Robertson, Susan. (1978). **Sex differences in expectancy before and after feedback.** 38(11-B), 5591-5592.

1289. Roman, Edward. (1986). **Racial differences and attributions: Black and White male students' judgments of causation, future success, and affect for the success and failure of Black and White peers on stereotyped-linked tasks.** 46(12-A, Pt 1), 3661-3662.

1290. Saliba, Akhee R. (1981). **Race recognition, personality judgment, preference, self-identification, and the relationship of self-concept.** 42(4-A), 1558-1559.

1291. Saundra. (1985). **The use of the discounting principle in preschool children.** 45(7-B), 2363.

1292. Steinberg, Marvin A. (1974). **Children's coping behaviors related to father absence.** 35(1-B), 490.

1293. Tapp, Marilyn C. (1976). **The social class and racial evaluations of four- and eight-year-old males in relation to their social class, race, and locus of control.** 36(10-B), 5238.

1294. Werton, Pamela C. (1976). **Sociodramatic play among three and four year old Black children.** 37(1-A), 185.

1295. Woal, S. Theodore. (1979). **The identification, development and evaluation of a method for modifying sex stereotyping of occupations by elementary level students.** 39(11-A), 6555.

1296. Zwiebel, Sarah. (1980). **The relation between maternal behaviors and aggression in sons: Black and Puerto Rican families.** 40(12-A, Pt 1), 6430.

SOCIAL PROCESSES AND SOCIAL ISSUES

1297. Adams, Darrell K. (1969). **Deviance, conformity, and expected consequences of aggression.** 30(6-B), 2921.

1298. Bienvenu, Millard J. (1968). **Effects of school integration on the self concept and anxiety of lower-class, Negro adolescent males.** 29(2-A), 692.

1299. Bolick. Edith M. (1980). **Race and gender awareness: An analysis of constant biosocial identities and attitudes.** 40(8-A), 4762.

1300. Bromwich, Rose M. (1967). **Some correlates of stimulus-bound versus stimulus-free verbal responses to pictures by young Negro boys.** 28(4-A), 1290–1291.

1301. Crane, Valerie. (1973). **Effects of Black or White adult modeling with or without rule structure on adopting a standard for self-control in six- to eleven-year-old black boys.** 33(7-A), 3372-3373.

1302. DeBord, Larry W. (1970). **The achievement syndrome among Negro and white culturally disadvantaged boys.** 30(10-A), 4558-4559.

1303. Freeman, Janie A. (1980). **A study of Black middle-class feelings and attitudes on male/female role identifications.** 40(7-A), 4254.

1304. Goldsmith, Arlene F. (1970). **The effects of verbal incentive, race, and sex of examiner of digit-symbol performance of Negro males and females.** 30(9-B), 4370-4371.

1305. Hayes, Edward D. (1970). **A comparative study of the manhood experiences of Black and White young adult males.** 31(5-A), 2105.

1306. Hurley, Robert B. (1973). **Race, fatherlessness, and vocational development: An exploration of relationships between membership in nuclear or fatherless families and level of occupational aspiration and expectation, self-esteem, extrinsic work values and person-orientation among a sample of Black and White adolescent boys.** 33(11-A), 6090-6091.

1307. King, Lewis M. (1973). **An experimental exploration of the relationship between self-reinforcement, self-esteem and locus of control in 9-11 yr. old Black males.** 33(7-B), 3310.

1308. Menchise, Donald N. (1972). **Racial bias as a determinant of literary preference and the relationship of selected variables to patterns of preference and rejection of literary works whose author's race is known.** 33(6-A), 2619.

1309. Muha, Michael J. (1985). **Crosscutting race, class, and gender group membership, group identification, and political attitudes.** 45(12-A), 3754–3755.

1310. Offut, Bobby R. (1972). **A comparison of self-perceived needs among Black and non-Black males attending an inner-city community college and those attending a suburban community college.** 32(12-A), 6813–6814.

1311. Rubin, Roger H. (1971). **Family structure and peer group affiliation as related to attitudes about male-female relations among Black youth.** 31(9-A), 4920–4921.

1312. Self, Ruthie L. (1979). **Black male/White female relationship: Implications for Black females.** 39(10-B), 5152–5153.

1313. Steigelmann, Val V. (1972). **Patterns of racial identity imagery in inner-city male children.** 32(8-B), 4872.

1314. Young, Robert L. (1982). **Race, sex, and guns: A social psychology of firearms ownership.** 43(6-A), 2113.

Social Structure & Social Roles

1315. Goodman, Jerry D. (1984). **The socioeconomic returns to education: An empirical assessment of alternative perspectives.** 44(9-A), 2896–2897.

1316. Hunt, Janet G. (1974). **Race and identity: A study of Black and White urban school boys.** 34(7-A), 4452.

1317. Long, Richard M. (1985). **A case study: Five illiterate Black men in a literate society.** 46(6-A), 1578.

Culture & Ethnology & Religion

1318. Broaddus, Raymond K. (1976). **Portrait of a Black man: Good or evil?** 37(4-B), 1967.

1319. Dukes, Lawrencella W. (1975). **The experience of being-me for Black adolescent males: A phenomenological investigation of Black identity.** 35(8-A), 5016.

1320. Fossett, Mark A. (1984). **Racial income inequality and market discrimination in metropolitan areas of the United States in 1970.** 45(3-A), 960.

1321. Griffin, Adrienne M. (1980). **The relationship of psychosexual security, self concept, and endorsement of ancient sexual beliefs about Black men to White supremacist attitudes.** 40(11-B), 5406.

1322. Klein, Katherine W. (1977). **The effects of racial, religious, and attitudinal similarity on behavioral intentions.** 37(11-B), 5880–5881.

1323. Lattimore, Vergel L. (1985). **Pastoral care strategies of Black pastors.** 45(7-A), 2053.

1324. McEwen, James L. (1985). **The relationship between cultural identification, the race-sensitive scale and selected MMPI scales.** 46(6-B), 2072.

1325. Sacks, Susan R. (1973). **Self-identity and academic achievement of Black adolescent males: A study of racial identification, locus of control, self-attitudes, and academic performance.** 34(6-B), 2911.

1326. Smith, Eleanor C. (1976). **Comparative survey of self-identity and racial perception in primary school age children from selected communities.** 37(3-A), 1391.

Marriage & Family

1327. Badaines, Joel S. (1973). **Identification, imitation and sex-role preference as a function of father-absence and father-presence in Black and Chicano boys.** 34(1-B), 403-404.

1328. Cazenave, Noel A. (1978). **Middle-income Black fathers: Family interaction, transaction, and development.** 38(12-A), 7593–7594.

1329. Cook, Margie B. (1981). **Communication confirmation and interpersonal satisfaction of mothers and their adolescent sons.** 41(8-A), 3319.

1330. Crawford, Albert G. (1976). **The stability of a man's family of origin, its causes, and its effects on his achievement: A test of Moynihan's theory.** 37(4-A), 2442.

1331. Daniel, Jerlean E. (1975). **A definition of fatherhood as expressed by Black fathers.** 36(4-A), 2090-2091.

1332. Davis, Debra L. (1986). **Psychosocial competence and stress among middle-class, Black and White, married and divorced, males and females.** 47(4-B), 1718.

1333. Green, Alice P. (1983). **Case studies of the impact of separation due to incarceration on Black families.** 43(12-A), 4050.

1334. Hoyte, Merle. (1976). **A study of the relationship between parenting, the self-concept and level of vocational maturity of the male adolescent.** 36(10-A), 6474-6475.

1335. Johnson, Evlyn L. (1983). **Mate selection: Preferences of Black single college males with reference to selected variables.** 44(6-A), 1693.

1336. Labrecque, Suzanne V. (1977). **Child-rearing attitudes and observed behaviors of Black fathers with kindergarten daughters.** 37(7-A), 4646–4647.

1337. Melton, Willie. (1977). **Self-satisfaction and marital stability among Black males: Socioeconomic and demographic antecedents.** 37(8-A), 5387–5388.

1338. O'Dowd, Mary M. (1974). **Family supportiveness related to illicit drug use immunity.** 34(11-A), 7360-7361.

1339. Samuels, Douglas D. (1977). **A study of the relationship between maternal anxiety and self-esteem of Head Start children.** 37(12-B, Pt 1), 6349.

1340. Smith, Dennis E. (1975). **Independence training of their male offspring by lower class Black mothers with high and low achievement motivation.** 35(7-A), 4262.

Political & Legal Processes

1341. Peterson-Lewis, Sonja M. (1984). **Evaluating the criminal offender: The effects of offenders' socio-economic status, academic achievement and color on personality attributions and sentencing.** 45(4-B), 1323.

1342. Unnever, James D. (1981). **Direct and structural discrimination in the sentencing process.** 41(9-A), 4172.

Psychosexual Behavior & Sex Roles

1343. Boxley, Russell L. (1974). **Sex-object choice in adult Black males: Perception of parental relationships and early sexual behavior.** 35(1-B), 495-496.

1344. Gossett, Ruth R. (1977). **So few men: A study of Black widowhood.** 38(5-A), 3086.

1345. Johnson, Julius M. (1982). **Influence of assimilation on the psychosocial adjustment of Black homosexual men.** 42(11-B), 4620.

1346. McDermit, William C. (1981). **White men loving Black men: An explication of the experience within on going erotic relationships.** 41(12-B, Pt 1), 4676–4677.

1347. McNair, Edward. (1984). **Changing sex roles and masculine role strain.** 45(3-B), 1061–1062.

1348. Smith, Patricia A. (1981). **Conceptions of masculinity and femininity among male and female Whites and Blacks.** 42(3-B), 1192–1193.

1349. Washington, James D. (1986). **Male gender role as a function of father absence, nurturance and race.** 46(8-B), 2828.

Drug & Alcohol Usage

1350. Bell, Beverly D. (1986). **Alcohol related expectancies and patterns of use in Black and White male college students.** 46(9-B), 3208.

1351. Pagan, Gilberto. (1985). **Social influences on the drinking behavior of Black and White male college students: A comparison of the laboratory and the natural setting.** 45(7-B), 2318.

1352. Capp, Larry D. (1980). **The role of race in judgments of dangerousness, mental disorder, and need for hospitalization.** 41(6-B), 2310.

1353. Elkin, Jay S. (1982). **The effect of observer and initiator race upon social perception: An attributional analysis.** 43(6-A), 1888.

1354. Gries, Leonard T. (1973). **Race and sex of the examiner and the elicited vocabulary of Black kindergarten children.** 34(1-A), 413-414.

1355. Hughes, Julius H. (1967). **Relationships between intolerance of ambiguity and values: White and Negro male college students.** 28(4-A), 1545–1546.

1356. Johnson, Betty S. (1975). **Imitation by children of model-performed behavior under a variety of stimulus conditions.** 35(8-B), 4219-4220.

1357. Mann, Joe W. (1972). **The effects of reflection and race on verbal conditioning of affective self-disclosure in Black and White males.** 33(6-A), 2717–2718.

1358. Rubincroit, Carl I. (1970). **Leadership in dyadic groups as a function of dominance and ethnic composition.** 31(4-B), 2265.

1359. Scott, William C. (1970). **The influence of contextual variables on the attractiveness of a stimulus target.** 30(11-B), 5266–5267.

1360. Unger, Hanne. (1972). **The effect of group pressure on members of different ethnic groups.** 33(1-B), 431.

Group & Interpersonal Processes

1361. Dirlam, Karen S. (1974). **An investigation of skin color as a salient variable in interpersonal preferences in dyadic and group social situations among elementary school children, Black and White, boys and girls.** 35(1-A), 96.

1362. Fleming, George R. (1976). **A comparative analysis of dyadic spatial interaction varying race and sex.** 36(9-B), 4753-4754.

1363. Floyd, Michael R. (1982). **Some effects of assertive statements delivered to Black college students.** 43(3-A), 672.

1364. Hamid, Rashid. (1976). **The modification of compliant behavior of Black males in biracial settings.** 37(4-B), 1970.

1365. Hare, Nathan. (1976). **Black male-female relations.** 37(3-B), 1435.

1366. James, Sherman A. (1974). **The effects of the race of the experimenter and the race of comparison norm on social influence in biracial cooperative problem solving dyads.** 34(12-B, Pt 1), 6258.

1367. La Boon, Sandra. (1975). **Self-concept congruence and cross-racial conflict management among Black and White males.** 36(6-B), 3124.

1368. Marcelle, Yvonne M. (1977). **Eye contact as a function of race, sex, and distance.** 37(7-A), 4238.

1369. Nettles, Reginald. (1985). **Situational factors, subjective expected utilities for consequences and assertive behavioral intentions.** 46(4-B), 1365.

1370. Nolan, Benjamin C. (1982). **Inside the decision making group: The effect of racial composition on three indices of group behavior.** 42(12-B, Pt 1), 4937.

1371. Summers, Marc D. (1974). **Effects of peer behavior, monetary incentive, and race of the peer on temporal persistence in fourth grade Black males.** 35(1-B), 491.

1372. Webber, Joseph R. (1975). **The influence of racial group composition on racial-aggressive humor appreciation: A test of reference group theory.** 36(1-B), 498-499.

Social Perception & Motivation

1373. Blakley, Dorothy T. (1977). **Internal and external locus of control and the perception of responsibility for interpersonal conflict among Black males and females.** 37(9-B), 4663–4664.

1374. Clark, Robert H. (1974). **Racial similarity as a factor in adult modeling of non-cooperative behavior.** 35(5-B), 2480.

1375. Clinkscales, Marcia J. (1976). **Black and White nonverbal dyadic behavior and attraction.** 36(8-A), 4846.

1376. Conto, Anthony D. (1978). **Deviance attribution, boundary maintenance, and deviant type-scripts.** 39(1-A), 504–505.

1377. Edwards, Angela R. (1976). **Conjunctive and disjunctive attributional patterns in competitive and cooperative situations in cross race dyads.** 36(11-B), 5863.

1378. Hill, Jannifer E. (1984). **Preconceptions and the Black male–female relationship.** 45(1-B), 402.

1379. Johnson, William E. (1976). **Imitative aggression as a function of race of model, race of target and socioeconomic status of observer.** 37(6-B), 3150–3151.

1380. Lacoste, Ronald J. (1976). **Preferences of three and four year old children for the facial features of the Negro and Caucasian races when skin color is not a racial clue.** 36(10-A), 6556.

1381. Onwuka, Golie T. (1979). **Effects of competition on motor skill performance and preference in relation to achievement motivation and anxiety.** 40(6-A), 3205.

1382. Roberts, George W. (1986). **Self-enhancement as a function of racial stereotypes.** 47(2-B), 854.

1383. Schneider, William E. (1975). **Black vs White social intelligence.** 36(6-B), 3069-3070.

1384. Wood, Nollie P. (1984). **Black trust: Coping among Black males.** 45(1-B), 371.

PERSONALITY

1385. Adams, Amelia E. (1973). **Clothing acceptance for the self and for others, and adherence to selected clothing norms as related to selected aspects of personality in a sample of Black college males.** 33(12-A), 7030.

1386. Allen, Juanita L. (1972). **The effects of repression-sensitization, race, and levels of threat on extensions of personal space.** 33(4-B), 1777.

1387. Baldwin, John W. (1981). **Racial differences on the Rorschach: A comparison of Black and White male Americans.** 41(12-B, Pt 1), 4649.

1388. Chepp, Theodore J. (1976). **The relationship of cognitive style to the attainment of success among selected disadvantaged, young adult, Black males.** 37(2-B), 948.

1389. Covington, Neil R. (1968). **Creativity in culturally deprived adolescent boys.** 29(5-A), 1608.

1390. Dale, Grady. (1976). **Dogmatism among Black seminarians: A pilot study.** 36(7-B), 3570.

1391. Darity, Evangeline R. (1978). **A comparison of fear-of-success imagery between Black male and female undergraduates.** 38(9-A), 5316.

1392. Everett, Moses L. (1982). **The effects of subject-figure racial similarity and dissimilarity on thematic apperception test production.** 43(2-B), 522.

1393. Howard, Lydia R. (1976). **An exploratory analysis of differences in assertiveness and self-disclosure in Blacks and Whites.** 36(11-B), 5795-5796.

1394. Hreshko, James L. (1977). **Antecedents of locus of control among young urban males: Race, residence, birth order, and family variables.** 37(10-B), 5354–5355.

1395. Jackson, Pamela R. (1973). **Self-conceptions in black male and female college students.** 33(9-B), 4509-4510.

1396. Losada, Gloria. (1985). **An exploratory study on the nature of symbolism.** 45(7-B), 2343.

1397. Nobers, Donald R. (1968). **The effects of father absence and mother's characteristics on the identification of adolescent White and Negro males.** 29(4-B), 1508–1509.

1398. Oudry, Yvonne M. (1974). **Reported emotional experiences in relation to ethnic and sex group membership.** 34(10-B), 5203.

1399. Rademaker, Timothy A. (1984). **Comparison of achievement motivation profiles between successful and less successful, Black and White, and male and female track and field athletes.** 44(12-A), 3630.

1400. Reeder, Ernestine N. (1978). **Clothing preferences of male athletes in relation to self-concept, athletic ability, race, socioeconomic status, and peer perception.** 38(9-B), 4179.

1401. Robinson, John W. (1978). **Locus of control in northern Black undergraduate male students.** 39(6-B), 3004.

1402. Rothenberg, Peter J. (1968). **Locus of control, social class, and risk-taking in Negro boys.** 29(1-B), 379.

1403. Sailes, Gary A. (1985). **Sport socialization comparisons among Black and White adult male athletes and nonathletes.** 45(8-A), 2664.

1404. Sale, Mary J. (1977). **The effect of self-instructional training on locus of control in sixth grade boys.** 37(7-B), 3629.

1405. Schmults, Theodore C. (1976). **The relationship of Black ethnicity to field dependence and adjustment.** 36(11-B), 5816.

1406. Stern, Frances. (1972). **Ethnicity and the acting out of aggression.** 33(4-B), 1773-1774.

1407. Williams, Maurice. (1979). **A comparison of sexual and racial differences in dating frequency, social anxiety and skills.** 39(12-B), 6151.

PHYSICAL AND PSYCHOLOGICAL DISORDERS

1408. Conrad, Carolyn T. (1986). **A conversational act analysis of Black mother–child dyads including stuttering and nonstuttering children.** 46(8-B), 2640.

1409. Cunningham, Madonna M. (1968). **Training concept learning with schizophrenic and nonschizophrenic culturally disadvantaged adults.** 29(2-B), 767-768.

1410. Etienne, Jerald F. (1968). **The relationship between language and employment of Caucasian, Negroid, and Spanish-American male educable mentally retarded adults.** 29(4-A), 1037.

1411. Grasso, Richard. (1975). **The relationship between the self concept and body concept in a disabled population, consisting of adult male and female, White and Black subjects from higher and lower socioeconomic levels.** 35(8-B), 4143–4144.

1412. Malon, James V. (1972). **The PAS study of delinquency and race.** 32(9-B), 5449.

1413. McClain, William A. (1972). **The readiness to transmit bad news by male adolescent delinquents as a function of age and sex of both communicator and target.** 33(1-B), 425-426.

1414. Moran, Patricia A. (1972). **The effect of father absence on delinquent males: Dependency and hypermasculinity.** 33(3-B), 1292-1293.

1415. Scallon, Richard J. (1969). **Field articulation: A study of the perceptual style of enuretic boys.** 29(11-B), 4369.

1416. Speck, Charles G. (1969). **Spontaneous visual expression and the problems of a child's adjustment: A case study.** 29(9-A), 3010.

1417. Sunshine, Nancy J. (1971). **Cultural differences in schizophrenia.** 32(2-B), 1197-1198.

1418. Wilkie, Charlotte H. (1970). **A study of familial expectations regarding work for the Negro schizophrenic male patient on convalescent leave.** 31(4-A), 1897.

Mental Disorders

1419. Fuller, William. (1983). **The definition, etiology and treatment of mental illness among adult Black males with middle and low socioeconomic backgrounds.** 43(9-B), 3073.

1420. Owens, Paula J. (1979). **The relationship between self-concept and psychopathology among Black American veterans in treatment.** 40(5-B), 2379.

Behavior Disorders & Antisocial Behavior

1421. Atwell, Wilbur M. (1977). **Anomie, perceived opportunity and drug addiction: A study of some correlates of drug addicted and non-addicted offending behavior.** 38(6-A), 3751.

1422. Austin, James B. (1981). **The relationship of locus of control to the academic performance of delinquent boys.** 41(8-A), 3483.

1423. Christian, Maureen M. (1979). **A comparison of D.C. offenders to other inmates in the Federal Bureau of Prisons.** 40(1-B), 442–443.

1424. Coleman, Philip P. (1982). **Separation and autonomy: Issues of adolescent identity development among the families of Black male status offenders.** 42(12-B, Pt 1), 4926.

1425. Davis, Charles E. (1984). **Child rearing patterns and job satisfaction of fathers with behavior disorder boys.** 44(7-B), 2227–2228.

1426. Gibbs, Jerome M. (1986). **Causative factors related to criminal involvement among young, low income, Black males.** 46(10-A), 2969–2970.

1427. Gottsagen, Mitchell L. (1974). **An analysis of the relationship between frustration, inhibition, and aggressive cue with overt aggressive behavior in delinquents.** 34(8-B), 4040.

1428. Jacobs, Rosevelt. (1976). **A study of drinking behavior and personality characteristics of three ethnic groups.** 36(11-B), 5796.

1429. Johnson, Phyllis T. (1986). **Verbal and physiological response patterns of homicidal adolescents to threatening situations.** 46(9-B), 3255.

1430. King, Gary T. (1973). **A comparison of Hand Test responses responses of aggressive and non-aggressive Black adolescents.** 34(4-A), 1736.

1431. Kirk, Alton R. (1977). **Socio-psychological factors in attempted suicide among urban Black males.** 37(9-B), 4757.

1432. Klimek, David E. (1974). **Censure sensitivity among Black and White delinquents, probationers, and nondelinquents.** 34(12-B, Pt 1), 6214.

1433. Kreuchauf, Gary A. (1978). **A typological study on institutionalized juvenile delinquents using hierarchical classification techniques.** 39(2-B), 956–957.

1434. Ludmar, Joan M. (1978). **Selected personality characteristics of Black and White male alcoholics in a state treatment facility.** 39(3-B), 1459.

1435. Magura, Stephen. (1980). **Explaining delinquency: A social systems approach.** 40(7-A), 4247–4248.

1436. Marowitz, Roberta L. (1982). **Psychosocial dynamics of Black rapists: A case study.** 42(11-A), 4946.

1437. Mayo, Michael A. (1985). **A comparison of MMPI diagnostic strategies to identify Black and White male alcoholics.** 45(10-B), 3340.

1438. Nobles, Joseph L. (1981). **MMPI and drinking pattern differences among Black/White male alcoholic rehabilitation patients.** 42(4-B), 1615–1616.

1439. Pomerantz, Arlyne E. (1978). **Sex role confusion, locus of control, direction of aggression, and delinquency in urban Black male adolescents.** 39(3-B), 1547.

1440. Roberts, Harrell B. (1983). **The psychological world of the Black juvenile delinquent: Three case studies.** 43(11-B), 3741.

1441. Robertson, John F. (1984). **The relationship of alcoholism and ethnicity to locus of control.** 45(5-B), 1577.

1442. Thomas, Ronald E. (1982). **Alcohol abuse among Black males in a detoxification center: A study of stress and social supports.** 43(4-B), 1271.

1443. Thompson, Cheryl L. (1978). **Perceptions of intrafamilial relationships in single parent lower-class families and male adolescent anti-social behavior.** 39(4-B), 1972.

1444. Tripp, Michael D. (1982). **Adolescents' attitudes and social judgments of delinquent behavior.** 42(12-A), 5251.

1445. Wallace, Joseph P. (1976). **Achievement motivation and modification of risk taking behavior of Blacks with criminal records.** 36(8-B), 4185-4186.

1446. Watson, Lawrence A. (1977). **Alienation and the addiction process: An investigation into the identification and the differential effects of various types of pre-drug conditions on the "preaddict" as he enters into and passes through the various stages of the life cycle of addiction.** 37(9-B), 4711–4712.

1447. White, Linda S. (1986). **The effect of child abuse and neglect on cognitive development of Black male children.** 47(4-B), 1759.

1448. Worthington, Christine F. (1977). **An analysis of WISC-R score patterns of Black adolescent male delinquents.** 38(3-A), 1315.

1449. Zipper, Barry O. (1973). **The personality and self concept characteristics of Negro and White delinquent and non-delinquent boys.** 34(1-B), 431.

1450. Zurrow, Stephen A. (1975). **The effects of self-awareness states upon and the attribution of responsibility in narcotic addicts.** 36(4-B), 1977.

Learning Disorders & Mental Retardation

1451. Mangum, Melvin E. (1976). **Familial identification in Black, Anglo and Chicano mentally retarded children using kinetic family drawing.** 36(11-A), 7343.

1452. Quantz, Richard A. (1980). **The effects of race and sex on the labeling of educable mentally retarded.** 40(9-A), 5004–5005.

1453. Sabol, Maxine V. (1981). **Selective attention in educable mentally retarded, learning disabled, and normal children: A comparative study.** 42(5-A), 2039.

1454. Tufano, Louis G. (1976). **The effect of effort and performance reinforcement on WISC-R IQ scores of Black and White EMR boys.** 36(9-A), 5961–5962.

Physical & Psychosomatic Disorders

1455. Abernethy, Alexis D. (1986). **Hypertension, stress, and affect: A study of anger.** 46(9-B), 3256.

1456. Johnson, Jake A. (1986). **A child with a physical disability in a nuclear Black family: A case study.** 47(5-A), 1660.

1457. Liem, Linda. (1981). **The relationship between anxiety, depression, denial of fear, and sick role expectations in Black, Hispanic, and White male first myocardial infarction patients.** 42(2-A), 859.

1458. Munder, Laura S. (1976). **Patterns of deficit in Black and White men with brain damage to the left, right, and both hemispheres.** 37(1-B), 442–443.

1459. Reed, Jesse A. (1982). **Gaze behavior of Black families with a hypertensive father during conflict and positive interaction situations.** 43(3-B), 883.

1460. Tracy, Octavious M. (1978). **Personality, coping, and defense in the etiology of essential hypertension.** 38(10-B), 5074.

TREATMENT AND PREVENTION

1461. Abston, Nathaniel. (1985). **The influence of patients' ethnicity and gender on ratings of suitability for various psychiatric treatments.** 46(6-B), 2053.

1462. Brathwaite, Noel A. (1984). **Relationship between psychosocial variables and adherence to medication regimens by Black hypertensive men.** 44(10-B), 3032.

1463. Goldring, Paul. (1969). **The initial interview with Negro adolescents.** 30(3-B), 1358.

1464. Paxton, Patricia W. (1972). **Effects of drug-induced behavior changes in hyperactive children on maternal attitude and personality.** 33(1-B), 447–448.

1465. Rhinard, Larry D. (1970). **A comparison of the effectiveness of nondirective play therapy and behavior modification approaches.** 30(12-B), 5696.

Psychotherapy & Psychotherapeutic Counseling

1466. Butler, Oliver T. (1980). **A study of the nonlexical differential speech behavior of White clients when paired with Black versus White therapists for psychotherapy-like sessions.** 41(5-B), 1906.

1467. Francois, Theodore V. (1978). **The engagement of adolescent Black males in psychotherapy: The relation of role induction, locus of control, and depression.** 38(12-B), 6147–6148.

1468. Mohamed, Ramona A. (1980). **Race, sex, and therapist's perceived competence.** 41(6-B), 2337.

1469. Smith, J. Otis. (1974). **The effect of a physical barrier and three levels of counselor greeting responses on the interpersonal trust of Black male college students from low income families during their initial interview.** 34(9-A, Pt 1), 5645.

Behavior Therapy & Behavior Modification

1470. Bosley, Florida M. (1982). **A study of the effectiveness of a stress management program on hypertension.** 43(5-A), 1432–1433.

1471. Carter-Nicholas, Doris E. (1982). **The differential effects of self-monitoring, self-reinforcement and performance standards on the diastolic blood pressure, body weight and urine (sodium) of Black hypertensive men and women.** 42(12-B, Pt 1), 4962.

1472. Eaves, Ronald C. (1975). **Stated reward preferences and effectiveness of reinforcement under performance conditions among Black and White disturbing and nondisturbing children.** 35(10-A), 6541.

1473. Joseph, Herbert M. (1982). **Black fathers and their sons: The impact of a modeling intervention.** 43(4-B), 1256.

1474. Wolf, Kenneth L. (1976). **The application of social modeling techniques in the development of job interview behavior with a heroin dependent population.** 37(5-B), 2535–2536.

Health Care Services

1475. Anderson, Glenn B. (1982). **Effects of ethnically varied deaf client vignettes, stage of interview and counselor hearing status on counselor empathy and counseling skills.** 43(4-A), 1043.

1476. Caldwell, Cleopatra H. (1986). **Motivation and patterns of medical services utilization among Black male veterans and non-veterans.** 47(6-B), 2670.

1477. Ness, Myrna K. (1981). **The effects of varying the race of the interpersonal partner on assertive behavior of Black male inpatients.** 42(1-B), 385.

1478. Sindos, Louise K. (1986). **Services needs and use among a population of single Black men and women.** 47(4-A), 1505.

1479. Stein, Steven J. (1981). **Client's perception of counselor trustworthiness, expertness, and attractiveness as a function of counselor race and dialect.** 42(6-B), 2552–2553.

1480. Taylor, Debra E. (1982). **The effects of counselor race, counselor sex, and client race on counselor preferences of male institutionalized juvenile delinquents.** 42(8-A), 3521.

1481. Thomas, Terra L. (1982). **The psychosocial network in treatment of emotional disorder.** 43(3-B), 889.

Rehabilitation & Penology

1482. Adams, Craig L. (1981). **The influence of counselor race, attire, and speech style on Black juvenile delinquents' perception of counselor attractiveness and ability to be warm, empathic, and genuine.** 42(3-A), 1324.

1483. Frye, Jerry B. (1987). **Self concept as related to behavioral and academic changes among juvenile offenders within a residential treatment center.** 47(7-B), 3091.

1484. Ingram, Jesse C. (1981). **Problem solving as a function of race and incarceration.** 42(5-A), 2032–2033.

1485. Newman, Judith. (1975). **The effect of modeling and model status on the verbal behavior of drug addicts in an interview.** 36(6-B), 3060–3061.

1486. Petersen, Jacquelyn L. (1976). **Correctional education model for underachieving young adult Afro-American male correctional clients from New York City.** 36(8-A), 5200–5201.

1487. Rickicki, John P. (1982). **An investigation of differences by race and security classification on responses to the impact questionnaire following a period of incarceration among a population of institutionalized male delinquents.** 42(12-A), 5259.

1488. Romero, Clarence. (1978). **Cooperative behavior of prison inmates towards peers and institutional staff utilizing the prisoner dilemma game.** 38(12-B), 6125.

1489. Wasserstein, Joyce R. (1985). **Alcoholic patients' perceptions of nonalcoholic and recovering alcoholic counselors during treatment.** 46(1-B), 318.

PROFESSIONAL PERSONNEL AND PROFESSIONAL ISSUES

1490. Roman, Frank D. (1974). **Measurement and modification of White counselor trainees' perceptions of Black male high school students.** 34(11-A), 6984–6985.

1491. Smith, Lois D. (1982). **The drinking practices of Black physicians.** 43(3-A), 932–933.

1492. Sussman, Marion B. (1973). **The development and effects of a model for training peer-group counselors in a multiethnic junior high school.** 34(2-A), 626–627.

1493. White, James O. (1973). **The assessment of a program in bibliotherapy for Black helpers.** 34(2-A), 628.

EDUCATIONAL PSYCHOLOGY

1494. Anderson, Carl E. (1970). **A study of selected psycho-social correlates of college student protesters and non-protesters.** 31(2-A), 606.

1495. Banks, Eugene M. (1975). **Career aspirations of Black male principals in large northeastern Ohio cities.** 35(11-A), 6958.

1496. Bell, David B. (1970). **The motivational and personality factors in reading retardation among two racial groups of adolescent males.** 31(2-B), 909–910.

1497. Brooks, Dalton P. (1976). **Student perception of teacher behavior in a tri-racial school district.** 37(1-A), 54.

1498. Bruininks, Robert H. (1969). **Relationship of auditory and visual perceptual strengths to methods of teaching word recognition among disadvantaged Negro boys.** 30(3-A), 1010–1011.

1499. Cole, Oscar J. (1973). **Children's academic motivation: An investigation of the effects of self- and social-evaluations.** 33(9-B), 4484.

1500. Crowl, Thomas K. (1971). **White teachers' evaluations of oral responses given by White and Negro ninth grade males.** 31(9-A), 4540.

1501. Day, Sherman R. (1968). **The effects of activity group counseling on selected behavior characteristics of culturally disadvantaged Negro boys.** 28(10-A), 3969.

1502. Dugas, Edmond A. (1971). **The influence of observers of the same race and a racially mixed audience on level of aspiration and gross motor performance of college males.** 31(9-A), 4516.

1503. Dukes, Phillip E. (1975). **Effects of race of experimenter, self-concept and racial attitudes on the performance of Black junior high school students.** 36(3-B), 1503–1504.

1504. Edwards, Curtis D. (1972). **Stress in the school: A study of anxiety and self-esteem in Black and White elementary school children.** 33(6-B), 2806.

1505. Ewing, Dorlesa B. (1971). **The relationship between anomie, dogmatism, and selected personal-social factors among asocial adolescent boys.** 31(10-A), 5197–5198.

1506. Garrity, Carla B. (1973). **Academic success of children from different social class and cultural groups.** 33(7-B), 3301.

1507. George, Flavil H. (1970). **The relationship of the self concept, ideal self concept, values, and parental self concept to the vocational aspiration of adolescent Negro males.** 30(11-A), 4772.

1508. Hall, John A. (1972). **The influence of school desegregation on the work values and occupational aspiration levels of twelfth-grade Negro males in Texas public high schools.** 32(10-A), 5545–5546.

1509. Halpern, Shelly. (1972). **The relationship between ethnic group membership and sex and aspects of vocational choice of pre-college Black and Puerto Rican high school students.** 33(1-A), 190–191.

1510. Heffernon, Andrew W. (1970). **The effect of race and assumed professional status of male lay counselors upon eighth grade Black males' perceptions of and reactions to the counseling process.** 31(4-A), 1575.

1511. Hoggard, Philip P. (1974). **Perspectives of Black teachers in predominately White schools in the Commonwealth of Pennsylvania.** 35(1-A), 101.

1512. Hood, Elizabeth F. (1972). **A study of the attitudes of Black high school male activists and Black high school male non-activists as related to the factors of social awareness, civil rights and institutional practices.** 32(11-A), 6575.

1513. Johnson, Joseph B. (1971). **A comparison of physical fitness and self-concept between junior high Negro and White male students.** 31(10-A), 5180.

1514. Jones, Alvin H. (1971). **An investigation of self concept using group counseling with Afro-American male ninth-grade students.** 32(6-A), 3031.

1515. Kandell, Alice S. (1967). **Harlem children's stories: A study of expectations of Negro and Puerto Rican boys in two reading-level groups.** 28(6-A), 2338.

1516. Katz, David. (1969). **The effects of a compensatory educational program on the vocational aspirations, expectations, self-concept, and achievement of selected groups of junior high school students.** 29(9-A), 2963.

1517. Kehres, Robert J. (1972). **Differential effects of group counseling methods with Black male adolescents.** 33(4-A), 1440-1441.

1518. Kovalkoski, John P. (1972). **Comparative preferences of retarded White and Black non-physically handicapped male adolescents toward normal White and Black physically handicapped male adolescents.** 33(3-A), 1046-1047.

1519. Lamar, Aaron L. (1972). **A comparative study of factors which contribute to the self-concept of Black freshmen in selected junior colleges in Alabama.** 33(3-B), 1270.

1520. Lao, Rosina C. (1969). **A study of the relationship of expectancy patterns to competent and innovative behavior of male Negro college students.** 30(5-A), 2151.

1521. Livingston, Loveless B. (1971). **Self-concept change of Black college males as a result of a weekend Black experience encounter workshop.** 32(4-B), 2423.

1522. LoMonaco, Leon J. (1969). **Response levels of disadvantaged ninth-grade Negro boys to both standard and oral-visual administrations of two vocationally relevant instruments.** 29(9-A), 3004-3005.

1523. London, Forestene L. (1975). **A comparative study of Black and White observer perceptions of videotaped verbal and nonverbal behaviors of Black and White (male-female) teachers in schools for adjudicated delinquents.** 36(3-A), 1451-1452.

1524. Lyles, Barbara F. (1971). **Familial ideological correlates of authoritarianism as related to internality-externality in Black male college students.** 32(6-B), 3621-3622.

1525. Mahan, Susan P. (1971). **The relationships between academic achievement and task-specific motivation, and school anxiety.** 32(1-A), 246.

1526. Marco, Millicent L. (1970). **Cognitive patterns of children with subnormal intelligence as they are related to associative memory, school achievement, and race.** 31(5-A), 2189.

1527. Meyers, Edna O. (1967). **Self-concept, family structure and school achievement: A study of disadvantaged Negro boys.** 27(11-A), 3960.

1528. Moates, Hugh L. (1970). **The effects of activity group counseling on the self-concept, peer acceptance and grade-point average of disadvantaged seventh grade Negro boys and girls.** 30(9-A), 3795-3796.

1529. Moore, Mary H. (1975). **Faculty, counselor, and student perception of the environment at Tallahassee Community College.** 35(9-A), 5823-5824.

1530. Robinson, Daniel C. (1979). **An investigation of the extent to which members of a single occupation (elementary teacher) show different or identical interests depending upon whether they are male or female or members of Black or Caucasian racial groups.** 39(8-A), 4766.

1531. Scheaf, William A. (1972). **The effects of paired-learning and Glasser-type discussions on two determinants of academic achievement and on reading achievement of male delinquents.** 33(1-A), 197-198.

1532. Showell, Diann R. (1975). **The reactions of student teachers and cooperating teachers toward children's oral language.** 35(11-A), 7047-7048.

1533. Smith, Mary B. (1972). **Effects of motivation on the level of aspiration of disadvantaged Negro boys.** 33(4-A), 1495-1496.

1534. Smith, Yvonne E. (1977). **The relationship of skin color and teacher perception of pupil behavior in the classroom.** 37(9-A), 5669–5670.

1535. Sobota, Catherine M. (1969). **The relationship between selected social and personal characteristics and academic achievement among male Negro adolescents.** 30(3-A), 1029-1030.

1536. Stugart, David B. (1971). **An experimental study investigating the effects of model race and model age-referent group upon the vocational information-seeking behaviors of male Black eleventh-graders.** 31(7-A), 3281.

1537. Thomas, Lionel C. (1978). **A study of differences in self-concept, vocational preferences, and school achievement among Black and White high school students.** 39(5-A), 2764.

1538. Wash, Brenda D. (1973). **The Black child's self-concept: A study of ten- and eleven-year olds varying in sex, socioeconomic background and integrated vs. segregated school settings.** 33(10-A), 5570.

1539. Woodard, Queen E. (1985). **Effect of father-presence and father-absence on the self-concept of Black males in special education and regular education classes.** 46(4-A), 951.

Curriculum & Programs & Teaching Methods

1540. Aitken, Eloise J. (1985). **Effects of an experimental achievement goals pilot program on mathematical achievement.** 46(4-A), 917–918.

1541. Cowan, Mae P. (1980). **An exploratory study on the effects of a structured social interaction program for reducing aggressive behavior among students of a desegregated elementary school.** 41(4-A), 1367–1368.

1542. Davis, Terence A. (1974). **A study of conceptual development in science education at two levels of verbalization.** 34(12-A, Pt 1), 7513.

1543. Devitt, Michael J. (1975). **Self-directed achievement groups: Improving motivation and self-concept of Title I junior high students.** 35(9-B), 4623-4624.

1544. Dixon, Jack H. (1985). **The employment goals of Black underprepared male students: Implications for adult vocational education.** 45(8-A), 2355.

1545. Dolan, Sandra L. (1976). **The effect of value-conflict discussion on the critical thinking and reading and adults.** 37(5-A), 2737.

1546. Dozier, Martha S. (1974). **The relative effectiveness of vicarious and experiential techniques on the development of moral judgment with groups of desegregated sixth grade pupils.** 35(4-A), 2045-2046.

1547. Dunn, Judith A. (1978). **The effect of creative dramatics on the oral language abilities and self-esteem of Blacks, Chicanos and Anglos in the second and fifth grades.** 38(7-A), 3907.

1548. Ferguson, Diana M. (1980). **The effects of oral reading and related language experiences on the reading readiness of kindergarten children.** 40(8-A), 4398.

1549. Galtelli, Barbara A. (1984). **A comparison study of oral language development programs at the kindergarten level.** 44(8-A), 2438.

1550. Guest, Sandra J. (1975). **Personality factors and attitudes toward mental illness in a college student companionship therapy program.** 35(7-B), 3580.

1551. Ibbott, Roy W. (1977). **A study of the effects of video-tape and audio-tape information presentation on listening comprehension for Black fifth grade male and female students.** 38(6-A), 3249-3250.

1552. Jackson, Charles L. (1974). **The effects of videotape feedback and audio-videotape feedback upon the acquisition and retention of sport type motor skills.** 34(9-A, Pt 1), 5689.

1553. Jackson, Micheal B. (1976). **Comparison of attitudes and effects of brief academic exposure on attitudes toward mental retardation of northern, southern, and southwestern Blacks.** 37(5-B), 2509–2510.

1554. Lenox, Mary F. (1976). **Black women: Student perceptions of their contributions.** 36(9-A), 5901.

1555. Leslie, Judith W. (1974). **An investigation of racial attitude formation.** 35(6-A), 3527-3528.

1556. Lowman, Betsy C. (1975). **The identification and modification of classroom behavior associated with internal and external loci of control among fourth grade students.** 36(6-A), 3517-3518.

1557. Majors, Elizabeth S. (1980). **The effects of a teacher-designed language arts program on kindergarten children: A comparative study.** 40(8-A), 4401.

1558. Marshall, James S. (1974). **The effects of Project BIG on self concept and Black pride of urban Black children at the fourth grade level.** 35(2-A), 804–805.

1559. Noel, Winifred S. (1976). **Experiencing as systematic training: Its effects on communication between Black and White high school students.** 37(4-A), 1995.

1560. Perry, Jesse. (1978). **Some effects of selected Black literature on the self-concept and reading achievement of Black male eighth grade students.** 38(9-A), 5318–5319.

1561. Railsback, Clem L. (1973). **A comparison of four automated auditory-visual techniques to teach the strong verbs to Black, male, adolescent dropouts.** 34(2-A), 561.

1562. Smith, Leonie. (1977). **Listening comprehension and reading comprehension of Black-English-speaking junior high school students in Black English and in standard English.** 38(4-A), 2095.

1563. Tubb, Peggy T. (1979). **The effect of intervention on the Paradigmatic Syntagmatic Language Inventory of seventh grade children.** 39(8-A), 4897–4898.

1564. Warfield, Eula F. (1981). **Forced desegregation and academic achievement of Negro male students in the school city of Indianapolis, Indiana.** 42(4-A), 1430.

1565. Wieseman, Robert A. (1975). **The effect of simulation gaming in the social studies upon student racial attitudes.** 36(3-A), 1286.

Academic Learning & Achievement

1566. Avinger, Juanita H. (1975). **An analysis of the oral language development of selected fourth-grade Black readers in relation to reading difficulties.** 35(11-A), 7023-7024.

1567. Cutrona, Michael P. (1974). **The relationship between working class mother attitudes toward education and the educational achievement of their children with regard to sex, race and residence.** 35(3-A), 1494.

1568. Doepner, Roland W. (1975). **A case study analysis of reading achievement among Black economically disadvantaged sixth grade boys.** 35(8-A), 4978–4979.

1569. Easley, Dorothy J. (1976). **A comparative study of the kindergarten child's comprehensive vocabulary development and readiness-to-read vocabulary development.** 36(8-A), 4988-4989.

1570. Ellis, Joyce T. (1975). **Academic performance and selected psychosocial factors of Black male and female students in a higher education program.** 35(7-A), 4247–4248.

1571. Exezidis, Roxane H. (1983). **An investigation of the relationship of reading comprehension, vocabulary, mathematical concepts, and computation on problem solving among Anglo, Black, and Chicano male and female middle school adolescents.** 43(7-A), 2264–2265.

1572. Favret, Renee. (1981). **The effect of attribution training and visual response cues on persistence following failure.** 41(11-B), 4283.

1573. Gale, Andrew. (1975). **Underachievement among Black and White male junior college students.** 35(12-B, Pt 1), 6070–6071.

1574. Hammond, Peirce A. (1975). **The relationship of literacy, race, and socioeconomic status to children's oral language.** 36(5-B), 2496.

1575. Hannel, Clarence W. (1986). **An analysis of the retention rate among seventh graders in a random sample of junior high schools in Texas.** 47(2-A), 363.

1576. Hill, Alfred W. (1977). **Examination of non-intellectual factors in achievement of Black disadvantaged males.** 37(10-A), 6330.

1577. Hill, Anthony L. (1978). **Motivational factors and academic achievement in Black and White low socioeconomic college students.** 38(12-A), 7171–7172.

1578. Houston, Gustie R. (1980). **An investigation of the relationship among the affective, parental, social and peer influences on achievement in mathematics of females and males among Black, Anglo, and Chicano adolescents.** 40(11-A), 5769.

1579. Johnston, Janet L. (1975). **The relationship between a measure of academic motivation and reading achievement in elementary school children.** 35(11-A), 6941.

1580. Kilpatrick, Ronald N. (1973). **A comparison of Black male high school students who graduated, with those who dropped out.** 34(5-A), 2218–2219.

1581. King, Nathaniel. (1974). **The interaction patterns and normative structure of a violent juvenile gang and its relationship to school achievement and attendance in an inner city.** 34(9-A, Pt 1), 5532.

1582. Kinnebrew, Robert K. (1985). **Achievement and persistence of postsecondary vocational-technical students as a function of ethnicity and sex.** 45(12-A), 3524.

1583. Lane, Patrick R. (1973). **Motivation to achieve in school, intellectual achievement responsibility, and academic achievement in urban Black third-grade students.** 34(1-B), 397.

1584. Marsh, Linda K. (1975). **Self-esteem, achievement responsibility, and reading achievement of lower-class Black, White, and Hispanic seventh-grade boys.** 35(10-A), 6514–6515.

1585. Mboya, Matthewson M. (1984). **A study of global self-concept, self-concept of academic ability, and academic achievement of Black and White high school students within differential school assignment patterns.** 45(5-A), 1286.

1586. McDonald, Charles R. (1974). **A study of the relationships between eight dimensions of school climate and pupil achievement in elementary reading and arithmetic.** 34(11-A), 6876-6877.

1587. Olivarez, Juan R. (1986). **Behavior ratings and school performance of Black, Caucasian, and Hispanic elementary male students.** 47(4-A), 1253.

1588. Quickenton, Arthur J. (1980). **Cognitive style and mathematics problem solving: An exploration of the relationship of field-dependence-independence to secondary school students' mathematics problem solving.** 40(7-A), 3905–3906.

1589. Sapienza, Philip J. (1975). **Race differences in fear of success and performance in competitive and non-competitive situations.** 36(5-B), 2483-2484.

1590. Scott, Valerie D. (1984). **The relationship between locus of control and grade point average for a disadvantaged college student sample.** 45(2-A), 470.

1591. Seidenberg, Pearl L. (1975). **Dialect and reading comprehension of lower class Black children.** 35(10-A), 6580.

1592. Shelton, Mary E. (1975). **The prediction of reading and arithmetic achievement of first grade students using an inventory of primary skills.** 35(8-A), 5137–5138.

1593. Shief, Rebecca J. (1981). **The effects of verbal reinforcement and race of tester on the task persistence of academically-deficient males.** 42(4-B), 1621.

1594. Spivey, William L. (1976). **A study of the self-concept and achievement motivation of Black versus White high school male achievers.** 36(9-B), 4711.

1595. Vance, Marilyn M. (1980). **Academic readiness characteristics of Black, urban preschool boys and girls of different socioeconomic backgrounds.** 41(4-A), 1505.

1596. Varadi, Marilyn M. (1974). **Achievement responsibility, attainment values, task persistence and academic achievement of Black fifth-grade boys.** 34(7-B), 3512.

1597. Vokurka, John F. (1975). **Socioeconomic and ethnic variables as they are related to the accuracy of aural comprehension in young children as a function of the dialect presented.** 35(9-A), 5976.

1598. Walsh, Daniel J. (1985). **A model for predicting academic achievement based on temporal aspects of children's item-naming.** 46(4-A), 889.

1599. Wolf, Randye L. (1980). **The effects of success/failure on personal space and subsequent task performance on Black and on White elementary school children.** 41(4-B), 1575.

1600. Zlotnick, Samuel J. (1976). **The effects of peer group acceptance and positive reference identification on the achievement of male sixth graders: A study of Negro students attending public schools in lower socioeconomic and residentially segregated communities.** 36(12-A), 7967-7968.

Classroom Dynamics & Student Adjustment & Attitudes

1601. Almaguer, Theodore O. (1982). **A study of the relationship between academic achievement and self-concept.** 43(3-A), 597.

1602. Barati Marnani, Ebrahim. (1982). **Comparison of preferred leadership styles, potential leadership effectiveness, and managerial attitudes among Black and White, female and male management students.** 43(4-A), 1271.

1603. Barnes, Freddie L. (1975). **The relationship of density and sex to self-concept and the cognitive and affective components of Black high school students' attitude toward school desegregation.** 36(6-A), 3496–3497.

1604. Bass, Leon. (1981). **A comparison of achievement and attitudes of Black male students attending co-educational and all male urban high schools.** 42(2-A), 589.

1605. Boone, Sherle L. (1976). **Language, cognition and social factors in the regulation of aggressive behavior: A study of Black, Puerto Rican, and White children.** 36(7-A), 4338.

1606. Brown, Perry W. (1981). **Case study of thirty matriculating and non-matriculating Black male high school graduates in a rural Southern community: A hypothesis generating study.** 41(12-A, Pt 1), 4991–4992.

1607. Butner, Barry. (1978). **Effects of prestige, peer, teacher and alternate culture teacher modeling on measures of honesty behavior of fifth & sixth grade Black males.** 39(3-A), 1430–1431.

1608. Chavez, Gene T. (1985). **Chicano, Black, and Anglo students' satisfaction with their university experiences.** 46(5-A), 1201.

1609. Cummings, Leonard O. (1980). **Social intelligence and classroom adaptive behavior.** 40(8-A), 4485.

1610. Dillard, John M. (1976). **A correlational study of middle class Black males' vocational maturity and self-concept.** 36(10-A), 6469.

1611. Flagg, Artemus. (1986). **Factors influencing college choice of Black males in middle Tennessee.** 47(2-A), 360.

1612. Gerbe, Thomas K. (1983). **Flow of influence to leadership from ten selected psychological and demographic variables for a national sample of high school seniors.** 44(5-A), 1386–1387.

1613. Goldwair, William C. (1978). **Value preference and critical thinking scores as they relate to completion of the undergraduate nursing curriculum at the Ohio State University, with special reference to minorities.** 39(2-A), 607–608.

1614. Harms, Norris C. (1977). **Relationships among learner self-concept, internality and ethnic group.** 38(5-A), 2724.

1615. Haynes, Norris M. (1981). **The influence of the self-fulfilling prophecy on the academic achievement and self-concept of Black marginal college students.** 42(5-A), 2031.

1616. Holowenzak, Stephen P. (1974). **The analysis of selected family background, achievement, and area of residence-school factors influencing differences in the educational plans and desires of twelfth grade males and females from six ethnic groups.** 34(11-A), 7045.

1617. Hoover, Velma O. (1986). **The dynamic interrelationship of critical identity images and school experiences: A comparative study of Black and White young women.** 46(10-A), 2971.

1618. Jameson, Anne S. (1974). **An analysis of self-esteem and academic achievement of tri-racial isolate, Negro and Caucasian elementary and middle school boys and girls.** 35(2-A), 722.

1619. Jennings, Valdea D. (1974). **The effects of salience of racial group membership on changes in Black and White adolescent boys' attitudes toward Black studies.** 34(8-A, Pt 1), 4872-4873.

1620. Jones, Charles H. (1973). **The relationships of self-esteem, general anxiety and test anxiety in Black and White elementary school student in grades four through six.** 34(3-A), 1131.

1621. Knott, James L. (1978). **Personality, interests and values among Black and White engineering and non-engineering students.** 38(9-B), 4519.

1622. Krehbiel, Gina G. (1984). **Sociometric status- and academic achievement-based differences in behavior and peer-assessed reputation.** 45(1-B), 355.

1623. Marotto, Richard A. (1978). **"Posin' to be chosen": An ethnographic study of ten lower class Black male adolescents in an urban high school.** 39(3-A), 1234-1235.

1624. McIntyre, Levi H. (1985). **A comparison of the infractions and punishments of Black and White male and female high school students.** 46(2-A), 527.

1625. Medley, Morris L. (1975). **Social class, family structure, academic performance, perceived maternal encouragement, and academic self-concept as determinants of college plans among Black, high school seniors.** 36(2-A), 1117.

1626. Mills, Donald B. (1985). **The achievement of student development tasks by male college scholarship athletes and non-athletes: A comparison.** 46(5-A), 1205.

1627. Molden, Sabrina A. (1981). **Achievement-related attributions associated with underachievement among young Black and White males.** 42(6-B), 2541-2542.

1628. Reynolds, Vinson B. (1973). **Black truancy: A study in values.** 34(2-A), 622-623.

1629. Rivero, William T. (1976). **Student grade perception as a function of trait anxiety in college freshmen.** 36(8-A), 4936-4937.

1630. Royer, Garry W. (1976). **Relationship of internal, powerful others, and chance locus of control to race, socioeconomic class, sex and perceived teacher behavior.** 36(11-A), 7309.

1631. Savage, Lonnie C. (1975). **A study of measures of Black alienation among a selected group of Black college students.** 36(4-B), 1931.

1632. Slayton, Wanda M. (1984). **Locus of control orientation of preschool children of low income families of various ethnic groups.** 45(4-A), 1031.

1633. Stanback, Bessie A. (1981). **Student behaviors in desegregated junior high school science classrooms.** 42(5-A), 2057.

1634. Stout, O. Hugh. (1974). **The effects of the meta-message of skin color and affective and neutral language: A replicative study.** 35(2-A), 810-811.

1635. White, David E. (1975). **The effect of hearing and viewing realistic picture story books on self-concept of first grade students.** 36(5-A), 2514.

1636. Williams, Velma H. (1976). **A survey of the career maturity of a select group of Black high school students.** 36(8-A), 5066.

1637. Zubrick, Stuart L. (1975). **The effects of sex-role identity on Black school children's attitudes toward school and teachers.** 35(12-B, Pt 1), 6122-6123.

Special & Remedial Education

1638. Bachrach, Jim N. (1978). **The effects of developmental therapy on emotionally disturbed males varying in race and socioeconomic status.** 38(7-A), 4086-4087.

1639. Conan, Marvin A. (1975). **Locus of control and academic self-concept as related to school performance and behavior in Black college students.** 36(3-B), 1500-1501.

1640. Dawes, Emma L. (1975). **Measures of academic aptitude, achievement, marks, attendance, and behavior of urban Black junior high school retarded educable males.** 36(6-A), 3402.

1641. Galbraith, Clotile B. (1984). **The relationship of auditory sequential memory tasks and deficits in reading performed by Black males in Grades 2, 3, and 4.** 45(6-A), 1690.

1642. Hughson, Howard. (1986). **The effect of the diagnostic label "mentally retarded" and racial labels on teacher expectations for pupil learning and social performance.** 46(12-A, Pt 1), 3658.

1643. Jensen, Mary K. (1974). **The influence of mode of presentation, ethnicity, and social class on teachers' evaluations of students.** 34(11-A), 7046.

1644. Lister, Dolores A. (1975). **The relationship of school placement of preadolescent mentally handicapped students to measured achievement and self-concept.** 36(6-A), 3408-3409.

1645. McIntosh, Janis H. (1980). **A comparative analysis of the reading status of special and regular students in the Waco Independent School District, 1971-78.** 40(8-A), 4508-4509.

1646. Reid, Dorothy K. (1975). **The effects of cognitive tempo and the presence of a memory aid on conjunctive concept attainment in educable mentally retarded boys.** 36(6-A), 3525.

Counseling & Measurement

1647. Adis, Warren. (1977). **A photographic analysis of the classroom environment.** 38(5-A), 2722.

1648. Berry, Grant M. (1978). **An investigation of the item ordering of the Peabody Picture Vocabulary Test by sex and race.** 38(11-A), 6642.

1649. Briley, Carl E. (1977). **The relationship between race, sex, type of problem and interpersonal trust in determining ethnic-racial preference for counselor.** 38(6-A), 3282-3283.

1650. Brooks, Ernest T. (1974). **The relationship between non-intellectual variables and college performance of Black college freshmen.** 34(11-A), 6860.

1651. Bufford, Raymond E. (1984). **The relationship of socio-economic status to self-disclosure among Black male high school students.** 45(2-A), 412.

1652. Holt, Curtis L. (1977). **Attitudes of leaders of groups with different life styles toward university counseling centers: A Guttman facet analysis.** 38(5-A), 2665–2666.

1653. Kaufman, Nadeen L. (1979). **Reversals and reading: Standardization and validation of the Horst Reversals Test for Black and White first grade children.** 39(10-A), 6065.

1654. Martin, Ila C. (1975). **Peer rating assessment of intelligence and social adaptability.** 36(2-B), 890.

1655. McDowell, Sonya L. (1978). **Verification of the Career Maturity Inventory Attitude Scale for use with Oregon twelfth grade students.** 39(6-A), 3534–3535.

1656. Reynolds, Cecil R. (1979). **Differential validity of several preschool assessment instruments for Blacks, Whites, males, and females.** 39(7-B), 3491.

1657. Rhett, William P. (1974). **Effects of a simulation game on autonomy and life career planning of Black senior high males.** 34(9-A, Pt 1), 5729.

1658. Robertshaw, Dianne W. (1983). **Sex and ethnic differences in aptitude indicator measurement models.** 43(10-A), 3298.

1659. Sanber, Shukri R. (1985). **Differential validity of standardized tests by gender and race: A comparison of study synthesis techniques.** 45(9-A), 2849.

1660. Seid, Lawrence G. (1978). **Self-concept metadimensions and vocational maturity among Black, male, community college students.** 38(7-A), 3965.

1661. Settles, Carl E. (1976). **The effects of two training modes on lay and professional therapy with Black adolescent males.** 37(5-A), 2704.

1662. Stevens, Edmund F. (1977). **Senior high school students' preferences for counselors in relation to dogmatism.** 38(6-A), 3299–3300.

1663. VanBuren, Janice J. (1980). **The effects of modeling, coaching, and coding on the assertive behavior of Black college students.** 41(3-A), 949.

1664. Walker, Patricia W. (1983). **Sex-role stereotyping as a factor influencing counselors' advising of Black male students to investigate selected allied health professions.** 44(2-A), 445.

1665. Weichun, William M. (1976). **Influence of racial background of the examiner on first grade Black pupils via a computer content analysis of verbal response to a school related task.** 36(8-A), 5166.

1666. Worthington, George B. (1986). **Use of the Kaufman Assessment Battery for Children as a predictor of achievement for students referred for special education services.** 47(3-B), 1291.

1667. Yankowitz, Robert B. (1983). **The structure of career maturity in Black male and female public high school seniors.** 43(8-A), 2562–2563.

1668. Berry, Charles C. (1974). **Changing employers and changing jobs: The career patterns of Black and White men.** 34(11-A), 7336–7337.

1669. Capuano, Sandra L. (1986). **The effects of culture upon MMPI responses: A comparison of industrially injured Black and Caucasian males.** 46(11-A), 3252.

1670. Carter, Swanson D. (1983). **The self-esteem and job satisfaction of Black male professional level college graduates as related to the racial identity of college attended.** 43(8-A), 2567.

1671. Cook, Verna S. (1971). **A comparison of work values of disadvantaged Black males with work values of advantaged Black males in an urban setting.** 32(4-A), 1848.

1672. Cotton, F. Jane. (1982). **A study of support given by superiors to male–female, and Black–White subordinates.** 42(12-A), 5063.

1673. Dodd, William E. (1972). **Background and situational factors related to anxiety in Negro test performance.** 33(4-B), 1835–1836.

1674. Feldman, Jack M. (1972). **Race, economic class, and job-seeking behavior: An exploratory study.** 33(1-B), 477.

1675. Frost, Olivia P. (1972). **A study of the effect of training upon the level of occupational aspirations and upon attitudes toward work for a group of young Negro men from low income families.** 33(5-A), 2494.

1676. Hoffman, Saul D. (1977). **Discrimination over the life-cycle: A longitudinal analysis of Black–White experience-earnings profiles.** 38(6-A), 3611.

1677. Jones, Thomas M. (1981). **Some psychological and personal variables related to the vocational development of Black male industrial workers.** 41(12-B, Pt 1), 4705.

1678. Levitin, Teresa E. (1972). **A social psychological exploration of power motivation among disadvantaged workers.** 33(5-A), 2495.

1679. Pecorella, Patricia A. (1976). **Racial inequalities in Army Reward Systems: A definition and empirical evaluation.** 37(3-B), 1474–1475.

1680. Roberts, William L. (1982). **Black and White managers in helping: Interaction effects of managers in responding to culturally varied subordinate vignettes.** 42(12-A), 5005–5006.

1681. Shirvanian, Hossein. (1984). **Factors affecting the level of Black male industrial workers' job satisfaction.** 44(9-A), 2902–2903.

Occupational Attitudes & Interests & Guidance

1682. Anderson, Alvin F. (1976). **An analysis of job placement patterns of Black and non-Black male and female undergraduates at the University of Virginia and Hampton Institute.** 36(7-A), 4248–4249.

1683. Baly, Iris E. (1985). **Assessing the vocational-educational decision-making patterns of low SES Black male high school seniors: A test of two models.** 45(9-A), 2850.

1684. Gilbert, Carol M. (1975). **Correlates of occupational goal-oriented behaviors and attitudes among urban, low income, Black, adolescent boys.** 36(6-B), 3120-3121.

1685. Gooden, Winston E. (1981). **The adult development of Black men: I & II.** 41(11-B), 4283–4284.

1686. Grace, Cynthia A. (1984). **The relationship between racial identity attitudes and choice of typical and atypical occupations among Black college students.** 45(2-B), 722.

1687. Nafziger, Dean H. (1973). **A Markov chain analysis of the movement of young men using the Holland occupational classification.** 34(1-A), 138–139.

1688. O'Brien, William F. (1975). **The concurrent validity of Holland's theory of vocational development using a sample of non-professional Black workers.** 36(6-B), 3010–3011.

1689. Pelham, Judy C. (1980). **Racial differences and attributes of career choice unrealism.** 41(4-B), 1485.

1690. Stokes, Leland E. (1978). **Effect of key figures on the occupational realism of Black male inner-city high school seniors.** 38(7-A), 3966.

1691. Thomas, Mark J. (1975). **An examination of the relationship between locus of control and vocational maturity, choice realism, and job knowledge among low socio-economic status Black and White male youth.** 35(7-A), 4264–4265.

Personnel Selection & Training

1692. Bowers, Robert F. (1975). **Measuring interpersonal value change in a federally funded manpower program.** 35(10-A), 6448.

1693. Kirnan, Jean P. (1986). **The relationship of recruiting source to applicant quality and subsequent new-hire success controlling for ethnicity, sex and age of the applicant.** 47(4-B), 1784–1785.

1694. Roskind, William L. (1975). **A longitudinal study comparing the chronically unemployed with other employees in an industrial organization.** 35(7-B), 3638.

1695. Sharar, Paul H. (1975). **Changes in the social adjustment of disadvantaged male high school dropouts as a result of vocational training and employment.** 35(10-B), 5091–5092.

Section IV. Subject Index

Subject terms in the Subject Index are taken from the *Thesaurus of Psychological Index Terms*. Those terms used to retrieve the records in this bibliography (Blacks, Negroes, human males, fathers, and sons) are not included in this index. *See* references are used to refer to preferred forms of entry, or from conceptually broader terms to narrower terms. *See Also* references alert the reader to more specific terms. Index terms are chosen to represent the most specific concepts and ideas in each document.

Enlistment (Military) [See Military Enlistment]

Enrollment (School) [See School Enrollment]

Environment [See Also Classroom Environment, College Environment, Communities, Ghettoes, Home Environment, Hospital Environment, Neighborhoods, Rural Environments, School Environment, Social Environments, Suburban Environments, Urban Environments, Working Conditions] 383, 1515

Environmental Effects [See Temperature Effects]

Environmental Stress 167

Enzymes [See Monoamine Oxidases]

Epidemiology 421, 434, 454, 971, 979, 994, 1011

Epithelium [See Skin (Anatomy)]

Equality (Social) [See Social Equality]

Equity (Payment) 1320

Equity (Social) [See Equity (Payment)]

Ergot Derivatives 1035

Eroticism 797

Error Analysis 1658

Essential Hypertension 1009, 1460

Ethics [See Personal Values, Social Values, Values]

Ethnic Differences [See Racial and Ethnic Differences]

Ethnic Groups [See Also American Indians, Asians, Hispanics, Mexican Americans] 25, 190, 388, 409, 508, 514, 673, 700, 847, 1025, 1110, 1149, 1174, 1252, 1398, 1405, 1450, 1492, 1497, 1509, 1584, 1605, 1616, 1618, 1643

Ethnic Identity 38, 63, 120, 154, 164, 208, 572, 662, 749, 845, 851, 857, 1059, 1234, 1279, 1290, 1299, 1319, 1325, 1405, 1431, 1558, 1614, 1616, 1670, 1686

Ethnic Values 176, 1251

Ethnocentrism 809

Ethnology [See Also Related Terms] 71, 76, 155, 156, 157, 163, 165, 179, 263, 271, 277, 313, 349, 356, 366, 367, 370, 495, 535, 536, 544, 546, 547, 550, 682, 697, 755, 758, 760, 774, 779, 781, 822, 826, 830, 832, 835, 848, 893, 894, 899, 900, 903, 904, 931, 932, 949, 954, 1033, 1089, 1090, 1091, 1093, 1098, 1099, 1103, 1105, 1108, 1111, 1229, 1241, 1248, 1300, 1305, 1313, 1355, 1358, 1410, 1412, 1415, 1417, 1505, 1510, 1513, 1515

Etiology 332, 441, 1419, 1460

Evaluation [See Also Educational Program Evaluation, Needs Assessment, Peer Evaluation, Personnel Evaluation, Self Evaluation, Treatment Effectiveness Evaluation] 299, 1532, 1643, 1654

Evaluation (Treatment Effectiveness) [See Treatment Effectiveness Evaluation]

Exceptional Children (Gifted) [See Gifted]

Exceptional Children (Handicapped) [See Handicapped]

Executives [See Top Level Managers]

Exercise 346

Exhibitionism 526

Exogamous Marriage [See Interracial Marriage]

Expectant Fathers 815

Expectant Parents [See Expectant Fathers]

Expectations [See Also Role Expectations, Teacher Expectations] 77, 92, 113, 279, 511, 594, 595, 605, 616, 624, 638, 683, 708, 790, 857, 915, 1108, 1134, 1185, 1231, 1288, 1292, 1297, 1350, 1369, 1418, 1457, 1471, 1500, 1511, 1515, 1520

Experience (Practice) [See Practice]

Experience Level (Job) [See Job Experience Level]

Experiences (Events) [See Also Early Experience, Life Experiences, Vicarious Experiences] 451, 992, 1546

Experiences (Life) [See Life Experiences]

Experiment Controls 468, 1201

Experimental Design [See Followup Studies, Longitudinal Studies]

Experimental Instructions 339, 778, 1231

Experimental Laboratories 268

Experimental Methods [See Stimulus Presentation Methods]

Experimental Replication 10, 62, 265, 864, 999, 1002, 1634

Experimentation [See Also Related Terms] 1091, 1248, 1503

Experimenter Bias 723

Experimenters 889, 927, 1196, 1354

Expert Testimony 869

Expressions (Facial) [See Facial Expressions]

Extended Family 863, 1284

External Rewards 41, 121, 305

Extinction (Learning) 1215

Extraversion 962

Extrinsic Rewards [See External Rewards]

Eye Contact 1368, 1459

Eyewitnesses [See Witnesses]

Eysenck Personality Inventory 44

Face (Anatomy) 389

Face Perception 200, 759

Face Recognition [See Face Perception]

Facial Expressions 761, 1283

Facial Features 296, 910, 917, 924, 1216, 1290, 1341, 1380

Facilitation (Social) [See Social Facilitation]

Factor Analysis [See Also Cluster Analysis, Item Analysis (Statistical)] 21, 34, 35, 47, 68, 195, 323, 726, 782, 1002

Factor Structure 664, 665, 1162

Factorial Validity 725

Factory Environments [See Working Conditions]

Fads and Fashions [See Also Clothing Fashions] 192

Failure [See Also Academic Failure] 540, 611

Familiarity 49, 385, 770, 890

Family Background [See Also Family Socioeconomic Level, Parent Educational Background, Parental Occupation] 151, 332, 360, 365, 381, 704, 1126, 1140, 1233, 1250, 1284, 1394, 1401, 1469, 1568, 1616, 1673, 1677

Family Counseling [See Family Therapy]

Family Life [See Family Relations]

Family Members [See Also Daughters, Husbands, Monozygotic Twins, Mothers, Parents, Spouses, Surrogate Parents (Humans), Wives] 174, 332, 969, 1303

Family Planning [See Also Birth Control, Contraceptive Devices] 222

Family Planning Attitudes 125, 252, 794, 867

Family Relations [See Also Childrearing Practices, Father Child Relations, Marital Conflict, Marital Relations, Mother Child Relations, Parent Child Relations, Parental Attitudes, Parental Role, Sibling Relations] 99, 117, 174, 194, 204, 227, 394, 607, 689, 792, 826, 863, 888, 969, 977, 1250, 1268, 1311, 1328, 1330, 1333, 1443, 1451, 1456, 1459, 1462, 1684

Family Size 864, 1142, 1261

Family Socioeconomic Level 1293, 1538, 1610

Family Structure [See Also Birth Order, Extended Family, Family Size, Father Absence, Matriarchy, Parental Absence, Patriarchy, Polygamy] 248, 310, 579, 969, 990, 1330, 1625

Family Therapy 1022, 1047

Family Violence [See Also Child Abuse] 238

Family [See Also Related Terms] 186, 342, 747, 780, 837, 838, 1333, 1418, 1524, 1527

Fantasy [See Imagination]

Fantasy (Defense Mechanism) 219

Father Absence 90, 97, 111, 112, 128, 135, 154, 218, 229, 267, 310, 373, 379, 579, 598, 704, 742, 1022, 1277, 1281, 1284, 1292, 1306, 1327, 1334, 1349, 1414, 1539, 1573

Father Child Communication 216

Father Child Relations 112, 218, 225, 226, 246, 788, 877, 1284, 1327, 1328, 1336, 1425, 1473

Fear [See Also Social Anxiety] 435, 1314, 1457

Fear of Success 308, 1186, 1391

Feedback [See Also Biofeedback, Visual Feedback] 107, 301, 581, 754, 1288, 1445, 1474, 1490, 1572

Feelings [See Emotions]

Felonies [See Crime]

Female Criminals 365

Females (Human) [See Human Females]

Introspection 1357
Inventories 2, 21, 24, 36, 565, 1244, 1667
Investigation [See Experimentation]
Involvement 512, 905
Iowa Tests of Basic Skills 654
Isolation (Social) [See Social Isolation]
Item Analysis (Statistical) 674, 1167
Item Analysis (Test) 654, 730, 1648
Item Bias [See Test Bias]
Item Content (Test) 1648
Item Response Theory 674

Jails [See Prisons]
Japan 51
Japanese Americans [See Asians]
Jews [See Judaism]
Job Applicant Interviews 678, 1474
Job Applicant Screening 1192
Job Applicants 1693
Job Experience Level 1174
Job Mobility [See Occupational Mobility]
Job Performance 683, 1173, 1175, 1177, 1182, 1418, 1694
Job Promotion [See Personnel Promotion]
Job Satisfaction 688, 699, 1095, 1169, 1172, 1182, 1425, 1530, 1670, 1681
Job Selection [See Occupational Choice]
Job Status [See Occupational Status]
Job Training [See Personnel Training]
Jobs [See Occupations]
Joy [See Happiness]
Judaism 634, 1174, 1322
Judgment 294, 1272, 1352
Jungian Psychology 1396
Junior College Students 1519, 1573
Junior Colleges [See Colleges]
Junior High School Students 69, 534, 543, 572, 600, 602, 616, 619, 620, 639, 641, 648, 657, 660, 664, 666, 672, 677, 1092, 1105, 1122, 1138, 1143, 1157, 1161, 1168, 1500, 1505, 1513, 1539, 1542, 1543, 1560, 1562, 1563, 1571, 1575, 1578, 1581, 1584, 1618, 1633, 1640, 1666
Junior High School Teachers 620, 657
Justice 871
Juvenile Court [See Adjudication]
Juvenile Delinquency 328, 329, 330, 338, 342, 350, 360, 361, 366, 367, 370, 394, 397, 411, 415, 419, 435, 444, 965, 978, 990, 1412, 1435, 1444
Juvenile Delinquents [See Also Male Delinquents] 8, 333, 334, 335, 395, 397, 416, 443, 507, 522, 524, 1078, 1261, 1413, 1426, 1432, 1449, 1483, 1531
Juvenile Gangs 400, 435, 1581

Karyotype Disorders [See Chromosome Disorders]
Kindergarten Students 52, 574, 598, 635, 647, 652, 668, 669, 1548, 1549, 1557, 1569, 1598

Kindergartens 568
Kinesthetic Perception 471
Kinship Structure 969
Knowledge Level 153, 853, 992, 1598

Labeling 1452, 1487, 1642
Laboratories (Experimental) [See Experimental Laboratories]
Laborers (Construct and Indust) [See Blue Collar Workers]
Language [See Also Dialect, Nonstandard English, Numbers (Numerals), Sentences, Sign Language, Vocabulary, Written Language] 59, 79, 1253, 1410, 1562, 1634
Language Arts Education [See Also Reading Education, Spelling] 1547, 1557, 1560, 1561
Language Development 1254, 1549, 1566, 1569, 1605
Language Disorders [See Also Aphasia] 1007
Language Handicaps [See Language Disorders]
Latent Trait Theory [See Item Response Theory]
Lateral Dominance 344
Latinos [See Hispanics]
Law (Government) [See Criminal Law]
Law Enforcement [See Also Adjudication, Incarceration, Legal Arrest, Legal Detention] 874
Law Enforcement Personnel [See Also Police Personnel, Prison Personnel] 260
Laws [See Also Drug Laws] 370, 855, 904, 951, 1176
Leadership [See Also Leadership Style] 277, 684, 928, 1026, 1358, 1554, 1612
Leadership Style 287, 688, 1169, 1602
Learned Helplessness 479
Learning Disabilities 19, 447, 449, 643, 646, 647, 1005, 1453, 1666
Learning Disorders [See Also Learning Disabilities, Reading Disabilities] 670
Learning Rate 1214
Learning Schedules [See Massed Practice]
Learning [See Also Related Terms] 91, 105, 757, 1227, 1409
Legal Arrest 9, 360
Legal Detention 1074
Legal Personnel [See Law Enforcement Personnel]
Legal Processes [See Also Adjudication, Competency To Stand Trial, Expert Testimony, Incarceration, Law Enforcement, Legal Arrest, Legal Detention, Legal Testimony, Probation] 499
Legal Testimony [See Also Expert Testimony] 868, 869
Leisure Time 195
Lesbianism 1652
Letters (Alphabet) 1215
Liberalism 234
Liberalism (Political) [See Political Liberalism]

Life Change [See Life Experiences]
Life Expectancy 1057
Life Experiences 377, 378, 403, 769, 980, 1677
Life Satisfaction 215, 1266
Life Span [See Life Expectancy]
Lifestyle 1652
Linguistics [See Also Grammar, Psycholinguistics] 104
Listening [See Auditory Perception]
Listening Comprehension 61, 1551, 1562, 1597
Literacy 1152, 1317
Literature [See Also Autobiography, Biography, Poetry] 299, 1560
Literature Review 161, 794, 882, 1159
Lithium Carbonate 461, 477
Local Anesthetics [See Cocaine]
Locus of Control [See Internal External Locus of Control]
Logistic Models [See Item Response Theory]
Longevity [See Life Expectancy]
Longitudinal Studies 357, 433, 603, 730, 856, 1126, 1265
Love 797, 1365
Lower Class 82, 119, 193, 194, 300, 318, 335, 354, 394, 568, 586, 597, 598, 615, 672, 767, 785, 801, 844, 1226, 1270, 1277, 1283, 1340, 1443, 1449, 1583, 1584, 1591, 1597, 1600, 1623, 1691
Lower Income Level 104, 218, 256, 579, 607, 648, 948, 990, 1094, 1632, 1675
Luminance Threshold [See Visual Thresholds]
Luria Neuropsychological Tests [See Neuropsychological Assessment]
Lymphatic Disorders [See Blood and Lymphatic Disorders]

Mainstreaming (Educational) 643
Major Tranquilizers [See Neuroleptic Drugs]
Maladjustment (Emotional) [See Emotional Adjustment]
Maladjustment (Social) [See Social Adjustment]
Male Criminals 231, 233, 365, 405, 407, 417, 427, 440, 1421, 1429
Male Delinquents 4, 7, 24, 25, 47, 278, 345, 351, 354, 372, 394, 400, 411, 412, 423, 435, 436, 446, 528, 976, 1414, 1422, 1424, 1427, 1433, 1439, 1440, 1448, 1480, 1482, 1487
Male Genitalia [See Penis]
Male Homosexuality 242, 877, 1343, 1345, 1346, 1652
Malignant Neoplasms [See Neoplasms]
Management Decision Making 1183
Management Development [See Career Development]
Management Methods 1170, 1694
Management Personnel [See Also Top Level Managers] 698, 1169, 1170, 1176, 1177, 1192, 1680

PsycINFO Coverage of the Journal and Dissertation Literature Focusing on Black Males in the United States

A preliminary search of the PsycINFO database for research on Black males in the United States (Evans and Whitfield, 1988) resulted in 3,003 journal and dissertation records in which the concept Black males (or synonyms) appeared; in 1,331 of these records (812 journal articles and 519 dissertations), Black males were the focus of the article or the population of interest. Refinements of the search strategy, based on preliminary output, resulted in 2,975 journal and dissertation records in which the concept Black males appeared and 1,371 records (829 journal articles and 542 dissertations) focusing on Black males in the United States. The following analyses are based on data from the latter search. Analyses were not made for the total dataset because it includes references in which Black males, although present in the research, were not the focus of the article or the population of interest (e.g., research in which Black and White male undergraduates were assessed as a homogeneous group).

The classification of the 1,371 records focusing on Black males in the United States were analyzed. As indicated in Table A-1, most (23.5%) of these references occurred in areas of educational psychology (including educational administration, personnel, and training; curricula, programs, and teaching methods; academic learning and achievement; classroom dynamics and student adjustment and attitudes; special and remedial education; and counseling and management).

PSYCINFO COVERAGE OF THE JOURNAL AND DISSERTATION LITERATURE FOCUSING ON BLACK MALES BY CLASSIFICATION

	1967-1971		1972-1976		1977-1981		1982-1987		TOTAL	
	No.	%	No.	%	No.	%	No.	%	No.	%
GENERAL PSYCHOLOGY	00	0.0	00	0.0	1	1.3	1	0.2	2	0.1
PSYCHOMETRIC	00	0.0	20	4.3	28	7.3	32	7.0	80	5.4
EXPERIMENTAL PSYCHOLOGY (HUMAN)	3	1.8	13	2.8	7	1.8	2	0.4	25	1.7
EXPERIMENTAL PSYCHOLOGY (ANIMAL)	00	0.0	00	0.0	00	0.0	00	0.0	00	0.0
PHYSIOLOGICAL PSYCHOLOGY	00	0.0	1	0.2	3	0.8	6	1.3	10	0.7
PHYSIOLOGICAL INTERVENTION	00	0.0	00	0.0	00	0.0	00	0.0	00	0.0
COMMUNICATION SYSTEMS	3	1.8	5	1.1	5	1.3	7	1.5	20	1.4
DEVELOPMENTAL PSYCHOLOGY	28	16.8	41	8.9	47	12.3	62	13.5	178	12.1
SOCIAL PROCESSES & SOCIAL ISSUES	23	13.8	59	12.8	77	20.1	63	13.7	222	15.1
EXPERIMENTAL SOCIAL PSYCHOLOGY	8	4.8	52	11.3	16	4.2	14	3.0	90	6.1
PERSONALITY	10	6.0	26	5.6	11	2.9	16	3.5	63	4.2
PHYSICAL & PSYCHOLOGICAL DISORDERS	35	21.0	49	10.6	47	12.3	91	19.8	222	15.1
TREATMENT & PREVENTION	11	6.5	24	5.2	29	7.6	48	10.4	112	7.6
PROFESSIONAL PERSONNEL & ISSUES	00	0.0	3	0.7	2	0.5	3	0.7	8	0.5
EDUCATIONAL PSYCHOLOGY	44	26.3	131	28.4	83	22.3	88	18.7	348	23.5
APPLIED PSYCHOLOGY	2	1.2	37	8.0	24	6.3	29	6.3	92	6.3
TOTAL	167		461		382		460		1,470	

Note: 99 records are classified in 2 categories. (Percentages are of column totals.)

A significant proportion of references (15.1%) occurred in areas of social processes and social issues (social structure and social roles; culture, ethnology, and religion; marriage and family; political and legal processes; psychosexual behavior and sex roles; and drug and alcohol usage. An additional 15.1% of the references occurred in areas of physical and psychological disorders (mental disorders; behavior disorders and antisocial behavior; learning disorders and mental retardation; speech and language disorders; and physical and psychosomatic disorders). Developmental psychology (including cognitive, perceptual, psychosocial, and personality development) accounted for 12.1% of the focused references.

Areas in which less than 2% of the references occurred included experimental psychology (1.7%), communication systems (1.4%), physiological psychology (0.7%), professional personnel and professional issues (0.5%), and general psychology (0.1%). Experimental psychology (human) includes the areas of perception and motor processes as well as cognitive processes, motivation and emotion, and attention and consciousness states. Communication systems includes language and speech as well as literature and art. Physiological psychology includes neurology and electrophysiology, physiological processes, and psychophysiology. Documents classified under professional personnel and professional issues include education; training; licensing; certification; peer review; job satisfaction; occupational stress; ethical standards; career opportunities; scientific communication; professional development; and interests, attitudes, and personality characteristics of mental health personnel. The few number of references classed in general psychology is expected, since records are usually classed in this category only if they are very general or unable to be classed in a more specific category.

An analysis of the journals in which the articles referenced were published indicated that 3.2% were published in *Psychological Reports*; 2.4% in the *Journal of Social Psychology*; 2.1% in the *Journal of Clinical Psychology*; 1.9% in the *Journal of Multicultural Counseling and Development* (formerly the *Journal of Non-White Concerns in Personnel and Guidance*); 1.6% in the *American Journal of Drug and Alcohol Abuse*; 1.4% in *Developmental Psychology;* and 1.3% each in the *Journal of Consulting and Clinical Psychology* and the *Journal of Personality and Social Psychology. The Journal of Educational Psychology* and *Educational and Psychological Measurement* accounted for 1% each of the references focused on Black males in the United States.

Reference

Evans, B. & Whitfield, J. (1988). The Status of Black Males in America: A Data Base Search. *American Psychologist*, 43, 401-402.

Search Strategy Used to Retrieve References for the Bibliography

James Whitfield, Brenda Evans, Carolyn Gosling,
Linda McKenney, Sarah Mulholland

The following is the refined search strategy executed on the PsycINFO database (through DIALOG) to retrieve journal and dissertation records on Black males in the United States published from 1967 to 1987. Each search statement is followed by an explanatory comment. Statements for updating this strategy and for searching for more recent research in the PsycALERT database are also provided.

?limitall/human, eng (Limits search to English language records with human populations.)

?s (black? ? or negro? or afr?( )american?)(f)(male? or m?n or boy? ? or masculin? or manhood or manliness) (Searches within the title, abstract, descriptors, identifier, and section heading fields for *free-text* [natural language] variations of the concept *Black males*. To minimize the retrieval of false drops [records with undesired connotations of the search concept, such as *Black*foot Indian *boys* and *black*jack, *male* college students] restricted truncation was used.)

	10687	BLACK? ?
	6244	NEGRO?
	2700	AFR?
	49812	AMERICAN?
	213	AFR?(W)AMERICAN?
	59980	MALE?
	20647	M?N
	9583	BOY? ?
	2437	MASCULIN?
	24	MANHOOD
	10	MANLINESS
S1	3082	(BLACK? ? OR NEGRO?) OR AFR?(W)AMERICAN?)(F)(((((MALE? OR (M?N) OR BOY? ?) OR MASCULIN?) OR MANHOOD) OR MANLINESS)

?s (africa? or egypt? or ethiopia? or kenya? or middle( )east? or nigeria? or south ( ) africa? or tanzania? or zambia? or england or great( )britain or carib? or jamaica? or haiti? or zimbabwe? or west( )indi? or barbados?)/ ti,id,de (Accesses records on foreign countries likely to include Black males in order to exclude non-US populations from the retrieval)

1933	AFRICA?/TI,ID,DE
144	EGYPT/TI,ID,DE
74	ETHIOPIA/TI,ID,DE
125	KENYA/TI,ID,DE
5005	MIDDLE/TI,ID,DE
958	EAST/TI,ID,DE
277	MIDDLE/TI,ID,DE(W)EAST/TI,ID,DE
688	NIGERIA/TI,ID,DE
1550	SOUTH/TI,ID,DE
1933	AFRICA/TI,ID,DE
572	SOUTH/TI,ID,DE(W)AFRICA?/TI,ID,DE
43	TANZANIA?/TI,ID,DE
84	ZAMBIA?/TI,ID,DE
1516	ENGLAND/TI,ID,DE
1063	GREAT/TI,ID,DE

	1045	BRITAIN/TI,ID,DE
	942	GREAT/TI,ID,DE(W)BRITAIN/TI,ID,DE
	56	CARIB?/TI,ID,DE
	108	JAMAICA?/TI,ID,DE
	25	HAITI?/TI,ID,DE
	16	ZIMBABWE?/TI,ID,DE
	1112	WEST/TI,ID,DE
	19150	INDI?/TI,ID,DE
	155	WEST/TI,ID,DE(W)INDI?/TI,ID,DE
	25	BARBADOS?/TI,ID,DE
S2	5501	(AFRICA? OR EGYPT? OR ETHIOPIA? OR KENYA? OR MIDDLE( )EAST? OR NIGERIA? OR SOUTH( )AFRICA? OR TANZANIA? OR ZAMBIA? OR ENGLAND OR GREAT( )BRITAIN OR CARIB? OR JAMAICA? OR HAITI? OR ZIMBABWE? OR WEST( )INDI? OR BARBADOS?)TI,ID,DE

?s s1 not s2 (Excludes non-US populations from free-text retrieval.)

	3082	S1
	5501	S2
S3	2975	S1 NOT S2 (Number of records in which the concept Black males (or synonyms) appeared in the title , descriptor, abstract, or section heading. A subset of these records is included in Section II of the bibliography.)

?s s3/ti,id (Limits free-text retrieval to the title and identifier fields of the record to obtain a dataset that *focuses* on Black males in the US. The presence of the concept in these fields indicate that Black males are the primary focus of the research or the primary population of interest.)

S4	1305	S3/TI,ID

?s (negroes or blacks)/de and (male?/ti,id,de or (fathers or sons or husbands or widowers)/de (Uses controlled vocabulary [index terms] as well as free text terms to search the title, descriptor, and identifier fields of records. Controlled vocabulary is from the *Thesaurus of Psychological Index Terms.*)

	5731	NEGROES/DE
	2898	BLACKS/DE
	34979	MALE?/TI,ID,DE
	1226	FATHERS/DE
	359	SONS/DE
	553	HUSBANDS/DE
	117	WIDOWERS/DE
S5	1084	(NEGROES OR BLACKS)/DE AND (MALE/TI,ID,DE OR (FATHERS OR SONS OR HUSBANDS OR WIDOWERS)/DE)

?s s5 not s2 (Deletes non-US populations from index term/descriptor search)

	1084	S5
	5501	S2
S6	1051	S5 NOT S2

?s s4 or s6 (Combines free-text and descriptor search retrieval)

	1305	S4
	1051	S6
S7	1411	S4 or S6

?s dt=book? or book/id,de (Accesses book records [books and book chapters were sporadically covered in the data-base until 1980])

	9568	DT=BOOK?
	7378	BOOK/ID,DE
S8	11059	DT=BOOK? OR BOOK/ID,,DE

?s s7 not s8 (Deletes book records from the dataset)

	1411	S7
	11059	S8
S9	1381	S7 NOT S8

?s s9/1967-1987 (Restricts retrieval to records published from 1967 to 1987)

	1381	S9
	475463	PY=1967 : PY=1987
S10	1371	S9/1967-1987 (Number of journal and dissertation records published from 1967 to 1987 in the database focusing on Black males in the United States.)

?s s10 and jn=dissertation? (Accesses the number of dissertations in the dataset)

	1371	S10
	113218	JN=DISSER?
S11	542	S10 AND JN=DISSER? (Number of dissertations in the focused dataset. A subset of these of these records is included in Section III of the bibliography.)

?s 10 not s11 (Deletes dissertations from dataset).

	1371	S10
	542	S11
S12	829	S10 NOT S11 (Number of references to journal articles focusing on Black males in the United States. A subset of these records is included in Section I of the bibliography.)

SEARCH NOTE: To retrieve records on Black males added to the PsycINFO database after the update for the present search (January 1988) use the following strategy:

?limitall/human,eng (Limits retrieval to English language records with human populations)

?s blacks/de and (male?/ti,id,de orr (fathers or sons or husbands or widowers)/de) and ud=8802:9999.   (This statement will result in a set of records labeled S1. To minimize non-US populations in the dataset, enter the following statements:

?s (africa? or egypt? or ethiopia? or kenya? or middle( )east? or nigeria? or south( )africa? or tanzania? or zambia? or england or great( )britain or carib? or jamaica? or haiti? or zimbabwe? or west( )indi? or barba-dos?)/ti,id,de (This statement includes country names [index terms] from the 1985 *Thesaurus* and will result in a set of records labeled S2.)

?s (algeria? or angola? or botswana? or east( )africa? or ghana? or ivory( )coast or libya? or morocc? or mozambique or senegal? or sierra( )leone or sudan? or uganda? or west( )africa? or zaire?)/ti,id,de (This statement includes country names added to the 1988 *Thesaurus* as new index terms and will result in a set of records labeled S3.)

?s s2 or s3 (Combines retrieval on selected countries and results in a set of records labeled S4)

?s s1 not s4 (Deletes non-US populations from records on males and results in a set of records labeled S5)

?s s5 not jn=dissertation? (Excludes dissertations from the retrieval)

SEARCH NOTE: To retrieve citations of recently published journal articles from the PsycALERT database, use the following strategy:

?limitall/human,eng (Limits retrieval to English language records with human populations)

?s (black? ? or afr?( )american?) and (male? or m?n or boy? ? or father? or son? or husband? or widower?) (PsycALERT statements are not qualified to specific fields since there are only 2 primary searchable fields [titles and descriptors] in PsycALERT. To exclude non-US populations, enter the country names as above.)